Latin American Documentary Narratives

Latin American Documentary Narratives

The Intersections of Storytelling and Journalism in Contemporary Literature

Liliana Chávez Díaz

BLOOMSBURY ACADEMIC
NEW YORK • LONDON • OXFORD • NEW DELHI • SYDNEY

BLOOMSBURY ACADEMIC
Bloomsbury Publishing Inc
1385 Broadway, New York, NY 10018, USA
50 Bedford Square, London, WC1B 3DP, UK
29 Earlsfort Terrace, Dublin 2, Ireland

BLOOMSBURY, BLOOMSBURY ACADEMIC and the Diana logo are trademarks of
Bloomsbury Publishing Plc

First published in the United States of America 2022
This paperback edition published 2023

Copyright © Liliana Chávez Díaz, 2022

Cover design by Eleanor Rose
Cover image: Untitled, 2017 © Edith Cota

All rights reserved. No part of this publication may be reproduced or transmitted in any form or by any means, electronic or mechanical, including photocopying, recording, or any information storage or retrieval system, without prior permission in writing from the publishers.

Bloomsbury Publishing Inc does not have any control over, or responsibility for, any third-party websites referred to or in this book. All internet addresses given in this book were correct at the time of going to press. The author and publisher regret any inconvenience caused if addresses have changed or sites have ceased to exist, but can accept no responsibility for any such changes.

Whilst every effort has been made to locate copyright holders the publishers would be grateful to hear from any person(s) not here acknowledged.

Library of Congress Cataloging-in-Publication Data
Names: Chávez Díaz, Liliana, author.
Title: Latin American documentary narratives: the intersections of storytelling and journalism in contemporary literature / Liliana Chávez Díaz.
Description: New York: Bloomsbury Academic, 2022. | Includes bibliographical references and index.
Identifiers: LCCN 2021022809 (print) | LCCN 2021022810 (ebook) | ISBN 9781501366017 (hardback) | ISBN 9781501366024 (epub) | ISBN 9781501366031 (pdf) | ISBN 9781501366048
Subjects: LCSH: Latin American prose literature–20th century–History and criticism. | Reportage literature. | Journalism and literature–Latin America. | Authors, Latin American–20th century–Interviews.
Classification: LCC PQ7082.P76 C47 2022 (print) | LCC PQ7082.P76 (ebook) | DDC 868.08–dc23
LC record available at https://lccn.loc.gov/2021022809
LC ebook record available at https://lccn.loc.gov/2021022810

ISBN: HB: 978-1-5013-6601-7
PB: 978-1-5013-7606-1
ePDF: 978-1-5013-6603-1
eBook: 978-1-5013-6602-4

Typeset by Deanta Global Publishing Services, Chennai, India

To find out more about our authors and books visit www.bloomsbury.com and sign up for our newsletters.

To my father, my first storyteller

*To my former colleague Alfredo Jiménez Mota,
who disappeared in Hermosillo, Mexico, in 2005,
and to all journalists who have disappeared while searching for true stories*

What can be said at all can be said clearly,
and what we cannot talk about we must pass over in silence.

      – Ludwig Wittgenstein, *Tractatus Logico Philosophicus* (2002 [1921], p. 3)

Contents

Figures	ix
Preface	x
Foreword	xii
Acknowledgements	xiv
Introduction	1
The journalist as storyteller	3
Intersections	7

Part I Courage

1 Naming the real	15
Non-fiction genres	18
Crónica	20
Literary journalism	24
Testimonio	27
Towards a theory of documentary narratives	32
The self	35
The other	38
2 Publishing to survive	45
Gabriel García Márquez chooses to hide	46
Newspaper fictions	50
The author and the sailor	52
Rodolfo Walsh's conversion to journalism	54
A story that never happened	60
Crafting the truth	65

Part II Belonging

3 Out of place	73
Elena Poniatowska: The lady behind the notebook	80
Lilus, Mariana and other strange women	85
A guilty *catrina* goes out	87
Carlos Monsiváis: A protestant reporter in a Catholic country	91

	The centre of all margins	94
	Mexico 'camp'	98
	The chronicler meets the people	101
4	A certain effect of truth	106
	Tomás Eloy Martínez and the Peronist palimpsest	108
	Memories and news	110
	A parody of journalism	112
	History and the fictions of Evita	115
	Deconstructing the myth	116
	Searching for a magical-realist corpse	121

Part III Listening

5	Local conversations in globalized times	135
	The journalist as protagonist	136
	Martín Caparrós around the world	141
	Juan Villoro's aftershock stories	145
	Approaching strangers: A dialogic method	152
6	Being there	159
	Who are you?	162
	Empathic listeners, unreliable narrators	165
	The potter's hand	167
	The vulnerable 'I'	171

Conclusion 177
  An erotics of testimony 178
  Is there a new other? 183

Apendix
  Interview 1: Cristian Alarcón (La Unión, Chile, 1970) 188
  Interview 2: Martin Caparrós (Buenos Aires, Argentina, 1957) 197
  Interview 3: Arturo Fontaine (Santiago de Chile, 1952) 213
  Interview 4: Francisco Goldman (Boston, United States, 1954) 221
  Interview 5: Leila Guerriero (Junín, Argentina, 1967) 225
  Interview 6: Elena Poniatowska (Paris, France, 1932) 238
  Interview 7: Santiago Roncagliolo (Lima, Perú, 1975) 252
  Interview 8: Juan Villoro (Ciudad de México, 1956) 266
References 273
Index 285

Figures

2.1 Newspaper main cover of Gabriel García Márquez's first publication of 'The Story of the Shipwrecked Sailor'. 'La Odisea del Náufrago Sobreviviente del "A.R.C. Caldas"' (The Odyssey of the Shipwreck Survivor from the 'A.R.C. Caldas'), *El Espectador*, Bogotá, 28 April 1955. Reproduction in whole or in part is prohibited. Unauthorized duplication is a violation of applicable laws. All rights reserved Copyright © 1955, Comunican S.A. Source: *El Espectador*   47

2.2 Section cover of Gabriel García Márquez's first publication of 'The Story of the Shipwrecked Sailor'. 'La Verdad sobre mi Aventura' (The Truth About My Adventure), *El Espectador*, Bogotá, 28 April 1955. Reproduction in whole or in part is prohibited. Unauthorized duplication is a violation of applicable laws. All rights reserved Copyright © 1955, Comunican S.A. Source: Biblioteca Nacional de Colombia   47

2.3 First page of Rodolfo Walsh's 'La Operación Masacre. Un libro que no encuentra editor' (Operation Massacre. A book that does not find an editor), Buenos Aires, 17 May 1955, p. 8. Source: Archive of the Ibero-American Institute, Prussian Cultural Heritage Foundation, Berlin   62

2.4 Cover of *Mayoría* magazine, featuring Rodolfo Walsh's Operation Massacre. Buenos Aires, 17 May 1955. Source: Archive of the Ibero-American Institute, Prussian Cultural Heritage Foundation, Berlin   64

3.1 Josefina Bórquez and Elena Poniatowska, photographed by Héctor García in Mexico City, February 1966. Source: Poniatowska's Luz y luna, las lunitas (Light and Moon, the Little Moons), Mexico City: Era, 1994, p. 61. Donación por parte de la Fundación María y Héctor García / Courtesy of the María and Héctor García Foundation   74

3.2 Book cover of Monsiváis's *Los rituales del caos* (The Rituals of Chaos), Mexico City: Era, 1995, illustrated by Rafael Barajas   76

4.1 Cover of *Panorama* magazine, issue 155, 14 April 1970. Courtesy of: Archive of the Tomás Eloy Martínez Foundation in Buenos Aires   111

4.2 First page of Juan Domingo Perón's memoirs by Tomás Eloy Martínez, in *Panorama* magazine, issue 155, 14 April 1970. Courtesy of: Archive of the Tomás Eloy Martínez Foundation in Buenos Aires   111

5.1 Newspaper cover of Juan Villoro's 'El sabor de la muerte' (The taste of death). Buenos Aires: *La Nación*, 2010   146

Preface

I started writing this book in a fairy tale British city called Cambridge, where Latin America's catastrophes and violent events seemed impossibly distant. I finished it under the Covid-19 global lockdown in Mexico, where doing intellectual work seemed to be a luxury more than ever. It is fitting then that the fieldwork research for this book started one rainy afternoon in 2013, in Chimalistac, the old upper-class neighbourhood of Mexico City, where the author Elena Poniatowska lives. While waiting for tea to be served by her maid, I asked her what it was like to be a reporter during the 1985 earthquake. She recalled: 'It was to do what you are doing: to ask questions, only in much more difficult circumstances, not sitting in an illuminated room, with flowers and books, waiting for tea, but on the street, standing, in circumstances of tragedy.'[1] Since the 1950s, Poniatowska has repeatedly left her comfortable house in order to ask all kinds of people all kinds of questions. What she does, like several other authors I have interviewed since then, is often complex work, which can nevertheless be described in these simple terms: she goes out and asks strangers questions.

Poniatowska compared her writing to that of an author living in Paris or New York, where they might write about the state of their soul; this is not so of an author living in Mexico. There, she said, reality assails you at every moment, from every angle, 'reality enters your house and overwhelms you'. It is not by chance that this phrase resonates with the words of the Argentinian Rodolfo Walsh, when he wrote, 'it could have happened a hundred kilometers away, it could have happened when I wasn't there' (Walsh 2013: 43),[2] explaining his reasons for embarking on the investigation that would result in his killing.

Before the coronavirus pandemic, I thought this book was going to be about the world we live in, and about certain (narrative) ways of making sense of it. In the wake of the pandemic, I believe that close, critical examination of narratives of reality – and the ways in which journalism conducts these examinations – is more important than ever. The global fear and suffering resulting from the spread of the virus will certainly lead to new ways in which literature and journalism attempt to make sense of this unexpected 'end of the world' experience. This book is now, however, a book about the pre-Covid world we used to live in. In particular, it is about the period from 1955 to 2010 in Latin America, and the way in which some authors attempt to make sense of its reality: by encountering other people face to face and writing about it. All the true stories studied here expose a degree of vulnerability in the authors and their informants, which is the inevitable risk of telling the truth about the self and others.

---

[1] In Spanish in the original. All translations are mine, unless otherwise noted in citations.
[2] 'Pudo ocurrir a cien kilómetros, pudo ocurrir cuando yo no estaba' (1969: 20).

In this study, I was compelled to respond to Edward Said's invitation to move out of the Western literary canon and search for otherness. The works I studied concern the other, but they are not seen through the 'imperial eyes' of the Spanish conquerors, nor through those of the European ethnographers or the American historians whose works have characterized notions of otherness (Pratt 1992). Rather, the other is seen through the eyes of a self who is, from a Western perspective, himself an other. I contend that this kind of other–self has to be rediscovered through the study of peripheral spaces of cultural production. And in this regard, maybe my fieldwork for this book really started one day in 2005, when I was a reporter at *El Imparcial* newspaper, in the Northern state of Sonora, Mexico, and my colleague Alfredo Jiménez Mota did not show up to his cubicle next door to mine. He was twenty-five years old, and he used to write about *narcotráfico* in our pompously called 'Special Investigations Unit'. Neither I nor the rest of the team believed that disappearing was a risk that could happen to us, for in that newsroom we were all young, passionate and, in retrospect, naïve journalists. Few years later, our country became one of the most dangerous places to practise journalism. I wrote this book thinking about all those who were never able to come back to their desks and finish their story, but also thinking about those who have been living in fear and still are doing what they love and feel compelled to do: to ask questions in order to find a truth. Although many of them have not called themselves authors, but 'only' journalists, their names should not be forgotten.

Foreword

Steven Boldy

Liliana Chávez, who was educated in literature and journalism in Mexico, and practised journalism there, wrote the basis of *Latin American Documentary Narratives*, grounded in often-harrowing Latin American realities, in the 'fairy-tale' [for some] city of Cambridge. From Cambridge she disappeared periodically to the Americas to conduct a series of in-depth interviews with authors from Argentina, Chile, Peru and Mexico. This was fertile ground for an academic project on the urgency of dialogue and storytelling, the pursuit of shifting truth in texts from 1950s to early 2000s. After Cambridge, Liliana's dialogues were enriched and widened in interactions with colleagues and students in New York, Berlin and Mexico City, and the development of projects on more specifically female experience such as her recent *Viajar sola*. What was 'merely' an excellent doctoral thesis developed in strength and nuance into a splendid final outcome and a future landmark in Latin American literary and social studies. Reflecting its own theme of intersection and fluid dialogue between genres and media, self and other, it is at once focused and unruly, structured and challengingly plural.

Beyond the guiding presence of Bakhtin and heteroglossia, Benjamin and the storyteller, Rama and transculturation, Bourdieu on cultural fields, an array of thinkers are introduced and clearly explicated throughout: philosophers, social scientists, political and literary theorists and essayists. Chávez displays conceptual rigour but no concessions to over-schematization as she follows through the labyrinthine evolution of texts from journalistic report or testimonial interview to highly complex multi-voiced or metadiscursive narratives. From García Márquez through Poniatowska to Roncagliolo, from Mexico and Argentina to cosmopolitan postmodern documentaries, the projects studied here overlap and diverge. LC studies their constant but diverse engagements with the other, with narration and truth, without imposing overly strict demarcations. She negotiates the slippery taxonomy of cognate testimonial narrative practices (*testimonio*, *crónica*, metadocumentary, new journalism, literary reportage and so on) with sense and tact. She extracts paths of intention and generic modes that she is able to draw on subsequently, while settling on her own favoured term 'documentary narrative'.

LC initially approaches writers in pairs, establishing communalities, teasing out difference: García Márquez and Walsh, Walsh and Tomás Eloy Martínez, Villoro and Caparrós. Playing on home ground and with locally informed irony, LC develops deliciously illustrated intertwined portraits of Elena Poniatowska and Carlos Monsiváis: aristocratic, foreign, guilty *catrina* longing to commune with the people and Protestant, sarcastic middle-class chronicler in a Catholic country. She follows their artful forging of legitimizing personae as mediators between popular culture and elite reader. While Poniatowska cultivates the air of the naïve interviewer of whom people will ask ¿qué preguntas va a hacer esta babosa ahora?', the detached observer Monsiváis is seen as 'another other' himself, offering a queer, camp reading of Mexican modernity. In their contrasting ways, they create a public space, a horizontal engagement with a national identity and popular culture previously generated vertically in Mexico by establishment figures from Altamirano to Bartra.

In the work of the Argentinians Rodolfo Walsh and Tomás Eloy Martínez, the backcloth is extreme political violence, surreal horror and nightmarish obfuscations of reality, where the writer faces real physical danger. The play between journalism and literature, fiction and reality, is observed diachronically as LC dissects multiple versions of a story from journalistic interview to literary narrative, from newspaper to book. Her reconstructing of the writing and rewriting process displays a confident grasp of political and editorial context and journalistic practice as she uses footnotes, paratexts and documents as generic shifters in these layered narratives.

A parallel process is followed in the analysis of a series of considerably later 'metadocumentary narratives', largely by journalist narrators: Guerriero, Alarcón, Roncagliolo and Fontaine. The development from the interviewing of the subaltern informant by a middle-class narrator to book-format text is plotted with sensitivity to the presence of the self-conscious narrator in the text. The focus here is on the fraught, physical act of interviewing, geographical displacement and a cosmopolitan, postmodern setting. In an age of democratic communications technologies, the encounter between self and other had become more of an act of negotiation. A new dimension of dialogue is introduced and foregrounded: the interview between LC and the author-interviewers (reproduced as appendix) and her canny interrogation of their accounts of their own moral and authorial stance. While the authors insist that they present themselves transparently, 'as themselves', in their books, LC draws out their fictional constructedness. The author interviews the subaltern with one voice and addresses his or her middle-class reader with another. LC acts firstly as interviewer and later as analyst, presenting her discourse to a yet another reader out in the academic world. This multidimensionality intriguingly reflects the dynamic nature of the texts characterized by LC as 'multiple selves exposing their desire for narration', 'an erotics of testimony', a 'new collective, heterogeneous and complex speech act'.

In her introductory pages, LC accepts 'Edward Said's invitation to move out of the western literary canon in search of otherness', and indeed the Latin American context she describes is characterized by the repression and censorship of authoritarian regimes and by searing class, cultural and racial difference. Her book is a sustained, multipronged, challenging and intelligent exploration of the literary figuration of truth in a rich selection of Latin American documentary texts over fifty years. While the earlier works are see as a 'veiled, baroque, alternative way of expressing anti-regime opinions without the risk of being censured', the later works are more postmodern and meta-literary in nature, but in all cases LC demonstrates exquisite sensitivity to tension and complexity and adopts unerringly appropriate critical approaches. Overall, she offers a masterful exploration of the paradoxes of the return to the book, to the literary, 'to tell a truth that, ironically, cannot be told through traditional journalistic formats'. In recent years, the fragility of truth has become more than evident in the wider Western world. The issues illuminated in this timely, intelligent and original book by Liliana Chávez are clearly far from 'other' to 'western' societies.

Acknowledgements

This book about dialogue would have not been possible without my own personal exchanges with many people, and to them I am deeply grateful for their time and words. First, I would like to express the greatest gratitude to my PhD supervisor at the University of Cambridge, Prof Steven Boldy, who has been a moral and intellectual support to me as I have continued my transatlantic academic adventure, even long after my graduation date. Also at Cambridge, I am grateful to professors Joanna Page, Geoffrey Kantaris, Rory O'Bryen and Brad Epps, from whom I have always received encouraging feedback and intellectual support. Thanks to my dearest female mentors Edith Negrín, Adriana Sandoval and Liliana Weinberg, at Universidad Nacional Autónoma de México, who accompanied me in the early development of my ideas, and warmly welcomed me back in Mexico.

Thanks to the scholars around the world who generously listened to my ideas and gave me valuable advice at various stages of my work, especially to Aída Hernández, Mónica Moreno, Hettie Malcomson, Oswaldo Zavala, Gabriela Polit, Aníbal González and Friedhelm Schmidt-Welle. Thanks also to the International Association for Literary Journalism Studies, where I found a unique shared enthusiasm for my topic of interest, and especially to Roberto Herrscher, John Bak, Ignacio Corona, Pablo Calvi, Rob Alexander, Bill Reynolds and Norman Sims.

I am deeply thankful for the generosity of the eight authors I interviewed for this book, who opened the doors of their homes, or sat patiently in a café, in order to share their stories with me: Elena Poniatowska, Leila Guerriero, Cristian Alarcón, Juan Villoro, Francisco Goldman, Arturo Fontaine, Martín Caparrós and Santiago Roncagliolo. Thanks also to those authors with whom I had informal discussions, and whose work is a great but inevitable absence here, in particular Gabriela Wiener. Special thanks must go to two Chileans: Diamela Eltit, whose literary workshop made me recall the reasons I write, and Pedro Lemebel, who took me by the arm for a walk around Santiago when he did not have much time left on Earth.

My eternal gratitude to my parents, José Trinidad Chávez Siordia and Elvira Díaz Gutiérrez, because even while living in a country which does not always encourage hopefulness, they have believed fiercely in education, mine in particular.

My personal and academic experience while writing this work would have not been the same without the communities I belong to. Thanks for the emotional support I always received from my fellows and friends at Fitzwilliam College, Cambridge; the Cambridge Mexican Society, and Cambridge-Mexico Solidarity; also, at Cambridge, my gratitude to the members of the Centre of Latin American Studies (CLAS), the Department of Spanish and Portuguese and the Department of Sociology. Special thanks to Julie Coimbra and Coral Neale, whose professional administrative support always went beyond expectations. I wish also to thank my colleagues from the research communities that made me feel welcomed back to Mexico: the Seminar Identities and Ruptures in Latin American Culture, and the Sociology of Culture Research Group, at Universidad Autónoma Metropolitana-Azcapotzalco, and the Espiral Seminar on Latin American Periodicals at Universidad Nacional Autónoma de México. I am equally thankful to my students at Universidad Autónoma Metropolitana in Mexico, whose debates reshaped my own views of the roles of literature and journalism in the present and future of Latin American societies.

This book is also the product of transcultural collaboration. I wish to thank Amy Martin at Bloomsbury for truly accompanying me in this journey, and Joanne Shortt Butler and Stevan Veljkovic for kindly and enthusiastically proofreading all these words. Thanks also to photographer Edith Cota for the cover image documenting my hometown.

The development of my research for this book took me from Mexico to the United Kingdom, and later to Spain, Germany, Argentina, Chile and the United States of America. It would not have been possible without the Cambridge Trust-CONACyT Scholarship, nor without the financial support of a Gibson Spanish Scholarship and a SEP Scholarship from Mexico. Travel grants from Fitzwilliam College, the Simón Bolívar Fund at CLAS, Santander Universities Fund, the Department of Spanish and Portuguese at Cambridge and the Ibero-American Institute in Berlin were also crucial for conducting fieldwork and presenting my findings at conferences. Thanks are also due to Fundación Tomás Eloy Martínez in Buenos Aires for the resources and information they generously assisted with. Turning my PhD thesis into this book was substantially aided by an Edmundo O'Gorman fellowship at the Institute of Latin American Studies, Columbia University, in 2020. Moreover, conversations there with scholars Frances Negrón-Muntaner, Graciela Montalvo and Daniel Alarcón motivated me to finalize this project. I extend my gratitude to these institutions, and the people working there, for allowing me to focus on two activities which are in many ways a luxury: reading and writing.

* * *

The author and publisher gratefully acknowledge the permission granted to reproduce the copyrighted material in this book.

An abbreviated version of Chapter 1 appeared in 2018 in *Textos Híbridos*, vol. 6. An early version of Chapter 2 was published in 2020 in *Literary Journalism and Latin American Wars. Revolutions, Retributions, Resignations*, edited by Aleksandra Wiktorowska, Margarita Navarro Pérez and Mateus Yuri Passos.

Most of the third-party copyrighted material displayed in the pages of this book are done so on the basis of 'fair dealing for the purposes of criticism and review' or 'fair use for the purposes of teaching, criticism, scholarship or research' only in accordance with international copyright laws, and is not intended to infringe upon the ownership rights of the original owners. Every effort has been made to trace copyright holders and to obtain their permission for the use of other copyrighted material. However, if any have been inadvertently overlooked, the publishers will be pleased, if notified of any omissions, to make the necessary arrangement at the first opportunity.

Introduction

Narrative becomes a problem only when we wish to give to real events the form of a story.

– Hayden White

Dialogue is the most basic form of communication among us, and yet it remains an enigmatic genre of speech. In daily contemporary life, the average citizen of the modern world is confronted with diverse modes of non-human-mediated interactions, from electronic cashiers and internet-based shopping to virtual reality games and social media for smartphones. The term 'IRL' (In Real Life) has been coined to describe human interactions outside virtual spaces. Furthermore, in the wake of our experience of the pandemic in 2020, it might appear that the development of 'intelligent' and affordable technologies assisting in bringing about face-to-face conversations are changing our everyday interactions. This book defends the importance of dialogue, both real and fictional, for our understanding of the contemporary world. Therefore, my approach inevitably departs from, and engages with, a Bakhtinean worldview of language: if the word is shaped by its social environment, I maintain that it is through our encounters with one another that human beings make sense of their world.

By relating the term 'world' to a certain reality that has been considered journalistic or newsworthy, I also seek to engage in current debates on world literature and to examine the place of Latin American literature in these debates. The Latin American documentary narratives I analyse here are based on global relations and transcultural exchanges, the history of which is linked to a postcolonial culture and intertwined with other narrative genres, particularly that of literary journalism. However, I agree with Mariano Siskind when he states, 'the world in Latin American world literary discourse is a space constituted by an antagonism that prevents its realization as a given totality of literary texts always already comparable to one another because of a supposedly common ground' (2014: 17–18). This book focuses on the 'differential specificity' of a marginal documentary trend that has formed its own alternative storytelling history and imaginaries at the margins of other more globally visible Latin American worlds.

My research, therefore, is primarily an interrogation of a particular narrative form: that of documentary narratives. I believe that the problems to be addressed regarding investigative journalism-based narratives are primarily ethical rather than textual, for I am in agreement with Aníbal González (1993), who notes that, stylistically, there is no way of differentiating journalistic narratives from fictional ones. However, in following the approach of Mikail Bakhtin (1981; 1987), I maintain that it is through stylistic analysis that it is possible to explore the implications of discourses that proclaim themselves to be acts of truth-telling. The focus of this study is thus on style, but only to the extent that style is a useful tool through which to view the dialogue between the documentary narrative and other social phenomena, within what is undoubtedly a diverse cultural field.

Because of their medial position in the literary and journalistic fields, Latin American documentary narratives question the capability of either to give a true account of society and individuals in times of uncertainty. These texts can be read, then, as baroque cultural products that reveal the inadequacy of language when it comes to giving reality a complete meaning – sometimes this applies in contradiction to their authors' intentions.[1] Beyond their stated intentions, I intend to demonstrate that these narratives exhibit the limitations of fully knowing the other. I conclude that the Latin American other has not changed since postcolonial studies began to observe them. The other is still the poor, the indigenous, the woman, the victim, the homosexual, the marginalized citizen in general. What has changed, however, is the self who tells the stories of these others. That is why these narratives offer an alternative response to the problem of telling the truth in complex contexts. In a world of instant, global communication, it is ironic that it is not such a common thing to do, to leave one's comfort zone, to listen to the account of a stranger and then to write about it.

To summarize, this book explores the relationship between journalism and the crisis of truth in contemporary Latin America, based on how the encounter between a journalist-narrator and his informant is represented in liminal, hybrid texts. These texts are a blend of many discourses, but journalism is the predominant influence. I focus mainly on textual representations of these encounters, as narrated by one of the participants. I then study how conversation functions as a research tool for the writer, and as a meaningful discourse technique produced in an intimate context, but represented and published as public dialogue. If, as Beth Jörgensen and Ignacio Corona (2002) have observed, there is a relationship between experience of crisis and the documentary impulse, then it might not be surprising that there has been a return to storytelling in books and the media, particularly in contemporary Latin America. Dialogue in our global era is still the essential and most effective form of human communication.

---

[1] I employ the word 'baroque' meaning a set of rhetorical strategies that generate a hybrid, polyphonic narration, but also implying a kind of playful attitude, sensibility or worldview that influences the position from which the author chooses to narrate, usually through the use of parody, highlighting the artifice of language. Although I will be relating some of these strategies to postmodern aesthetics (particularly in the case of Tomás Eloy Martínez), I am mostly basing my use of the term on Severo Sarduy's semiological theorization regarding which baroque aesthetics can be historically traced in Latin American narrative back to colonial times. In the twentieth century, these aesthetics surface in what he calls a '*neobarroco*' style, which is evident in the way some authors (e.g. João Guimarães Rosa, Alejo Carpentier) use intertextuality, intratextuality and other rhetorical games, by which the superabundance, the waste and pleasure transmitted through language, is equated with eroticism (2013). Although this concept has been mostly used in Latin American cultural studies, Sarduy relates it to other equally hybrid aesthetics, such as the camp and the kitsch, which I explore in Chapter 3, in connection with Monsiváis's *crónicas*. Bakhtin's concepts of *heteroglossia* and *carnival* are also discussed by Sarduy as distinctive features of contemporary Latin American narratives.

The journalist as storyteller

While flesh-and-blood, face-to-face dialogues may be going out of fashion, there is simultaneously a growing fascination with true stories and an evident increase in the technologies and formats that allow us to document reality in detail. These include digital photography and documentary films, reality television, talk shows, films inspired by real-life events, blogs and other electronic media, plus the more conventional biographical genres. Literary prizes, traditionally awarded to fiction writers, have begun to recognize non-fiction writing, the clearest example of which is the 2015 Nobel Prize for Literature, awarded to Svetlana Alexievich, 'for her polyphonic writings, a monument to suffering and courage in our time' ('The Nobel Prize in Literature 2015' 2014). Two years before, Mexican journalist and testimonial author Elena Poniatowska was awarded the Premio Miguel de Cervantes, the most prestigious literary award in the Spanish-speaking world.

In the context of the rise of social media, people interact in a world overloaded daily with data of all kinds, which, perhaps ironically, has generated a crisis of trust and truth. Acts of extreme violence between groups and individuals worldwide continually demonstrate that this is not a world in which one can tell the truth – or certain truths, at least – without risks. It is not surprising then to hear Walter Benjamin's words take on new significance against a backdrop of renewed interest in storytelling:

> Every morning brings us the news of the globe, and yet we are poor in noteworthy stories. This is because no event any longer comes to us without already being shot through with explanation. In other words, by now almost nothing that happens benefits storytelling; almost everything benefits information. Actually, it is half the art of storytelling to keep a story free from explanation as one reproduces it. [...] the narrative achieves an amplitude that information lacks. (1999 [1955]: 89)

For Benjamin, the modern world privileges information as a form of communication. Thus, there is, in his view, a certain scepticism towards the press and nostalgia for storytelling as a way through which knowledge and culture were transmitted.[2] Nevertheless, I believe that the storyteller has returned, ironically, through the dreaded press itself. He can be most clearly identified in those discourses that represent the 'real' story of a journalist-narrator, who, in their search for a truth, must have a face-to-face encounter with the other. In listening to this other and writing about him or her, the contemporary storyteller may act as Benjamin's craftsman, fashioning – in a unique manner – a human life, 'the raw material of experience' (107). Roberto González Echevarría raised a similar point within the Latin American context when he proposed that the origin of narrative in the region, after the Spanish conquest, must be found in

---

[2] Benjamin was aware of the documentary trend going on in Europe, as developed in the Soviet Union with the popularization of 'factual literature' or 'factography'. Benjamin's 'The Author as Producer' was a response to Sergei Tretyakov's 1931 presentation on factography at the Society for Friends of the New Russia in Germany (Hartsock 2016).

the aim to mimic discourses of authority, especially those founded on law and science. For González Echeverría, even contemporary Latin American literature maintains a link with this colonial history through a complex appropriation of documents and archives:

> Is a move beyond the Archive the end of narrative, or is it the beginning of another narrative? Could it be seen from within the Archive, or even from the subversions of the Archive? Most probably not, but if one form of discourse appears to be acquiring hegemonic power it is that of communication systems. Perhaps a new masterstory will be determined by them, but it is difficult to tell with any degree of certainty from the Archive. (1990: 186)

This book revisits the trajectory in Latin America of some of those forms of communication identified by Benjamin and González Echeverría as narratives beyond the literary. I refer to these as 'documentary narratives'. They encompass all literary modes of discourse that, in aiming to represent reality, exist in varying degrees of dialogue with journalism.

Nevertheless, the particular focus of this book is true stories narrated by a first-person witness, who is the journalist searching for first-hand accounts of an event, and who sometimes becomes the protagonist of such stories. Even since the turn of the twenty-first century, in Latin America it is still possible to find Benjamin's storyteller disguised as a *flâneur*, a chronicler or *cronista*. He, and sometimes she, is able to get away from home in order to listen to a selected other, to witness certain realities, to walk around and finally to return and write about it. In other words, these writers are able to generate experience. As described by Beatriz Sarlo, another follower of Benjamin, testimonial narratives are inherently linked to an embodied, collective experience of being in the world:

> The narration of the experience is linked to the body and the voice, to a real presence of the subject in the scene of the past. There is no testimony without experience, but neither is there an experience without narration: language liberates the muteness of the experience, it redeems experience from its immediacy or from its oversight and transforms it in the communicable, that is, the common.[3]

The very presence of this kind of storyteller in the media demonstrates their anachronistic nature. This is because the contemporary Latin American storyteller is in debt to a rather old journalistic narrative tradition, which is in itself a product of modernism that has – surprisingly – survived postmodern trends. It is no wonder that

---

[3] 'La narración de la experiencia está unida al cuerpo y a la voz, a una presencia real del sujeto en la escena del pasado. No hay testimonio sin experiencia, pero tampoco hay experiencia sin narración: el lenguaje libera lo mudo de la experiencia, la redime de su inmediatez o de su olvido y la convierte en lo comunicable, es decir, lo común' (2006: 29).

there is a nostalgia in this kind of narrative, for the authors seem to write in order to register the moment they are witnessing, and to not let time move on.

A story is always told to a specific listener, however. The account of oneself is, as Judith Butler (2005) states, always an account given *to* someone. It is then an account passing through the body of the storyteller, who cannot avoid leaving traces of his or her own self on the material. From a philosophical perspective, giving an account of oneself thus always implies a certain degree of confession. Facing the listener, the confessor is exposed in his or her vulnerability (Butler 2005; Cavarero 2000). From a literary perspective, however, contemporary documentary narratives can be linked with what Linda Hutcheon (1980) has called 'narcissistic narratives', due to the predominant presence of a self-referential or auto-representational narrator. This kind of self-mirroring, metafictional narrator has been studied widely, particularly as a characteristic of postmodern literature (McHale 1987; Hutcheon 1988). Nevertheless, I have found that there has been no equivalent attention paid to the use of this kind of narrator within the specificities of non-fiction. This is, of course, part of the 'critical marginalization' that literary journalism and similar forms have received historically (Hartsock 2016; Nance 2006). On the other hand, from the perspective of journalistic practice, the use of the first-person narrator is still a cause of passionate debate in professional encounters, at least in the Latin American context.

Recent approaches to the study of testimony as a socio-literary genre demonstrate a wider interest in the ethics of representation (Nance 2006), acknowledging the return of the storyteller (Dragas 2014) and the rise of the subjective turn (Arfuch 2002; Sarlo 2006). Alternative perspectives prefer to focus on self-representation alone, in the study of genres such as autobiography and memoirs (Molloy 1991). This study, however, focuses on dialogue; that is, the moment in which the encounter between the self and the other generates a clash of different worldviews. In the cases analysed here, this encounter borrows the methodology and stylistic form of the journalistic interview.[4] The macro-genre that I term 'documentary narratives' also gives rise to questions of self-representation, but the focus remains on how the first-person narrator impacts on the presentation of the other.

The representation of the other is addressed in this book, particularly in Chapter 1, as part of the study of the genre of *testimonio*. The other in this context does not, however, conform precisely to the definition used by subaltern studies and postcolonial theory. This view defines the other mostly in terms of race, gender and geographic differences, for the other is the one who is not a European (or Western) white man (Said 2003, Todorov 1992). In cases such as those analysed here, however, this definition is not specific enough. This is because the narrative self is also someone who could be seen as the other from the traditional perspective; therefore, further theorization is needed to define this 'new' other. Additionally, in this kind of narrative,

---

[4] I use 'interview' to refer to the actual conversation between the journalist and the informant, but also to name the journalistic genre *entrevista de perfil, semblanza*, portrait or profile. This is a written piece which is rarely a mere transcription of the real conversation with an informant, but a mixture of first-hand testimonies, citation of documents and the journalist's observations and opinions.

a public intellectual generally makes an ethical intention to tell a version of the truth, and in this my definition of documentary narrative intertwines with Kimberly Nance's (2006) definition of testimonial narratives. Both testimonial and documentary might seek justice, although for different reasons and through diverse research methods. My proposed definition also connects with Pablo Calvi's historical study of the particularities of Latin American literary journalism (2019), in which he identifies a strong drive for social and political action implicit in these narratives. Whether or not these ethical intentions are fulfilled by the works, however, depends on the degree of freedom of the particular time and place in which their stories circulate.

For the purposes of my research, I use a rough working definition of the other, which oscillates between Tzvetan Todorov's (1992), Ryszard Kapuściński's (2007) and Emmanuel Levinas's (1984, 1972) views on the question. When I refer to the other, then, it is to name the subject who does not write his or her own story but tells it to a (narrative) self, who is somehow different from him. I have found out that generally, although not always, this difference is based on social class. The authors analysed in this book use the concept in rather ethnographical terms; the other for them is the source of their stories or the informant who eventually becomes their (fictional) character. In a similar line of thinking, I refer to the otherness as the circumstances or context within which this subject acts and which differ from the authors' comfort zones.

In the following chapters, I analyse a variety of texts that have been classified as non-fiction, *crónicas*, *periodismo narrativo*, literary journalism or non-fiction novels, and which were published in the Spanish language between the 1950s and the 2000s. As a way of distinguishing these works from similar, *testimonio*-based literature, I refer to my corpus of study as 'documentary narratives'.[5] I am deeply aware of the exhaustive critical effort to classify and determine the specific nature of each non-fictional variant, and so I offer a summary of the main, relevant concepts in the first chapter.[6] It is not my aim, however, to impose another classificatory mark upon them, and, therefore, my term is not meant to be exclusive, nor a generic classification either, although it may overlap with traditional categories. I use 'documentary narratives' because it is the term which best defines the corpus I have identified, in order to illustrate my own research interests and arguments.

The selection of the corpus was based primarily on the authors' use of journalism, either as a research technique during fieldwork or as a discourse in dialogue with

---

[5] A similar term, albeit in its singular form, has been used by David Foster (1984) and by Julio Rodríguez-Luis (1997) with its Spanish translation *narrativa documental*. Although their works have been influential for mine, each term is based on different assumptions, theoretical perspectives and corpora; therefore, they cannot be considered synonyms. I discuss these concepts in Part III of this introduction. My concept does include some of Foster's case studies, but omits others.

[6] For foundational theoretical works on the subject, see, among many others, Johnson (1971), Zavarzadeh (1976), Hellman (1981), Foley (1986) and Hartsock (2016). For in-depth genre discussions in the Spanish American context, see Acosta Montoro (1973), Amar Sánchez (1992), González (1993), Rodríguez-Luis (1997), Chillón (1999; 2014), Herrscher (2012) and Carrión (2012). More recently, Roberts and Giles (2014) proposed a theoretical framework for non-fiction narrative which claims to identify and analyse 'any given text in this genre', based on a typology of ethnographic realism and cultural phenomenology.

others within their narrative. Secondly, these are works written in the first person, by a self-reflective narrator, who is usually depicted as a journalist or, more broadly, an investigator. They are all metafictional narratives – or more accurately, *metanonfictional* – for they demonstrate an awareness of their discursive nature. Because of their hybrid stylistic nature and their time of publication, they generally oscillate between modern and postmodern trends.

Although there is currently a boom in print and online media specializing in literary journalism in the region, I will focus on works published in books, and specifically those presented as a full-length story, and not short *crónicas* collections. I found that, at least in Latin America, the book still has a higher literary prestige, and it is a much more adequate format for the transmission of this kind of story. By publishing their story in a book, the authors have felt at liberty to reveal their ideas, as well as to experiment with language in a way that would be difficult to do in newspapers or magazines for a variety of economic, logistic and political reasons. It is not by chance, I suspect, that there has been a return to the book as an alternative medium through which to tell a truth that, ironically, cannot be told through traditional journalistic formats.

I intend to explore these narratives as a particular cultural phenomenon of contemporary Latin America, rather than to present an in-depth, case-by-case study of each. However, I focus on the investigative and literary work of the authors Gabriel García Márquez (Colombia), Rodolfo Walsh (Argentina), Carlos Monsiváis (Mexico), Elena Poniatowska (Mexico), Juan Villoro (Mexico), Martín Caparrós (Argentina), Santiago Roncagliolo (Peru/Spain), Leila Guerriero (Argentina), Arturo Fontaine (Chile), Cristian Alarcón (Chile/Argentina) and Francisco Goldman (Guatemala/the United States). Some of the authors are related to the Boom or Post-Boom literature, while some others are better known as journalistic chroniclers, as they are part of the group called 'Nuevos Cronistas de Indias'.

I do not intend to take a historical approach, for almost all the authors are still alive and actively producing, but the structure of my chapters might allow us to trace an 'evolution' of the documentary mode in themes and style. I consider 1968 a symbolic point of departure for my study of these 'contemporary' documentary narratives, since it is the time of the Mexican student protests and the Tlatelolco massacre, which motivated a rise in the already-established genre of testimonial narratives. Along with the influence of New Journalism as a phenomenon simultaneously related to social movements in the United States, this testimonial mode continued to pervade the representations of other major conflicts and catastrophes throughout the ensuing decades in Latin America: through the 1985 Mexico City earthquake, the Sandinista war in Nicaragua, Videla's dictatorship in Argentina and Pinochet's rule in Chile.

Intersections

Broadly speaking, the relationship between journalism and literature has been studied in diverse academic fields, such as literary, cultural, social and media studies. Against the general consensus regarding the hybrid nature of the subject, the academic approaches to it have been constrained by discipline in terms of their research methods and distribution of knowledge. This book, therefore, aims to fill a gap regarding the theorization of the role of documentary and/or journalistic discourse in Latin American literature by using a hybrid methodology. I base my reflections primarily on a textual analysis of the selected texts, borrowing concepts from literary, cultural and philosophical studies. Furthermore, I consider the journalistic practices that produce the raw material for the narrative. Thus, I also employ a sociological approach to address the authors' intentions and working processes. During fieldwork in Mexico, Argentina, Chile and Spain, I conducted in-depth semi-structured interviews with selected writers, as well as participant observation. Additionally, archival research was particularly important for my development of a palimpsestic reading of some texts that were originally published in newspapers or magazines.

As I intend to go beyond traditional discussions of genre regarding the degree of fictionality embodied by this kind of text, I will inevitably depart from some personal assumptions. Mainly, I assume that my selected texts are true stories about real people. I am concerned with the study of these texts as acts of speech, of truth-telling, particularly in circumstances in which freedom of communication is at risk. I assume, then, that these texts are products of a (journalistic) investigation, and I believe in the individual ethical intention to tell the truth, as espoused by a self-conscious author. It is not my intention to validate their claims of truthfulness, but to understand why it is so important for these authors to claim truthfulness.

This hybrid approach, both synchronic and diachronic, aims to contribute to the recognition of at least two documentary traditions, or generations, in the region. These generations of course overlap in a number of ways, and the relationship between them should be seen as a process, or continuum, of the same *fin de siècle* chronicle movement, rather than pitching them as two opposing groups or periods. For my aims in this analysis, however, I group authors according to the period of time when they had their most representative production. The three parts into which this book is divided are based on this classification.

The first part of the book, comprising this introduction and Chapters 1 and 2, gives a historical overview of the diverse genres under which what I call 'documentary narratives' have been studied before. These genres are *testimonio*, *crónica* and literary journalism. I also develop my own theoretical approach in order to propose a new reading of Latin American true stories which considers the process of production and the implications of the encounter between the journalist and his or her informant.

Chapter 1 critically reviews theoretical discussions and proposes an approach to the topic that brings to the light stylistic and ethical differences in the works of the authors I study. Chapter 2 focuses on works published in the 1950s, which I consider to be the immediate antecedents of contemporary documentary narratives, for their authors created two important trends for future generations. These are Gabriel García Márquez's *Relato de un náufrago*, which inspired a more 'literary' vein for the telling of true stories in the region, and Rodolfo Walsh's *Operación Masacre*, an exhaustive investigative piece, more in the tradition of reportage which still influences literary journalists today.[7]

Part II, comprising Chapters 3 and 4, analyses documentary writers of the 1970s–80s, who are considered to be the founders of the contemporary Latin American chronicle. Chapter 3 focuses on two Mexican chroniclers and public intellectuals, Elena Poniatowska and Carlos Monsiváis. I analyse how the physical position of the body in public space (e.g. squares, streets) affects the writers' perception of reality, particularly in texts that seek to understand national culture. In Chapter 4, I explore questions of journalistic intentionality in the literary work of the Argentinean writer, Tomás Eloy Martínez, particularly in his novels on Juan Domingo and Eva Perón. Based on my findings in his private archive, I demonstrate how the blend of journalism and literature can communicate a deeper truth in times of uncertainty and censorship.

These authors are part of a generation that was clearly influenced by modernist models, both in writing style and in the conception of the role of the author as public intellectual. Interested in popular culture and modernity, however, they go beyond the *modernistas* by innovating forms for representing oral speech, influenced by anthropological discourse and the techniques of the period. They have used the medium as a platform to express their political opinions, and they became popular as leaders of public opinion. Although they publish frequently in newspapers and magazines, their texts are rarely 'news' or other journalistic genres. Their writing frequently crosses borders with the essay, in their intention to explain or criticize what they see. Like the *modernistas* at the beginning of the twentieth century, they were an intellectual elite, mediating between powerful and non-powerful groups within society. Documentary authors from this generation witnessed the transition from authoritarian regimes, such as the dictatorships in the Southern Cone, civil wars in Central America and the ruling of the PRI Party in Mexico, to a democratic era in the region. It is possible to imagine that, within this context, documentary narratives flourished initially as a veiled, baroque, alternative way of expressing anti-regime opinions without the risk of being censored.

Part III of this book focuses on a second group of writers from the 1990s to 2000s, who are mostly journalists searching for new methods in research and narration. Chapter 5 examines the encounter with strangers in the travel accounts of the Mexican Juan Villoro after experiencing an earthquake in Chile and the Argentinean Martín Caparrós talking with immigrants around the world. I study the cosmopolitan perspective of the writer in relation to remote localities within a globalized context.

Chapter 5 contrasts the documentary intentions of Latin American authors with their textual self-representation. It is based on textual analyses of life stories published after 2000 and on in-depth interviews with Leila Guerriero, Cristian Alarcón, Arturo

---

[7] Although it is not common in everyday English, the word derives from the French *reporter* and refers to a journalistic presentation of an account ('reportage' *OED*). In this book, however, 'reportage' is used as a literal translation from the Spanish *reportaje*, which refers to a specific journalistic genre, usually lengthy and based on in-depth investigation; it is always signed (Bastenier 2009: 86). It can be equivalent to a news story or feature.

Fontaine and Santiago Roncagliolo. Contrary to the authors' intentions of documenting others' lives, I conclude that these stories offer an interrupted account of oneself, that is, the account of a contemporary storyteller pursuing a rarely fulfilled desire: that of truly getting to know the other.

The authors of this final part were born symbolically with the establishment of the Fundación para un Nuevo Periodismo Iberoamericano (FNPI), created in 1994 by Gabriel García Márquez and a group of writers linked with the former generation. Their writing is more related to reportage and to investigative journalism. They focus on the ethics of detailed research and verifiable information more than the innovations in form pursued by the earlier group. Some of them claim continuity with the original 'cronistas de Indias', and thus they have self-identified as 'nuevos cronistas de Indias'. Although they usually deny any connection with the postmodern turn, they often display at least one characteristic of what Linda Egan (2001) calls *postmodern journalism*: a rhetoric of anti-rhetoric; the exposure of the deceptive transparency of traditional journalism's mythical objectivity – mostly through controversial use of the autobiographical and metahistoriographical 'I' – and the undocumented representation of the thoughts of others. In Latin America, this period coincides with huge economic crises, like those of 1994 in Mexico and 2001 in Argentina, and seismic political changes, such as the presidencies of Hugo Chávez in Venezuela, Lula da Silva in Brazil and Evo Morales in Bolivia. These events marked an era of uncertainty that indicates a major crisis of trust in institutions. At the same time, this period has seen the rise of internet-based media and other communication technologies that have created alternative spaces for collective and individual expression beyond the mainstream media.

In the conclusions I state that while scholars have focused on the rhetoric and history of this kind of narrative, my reading considers the real, physical dialogue between the journalist and the other. I argue that the representation of this physical encounter between the self and the other through novelistic techniques influences the pact with the reader and challenges the notion of truthfulness. I conclude that documentary narratives can be a tool for the transmission of knowledge and an alternative medium for generating public debates in societies affected by political and social instability. In a world overwhelmed with data production, but also immersed in violent acts against those considered 'others', I argue that storytelling is still an essential form of communication between individuals, classes and cultures.

The book includes an appendix containing edited and translated transcripts of the interviews that I conducted in Spanish with eight Latin American authors: Elena Poniatowska, Leila Guerriero, Cristian Alarcón, Arturo Fontaine, Santiago Roncagliolo, Francisco Goldman, Martín Caparrós and Juan Villoro. These interviews are arranged in three thematic sets of semi-structured questionnaires, although the order changes depending on the degree of trust and empathy developed with each author and the time we had, as I tried to respect the natural rhythm of each interaction. In the first part, I asked similar questions about the beginnings of their literary and journalistic career and their definition of what they do (whether they call their work documentary narrative, *crónica* or something else). The second part focused on their investigative and creative process for non-fiction stories, and the third one was about the specific work I was interested in analysing.

I am conscious of the ethical pitfalls, and even the postmodern irony that such a transdisciplinary study might entail, in considering both literary analysis and in listening to and interpreting what some major authors have said – and want to say – about their own storytelling. After all, this is a book focusing on metanarratives, and in approaching oral sources I have unavoidably added another layer of information and complexity to the study of dialogue between the self and the others. Interviewing cultural elites is a challenge for any researcher. Although our conversations took place out of the public eye, in the surroundings of their everyday life, I was aware of their role not only as literary authors but as public intellectuals, who were used to being interviewed – albeit normally for the media and not for academic research (some of them were genuinely surprised to learn that they were being studied in a thesis). Of course, their diverse positions in both the cultural fields of journalism and literature influenced their self-representation and their responses to my questions.[8] Furthermore, the reader must have in mind that their testimonies, of course, were told to that specific 'other' who was me. At the time of our encounters, I was a PhD student from Cambridge, a former journalist and one-time *tallerista* (fellow) of the Fundación Gabo (for I approached some of them through personal and professional networks), and a young middle-class Mexican woman living in the United Kingdom, and who talked to them in the most standardized Spanish possible.[9] I sensed that every author was influenced differently by each of these social categories, into which they sought to accommodate their listener during our sessions. Beyond the acknowledged tensions and differences present in our conversations, however, it is my view that these interviews somehow manage to replicate the desire for self-narration and storytelling, which is also present in the works I analyse here. This hybrid approach to both the author and the narrator was for me a matter of research ethics. I believe that experiencing these encounters with the authors as 'the other' was also a form of expressing respect for the words of all the individuals involved in the real stories that I write about here.

---

[8] When I asked Villoro about his entry into the journalistic profession, for example, he started by acknowledging that the story might sound 'repetitive', assuming perhaps that the readers of this interview would be the same public he is used to.
[9] Coming from different countries, we all talk in diverse dialect varieties of Spanish, which of course was funnier during the conversations than it was while doing the transcripts and translations.

Part I

Courage

1

Naming the real

La Habana, December 1960. Rodolfo Walsh and Gabriel García Márquez were working together in the news agency Prensa Latina, headed by the Argentinian journalist and guerrilla leader Jorge Masetti. The Cuban Revolution had just won against the dictatorship of Fulgencio Batista, and Fidel Castro's new socialist government was dealing with the American embargo over the island. One day Walsh deciphered an encoded telegram sent from a CIA agent in Guatemala to Washington. The message was a detailed report of the US plans to invade Cuba, including the address in Guatemala where an army was being trained. Masetti decided to send Walsh to Guatemala as an undercover reporter, disguised as a protestant priest. The plan failed because Walsh's real identity was discovered in Panamá, but Masetti did not give up. Months later, Masetti and García Márquez were in Guatemala City's airport, drinking a beer while waiting for a connecting flight to Peru. Masetti wanted to go outside the airport and look for the training field. Nevertheless, García Márquez convinced him to have 'common sense' and proposed a consolatory task: to co-author a 'detailed account based on so many truths that we knew because of the encoded messages, but making believe that it was information obtained by us through fieldwork after a clandestine trip to the country'.[1]

Latin America might never have been a safe place to be a journalist, but what García Márquez's anecdote shows is that the limits between fiction and reality are not only a matter of rhetoric but of ethics. Against the impossibility of telling the truth without risking one's own life, García Márquez finds in fiction a moderate solution: 'safe from the risks of that childish prank, [Masetti] ended up accepting that we, the calm liberal guys, sometimes had a larger life'.[2] On the contrary, Walsh, like Masetti, defends his own concept of journalism, even until its final, tragic consequences: 'it happens that I believe, with all naivety and strength, in the right of any citizen to spread the truth he knows, no matter how dangerous it is.'[3]

---

[1] 'Un relato pormenorizado con base en las tantas verdades que conocíamos por los mensajes cifrados, pero haciendo creer que era una información obtenida por nosotros sobre el terreno al cabo de un viaje clandestino por el país' (García Márquez 1981: par. 6).
[2] 'A salvo ya de los riesgos de aquella travesura pueril, [Masetti] terminó por admitir que los liberalitos tranquilos teníamos a veces una vida más larga' (par. 7).
[3] 'Sucede que creo, con toda ingenuidad y firmeza, en el derecho de cualquier ciudadano a divulgar la verdad que conoce, por peligrosa que sea' (1957: 9).

These two extreme images of the self, the intrepid and serious investigative reporter and the cynical creative author, are present to diverse degrees in the construction of the narrators of Latin American documentary discourses. In *Latin American Adventures in Literary Journalism* (2019), one of the few academic books regarding the history of this genre in the region published so far, Calvi explores the role of both Walsh and García Márquez within the context of the Cuban Revolution, proposing that their 1950s works represent the roots of the *testimonio* genre and show the historical tension between politics, literature and journalism in Latin America. While looking for differences between US and Latin American literary journalism, Calvi focuses on what he calls the 'concealing narrator' as opposed to the first-person narrator popularized by the 1960s American New Journalism. Nevertheless, since the final decades of the twentieth century there has been a boom in the first-person journalist-narrator that is perhaps anachronic if we compare it with similar, earlier American narrative trends, but nonetheless unavoidable as an ethical response to state and organized criminal violence against journalists and civil society in general. This phenomenon has been particularly striking in the case of Mexico, as Gabriela Polit states in *Unwanted Witnesses. Journalists and Conflict in Contemporary Latin America* (2019). Focusing on female journalists currently working in Mexico, Argentina, and Colombia, from the perspective of the sociology of emotions, Polit's ethnographical and literary research explores the effects of trauma in reporters who have been covering stories of violence and mourning in their countries. Although Polit's corpus and theoretical approach differs from mine, as she focuses on those who are, in the journalistic jargon, '*periodistas de a pie*' (journalists down to earth, everyday life reporters), I believe this book contributes to the same debates I address here. In particular, concerning the ethical role of journalists in the region, and regarding what Polit terms the 'rebranding' of the *crónica* genre by some chroniclers (such as Leila Guerriero, whose work I analyse in Chapter 6) as a 'survival strategy', for obtaining prestige in the literary field through book publishing (Polit: 15-17). While Polit looks mostly to the investigative works of *periodistas de a pie*, I explore more hybrid works, usually written by what Viviane Mahieux (2011) calls 'accessible intellectuals', within the *modernista* tradition of literary authors publishing in newspapers, who thus develop a sense of closeness with their readership. In my view, these two types of *cronistas* are two faces of a contemporary phenomenon by which, because of the risks that telling true stories entails in the region, journalists are becoming authors and, sometimes, vice versa. Although sometimes positioned at opposed poles, they all are social and political actors on a hybrid and complex cultural field, who are writing long-format stories, normally independently from mainstream media, based on exhaustive fieldwork and using the resources of fiction. And these stories, usually published in books or multimedia digital formats, cannot be read merely as aesthetic products but as responses to social problems. Their storytelling techniques – as Polit shows in her research, and as I demonstrate in mine – are in the service of their emotional, creative need to express while witnessing traumatic events, and of their empathetic relationship with their informants while pursuing social justice.

I thus agree with Calvi and Polit that the historical particularities of this genre in Latin America have to be understood in relation to the constant political instability of the region, and the authoritarian and conservative regimes that have controlled free speech and the press since the nineteenth century, all of which has certainly made journalism a highly dangerous activity.

Like Calvi, I recognize that a third-person narrator or fictional first-person narrator was preferred by early literary journalists writing under oppressive political circumstances. However, I also think that contemporary documentary narratives in the region have seen a strong switch to the use of the self-referenced, first-person narrator, and it is within this trend that I find the most *literary* examples of today's literary journalism. This study thus departs from the point at which Calvi's book ends – that of the non-fiction of the 1950s, with its strong ideological aims – in order to explore new narrative trends in 'democratic' and neoliberal Latin America, for as Polit argues, 'contemporary *crónica* (and especially urban *crónicas* dealing with social suffering) is the genre that has defined Latin American neoliberal expansion' (2019: 13).

Regardless of the self-designated role of the narrator within the narrative, I argue that what the storyteller has become, at least in the Latin American setting, is an essential figure through which true stories reconstruct reality. By the last two decades of the twentieth century, there was clearly a new way of representing reality in Latin American fiction. In fact, those years were a time of censorship and mistrust in authority in Latin America, a time of dictatorships, exile, and civil wars. It is this background that might have inspired Mario Vargas Llosa's theory on *sociedades cerradas* (closed societies), that is, societies in which literature and history can no longer exist independently. In a society highly controlled by the state, Vargas Llosa proposes that literature and history are able to exchange identities like in a masquerade ball (1990: 17–18).

This was also the time in which the rise of the postmodern novel met the Boom, with its purpose of destroying the hierarchical difference between historical and fictional discourse. Regardless of the declared death of the author, in Latin America the role of the writer as an important public figure in society has endured from the modern to the postmodern era. The social value of the *grandes firmas* (great signatures) led to the recognition of certain documentary narratives, written by established fiction authors (González 1993).

Latin American non-fiction was also influenced by avant-garde literature, whose writers questioned the prestige and power of journalistic discourse. Authors experimented with language in order to represent a diversity of discourses, particularly those that were part of everyday life. The difference is in what Aníbal González calls 'a return to ethics', during the 1980s. The post-Boom writers, including the documentarists, used journalism either as a thematic resource or a motif within their works. The journalistic value system was thus employed as a way to question facts. This attitude towards social reality was understandable if one considers that most of these authors had a personal involvement with politics. For Aníbal González, journalism is no longer an emblem of truthfulness, as it was to Modernism, but a narrative strategy:

> In today's Spanish American narrative (from the 'boom' to the 'postboom') journalistic discourse is assimilated quite freely and openly as one of many elements in a textual repertoire that contributes to the narrative. This does not

mean that journalism is no longer significant in fictional narrative; rather, whenever journalism is alluded to or otherwise 'grafted' onto the fictional text, its significance becomes more complex and varied. (2006 [1993]: 108)

From a literary and historical perspective, journalism might be a link between modern and postmodern literary production in Latin America. As a modern product itself, journalism in documentary narratives can be seen as a value system, raising ethical considerations regarding writing. At the same time, it can be read as a parodic discourse used to question the relationship between the author and the other, the fictional and the 'real' world. Although journalism has been practised since medieval times, its definition, objectives and methods have undergone constant change across times and cultures (Davis 1983). If any characteristic has remained as an essential condition for journalism to exist, it would be to tell stories that are new, relevant and (apparently) true. I, therefore, use the word here both in the sense of social discourse and a method of investigation which claims to seek the truth, one which is transmitted through a public platform, regardless of the obviously subjective approach that each author, publisher and consumer of journalism brings to the practice.

I argue, however, that journalism, as used by documentary narratives, exhibits the impossibilities of truthful representation. If it is clear that by inserting journalistic discourse into a literary work, the author problematizes the notion of truth, then what I am interested in questioning here is not the nature of the discourse per se, nor the traces of journalism in a literary story, but the traces of those flesh-and-blood selves involved in the plot.

Non-fiction genres

The non-fiction genre was born from a time of crisis and disorder (Zavarzadeh 1976). Hartsock (2016) traces the origins of literary reportage – which would later inspire American New Journalism – as a proletarian, literary genre used in the late 1920s by the workers' movements in Germany and the Soviet Union.[4] Nevertheless, deciding upon a name for narratives based on true stories has long been a source of debate among practitioners and researchers. According to my interviewees, it seems that the former are less worried than the latter about assigning a label to their work. For Santiago Roncagliolo, for example, there is no difference between *no ficción*, *reportaje*, *crónica* or *periodismo*, but they are all different from the novel in methodology: 'one involves going out searching and the other involves locking yourself in your room and inventing'. Leila Guerriero defines her work as like that of a documentary film, 'it is a documentary, but in written form', while Cristian Alarcón considers himself a *cronista* (a chronicler) and a 'storyteller of the real'. Although considered the *cronista*

---

[4] Another interesting account of the history of non-fiction in relation to the Latin American context is given by Amar Sánchez (1992).

par excellence in contemporary Latin America, Martín Caparrós confessed that he still cannot decide how to define his own writing: 'I say it is a chronicle-essay, a chronicle that thinks, an essay that tells, but I would like to find a synthesis, I still have not found it.'

Linda Egan (2001) collected some names used for this type of discourse. In Spanish, these texts are called *periodismo de autor, ficción documental, sociología auxiliar, crononovela, socioliteratura, metaperiodismo, periosía, periodismo cultural, relato de no–ficción, periodismo interpretativo, neocostumbrismo, no (crónica)vela*. In English, the related concepts include transfiction, faction, transformation journalism, creative non-fiction, documentary narrative as art, apocalyptic documentary, paraliterary journalism, mid-fiction, metareportage, liminal literature, radical news analysis, higher journalism, journalit, postmodern journalism, parajournalism, participatory journalism, the new non-fiction, poetic chronicle.

For John Bak (2011), the differences in the terms, across languages and eras, are the result of the intentions of the texts, and also of the cultures in which they are embedded. Latin American documentary-like narratives demand to be read in their specific context. In the first place, because they claim to be produced in a field that expands beyond the realm of the literary. Their writers usually claim not to have artistic intentions, but rather a commitment to truth-telling. At the same time, while they are published in journalistic spaces, these works employ more flexible ethical standards than American or British journalism.[5] These authors are also well-known fiction writers, and, additionally, they are often socially and politically committed to issues in their countries, and most of them act as public intellectuals.

Beyond the specialized Latin American studies on specific, related genres – which I will discuss briefly in this section – critics have identified a trend towards the documentary effect that could have particular resonance for the region. Nevertheless, the names applied to similar narratives diverge. For example, David Foster's concept of 'documentary narrative' includes 'those texts in which a credibly real story is given an explicit narrative framework by an intervening narrator' (1984: 53). Foster's corpus focuses mostly on fiction, for he considers the best practitioners of this trend to be well-known novelists. On the contrary, Julio Rodríguez-Luis thinks that 'documentary narrative narrates certain events – that could be organised in such a way as to create a biography – that have taken place, and the authenticity of which the author wishes to be evident'.[6] His taxonomic study, therefore, focuses on the degree of intervention of the author, who he calls *mediador* (mediator). For Foster, this narrative is in opposition to the traditional concept of literature because it is not its intention to transform reality in any artistic manner.

---

[5] Some of the authors interviewed, for instance, claimed not to use voice recorders, and fact checking is not a common practice in Latin American media.

[6] 'La narrativa documental relata ciertos hechos –que pueden organizarse de modo que conformen una biografía– que han tenido lugar y cuya autenticidad quiere el autor que resulte evidente' (Rodríguez-Luis 1997: 84).

Clearly, when reading these narratives after the experiments of the postmodern era, one cannot avoid a certain scepticism. Narrative strategies such as the configuration of a self-conscious, metafictional narrator or diverse modes of intertextuality, for example, can be read as typical postmodern devices rather than a way of emphasizing the act of witnessing. Nevertheless, I agree with Amar Sánchez (1992) and Frus (1994), that non-fiction raises political and historical issues that should be analysed along with discursive strategies. It is precisely because literary journalism, used as a synonym or subgenre of the non-fiction genre, was born as a subversive form in an age of uncertainty that its content should read through this form, so as to question what we mean by literature and by journalism. For Frus, non-fiction is part of a complex public discourse, and therefore its literary strategies are more than stylistic attributes. This point of view coincides with the declared intentions of the authors I interviewed for this book, as they stated that they included, for instance, a first-person narrator mostly because of their intention to show themselves as witnesses to the events they narrate.

As stated earlier, it is not my intention to become embroiled in a discussion of genres and disciplines that has already been a significant part of the debate surrounding this field. Therefore, what follows is a brief critical description of three major genres that I have identified as the most influential for the kind of writing I am focusing on.

Crónica

Criticism usually associates this genre with newspapers, for journalistic discourse has legitimized fiction authors who practise *crónica*, as well as establishing the standards for its writing (Reynolds 2012). From a wider perspective, the origins of this writing form can be found in Classic epic and in the work of the historical chroniclers of the Middle Ages in Europe (Benjamin 1999). However, the term 'chronicle' as a literal, albeit imprecise, translation from the Spanish *crónica*, was first used in the American colonies to designate the conquerors' and missionaries' reports on new discoveries to the Spanish kings. By using the Spanish word, *crónica*, critics such as Aníbal González and Susana Rotker (1999) highlight the difference between any type of *chronicle* and the kind of writing that refers to a particular Spanish American literary tradition. Moreover, Mahieux (2011) expands awareness of the genre to Brazilian authors of the 1920s and 1930s writing in Portuguese, such as Mário de Andrade, Machado de Assis and later Clarice Lispector.

During the first decades of the independent nations, the chronicle appears again, this time as a tool for constructing national identities and educating citizens. The writer as an intellectual mediating between *la ciudad letrada* (the lettered city) and *el pueblo* (the people) found a way to represent and even to create the nation through the chronicle.[7]

---

[7] This is the age of foundational works for Latin American literature, such as Juan Domingo Sarmiento's *Facundo: Civilización y Barbarie* (1845) in Argentina and Euclides da Cunha's *Os Sertões* (1902) in Brazil. These texts are not only literary but social proposals aiming to establish modernity on the continent (González 1983).

Nevertheless, scholars agree that the *modernista* writers at the beginning of the twentieth century were actually the inventors of the contemporary *crónica*. Rotker considers the Latin American *crónica* to be a mixed genre: the result of the encounter between literary and journalistic discourses. Based on Roman Jacobson's communication theory, Rotker states that in *crónicas* the poetic and referential functions have the same level of importance. It is not by chance that these authors, usually fiction writers, published their *crónicas* in newspapers, as it was the modern medium par excellence.

Crónica, as it was originally practised by the *modernistas*, can be defined as 'a short piece, published in a journalistic venue and produced in a polished literary style' (Reynolds 2012: 3). A broader and more contemporary concept of the genre, however, is given by Ignacio Corona and Beth Jörgensen: 'the genre is adaptable and elastic in form, an invitation to writers to mix an extratextual reality with artful fictional touches' (2002: 5).

Whereas in the literary field its study has been traditionally neglected, in the journalistic one, it has a privileged place as representative of public opinion: 'the chronicle, along with the literary article, became the most aesthetically elaborated section of the newspaper, serving a function of enlightened entertainment amid the predominant documentary information' (Jörgensen and Corona 2002: 7).[8]

The chroniclers have also theorized on the genre, perhaps in their aim to legitimize their own position within such an unstable field, or as to substitute for the lack of literary prestige. For most of them, the main element involved in the concept is time. For example, Carlos Monsiváis ([2006] 2010a) thinks that the chronicle reclaims literature in an anti-intellectual environment, that of the press, whereas Juan Villoro defines it as 'literature under pressure'.[9] On the contrary, Peruvian editor Julio Villanueva Chang argues that 'a chronicle is no longer a literary and fun form through which to be informed of events but it is, overall, a form of "getting to know" the world'.[10] According to Villanueva, the *crónica* should avoid the use of the first person, while Colombian editor Darío Jaramillo Agudelo considers the 'I' to be a distinctive device of the chronicle and describes it as 'a long narrative of a true incident, written in the first-person or with the visible participation of the narrative self, about events or individuals, or unusual, unexpected, marginal, dissident groups, or about shows or social rituals'.[11]

---

[8] Carlos Monsiváis's introduction to his own 1980 anthology of Mexican chronicles is recognized as one of the first formal attempts to legitimize the genre. Three years later, Aníbal González published the groundbreaking academic study *La crónica modernista hispanoamericana* (1983). It was followed by Susana Rotker's *La invención de la crónica* (1992), which became very influential among practitioners, for it was reprinted in 2005 by the FNPI, as a handbook for journalists, with a prologue by Tomás Eloy Martínez. It is only in recent decades that the variety of academic books on the topic has increased. See, for example, Bencomo (2002), Jörgensen and Corona (2002), Bielsa (2006), Aguilar, Darrigrandi, Méndez and Viu (2014), Mahieux (2011), Reynolds (2012), Angulo Egea (2014, 2017) and Polit (2019).

[9] 'Literatura bajo presión' (Villoro 2011: 578).

[10] 'Una crónica ya no es tanto un modo literario y entretenido de "enterarse" de los hechos sino que sobre todo es una forma de "conocer" el mundo' (2011: 590).

[11] 'Una narración extensa de un hecho verídico, escrita en primera persona o con una visible participación del yo narrativo, sobre acontecimientos o personas o grupos insólitos, inesperados, marginales, disidentes, o sobre espectáculos y ritos sociales' (17).

While *cronistas* coming from a more literary background emphasize how quickly these texts can be written, *cronistas* with a stronger background in journalism find space and time in this genre that they cannot have in traditional news writing. These opposed perspectives are understandable, since the former may be comparing the *crónica* with the novel, while the latter compares it with the news. However, this further demonstrates the complex conception of the genre in terms of its production.

There are claims from some practitioners and academics that the Latin American chronicle remains a marginal genre. In fact, some authors, such as Caparrós, agree that the word 'cronista' was used in the newsrooms to refer to the lower level of reporters, that is, an apprentice or a mere informer who would take notes in order for others to write the news (see Interview 2). Nevertheless, by the end of the twentieth century, there was a renewal of interest in the *crónica* that had not been seen since *Modernismo*.[12] International publishing houses like Penguin Random House Group, Alfaguara, Anagrama and Planeta have launched their own collections, some of them edited by renowned authors within the field; mass media and institutions related to the genre have also published selected *cronistas*.[13] The current editorial boom in chronicle collections is thus an example of the way in which this hybrid form aims for literary prestige. It fact, in these anthologies, those authors who are already established are featured repeatedly.

Fundación Gabriel García Márquez para el Nuevo Periodismo Iberoamericano (better known as 'Fundación Gabo' and taking over from the former Fundación para un Nuevo Periodismo Iberoamericano) has also played an important role in organizing workshops, prizes and professional encounters for young journalists across the Spanish-speaking countries. From its headquarters in Cartagena de Indias, Colombia, this foundation has become the influential journalistic elite of the region. As a result of seminars and conferences organized by this foundation, for instance, a group called Nuevos Cronistas de Indias was created in 2008. Officially, the group has twenty-six members from Latin America and Spain, born between the 1950s and 1980s, including some of the authors studied in this book: Guerriero, Caparrós, Villoro, Alarcón and Goldman.[14]

---

[12] Mass media publications interested in what is called 'investigative journalism' have been opening up more spaces for the genre. Some examples are print magazines as *Etiqueta Negra* in Peru, *Gatopardo*, *Emeequis*, *Letras Libres*, and *Proceso* in Mexico, *Soho* and *Lamujerdemivida* in Colombia; and online media as *Cosecha Roja* and *Anfibia* in Argentina, *Sinembargo.mx*, *Animal Político* and *El Barrio Antiguo* in Mexico, *The Clinic* in Chile or *El Faro* in El Salvador.

[13] The most relevant anthologies have been edited by Monsiváis (2010a), Martínez (2006), Samper Ospina (2008), Jaramillo Agudelo (2012), Fonseca and El-Kadi (2012), Carrión (2012) and Alarcón (2015). Some academic publications also include a selection of chronicles or reflections of their writers, besides a variety of critics reflecting on the topic, such as Jörgensen and Corona (2002), Aguilar, Darrigrandi, Méndez and Viu (2014) and Angulo Egea (2014). Although all these texts have published chronicles in Spanish, some of them include Brazilian authors in translation. Brazil certainly shares in this editorial boom – as an example, see Ferreira dos Santos (2005).

[14] In an updated version of the Nuevos Cronistas' website, authors Elena Poniatowska and Santiago Roncagliolo are also included. See nuevoscronistasdeindias.fnpi.org for the full list of authors in this group.

In terms of authorship, today's chroniclers are an elite, much as they were in the *modernista* era. If they do not all portray the glamorous lifestyle that their forerunners did, they still claim a connection with this heritage, as a means of distinguishing themselves from everyday news reporters. In Villanueva's words, *crónica* is still 'an aristocratic genre with hopes for a pop culture audience'.[15] Nevertheless, the main difference from past generations might be that contemporary chroniclers consider their research methods to be as important as the narrative style they use. The *reportería* or *reporteo*, and therefore the documents, images and voice recordings they obtain during it, seem to be the base on which they establish their credibility.

Furthermore, it is important to acknowledge that the field of the *crónica* has been traditionally dominated by males. In one of the first anthologies on the topic, *A ustedes les consta. Antología de la crónica en México* (You will attest. Anthology of the chronicle in Mexico, Monsiváis 1980), there are only three women among the thirty-seven selected writers: Elena Poniatowska, Carmen Lira and Magali Tercero. In the more recent anthologies (Jaramillo Agudelo 2012; Carrión 2012; Angulo Egea 2014), the situation has not changed: for every ten male chroniclers, there are on average two women published. Within the subgenre of travel writing (*crónica de viaje*), a striking example is *Con la sangre despierta* (2009), edited by Juan Manuel Villalobos: there is only one women, Alma Guillermoprieto, out of eleven chronicle authors who he invited especially to be a part of this collection. However, some exceptions are anthologies focusing only on female *cronistas*, such as *Mujeres que viajan solas. 15 cronistas frente a las aventuras que marcaron sus vidas, desde París al Amazonas* (Women who travel on their own. 15 chroniclers facing life-changing adventures, from Paris to the Amazon, 2013), edited by Ana Pizarro, and the special issue of *Altaïr Magazine* 'A bordo del género. Cruzando fronteras' (On board of gender. Crossing borders, 2017).[16]

As the term *crónica* continues to be used without a consolidated definition, it is usual among academics to mix its literary history with that of other documentary or testimonial-like genres. If some defend the *crónica* as a uniquely Latin American genre, others have been trying to integrate it into a particular form of journalism or literature. For instance, María Angulo Egea (2014) uses the term *periodismo narrativo* (narrative journalism) as the equivalent in Spain of what in Latin America have been named as *crónica*, whereas Egan views the chronicle as a synonym of *literary journalism*, which for her would be a subgenre of non-fiction. Furthermore, Calvi describes *crónica* as an 'early form of Latin American nonfiction' (2019: 85), considering the genre in its modernist phase only as a precedent of literary journalism.

There are other scholars, including myself in the context of this book, who prefer to view the *crónica* within a broad spectrum of non-fiction narratives as they

---

[15] 'un género aristocrático con ilusiones de un público pop' (603).
[16] For more about the female travel experience in Latin America represented through diverse documentary genres, see my book *Viajar sola: identidad y experiencia de viaje en autoras hispanoamericanas* (To travel alone: identity and travel experience in Spanish American female authors, 2020). For the relationship between *crónica*, violence and investigative journalism in the work of contemporary female Mexican journalists, see Polit (2019).

analyse the representation of the 'world' in Latin America. In this line of thought, studies such as those of Beth Jörgensen (2011) and Gabriela Polit (2019) on Mexican non-fiction writing, often include *crónicas* in corpora that also consider other works dealing with social realities but which are traditionally classified as literary, ethnographic or journalistic. In my view, this hybrid approach to contemporary *crónica* should be less about searching for their *modernista* writing roots and more concerned with possible connections to an equally modern Latin American cultural phenomenon that Ángel Rama (1982) once identified as '*transculturación narrativa*' (narrative transculturation).[17] Looking at a variety of literary Latin American works, from Gilberto Freyre, Mário de Andrade, Mariano Azuela and Juan Rulfo to César Vallejo, José María Arguedas, Alejo Carpentier and Jorge Luis Borges, Rama traces an alternative artistic tradition that oscillates between the avant-garde and the regional, and between the fantastic and the critical-realism in order to represent the unequal social transformations they witnessed. Rama states that Latin American writers, as well as painters and musicians, have created hybrid or transcultural products as an artistic solution to reconcile modernity with tradition (1982: 29). In an updated interpretation of Rama's transculturation theory, Siskind (2014) sees in Latin American modernist authors, usually chroniclers, an anxiety over not being able to fully reach modernity and links it to the construction of a cosmopolitan author, who oscillates between 'the world' and local culture. I believe the history of *crónica* genre, at least in its contemporary stage, aligns with Rama's theory as well as with Siskind's view on cosmopolitanism. Chroniclers are both witnesses to and actors within a reality they intend to make sense of in order to communicate it out to the world, and for that they must create new forms of expression that integrate the local and the global. By considering *crónica* as a modern, transcultural mode of representing reality, within a wider spectrum of non-fiction narratives, we might be giving this genre an anachronistic position in the Latin American cultural field, but it is more interesting to think of the reasons why contemporary authors choose to take a nostalgic view of the world.

Literary journalism

Even though the genre has been gaining prestige among practitioners since the 1960s, literary journalism is still looking to consolidate its place as a field of study in American academia. Although some scholars study literary journalism within English and comparative literature departments, it is integrated most commonly into the fields of media and cultural studies. An example of this is the foundation of the International

---

[17] The concept *transculturación narrativa* was based on Fernando Ortiz's neologism *transculturación* referring to a particularly Cuban form of cultural appropriation. Opposed to the widespread anthropological term 'acculturation' to describe the process of individual or social acquisition of a new culture, Ortiz uses 'transculturation' to name 'the different phases of the transitive process from one culture to another' (Ortiz [1963] 1987: 96, my translation), in which, nevertheless, there is a loss of the former culture (*desculturación*) but also the creation of new cultural phenomenon (*neoculturación*).

Association for Literary Journalism Studies (IALJS) in 2006, after the first International Conference on Literary Journalism in Nancy, France. For this association, literary journalism is synonymous with reportage, and it is thought of as 'journalism that is literature' ('About Us', International Association for Literary Journalism Studies).[18]

As a writing style, it is related to long-form journalistic genres, such as reportage, profiles and the feature story. The IALJS considers the following terms to be synonymous with their definition of American literary journalism: literary reportage, narrative journalism, creative non-fiction, New Journalism, *Jornalismo Literário, periodismo literario, Bao Gao Wen Xue*, literary non-fiction and narrative non-fiction.

Some critics study this form as a kind of non-fiction, that may also have derived from postmodern metafiction (Frus 1994; Zavarzadeh 1976; Hellmann 1981). Others consider it a completely new genre (Wolfe 1973), a subgenre of the novel (Hartsock 2016) or even an academic discipline in its own right (Bak 2011). To avoid the traditional aesthetic values implied when using concepts in which the adjective *literary* precedes *non-fiction* or *journalism*, Phyllis Frus (1994) opts for the term *journalistic narrative*. In referring simply to writing that is about 'newsworthy subjects' (Frus 1994: ix), the term offers a wider space for the positioning of all kind of hybrid texts between literature and journalism, with emphasis on both content and form. In spite of their diverse names, all these concepts are generally used indiscriminately to refer to a type of journalism that can be valued as literature because of its narrative qualities. Literary journalists use dialogue, monologues, descriptions, allegories, metaphors, intertextuality and other constructions, in order to recreate the events aesthetically.

In the United States, literary journalism has been published widely in print and online journalism since the flourishing of the New Journalism movement in the 1960s, led by authors such as Tom Wolfe, Norman Mailer and Truman Capote.[19] According to Johnson (1971), New Journalism was born as an alternative way of writing about reality, in opposition to the established mass media. Therefore, it implied a complete change in journalistic practice. One of the main characteristics of this form was the inclusion of sociological and political commentaries, which signposted a subjective perspective, for 'it is the writing itself – its style and technique, its expression of the writer as a person, and its record of human events – that is central' (xi–xii). Although

---

[18] Since 2009, the IALJS has sponsored the peer-reviewed journal *Literary Journalism Studies*. They mostly publish papers analysing American texts; there have been just three papers and one interview published on Latin American literary journalism. Nevertheless, their 2015 annual conference in Puerto Alegre, Brazil, was the first one to be held in a Latin American country and to offer space for presentations in Spanish and Portuguese. As a participant, I observed that there is still a need to legitimate, academically, the connections between *crónica* and literary journalism.

[19] Tom Wolfe is recognized as the one who coined the term 'New Journalism' in 1973, when he published the movement's first anthology, along with Michael L. Johnson. However, by that time Johnson had already published a theoretical book analysing the works of Wolfe, Mailer and Herr, under a very similar title: *The New Journalism. The Underground Press, the Artists of Nonfiction, and Changes in the Established Media* (1971). For Hellmann (1981), New Journalism was symbolically born in 1965, when Tom Wolfe's *Kandy-Kolored Tangerine-Flake Streamline Baby* and Truman Capote's *In Cold Blood* were published. By then, however, Capote had already coined his own term: 'nonfiction novel'.

innovations in journalistic writing style seem to be an inherent condition for this movement, there is also an ethical condition for its existence. For Johnson, at the root of this new way of telling facts there is a renewed commitment to honesty and thoroughness as important values of journalistic practice. Hence, a free press is a basic condition for New Journalism to exist.

In the European context, this kind of text was called *literary reportage*. Both movements, however, have their origins in the literary realism, as well as in the journalism, of the nineteenth century. The difference in the terms might be based on the intentions of the texts. On the one hand, American New Journalism has explored innovations in form, but remains rooted in detailed, objective research. European writers, on the other hand, have found, through reportage, a way to express themselves in a more interpretative style, and to write about censored topics, following an ideological, journalistic tradition (Bak 2011).[20] It is possible that the contemporary Latin American *crónica* is a blend of both American and European traditions, and, thus, it is difficult to incorporate all documentary-like works into the realm of literary journalism. If the existence of a free press is a critical condition for literary journalism to exist, then emblematic Latin American non-fiction narratives written or published in censored environments – or in exile, without signature, or disguised as fiction – would not exactly fit into this category.

Nonetheless, I sense that when the term 'literary journalism' is preferred over chronicle, it has more to do with the international dissemination of the work than with the scholar's genuine intention, or that of the *cronista* himself, to mark a difference between the terms. In the Spanish American context, Roberto Herrscher (2012) uses the term *periodismo narrativo* to refer to true stories told with 'the arms of literature'[21]; however, as he is a member of the IALJS, Herrscher's practice-based work has contributed to stablishing a closer relationship between *crónica* and literary journalism in international studies of the genres.

Regardless of the many practitioners, editors and scholars publishing reflections about this genre within the Latin American context, until Calvi's book, mentioned earlier, there has not been much theoretical research considering the place of Latin America in a still-incomplete global history of literary journalism. This might be due to the fact that this term has been more widespread among American academics or scholars publishing mainly in English. However, it is notable that academics from the Spanish- and Portuguese-speaking worlds studying *crónica* are using the term 'literary journalism' as a sort of English translation of the genre when publishing internationally. An interesting example in this regard is the edited book, *Literary Journalism and Latin American Wars* (2020).[22] In the introduction, Aleksandra Wiktorowska opts to gather all the works studied under the label of 'reportages' when she states:

---

[20] For more on contemporary literary journalism around the world, see Norman Sims (1990; 2007), Bak and Reynolds (2011), and Keeble and Tulloch (2012).
[21] 'Las armas de la literatura'.
[22] The book is part of the series ReportAGES, aiming to reflect on literary journalism based on the coverage of wars across the globe and edited by another IALJS member, John Bak.

Born from colonialist and postcolonialist affronts and affinities with European and North American traditions, as well as from specific nationalistic needs, cultural as well as political, Latin American literary journalism is arguably a direct product of the people's volatile past. Be it a specific *reportaje, testimonio* or *crónica* or a more general *no ficción, periodismo narrativo, jornalismo literário* or *periodismo literario* (depending on the nation and the language referenced), these reportages stroke more often than calm the political and social unrest frequently associated with the development of South and Central America. (1–2)

Wiktorowska notes that a distinctive characteristic of Latin American journalism, in comparison with its 'North American cousin', is that it has always been politically engaged. This particular kind of literary journalism has been called in Spanish *reportaje comprometido*, and it is the equivalent to the French *journalism engagé* and the Polish *reportaż zaangażowany* (Wiktorowska 2020: 4). Calvi has also noted the main difference regarding American literary journalism, which is linked to another stylistic difference: the use of the narrative 'I' (2019: 199–201). While American New Journalists popularized the authorial stance by narrating mostly in the first person, according to Calvi, Latin American authors opted for a third-person narrator for contextual and ideological reasons. These are linked to another genre endemic to the region, *testimonio*, which has shared roots with literary journalism following on from the Cuban Revolution triumph period. I pursue the details of the relationship between *crónica*, literary journalism and testimonial narratives in next section.

Testimonio

Testimonio is a word charged with complex and sometimes contradictory meanings in the history of Latin American literature. In its literal translation as 'testimony' it evokes the legal narratives used to bear witness in a judicial process, and in this sense is linked in recent history to the oral transcripts of the *Comisiones de la Verdad* (Truth Commission Trials) across Latin America, and with the testimonial discourse derived from other collective traumatic events, from the dictatorships of the Southern Cone to the Holocaust (Sarlo 2006, Nance 2006). Nevertheless, I refer here to the particular, Latin American socio-literary genre, that has been called *novela-testimonio, testimonial novel* or simply *testimonio*.

The *testimonio* genre is formally related to different modes of narrative, such as autobiography, biography, confessions, memoirs, letters and diaries. Furthermore, its origins have been traced back to the same works as those often cited in evaluating the roots of the Spanish American *crónica*, that is, the discovery accounts of the Americas written by missionaries or military men for the Spanish kings, usually called *crónicas de Conquista* (Nance 2006: 167). However, the main difference with other fictional and non-fictional genres might be its strong sociopolitical engagement as a sine qua non condition for its legitimation. I therefore refer to *testimonio* as it has been described by John Beverley: 'The situation of narration in *testimonio* has to involve an urgency to communicate a problem of repression, poverty, subalternity, imprisonment, struggle for survival, and so on, implicated in the act of narration itself' (1996 [1989]: 26). Due to the fact that the narrator is often illiterate, or is not a professional writer, the process of writing a *testimonio* involves recording, transcription and editing by an intellectual, generally a well-known novelist or experienced journalist.[23]

In 1966, Miguel Barnet published *Biografía de un cimarrón*, defining it as the first *novela-testimonio*. By then, there had been two other books published first in newspapers, and current research considered them as important precedents of *testimonio* as well as of literary journalism: Gabriel García Márquez's *Relato de un náufrago* (The Story of a Shipwrecked Sailor), published in 1955 in Colombia, and Rodolfo Walsh's *Operación Masacre* (Operation Massacre), published in 1957 in Argentina (Calvi 2019, Nance 2006). I will present my own analysis of these seminal works in next chapter; however, it must be said that the most significant influence these authors had on the development of *testimonio* might not have been the testimonial style they use in these early works, which is certainly present, but rather their own political engagement with the Cuban Revolution during their journalistic activities there as founders of the news agency Prensa Latina. Under Fidel Castro's brand new government, *testimonio* became part of a political program focusing on allegorical stories that aimed to encourage social advancement (Calvi 2019: 200).

The genre of *testimonio* was consolidated with the incorporation of the testimonial category into the prestigious Premio Casa de las Américas in 1970. By this time, the Cuban Revolution (1953–9) had triumphed and campaign diaries were popular, such as those by Ernesto 'Che' Guevara. It was a time in which freedom of speech was being negotiated, against the international backdrop of the Cold War (Franco 2002). In the intellectual field, theories about the West and the representation of otherness were emerging, particularly those developed by the cultural anthropologist Clifford Geertz and the sociologist Edward Said.[24]

The *novela-testimonio* shares its documentary mode with other literary trends developed throughout the same period, such as New Journalism, the Latin American Boom and the postmodern novel.[25] Regardless of the realistic mode that the *testimonio* can share with the 'new historical novel', which was also in fashion at the time, the evolution of the testimonial novel should be viewed as a different phenomenon. In a polemical piece, Seymour Menton (1993) describes it as a trend that had declined

---

[23] For Beverley, all kinds of narratives where the *testimonio* is invented or reworked 'with explicitly literary goals' (38) are not *testimonio* but pseudo–*testimonio*. These kinds of works are more linked with postmodern literature, an aesthetic that testimonial theorists reject. This observation could be highly problematic and leads to confusion about the literary value that he paradoxically claims for *testimonio*. Under these non-*testimonio* texts, he even includes Barnet's testimonial novel and Capote's non-fiction novel.

[24] In fact, one of the most important academic interpretations of *testimonio* came from the Latin American Subaltern Studies Group. Founded in America by John Beverley, Ileana Rodríguez and other scholars, it was based on the Subaltern Studies Group among whose associates was Said.

[25] Williams (1997) considers postmodernism in Latin America to be related to the historical and political situation of the region, as shown in the novels of writers such as Guillermo Cabrera Infante, Manuel Puig, Ricardo Piglia, Salvador Elizondo, Carmen Boullosa, José Emilio Pacheco, Diamela Eltit, Sylvia Molloy, among others.

by the 1980s and that 'never attained the high productivity, the great variety and the outstanding artistic quality of the New Historical Novel' (190–191).

Although emerging from the tradition of social realism, *testimonio* is not defined as a novel, and therefore its fictional nature is overlooked. But, like the *archive novel* (González Echevarría 1990), *testimonio* also claims to form a pact of truth with its reader.[26] It is not surprising, then, that legal terminology was incorporated into this form: 'The position of the reader of *testimonio* is akin to that of a jury member in a courtroom. Unlike the novel, *testimonio* promises by definition to be primarily concerned with sincerity rather than literariness' (26). In contrast to Lukács's (1978) notion of the novel as a grand narrative seeking universal truth through the representation of a whole society, the theorists of *testimonio* make a claim for the importance of specific, localized stories. This is why Beverley defines *testimonio* as 'a nonfictional, popular–democratic form of epic narrative' (Beverley: 27). The traditional role of the writer as one who speaks on behalf of the 'voiceless' has, therefore, vanished. The erasure of the function of the author, who is just a compiler, is one of the main characteristics of a testimonial style. George Yudice states that 'the *testimonialista* gives his or her personal testimony "directly", addressing a specific interlocutor' (1991: 42). These debates concerning sincerity and literariness, nonetheless came to a head with the controversy following Elizabeth Burgos's *Me llamo Rigoberta Menchú y así me nació la conciencia* (translated as *I Rigoberta Menchú: An Indian Woman in Guatemala*, 1983).[27]

Against Yudice and Beverley's concept of the author as an objective mediator, some critics studied the aesthetic and ethical implications of the role of the writer, mainly during the processes of transcription and edition (Vera León 1992; Sklodowska 1993). For them, the testimonial pact is complex because there will always be a tension between the worldview of the writer and that of the informant: 'it is evident that between the codes of truthfulness of the witnesses and of the editors, there is a gap, which is due to their different cognitive positions towards the world.'[28]

Although *testimonio* has been written about and studied from different points of view, an aspect agreed by all relevant actors to be inherent to the genre, is that *testimonio* is not only a discourse but an *act* that implies solidarity. '*Testimonio* is a means rather than an end in itself' (Beverley 1996: 279), and a way to understand experience and to preserve memory (Randall 1992).

---

[26] González Echevarría (1990) uses *archive novel* as a metaphor, coming from the language of the law to define a type of Latin American novel that creates a modern myth based on an old form, generally represented by an unfinished manuscript and an archivist/compiler. As an archive that accumulates and classifies information, these novels tend to go back to the origins of Latin American history, representing the relationship between legitimacy and power.

[27] The book was based on interviews with Rigoberta Menchú, conducted and edited by the Venezuelan anthropologist Elizabeth Burgos. After being awarded the Nobel Peace Prize in 1992, Menchú declared that Burgos did not tell all of her story. In 1999, anthropologist David Stoll published *Rigoberta Menchú and the Story of All Poor Guatemalans*, in which he claimed that some facts had not happened exactly as Menchú narrated them.

[28] 'Es evidente que entre los códigos veredictivos de los testigos y de los editores hay un hiato que se debe a sus diferentes posturas cognitivas frente al mundo' (Sklodowska 1993: 86).

In contrast with its definition as a new genre between the 1960s and the 1980s, current scholarship considers *testimonio* to be a subgenre of Latin American non-fiction literature. Some academics remain drawn to traditional testimonial works for the way their position beyond the literary realm seeks to make a difference regarding human rights violations. For instance, in her book *Can literature promote social justice?* (2004), Kimberly Nance analyses a wide spectrum of testimonial narratives and updates Beverley's now classic definition of the genre: '*testimonio* will be defined as the body of works in which speaking subjects who present themselves as somehow "ordinary" represent a personal experience of injustice, whether directly to the reader or through the offices of a collaborating writer, with the goal of inducing readers to participate in a project of social justice' (7). Nance's definition goes beyond the written discourse and considers also the presence of testimonies in film, television, the arts and even architecture. She concludes that *testimonio* must be considered in its collective nature, that is, as a social project involving a community of speakers, writers, readers and critics. While remaining sceptical about the concrete effects that testimonial narratives can have on society and justice, Nance highlights their importance as an alternative tool that invites readers to act. Between the old 'poetics of solidarity' that turned out to be a fantasy and the new 'poetics of isolation', Nance proposes a 'prosaics' of *testimonio* that could restore its political potential (158). Beyond the shared origins and stylistic coincidences, I consider this characteristic to be the ethical link between *crónica*, literary journalism and *testimonio*: they have in common an intention to tell the truth, and they invite people to do something with it.

Finally, other scholars have moved towards a less politically charged speech, proposing that *testimonio* should be analysed as any other hybrid discourse. They prefer to use concepts such as the *testimonio mood* or *storytelling* to refer to life narratives based on real experiences:

> It is time for testimonio de jure of scholarship to move forward because testimonio de facto on the ground has undergone a profound metamorphosis and many migrations: from discipline to discipline and border to border; from text to textiles, radio, and graphic art; from transcribed and written to spoken, public, and performative; from fixed contexts to interactional ones; and from nonfiction to fiction and film. Included in these movements is the key figure of the *testigo*, or eyewitness. In the informant role, the eyewitness described in these pages may be invented, false, hidden, or disengaged while living in insile (internal exile), or even nonhuman. (Detwiller and Breckenridge 2012: 2)

Coinciding with Nance, this definition liberates *testimonio* from the written form, allowing for the exploration of a variety of media in which *testimonio* could find a new place. It is interesting to note also that *testimonio* is no longer attached to a particular person or locality, but rather it can be found at the intersections of self, community and geopolitical borders.

The traditional concept of *testimonio* as a tool for social action remains, in whatever way, useful as a form of expression for individuals in marginal communities, such as indigenous villages, urban peripheries or prisons. If it is true that there is still a high percentage of illiteracy and poverty in Latin America, technology and new media allow more possibilities for the self-expression of the other who, without any need of a mediator, can now become the author of their own story. For instance, projects such as *Tejiendo nuestras raíces* (Knitting our roots, 2010), an audiobook of testimonials in Spanish and Mayan, are recovering myths and worldviews of native cultures as well as details of everyday lives. These new practices challenge the traditional definition of *testimonio* as mediated speech and lead us to question, again, the politics of representation.

From a media studies perspective, Beatriz Sarlo (2006) analyses documentary texts and films in order to criticize the excess of testimony in contemporary representations of the past. Although it is true that testimonial accounts have been essential to the reconstruction and validation of cases of human rights violations, it is important to critically examine the ethical implications of the first-person narratives, when testimonies are the only source, or the most trustworthy one. She analyses, for instance, the artistic representation of disappearances during the Argentinian dictatorship, as described by the children of the victims, and which have been seen as part of a post-memory trend. For Sarlo, however, in the twenty-first century there is no *posmemoria*, just another form of memory in which an event has to be precariously reconstructed through disorganized pieces of information, because it is the only way to tell the stories of those who were silenced and murdered:

> The first person is essential in order to restore what was removed by the violence of state terrorism; but at the same time, one must not ignore the questions that arise when this person offers their testimony about what never would have been known otherwise, and also many things where she, the first person, cannot claim the same authority.[29]

But testimonies respond to the needs or trends of the public sphere, and in the established *teatro de la memoria* (theatre of memory) the other who speaks is no longer the poor; the illiterate; the exploited, but rather the female; the marginal; the subaltern; and the young. Nonetheless, it is only by the means of fiction, Sarlo concludes, that one can say what has not been said already, what the victim was not able to document: 'literature, of course, does not dissolve all the problems set out here, but in it a narrator always thinks from outside the experience, as if humans could take control over the nightmare and not simply suffer through it.'[30] It is worth noting that Sarlo refers to

---

[29] 'La primera persona es indispensable para restituir aquello que fue borrado por la violencia del terrorismo de estado; y al mismo tiempo, no pueden pasarse por alto los interrogantes que se abren cuando ofrece su testimonio de lo que nunca se sabría de otro modo y también de muchas cosas donde ella, la primera persona, no puede reclamar la misma autoridad (162).'

[30] 'La literatura, por supuesto, no disuelve todos los problemas planteados, ni puede explicarlos, pero en ella un narrador siempre piensa desde afuera de la experiencia, como si los humanos pudieran apoderarse de la pesadilla y no sólo padecerla' (166).

fiction and literature as synonyms, which is not uncommon but is the kind of practice that makes it difficult to conduct an analysis of non-fictional narratives as literature.

Towards a theory of documentary narratives

Francisco Goldman's *The Art of Political Murder. Who Killed Bishop Gerardi?* (2007) uncovers the case of Bishop Juan Gerardi, murdered in Guatemala in 1998. Although the text is written in the first person, it is hard to find an explicit representation of the journalist at work. References to the process of investigation are used in this case not to tell of his own experience as a reporter approaching others, but to provide information that confirms his involvement with the topic. It is only in a paratext, in the afterword, that Goldman represents himself in relation to the case. He closes with a scene in which he meets Judge Yassmín Barrios, who had received several threats during politically charged cases:

> She didn't seem to register my name, though maybe she did, because turning back to Mario, she asked him, 'And when is that book on the case coming out in Spanish?' Mario told her that the person who'd written it was standing next to her. She was astonished, and thanked me, and I replied that I'd done nothing but narrate as faithfully as I could what she and many others had accomplished in the case. She spoke about her inability to 'understand people who live by denigrating the truth.' Then she gestured to her police bodyguards, and said that there was a *patrulla*, a police patrol car, waiting for her around the corner.
>
> 'As you can see,' Judge Yassmín Barrios said, 'I gave up my own freedom so that other people can have justice – so that other people can be free to say what they believe'. (381)

The scene depicts two characters who have been involved in telling the truth about others, but from different positions. In comparison with the judge who has to live surrounded by bodyguards, the writer is much safer. By including the judge in his narrative, as well as other people who risked their lives for the case, Goldman becomes not only the one who listens for the truth of Gerardi's case, but for the truth of the tales of all those who cannot tell the full story.

Born in Boston to a Catholic, Guatemalan mother and an American, Jewish father of Ukrainian ancestry, Francisco Goldman is personally and professionally linked to Latin America. Goldman is aware that, in contrast with colleagues publishing from within Latin America, he can be a more committed listener: 'I felt that these kids needed someone to tell the truth; I was the only one who was in a position to do it and I felt very compelled to do so' (Interview 4).

In unstable societies, in which journalism has become a dangerous profession and the media are censored, transmitting the other's truth is always a risk. Goldman is aware of the privileges of publishing his true stories abroad: 'I have never had much sympathy for the *gringo* point of view, neither then nor now, but it is another way [of doing journalism], you are more detached' (interview 4). As opposed to the American New Journalism, which has a long tradition of employing the first-person narrative, the Latin American writer cannot aim to tell the truth of others without risking censorship, or even death. These writers therefore speak from the position of someone who, in order to tell the story of others, must tell their own story too. In contrast with authors publishing abroad, such as Goldman, Latin American writers need to include themselves in the narrative, for being a witness can supplement a lack of official information, or of a trustworthy legal process. This might explain why these authors are more concerned with modes of telling the truth that entail fewer risks, than with delivering 'objective' information.

Rather like the priest hearing confession, the journalist acts as a responsible listener. What documentary narratives show, however, is that there is a contradiction between the aim of the journalist-narrator to express himself, and his will to say what people trust him to say. This is why I find that, in documentary narratives, the narrator is configured as both a storyteller and a professional listener. This phenomenon is especially seen in self-reflexive narratives which employ metafictional techniques, and which I would call 'metadocumentary narratives'.

If truth is a social construct, as Michel Foucault (2012) claims, then in Latin America this truth will have a different mode through which it can be told. One must attend to the particularities of the context in which documentary narratives are produced. The four modalities of the truth-teller as categorized by Foucault – prophet, sage, technician, parrhesiast – are combined in different ways by each culture or society. In the particular case of Latin America, I believe that writers who aim to tell true stories have to combine the role of the sage, 'the subject who tells the truth but has the right not to speak' (88), with that of the technician and the parrhesiast, that is, the ones who tells the truth.[31] The act of questioning, for example, is a way of combining the role of the sage with that of the parrhesiast. Depicting themselves as interviewers, and thus letting the other speak through their responses, may provide a way without taking too much risk.

The act of telling the truth, or *parrhesia*, involves a pair: a speaker and a listener. The risk in telling the truth is always on the side of the *parrhesiast*, the speaker who needs courage to tell the truth about himself even if that may involve angering the listener, breaking a connection or experiencing hostility. The receiver of this truth is an expert in listening, like a technician or a teacher. In theory, this *teckne* passes the knowledge to society without putting himself at risk.

The activity of listening to someone else's truth involved several people in Ancient Greece, and in Christian culture was a responsibility shouldered by the confessor or

---

[31] Foucault defines *parrhesia* as 'the courage of truth in the person who speaks and who regardless of everything takes the risk of telling the whole truth that he thinks, but it is also the interlocutor's courage in agreeing to accept the hurtful truth that he hears' (13). The concept is opposed to the art of rhetoric, in which the way of saying things does not affect or determine the relations between individuals, and it does not involve any link between the speaker and what he states. For Foucault, the rhetorician is 'an effective liar' and a parrhesiast is 'the courageous teller of a truth'.

spiritual director. In modern societies, Foucault notes, the role is practised by the doctor, psychiatrist, psychologist or psychoanalyst. Nowadays, I argue, the journalist can also act as a professional listener who transmits the true story entrusted to him.

Nevertheless, in Latin America the journalist-narrator is in a highly vulnerable position, for their role vacillates between that of the idealized, professional who listens to a parrhesiast, and that of being the parrhesiast themselves. This is because telling the truth is a risk for them too, but they feel a responsibility to tell it.[32] The assassination of Rodolfo Walsh is perhaps the most iconic example of this situation (see Chapter 2), but there are yet more contemporary cases of journalists who have disappeared after reporting and publishing documentary narrative books, like the Mexican Javier Valdez Cárdenas, who wrote about the 'war on drugs' from his native Sinaloa. It is not out of mere fascination with literature, at least not in all cases, that Latin American authors opt for storytelling as a strategy for communicating certain information, it is a mode without the risks that other modes of truth-telling might imply. To publish a book, rather than an article in a newspaper or magazine, can also be a way of avoiding media censorship or heightened attention while writing about particularly sensitive topics.

While Foucault dedicates more space to the role of the speaker, the truth-teller, Judith Butler (2005) focuses on the receiver of the confession. For Butler, giving an account of oneself is an embodied phenomenon that involves more than one person, since one must always tell the truth to another. It is my view that documentary narratives are not a medium to 'let the other speak' – at least not to the same ideological degree that it was for the *testimonio* authors of the 1960s – but they are the textual evidence of a dialogue between two selves exposed at a moment of vulnerability to a reader. For even if this dialogue is never equal and fails in its ambition of getting to know the other, it is still a valid response to the human search for truthfulness in uncertain times, and it is evidence of the enduring question of how we can approach each other, in both private and public spheres.

By representing versions of themselves in other people's stories, writers are nonetheless not only building up their authority within the text, but also claiming their right to belong to a certain cultural field. Certainly, the point of view of the author affects the representation of reality, and this is not only a matter of narrative strategy but also the result of the embodied, real and complex experience of encountering the other. In order to ask the other 'who are you?', as Butler proposes, one must first give an account of oneself, recognizing one's differences from the other. This might not be a conscious, creative process or a deliberate narrative strategy for writers who conceive of their task as a service to others' testimonies. It is, however, a process that is irrefutably dialogic. This is why I maintain that the texts and the authors analysed in the following pages offer both an aesthetic and an ethical response to the problem of truthfulness and communication in uncertain times, as well as a challenge to continue the endless dialogue between the world and the word. Writing perhaps at

---

[32] An illustrative example is that of Roncagliolo's *Memorias de una dama* (2009).

the end of the world, documentary authors respond to their 'cosmopolitan desire' (Siskind 2014 and 2019) on their own terms: by offering a hybrid narrative that can be read as an updated version of what Fernando Ortiz (1963) called '*neoculturación*', for these works are a new cultural product that emerges from the interactions of many individuals and societies.[33] Within this postcolonial framework, it may also be useful to revisit Severo Sarduy's reflections on the '*neobarroco*' as the (literary) art of the unbalanced, recherché or affected artifice, that of transgression, revolution and rupture (2013 [1972]: 426).This is particularly the case, when focusing on rhetorical strategies used by authors who are closer to the Latin American novel tradition of the Boom and Post Boom, or those who attempt to address issues about or embedded in popular culture through the lens of a melodramatic (parodic or not) sensibility[34].

The self

Santiago Roncagliolo's *La cuarta espada. La historia de Abimael Guzmán y Sendero Luminoso* (The fourth sword. The story of Abimael Guzman and the Shining Path, 2007) begins with a self-reflective narrator responding to a rhetorical question. A shameless and ironic Santiago Roncagliolo-as-narrator explains his reasons for getting involved in the journalistic investigation that makes up the book:

> Why a reportage on Guzmán? Because it sells. Or because I think it sells. Or because it is the only thing I can sell. I have always been a mercenary of words. Writing is the only thing I know how to do and I try to monetise it. I now live in Spain and I am trying to make myself a place as a journalist. I need something novel, and the hot topic in the last year, after the 11-M, has been that of terrorism.[35]

In an attitude that resembles that of a *modernista* chronicler, this narrator shows his awareness of the commercial value that words hold for newspapers. The journalistic field whence Roncagliolo is speaking, however, is no longer the romantic, Bohemian scenario that previously served as a platform for the Spanish American *modernista* authors, lending them social popularity and literary prestige (Reynolds 2012).

---

[33] Focusing on recent Latin American fiction about violence, such as the works of Roberto Bolaño, Siskind revisits his own idea of 'deseo de mundo' (desire for the world) to propose a new view on cosmopolitanism at 'the end of the world' and the 'overwhelming experience of loss that defines the very contemporary sense of crisis' (2019: 206).

[34] For a deep sociohistorical study of the relationship between baroque aesthetics and the Spanish colonies, see Bolívar Echeverría (2017), and for a contemporary insight into melodrama and popular culture in Latin America, see Hermann Herlinghaus (2002).

[35] '¿Por qué un reportaje sobre Guzmán? Porque vende. O porque yo creo que vende. O porque es lo único que puedo vender. Siempre he sido un mercenario de las palabras. Escribir es lo único que sé hacer y trato de amortizarlo. Ahora vivo en España y trato de hacerme un lugar como periodista. Necesito algo novedoso, y el tema de actualidad en el último año, tras el 11–M, es el terrorismo' (23).

It is true that *crónica* is still, as a genre, mostly published in newspapers by intellectuals who 'enjoy a recognised position in the field of restricted production' and manage 'to overcome the isolation of the written word' (Bielsa 2006: xii). The contemporary press, however, is not as well-disposed towards fiction authors as it used to be, or at least not universally. What Roncagliolo's metafictional narrator demonstrates in this quoted passage, is that an ambitious author, who aims to make a living from journalism – and not an occasional *cronista* – must obey the rules of the market and look for a story that sells. This cynical narrator, thus, represents what I see as a generational change in Latin American authors interested in 'giving voice to the other'. If the documentarist goes out of his comfort zone and risks his security in order to encounter the other, it is less because of a social or ideological commitment to the topic – that past testimonial authors would have claimed to be motivated by – and more because the topic is newsworthy.[36]

Another difference is that today's documentary authors have found that the traditional format of the book, rather than any mass media, is the best platform for telling true stories. Two years before publishing *La cuarta espada*, in October 2005, Roncagliolo published a journalistic article on Abimael Guzmán in the Spanish newspaper *El País*. Divided into two chapters, the story is told in the third person, without any allusion to the author's personal experience or opinions on the topic. Parts of the information, and of the text itself, were repurposed for the book. The main stylistic difference was the first-person narrator. By inserting the self into the narrative, the new story became a dialogue between the protagonist and the journalist, even if the former never gave him an interview. Roncagliolo chooses the book to tell the complete, true story of Sendero Luminoso, rather than one of the more influential Spanish newspapers.

Metafiction as a self-reflective narrative technique has been used and debated in the postmodern era, largely by the social scientist, and particularly in fields such as anthropology, ethnography and history. However, traditional journalism has paid less attention to theoretical discussions on the role of narrative in the construction of discourse, and thus in the construction of reality through language. In a field that assumes a transparent style of writing, what Barthes (1953) called 'degree zero' – experiments with storytelling structures and general narrative techniques – can be found less in everyday, breaking news and more in what in journalistic jargon is called 'soft news'. This experimentalism is found particularly in interpretative genres such as the opinion piece, column, *reportage* and *crónica*.

According to Pierre Bourdieu's theory on the field of cultural production (1993), cultural producers move between two poles in the field: the autonomous and the heteronomous. The first one is the space for those artists who are more concerned with autonomy, while the second one is the space of popular culture and bourgeois art, and its producers are more driven by economic interests than those on the autonomous

---

[36] The idea of a 'comfort zone' is of course highly subjective. In the case of Roncagliolo's narrator, journalism represents a sort of dignified salvation from his impoverished life as an illegal Peruvian immigrant in Spain.

pole. In the case of the literary subfield, the struggle can be defined as a battle for the monopoly of literary legitimacy, or 'the power to say with authority who are authorised to call themselves writers' (41). This is not wholly different for the journalistic field, for in a later work, *On Television and Journalism* (1998), Bourdieu locates the journalistic field between the market and the intellectual pole. Journalists might have more or less freedom to say what they wish, depending of their specific role or position in the field. This position is determined by the level of control of both the particular media interests and the journalists' sense of self-censorship.

If one considers that culture is a field in which its producers are in a constant struggle for power (Bourdieu 1993), the corpus I am analysing in this book, as documentary narratives, are inevitably situated in a liminal space. Its authors can be placed in diverse positions on the field of cultural production. Their positions, I would suggest, depend more on their cultural affiliations and prestige, in both the literary and the journalistic fields, than on the peculiarities of their writing. In the case of the Latin American cultural field, in which belonging to the literary subfield has traditionally been much more prestigious than having a place as a journalist, it is not surprising that the 'literary' element of documentary narratives makes their position ambiguous in terms of authority.[37] Writers like Guerriero, Caparrós, and Villoro, recognized in the interviews I conducted that they usually do not have disagreements with editors, and that they normally publish their texts as they wish. They also have the freedom to choose or propose their own topics, and enough time to develop them, at least in comparison with writing up the daily news. This is not the case, however, for common reporters working to the pressures and interests of editors and media owners.[38]

Despite Roncagliolo's cynical self-representation as a *reportero en apuros* (reporter in distress), the Latin American *cronistas* can be considered an elite in the journalistic field, and thus their actions are closer to the autonomous pole of the cultural field of production. As I stated before, since the creation of the FNPI, there has been an increase in workshops, conferences and even festivals at which recognized chroniclers from all over the region get together to share their experiences and teach 'the craft' to young journalists.[39] This new situation seems to be challenging the supposedly marginal status of the *crónica*, as Cristian Alarcón told me:

> I have a critical view of the centrality that the genre of chronicle has taken on in Latin America, because I think we can say that there is a liberal chronicle and a

---

[37] According to Esperança Bielsa (2006), the *crónica* as genre was not independent of the Latin American literary field until the 1960s.

[38] Based on interviews with selected *cronistas* from Mexico City and Guayaquil, Bielsa also concluded that they are usually not full-time journalists but writers with an 'in-between position' who have the freedom to work beyond the conventional press limitations of space and time: 'Cronistas enjoy a degree of relative freedom in a medium in which their work is recognised as creative or literary journalism, and is not subject to the same kind of demand and limitations as predominantly informative reporting. It is thus possible to argue that most *cronistas* experience a privileged position when compared to the journalists who cover news' (85).

[39] Other important venues for this kind of training are Mexico and Argentina. In Buenos Aires, for example, the Fundación Tomás Eloy Martínez regularly offers workshops led by recognized authors.

purist chronicle. I believe that there is a liberal chronicle that is obsessed with the rituality of style, that attempts to claim it is ultra-literary or supra literary, abandoning the political roles of the nonfiction or documentary text.... The quests of many chroniclers are stranded in this literary aspiration: a liberal ambition of singularity, without any commitment to the idea of deep inquiry and research, where the first subject of investigation is the chronicler, the self itself. (Interview 1)

Nevertheless, if in the journalistic field these Latin American authors are considered an elite, in the literary field they are still marginal. For instance, they have less likelihood of success when competing with fiction writers for prizes, peer recognition, social prestige and even less in terms of publishing opportunities.

Documentary writers, therefore, have to play two games simultaneously in order to legitimate themselves within both fields. On the one hand, for the journalistic field they emphasize the ethics of their work, conducting long and detailed investigations. Finding the balance between fidelity to the 'voice' of the informant and 'good' storytelling has been particularly challenging for journalists who also wish to experiment with form, for there is a risk of falling into stereotypes in the characterization of the other. Based on her anthropological research on non-fiction narratives about violence in Colombia and Mexico, Gabriela Polit thinks that journalism becomes a trap, because even if not all documentary authors are pursuing originality in their writing, they struggle with representation and try to avoid portraying the cliché of the victim, for instance (Polit 2013: 174–6).

For the literary field, on the other hand, they consciously craft their authorial presence through the construction of a first-person narrator. For it is true that authors use the first-person narrator to create verisimilitude – they depict themselves as witnesses to the story they are telling – and they also use the 'I', to claim authority in a cultural field that still does not give them full acknowledgement.

The other

Documentary narratives, particularly metafictional ones, are never unmediated testimonies. They are neither biographies, nor conventional journalistic profiles, but a collective product, a mix of several accounts of dialogues between at least two participants. These dialogues, I propose, can be read as a metaphor for contemporary attempts at communication between strangers. There is a rhetoric of alterity that highlights values such as empathy and altruism. Nevertheless, a close reading of the selected works, focusing on the representation of the dialogues as products of real encounters, shows that there is an unsolved tension between the self and the other. I believe this is due to the stylistic and ethical challenges that a text dealing with at least two fields – the journalistic and the literary – inevitably imposes on the author.

Latin American literary journalists have created a self-referenced character for themselves, who is usually a trustworthy, cultivated, cosmopolitan, intellectual, middle-class, progressive, open-minded man (or sometimes a woman), who is interested in marginal people and social problems. Within their own texts, they are intrepid reporters and sensitive detectives; they are, in short, the heroes of their stories. This 'I' in literary-journalistic narratives is closer to an autobiographical voice, and therefore there is a tension between what Robert Burroughs calls the 'eyewitness' and the 'I-witness' (in Berger and Luckman 1967). Beyond the information the journalist gathers in the field, that which becomes the unquestionable evidence in the text is the self who witnessed something: the storyteller who comes back home to relate what he saw or heard.

Narratives that fall between fields need to be studied with a consideration of the physical, concrete conditions of the real encounters between the author and his or her informants. These real encounters, which become part of the narrative, problematize a reading contract based on credibility: if the author declares 'I was there', the reader is invited to believe it. The author, then, acts less like an isolated, (post-)modernist novelist, and more like Benjamin's storyteller: 'The storyteller takes what he tells from experience – his own or that reported by others. And he in turn makes it the experience of those who are listening to his tale' (87).

If 'real-life' has always been a popular chronotope (Bakhtin 1981), it is in documentary narratives that the limits and consequences of using this setting are most evident. This is particularly clear in the Latin American cultural field, in which even before the Boom movement writers used tools from the social sciences to approach a reality within their countries that they could not relate to directly. Writers have used anthropological research methods, specifically ethnographic techniques, such as the field interview, participant observation and the life story (González 1993; Corona 2002). Framing facts through this kind of narrative, particularly in politically difficult times, has been a way through which writers make sense of reality and preserve stories that otherwise would have disappeared, for, as Bruner notes, when analysing how people give meaning to their experiences: 'if we were not able to do such framing, we would be lost in a murk of chaotic experience and probably would not have survived as species in any case' (1990: 56).

As all the selected texts depart from a journalistic, or semi-journalistic investigation, I have chosen to focus on a particular form of framing reality: the testimony that results from a dialogue or interview. In order to do so, I apply Mikhail Bakhtin's reflections on speech genres and style as a social phenomenon, individualized by each author's particular use of language.[40] Although I conduct a literary analysis, I do not intend to read the chosen corpus as novels.[41] I rather read each of these texts as what Bakhtin has defined as an 'utterance', that is, an individual, concrete use of language, here generated within a specific genre. These acts of speech, called 'documentary narratives' throughout my analysis, are, therefore, the result of various dialogues: first, between

---

[40] Bakhtin defines speech genres as 'relatively stable thematic, compositional, and stylistic types of utterances', developed in a particular social sphere (1987: 64).

[41] I refer here to the works not defined as novels. The only self-stated novels that I analyse are Arturo Fontaine's *La vida doble*, Poniatowska's *La 'Flor de Lis'* and Martínez's *La novela de Perón* and *Santa Evita*.

the informant and the writer, and second, between the writer and the reader, and, on another level, between the journalistic and the literary genres. All these diverse voices and genres clamour alongside one another in the text, for each speech represents a particular worldview.[42] I agree with Bakhtin, that rather than considering the work to be a closed monologue, we should approach it as 'a rejoinder in a given dialogue, whose style is determined by its interrelationship with other rejoinders in the same dialogue (in the totality of the conversation)' (1981: 274).[43]

By focusing on style, as conceived by Bakhtin, I have found that the ethical intentions of the documentary authors do shape their narratives and their pact with the reader. Their words cannot avoid being conditioned by the other's words, even when they are appropriating them by means of writing. That these narratives are the product of real encounters between at least two people, the author and the informant, cannot be ignored. They are, then, the most literal example of Bakhtin's idea of *dialogization* in speech:

> Language is not a neutral medium that passes freely and easily into the private property of the speaker's intentions; it is populated – overpopulated – with the intentions of others. Expropriating it, forcing it to submit to one's own intentions and accents, is a difficult and complicated process. (1981: 294)

What I propose, therefore, is that documentary narratives should be read as performative speech acts, in which multiple and highly diverse worldviews clash. A reading like this can show that questions of self-representation are inevitably linked to the participants' real identities.

Self-identity is always changing according to circumstance, but it can be observed in the way that individuals perform tasks, or in their behaviour in concrete situations (Goffman 1974). Therefore, an approach that focuses on the dialogical nature of these texts as a representation of the real can reveal, to a certain degree, the identities of the self and others, beyond the fiction. The traces of the relationship between the self and the other are, therefore, exposed in the representation of the narrative dialogues, for the story shared is never just of one self but the result of particular encounters between particular individuals. This is proven by the different kinds of relationships

---

[42] Critics who defend literary journalism as a literary subgenre, like Hartsock (2016), use Bakhtin's theory of the novel as support for their arguments. Although it is true that defining the novel as a hybrid form that mixes diverse speeches from real life (*heteroglossia*) can allow non-fiction forms to be considered as such, I do not think that Bakhtin included texts that claim to document real-life speech in his own definition of the novel. First, because for him the division between 'artistic' and 'extra artistic prose' is quite clear, and he includes journalism as well as philosophy and other 'moral' speeches in the 'living rhetorical genres'. Second, because to consider a reading of these texts as novels would imply, according to Bakhtin's theory, a transformation of any element coming from the realm of the real life into objects or characters, and this is precisely the opposite of what authors intend to do with documentary narratives.

[43] For Bakhtin 'any research whose material is concrete language . . . inevitably deals with concrete utterances (written and oral) belonging to various spheres of human activity and communication' (1987: 62).

that authors develop with their informants, some of which might continue after the story is published. These relationships seem to depend on the level of similarities found between the participants. For example, in the case of Leila Guerriero, those similarities depend on intellectual or artistic interests, although she said she usually does not follow up any relationship after the publication of her texts. Others might go so far as to develop a long-term friendship, like Elena Poniatowska, or to create family bonds, like Cristian Alarcón, who adopted the child of one of his informants (see Appendix).

The device that makes it possible for contemporary documentarists to connect both the social and textual spheres in which they act is the interview.[44] The interview, as used in the selected texts, is in itself a hybrid speech genre. It incorporates an oral conversation, generated in a particular social sphere and later reorganized by only one of its participants. This speech is then incorporated into written speech, which is intended for another social sphere. The interview is also complex in its function, for it is a method of research, and also, when incorporated into the text, it becomes a stylistic, literary device.

Through the interview, authors strengthen verisimilitude. Quoting – directly or indirectly – the other's speech becomes essential for the pact of credibility with the reader, because, ironically, it is only through the manipulation of the information gathered by the encounter with others that the author is able to tell the truth:

> It could be said that facts exist to the extent in which they are told, someone has registered something about them and then it is possible to proceed towards their reconstruction. The truth is what emerges from those testimonies, out of their assembly, and it is not in a reality of which one can give a faithful account, but it is the result of the construction.[45]

The truth coming from the other's speech, however, is transformed through narrative into a *fictional truth* (Riffaterre 1990). This is because testimonies act in the text as symbolic stories, in the way that any other literary text inserted would do. Transformed from real into symbolic stories, they tell a truth about certain aspect of reality in a way that is memorable and meaningful. This explains why there is an obsession among documentarist authors with finding the individual story that stands as an exemplar for the theme they aim to address, as expressed by Alarcón regarding his own working process: 'I think one knows that one has a great story not because the story itself

---

[44] I refer to the genre of interview in its broadest sense as a conversation intended to be recorded somehow and later used by one of the speakers as a source for his or her book. This is because some of the authors I studied do not conduct formal, well-structured interviews but opt for a more flexible ethnographic-like method of gathering testimonies. For an in-depth analysis of the interview as speech genre in contemporary societies, also applying Bakhtin's theory, see Arfuch (1995). For the specific use of the interview in journalistic genres, see Halperín (1995).

[45] 'Podría decirse que los hechos existen en la medida en que son contados, alguien ha registrado algo sobre ellos y entonces se puede proceder a su reconstrucción. La verdad es la que surge de esos testimonios, de su montaje, y no está en una realidad de la que se puede dar cuenta fielmente, sino que es el resultado de la construcción' (Amar Sánchez: 34).

is good but because there is a character that is worthy and that will be memorable' (Interview 1).

Testimonial-like narratives tell the interviewee's story, but also show a trace of the encounter, as remembered by the interviewer. Riffaterre's fictional truth can, thus, relate to Adriana Cavarero's concept of a *narratable self*, for both interviewer and interviewee are exposing an equal desire for narration:

> The narratable self's desire for narration manifests itself in autobiographical exercises in order to entrust one's own story to another's storytelling [. . .] what is at stake is not an assessment of qualities, or the frequency of a biographical response. Rather, the point is that I become for you a narratable identity, someone whose story you can tell, since my identity is by now in the care of this story that you know by heart. (114)

Stylistically, the presence of the other in the narrative is represented by quotation marks or dialogue markers. According to Riffaterre, quotations are symbols of the text's limits because they are used to signpost the intersection between the world and the word. They also show the limits between the authority of the writer's and the other's speech. To quote is to demonstrate awareness of otherness, but also to state the degree of authority that each speech has. That is why editing becomes the most creative element in documentary narratives, because it displaces the experience of the encounter and its recorded evidence to fit the will of the author. The author's decisions regarding the representation of the other are primarily stylistic, as Leila Guerriero explains: 'I believe that when one perceives that there are things that have to have a stronger narrative tension it is not a very good idea to give the voice to the protagonist of the matter, it depends. There are no rules with that' (Interview 5).

It is through the process of editing, thus, that the other's story becomes the self's story too. During interviews, authors place great emphasis on the carefully crafted process of editing the words of others. I see this as less because they might need to defend themselves against a fact-checker – since this is not a common practice in Latin American media – and more because the transcription of the recorded voice of others is a way of showing respect for their stories. To take care of the story entrusted to them is part of the ethics of the profession, according to Alarcón:

> There is a respect for the way of speaking, that is for the forms of language, and nor are they mechanical reproductions. It is certainly a more polished language, more accessible, but in which the work is that of the ear, that of being able to respect the melodies that in the end are essential to the discourses and they are key for the existence of the other. (Interview 1)

Nevertheless, Alarcón would recognize, along with others, that he does not transcribe the testimonies verbatim. Furthermore, novelist Arturo Fontaine felt that the victims generally did not possess the kind of language he thought was most effective for expressing their stories. Therefore, to let the other speak is an ethical problem that can be reflected through style. A simple decision about the way in which the testimonies are included in the text becomes essential for our interpretation of the work. There is, then, an evident linguistic tension in the dialogues. They expose the unavoidable differences between the self and the other. After all, these encounters are not as smooth and idyllic as may be imagined by testimonial theory:

> As a living, socio-ideological concrete thing, as heteroglot opinion, language, for the individual consciousness, lies on the borderline between oneself and the other. The word in language is half someone else's. It becomes 'one's own' only when the speaker populates it with his own intention, his own semantic and expressive intention. Prior to this moment of appropriation, the word does not exist in a neutral and impersonal language (it is not, after all, out of a dictionary that the speaker gets his words!), but rather it exists in other people's mouths, in other people's contexts, serving other people's intentions: it is from there that one must take the word, and make it one's own. (Bakhtin 1981: 293–4)

Although it might be true that the author's intention is to respect the other's story, and that during the real encounter the dialogue might appear equal, there is something lost and something else added in the process of translation from oral to written speech. If, during fieldwork, the author acts mostly as a listener, during the process of writing he or she transforms the journalistic interview into a literary dialogue, and it is in this that the differences between the self and the other emerge.

It is important, however, to acknowledge the ethical pitfalls that this kind of practice is exposed to, for the dialogue represented here, the interview, is an irregular genre, between oral and written speech, and between the social and literary spheres. The interview, as a paradigm of the dialogical nature of speech, places its actors in an uneasy position, for their roles are constantly shifting. The listener, who is never passive, eventually becomes the speaker (Bakhtin 1987).

Furthermore, as the conversation moves from the private to the public sphere, the reader, 'the third person included' (Arfuch 1995), joins the conversation. In this regard, one must consider that whereas in Europe the novel was born as a popular, mass form of entertainment that aimed to reflect the everyday life of common people (Bakhtin 1981), in Latin America this form, like any other literary genre, was produced and consumed by the elites. In their emergence from popular culture, documentary narratives – while not as openly popular – might be seen as an alternative way of revealing the diversity of voices and identities within the masses, a way that allows these voices to speak from their own positions of diversity. Additionally, the journalistic genre, particularly the interview, can also set the tone for contemporary literature in the region.

As there is an unresolved tension between the self and the other, shown in their own communication process, there is also an unavoidable betrayal of the other by the author. If, following Bakhtin and Cavarero, one's story is always attended to, and shaped by the listener, there will be a discrepancy between a testimony confessed to the writer and the version of it that the reader finally receives. As I hope to demonstrate throughout this book, the real encounter between the journalist and the informant cannot be separated from its narrative representation. This is because in contrast to other truth-telling situations in which there is a real story to tell (e.g. confession, therapy, legal process), in the case of documentary narratives, what generates the encounter is the desire for narration.

To summarize, documentary narratives are a means of exploring the difficulties of the encounter with otherness. In representing diverse individuals in dialogue, transmitting a 'living impulse' as Bakhtin would say, these texts show that each voice carries its own perspective on the world. These perspectives or worldviews do not interconnect smoothly with each other, as in a traditional fictional style. They clash, they collapse into each other, producing a new collective, heterogeneous and complex speech act.

2

Publishing to survive

Before the New Journalists in the United States began questioning their society and the way mass media represented reality, in Latin America there had been two paradigmatic cases for the relationship between literature and journalism.[1] By the mid-twentieth century, Gabriel García Márquez (Aracataca 1927–Mexico City 2014) had published *Relato de un náufrago* (1955/1970), and Rodolfo Walsh (Lamarque 1927–Buenos Aires 1977), his *Operación Masacre* (1957/1972). Both are stories of survivors, but they present two different approaches to the task of journalists in censored environments. Their use of literary strategies to reproduce real testimonies allows for an interesting comparison, especially regarding the complex relationship between the journalist-narrator and his or her informants, and the risks authors have to take in order to tell a true story.

Relato de un náufrago and *Operación Masacre* point to one aspect of the polemics involved in the ethics of *testimonio*: the legal question of authorship. In this sense, they can be seen as seminal works in the *testimonio* tradition, and in that of the documentary narratives that appeared in Latin America during the closing decades of the twentieth century.[2] In her 'Brief history of Latin American Testimonial Narrative', Nance considers *Operación Masacre* an antecedent of the *testimonio* genre even when she classifies it as a 'nonfiction novel'. For her, *Operación Masacre* shares a status with other sociological or anthropological works that also narrate experiences of injustice, such as Ricardo Poza's *Juan Pérez Jolote* (1952) and Oscar Lewi's *The Children of Sánchez* (1961); however, these works differ from *testimonio* because they lack an explicit call to action, and their preference is for the 'perspective of a third-person observer' (167). It is then evident that the stylistic choice of the narrative person (third or first) becomes political and essential for establishing genre boundaries. Nonetheless, in my view it is not the grammatical 'I' that is wholly responsible for determining a genre, but the worldview that the narrator

---

[1] In *The New Journalism*, published in 1973, Tom Wolfe mentions Gabriel García Márquez as part of the Neo-Fabulists, along with authors such as John Barth, Jorge Luis Borges, John Gardner, James Purdy, James Reinbold and Alan V. Hewat. For Wolfe, these writers proposed a return to storytelling as a form that was part of the origins of literature. Of course, by then García Márquez had already published *Cien años de soledad* and was internationally known. Wolfe may not have been fully aware that the father of the Boom, only four years his senior, had a similar interest in exploring new forms of journalistic writing.

[2] For more about Walsh and García Márquez's political involvement with the *testimonio* tradition, see Calvi (2019).

expresses through his or her level of intervention in the testimonials of others, regardless of whether the account is written in the first or third person.

By reading Walsh's and García Márquez's works as palimpsests, that is as a product of multiple layers of texts printed in diverse formats, this chapter demonstrates how deeply interconnected the practice of journalism as procedure for truth-telling and the authors' understanding of writing as a form of self-expression are in documentary narratives. These narratives, I argue, are able to transform the reality in which they are produced, if not at the societal level, then within the lives of their producers: the journalists and the informants.

On the one hand, the initial publication of the stories in newspapers demonstrates the social and personal consequences that a story that aims to adhere faithfully to real facts in a particular political context can have. On the other hand, published as books, the stories highlight questions of the representation of reality. The relationship between the journalist and his or her informant is always problematic, and cannot be resolved; nor can it be ignored. The dialogue can be as friendly and close as the participants allow it to be. However, the question of who owns the story exists to remind us that the dialogue is never equal. By their interaction with the subject, the writer appropriates the other's words; the story no longer belongs to the one who lived it, but to the one who writes it. What *Relato de un náufrago* and *Operación Masacre* ultimately rely on, I believe, is that a reader seeking an understanding of silenced or ignored facts in a repressed society will value the ethical intention to tell the truth.

Gabriel García Márquez chooses to hide

On Thursday 28 April 1955, *El Espectador* newspaper in Bogotá, Colombia, published a special supplement, in eight columns: 'La Odisea del Náufrago Sobreviviente del "A.R.C. Caldas"' (The Odyssey of the Shipwreck Survivor from the 'A.R.C. Caldas') (see Figure 2.1). Under this title, there is a half-page, colour illustration of a man in the middle of the sea. He defends himself against the sharks surrounding his small boat with nothing but an oar. The second half of this cover presents three black-and-white photographs of the survivor before and after his adventure, with small print announcing that the story will be published in fourteen parts over the following days: 'La Verdad sobre mi Aventura' (The Truth About My Adventure). The subtitle reads: 'Por el marinero Luis Alejandro Velasco, exclusivo para El Espectador' (By the sailor Luis Alejandro Velasco, an exclusive for *El Espectador*) (see Figure 2.2). Despite the (perhaps conscious) editorial decision to let readers assume that the story was written by the survivor himself, the text was not signed at all, and it was actually written by a young journalist who would go on to win a Nobel Prize for Literature: Gabriel García Márquez. The initially obscured authorship is not the only element related to fiction in this publication (which links Velasco's adventure with that of the mythic Odysseus), but it would prove the most problematic for its author.

Figure 2.1 Newspaper main cover of Gabriel García Márquez's first publication of 'The Story of the Shipwrecked Sailor'. 'La Odisea del Náufrago Sobreviviente del "A.R.C. Caldas"' (The Odyssey of the Shipwreck Survivor from the 'A.R.C. Caldas'), *El Espectador*, Bogotá, 28 April 1955.

Figure 2.2 Section cover of Gabriel García Márquez's first publication of 'The Story of the Shipwrecked Sailor'. 'La Verdad sobre mi Aventura' (The Truth About My Adventure), *El Espectador*, Bogotá, 28 April 1955.

It was not until 1970, when García Márquez had become a well-known fiction writer, that Tusquets publishing house printed the story as a book, entitled *Relato de un náufrago que estuvo diez días a la deriva en una balsa sin comer ni beber, que fue proclamado héroe de la patria, besado por las reinas de belleza y hecho rico por la publicidad, y luego aborrecido por el gobierno y olvidado para siempre*.[3] Nevertheless, the story behind the initial publication of *Relato de un náufrago* is the story of García Márquez's transition from full-time journalist to full-time author. Like many others from his generation, García Márquez saw in journalism a way of earning a living while pursuing his literary career, although it is evident that journalism also influenced his fiction (Gilard 1987; Vargas Llosa 1971).[4]

---

[3] Translated into English by Randolph Hogan in 1986 as *The Story of a Shipwrecked Sailor who drifted on a life raft for ten days without food of water, was proclaimed a national hero, kissed by beauty queens, made rich through publicity, and then spurned by the government and forgotten for all time*. All the translations quoted here come from the 1989 reprint of this book by Knopf in its ebook version published by Apple Books.

[4] For an updated reading of the cultural and publishing context that facilitated García Márquez's works becoming internationally popular in the context of world literature, see Siskind (2014).

García Márquez began his literary and journalistic career almost at the same time: he published his first short story 'La tercera resignación' (The Third Resignation) in 1947 in *El Espectador*, and one year later he was working in *El Universal* newspaper in Cartagena de Indias. He had had to interrupt his undergraduate studies in Law at Universidad Nacional de Colombia in Bogotá, because the university was closed after the murder of Jorge Eliécer Gaitán, a presidential candidate from the Liberal party. On the Colombian coast, he became so engaged with journalism that he never returned to law school. However, he did not always work as a reporter, but he also wrote anonymous and routine news stories; he was better known for his humorous columns, editorial pieces and film reviews (Gilard 1987). This was not at all coincidental, as after Gaitán's murder, violence became part of everyday life in the country. Within this context, the media preferred to publish frivolous news, and journalists got used to writing in a careful, indirect manner (Méndez 1992).

The story of the sailor appeared during the dictatorship of Gustavo Rojas Pinilla, whose rule was imposed by military coup in 1953. Returning to Colombia from the United States, the military destroyer *Caldas* was shipwrecked in the Caribbean and eight sailors disappeared in February 1955. The twenty-two-year-old Luis Alejandro Velasco was the only survivor. After ten days alone in the sea, Velasco appeared on a Colombian beach and became a celebrity. By the time he met the twenty-eight-year-old reporter García Márquez, he had already told almost everything about his adventure to the media. What he had not related, however, was what he finally confessed to García Márquez following days of long interviews: the shipwreck was not caused by a storm, as the official version communicated by the government had said. It took just a strong wind to wreck the overloaded vessel; the military ship was illegally transporting televisions, refrigerators and washing machines, which the sailors bought in the United States for their families in Colombia.

At the beginning, the informant, the other, was not important – Was he ever? 'When Luis Alejandro Velasco showed up of his own accord to ask how much we would pay him for his story, we took it for what it was: a rehash' (García Márquez 1989: 14).[5] On the one hand, there is a glimpse here of the journalistic environment in mainstream media, where the decision to tell a story or not has usually been a matter of money. On the other hand, the shipwrecked man knows that his story could be economically valuable and negotiates his testimony.

The sailor's story was, therefore, treated as a commercial product for which the newspaper and the journalist involved invested time and money. Nonetheless, García Márquez adds emotions to the equation when, immediately after relating his first impressions of the informant, he recreates the Bohemian environment that connects journalists with fiction writers: 'but on a hunch, Guillermo Cano caught up with him on the stairway, accepted the deal, and placed him in my hands. It was as if he had given me a time bomb' (15).[6] Therefore, the origins of the story were not only based on

---

[5] 'Cuando Luis Alejandro Velasco llegó por sus propios pies a preguntarnos cuánto le pagábamos por su cuento, lo recibimos como lo que era: una noticia refrita' (García Márquez 2013: 12).

[6] 'De pronto, al impulso de una corazonada, Guillermo Cano lo alcanzó en las escaleras, aceptó el trato, y me lo puso en las manos. Fue como si me hubiera dado una bomba de relojería' (13).

a pragmatic decision regarding profit and the desire to sell the story. There was a gut feeling, *una corazonada*, that the story had an intrinsic value, like any piece of fiction.

After talking with Velasco, the writer's image of him changed. From being a man capable of inventing anything in order to obtain money, he was now described as a hero and a good storyteller:

> My first surprise was that this solidly built twenty-year-old, who looked more like a trumpet player than a national hero, had an exceptional instinct for the art of narrative, an astonishing memory and ability to synthesise, and enough uncultivated dignity to be able to laugh at his own heroism. (16)[7]

The moral interpretation of the character, even the admiration of sorts, contrasts with the distant point of view used to present Velasco in their first encounter. However, there is still a sense of irony, for the informant is never the standardized character the journalist had created for him. García Márquez is surprised that a simple young boy that does not look like a hero could nevertheless be one, and could also be a good storyteller.

At the time he met the sailor and was forced by his editor to work on a story he did not like, García Márquez might have been less experienced than his colleagues were in reporting and dealing with informants, but he was certainly not naïve. He was a member of the Grupo de Barranquilla, a Bohemian group that he joined when living in Barranquilla; it was comprised of journalists and fiction writers. They would gather in bars and cafés to discuss political and social problems, as well as literature. It was at the suggestion of members of this group that García Márquez read foreign authors who would influence his future works, such as Faulkner, Woolf, Dos Passos, Steinbeck, Caldwell, Huxley and Hemingway (Gilard 1987).[8] García Márquez remembers his formative years as journalist in quite a romantic fashion, showing how the process of becoming a journalist did not differ much from that of becoming a fiction author:

> Some fifty years ago, Journalism Schools were not in fashion. One learned in the newsrooms, in the pressrooms, in the coffee shops nearby, in the Friday night parties.... The self-taught are usually greedy and fast, and those from those times were extremely so in order to keep opening space in our lives for the best job in the world – as we used to call it.[9]

---

[7] 'Mi primera sorpresa fue que aquel muchacho de veinte años, macizo, con más cara de trompetista que de héroe de la patria, tenía un instinto excepcional del arte de narrar, una capacidad de síntesis y una memoria asombrosas, y bastante dignidad silvestre como para sonreírse de su propio heroísmo' (13).

[8] *Relato* has been compared with Hemingway's *The Old Man and The Sea*, which was published beforehand (Foster 1984). In fact, Vargas Llosa (1971) compares the journalistic career of García Márquez with that of Hemingway.

[9] This is my translation, although an edited version of this article, which does not contain all the content quoted here, has been published in English as 'The best job in the world' in vol. 26, issue 3 of *Index on Censorship* (1997: 77–80). 'Hace unos cincuenta años no estaban de moda escuelas de periodismo. Se aprendía en las salas de redacción, en los talleres de imprenta, en el cafetín de enfrente, en las parrandas de los viernes. ... Los autodidactas suelen ser ávidos y rápidos, y los de

In fact, the experience that García Márquez had during this time could be compared with what Tom Wolfe describes for the American journalists in the same period:

> By the 1950s The Novel had become a nationwide tournament. There was a magical assumption that the end of World War II in 1945 was the dawn of a new golden age of the American Novel, like the Hemingway-Dos Passos-Fitzgerald era after World War I. There was even a kind of Olympian club where the new golden boys met face-to-face every Sunday afternoon in New York, namely, the White Horse Tavern on Hudson Street. . . . Ah! There's Jones! There's Mailer! There's Styron! There's Baldwin! There's Willingham! In the flesh – right here in this room! The scene was strictly for novelists, people who were writing novels, and people who were paying court to The Novel. There was no room for a journalist unless he was there in the role of would-be novelist or simple courtier of the great. There was no such thing as a *literary* journalist working for popular magazines or newspapers. If a journalist aspired to literary status — then he had better have the sense and the courage to quit the popular press and try to get into the big league. (1973: 8)

It was not by chance that this kind of cultural environment was shared in Colombia by the Barranquilla group. Later on, García Márquez would declare that 'journalism is a literary genre',[10] which of course relates to Wolfe's concept of the 'new journalism'. Considering this context and García Márquez's awareness of the effects of the literary discourse upon the journalistic one, my views coincide with Foster's, in that *Relato* is an example of the continuity between 'imaginative literature' and 'documentary' in Latin America.

Although the book was published when *testimonio* was at its peak as a new Latin American genre, *Relato* could hardly be considered a part of this specific tradition. Primarily, because the original story appeared in the newspaper before Barnet's *Biografía de un cimarrón* (1963), which was considered the beginning of *testimonio* narrative. But also because García Márquez's intentions were journalistic rather than anthropological: 'this book is a journalistic reconstruction of what he told me' (13).[11] Nevertheless, it is interesting that, as with Rigoberta Menchú's famous controversy, *Relato* highlights one of the disputes that haunt *testimonio* as a genre: the legal question of authorship.

Newspaper fictions

After the story was published, the sailor lost his job and the newspaper responded to government censorship by sending García Márquez to Europe to work as a

---

aquellos tiempos lo fuimos de sobra para seguir abriéndole paso en la vida al mejor oficio del mundo –como nosotros mismos lo llamábamos' (1996: 7–8).

[10] 'El periodismo es un género literario' (1996: 7).

[11] 'Este libro es la reconstrucción periodística de lo que él me contó' (2013: 11).

correspondent. A text he did not sign was the one that ended his journalistic career but that, in a sense, inaugurated his literary career. Also in 1955, García Márquez published his first novel, *La hojarasca* (Leaf Storm), but he would hardly ever return to journalism, with the exception of two non-fiction works: *La aventura de Miguel Littín clandestino en Chile* (Clandestine in Chile: The Adventures of Miguel Littín, 1986), a first-person testimony of Miguel Littín, a Chilean film director in exile during Augusto Pinochet's dictatorship, who clandestinely returns to Chile in order to film a documentary about everyday life under the dictatorship; and *Noticia de un secuestro* (News of a Kidnapping, 1996), about kidnappings in Bogotá that had been organized by the drug trafficker Pablo Escobar. Although these real stories share a violent context with Velasco's, they are focused on the testimonies of the friends of the author, and they are cases in which the author was clearly politically invested.

The book version of the sailor's story, published by Tusquets in the 1970s, was identical to the original except for an added prologue by the author, entitled 'La historia de esta historia' (The story of this story). I argue that it is precisely this paratextual device that transformed – both literarily and legally – Velasco's story into García Márquez's one. The original text was published as if Velasco had written it, for there was no mention of García Márquez as author of the text. Later, in his own memoirs, García Márquez gave his explanation; he was not interested in writing the story, so he had no interest in receiving recognition as the author:

> I informed him, depressed but in the best possible style, that I would write the article out of obedience as his employee but would not put my name to it. Without having thought about it first, this was a fortuitous but on-target determination regarding the story, for it obliged me to tell it in the first-person voice of the protagonist, in his own style and with his own ideas, and sign it with his name. (García Márquez 2004: 838)[12]

Choosing not to sign their texts is a common practice among journalists who wish to convey their disagreement with an assignment. Although García Márquez seems to protest in this way, he goes further and makes the issue of authorship more complex: he actually gives the text an author, but a fictional one. After interviewing Velasco, García Márquez realized that it was a good idea to give the story a first-person narrator. He decided to use a fictional device for what was intended to be a journalistic discourse.

The function of the prologue to the book is therefore to assign names: to name the real (and legal) author of the story, as well as to name the nature of the narrative. By describing the creative process behind the story, García Márquez reveals himself as its creator, while by naming his creation as *reportaje*, García Márquez also establishes a new pact with the reader. According to some critics,

---

[12] 'Le advertí deprimido pero con el mejor estilo posible que sólo haría el reportaje por obediencia laboral pero no le pondría mi firma. Sin haberlo pensado, aquélla fue una determinación casual pero certera para el reportaje, pues me obligaba a contarlo en primera persona del protagonista, con su modo propio y sus ideas personales, y firmado con su nombre' (García Márquez 2002: 564).

markers of the book version's literariness (against the journalistic reading of the original text) are the change in the title, and the transformation of the fourteen instalments into chapters (Díez Huélamo in Rivas 2011). According to Ascención Rivas (2011), one of the major modifications of the pact with the reader is the change in printing format: from newspaper to book. Further to Rivas's observation, I argue that the inclusion of the prologue is the main literary device used by García Márquez in his claim to authorship of the anonymous press text. Although he avoids using the word 'literature' to describe *Relato*, David Foster thinks that the work only functions as a documentary narrative in its book version, for the original publication is only 'a detailed description of the hardships faced by an individual', a conventional newspaper's 'human-interest story' (1984: 49).

The author and the sailor

The prologue to *Relato* claims textual authority for García Márquez, even when his declared aim is to present the story as a dialogical product: 'there are books that are not about the one who writes them but about the one who suffers them.'[13] Beyond his own sense of guilt, or social awareness, regarding his old informant, García Márquez's prologue was in actual fact claiming the copyright, merely by attaching his name to it. For it is true that he might have underestimated the text once, when he considered Velasco's story a rehash, but fifteen years later he had reconsidered and thought it was worthy of publication (15). In the prologue, the author is aware that he is able to publish the story – this time with his signature and with no more risk of exile – precisely because of his own fame. 'I find it depressing that the publishers are not so much interested in the merit of the story as in the name of the author, which, much to my sorrow, is also that of a fashionable writer' (20),[14] he wrote in 1970 from Barcelona.

The original prologue ends with a sentence that was erased from later editions: 'The copyright, as a consequence, will be for the one who deserves it: the anonymous compatriot who had to suffer ten days without eating and drinking in a raft to make this book possible.'[15] Velasco did receive money from the sales of *Relato* during the thirteen years following the publication of the first edition (García Márquez 2002). Nevertheless, this agreement with the publishing house ended in 1983, when Velasco initiated a trial against García Márquez, claiming to be the co-author of the book and, therefore, claiming additional earnings from editing and distribution. The trial ended

---

[13] This is my translation, as this part is not reproduced in the English version. 'Hay libros que no son de quien los escribe sino de quien los sufre, y este es uno de ellos' (12).
[14] 'Me deprime la idea que a los editores no les interese tanto el mérito del texto como el nombre con que está firmado, que muy a mi pesar es el mismo de un escritor de moda' (16).
[15] 'Los derechos de autor, en consecuencia, serán para quien los merece: el compatriota anónimo que debió padecer diez días sin comer ni beber en una balsa para que este libro fuera posible' (García Márquez in Mudrovcic 2005: 162).

eleven years later, when the court ruled that García Márquez was the sole author of the work (Mudrovcic 2005).[16]

Discussing the complex interviewer–interviewee relationship, and the ever-present possibility of a betrayal of the informant's trust, Janet Malcolm (1997) argues that there is no moral justification for the journalist's work because the relationship between the journalist and the informant is never naïve. In practice, when a journalist is interested in someone's story, the closeness to his informant is inevitable, but it cannot be confused with a faithful friendship. At the end of the day, the writer will select and even change the subjects' words in order to privilege the story that he wants to write. In his memoirs, García Márquez admitted that he looked for contradictions in Velasco's story:

> The interview was long and thorough and took three exhausting weeks, and I did it knowing it was not for publishing raw but needed to be cooked in another pot: a feature article. I began with some bad faith, trying to have the shipwrecked sailor fall into contradictions in order to reveal his hidden truths, but soon I was certain he had none. (García Márquez 2004: 839)[17]

There has always been tension between journalists and their informants, and it is known that a journalist is not a friend you can trust, but Malcolm asks: Why, then, do people still want to be interviewed by journalists? And the answer seems to be simply: people want to tell their story; they want to be listened to by someone who seems really interested in it. 'The subject is Scheherazade. He lives in fear of being found uninteresting, and many of the strange things that subjects say to writers – things of almost suicidal rashness – they say out of their desperate need to keep the writer's attention riveted' (Malcolm: 20). The only ethical solution to this dilemma, according to Malcolm, would be to write only about subjects whose story is already interesting, so the non-fiction writer can limit himself to recounting what the subject tells. That was what García Márquez did with Velasco's testimony:

> In twenty daily sessions, each lasting six hours, during which I took notes and sprang trick questions on him to expose contradictions, we put together an accurate and concise account of his ten days at sea. It was so detailed and so exciting that my only concern was finding readers who would believe it. (García Márquez 1989: 16)[18]

---

[16] García Márquez did not use a voice recorder – a recent invention at that time – because according to him they were heavy and difficult to use, and he preferred just to take notes; however, he stated that the trial included documentary evidence (2002: 552–73).

[17] 'La entrevista fue larga, minuciosa, en tres semanas completas y agotadoras, y la hice a sabiendas de que no era para publicar en bruto sino para ser cocinada en otra olla: un reportaje. La empecé con un poco de mala fe tratando de que el náufrago cayera en contradicciones para descubrirle sus verdades encubiertas, pero pronto estuve seguro de que no las tenía' (2002: 564–65).

[18] 'En veinte sesiones de seis horas diarias, durante las cuales yo tomaba notas y soltaba preguntas tramposas para detectar sus contradicciones, logramos reconstruir el relato compacto y verídico

The Colombian author seemed to represent the informant's speech with such fidelity that the interviewee claimed authorship himself, as noted. The decision to write in the first person was apparently a matter of narrative strategy – although given the possibility of censorship, it might also have also been an ethical decision – and thus was one of the arguments used against García Márquez in the legal conflict with Luis Alejandro Velasco. What is of interest for the purposes of this analysis is that during the trial the character in the story became, once more, a person. The other, thus, was able to obtain the power to speak without the mediation of the author, who had represented his words before. When the legal fight for authorship was over, Velasco declared to the media:

> The text has around 60 or 70 per cent of my own vocabulary. My interest has not been to quarrel with García Márquez, for we are bounded like the Siamese twins are by the belly button. I have wished to encounter him so we could analyse the situation together. I don't want to be a black birth mark in his glory.[19]

What Velasco was not aware of, maybe, is that the encounter that mattered had already happened, and it was not a face-to-face encounter like the first one, which itself had never been on equal terms. The encounter between the journalist and the informant was depicted in the book's prologue, and it was not an encounter between two persons, but the representation of two characters according to the memory of only one participant.

Rodolfo Walsh's conversion to journalism

'Can I go back to playing chess?' (Walsh 2013: 24),[20] asks Rodolfo Walsh after witnessing a murder on the other side of his wall, through the front-facing window of his house in La Plata, Argentina. Earlier during that night in 1956, his chess game in a café was interrupted because of a shoot-out between military and civilian groups. Nonetheless, he tries to forget the violent events and continue his bourgeois lifestyle: that of a novelist making a living from journalism. Six months later, while drinking

---

de sus diez días en el mar. Era tan minucioso y apasionante, que mi único problema literario sería conseguir que el lector lo creyera' (2013: 13).

[19] '[E]n el escrito hay léxico mío en el 60 o 70 por ciento. Mi interés no ha sido pelearme con García Márquez, pues quedamos ligados como dos siameses por el ombligo. He querido encontrarme con él y entre los dos analizar la situación. No quiero ser un lunar negro en su gloria' (Velasco in Mudrovcic 2005: 163).

[20] All translations from Walsh's *Operation Massacre* are from the 2013 Seven Stories Press edition, Apple Books digital version, translated by Daniela Gitlin. '¿Puedo volver al ajedrez?' (2009a: 20). Unless stated otherwise, all of Walsh's quotations are from *Operación Masacre. Seguido de La campaña periodística*, edited by Roberto Ferro (2009c), which reprints the 1972, fourth edition of the book. Ferro provides a detailed chronology of the process of Walsh's investigation.

beer in a bar, he hears about the survivor of a military shooting. This time he decides to learn more, so he asks to meet the man.

Looking for the first time at his informant, Juan Carlos Livraga, Rodolfo Walsh enters into the story of Livraga and his fellow survivors as if he were entering into a novel. He listens, and he believes the storyteller: 'Livraga tells me his unbelievable story; I believe it on the spot. And right there the investigation, this book, is born' (46).[21] The first face-to-face encounter between Rodolfo Walsh and the survivor Juan Carlos Livraga took place on the evening of 21 December 1956, in Livraga's attorney's office in La Plata. Evidently that moment, which would change Walsh's life, left a vivid impression on the author, when he remembers in the prologue to the 1969 edition of *Operación Masacre*: 'I look at that face, the hole in his cheek, the bigger hole in his throat, his broken mouth and dull eyes, where a shadow of death still lingers. I feel insulted, just as I felt without realizing it when I heard that chilling cry while standing behind the blinds' (46).[22]

Walsh realizes that looking at the man covered in blood in the other side of his wall generated a similar feeling to that experienced when looking at Livraga's mutilated face. It is significant, however, that the epiphany, the life-changing moment, is an encounter in which Walsh is able not only to acknowledge the physical presence of the other, but an encounter in which he addresses a man by name, asking for his story – and then listening to it.

Whether it can be found within the plot, or in a paratext of the work, the representation of the encounter between the self and the other is a recurring motif in the documentary narratives analysed in this book. This encounter can take place on the road, in the streets of big cities, in the squares of small villages, in houses, prisons, airports, cafés or bars. All are meeting places of social and literary significance. This encounter would, generally, be between an educated middle- or upper-class author, and a marginalized other. This kind of encounter is recognizable from other disciplines, such as history and anthropology. Clearly, there is therefore much more going on beyond the face-to-face encounter with a stranger. Why does it matter that the author states that his or her story is a true story? And, departing from the assumption that what he or she writes is 'real', what impact do documentary narratives, as a cultural phenomenon, have on the world they depict?

Although it is not my intention to judge whether or not documentary narratives should be considered literature, I pursue this study from the assumption that, ironically perhaps, the element that makes these stories true is precisely the most fictional one: the representation of the self in search for truth. Therefore, this is the exact problem I wish to address. Considering that there is nothing in the style of written/literary journalism that distinguishes it from fictional narrative (González 1993), then what, for me, is

---

[21] 'Livraga me cuenta su historia increíble; la creo en el acto. Así nace aquella investigación, este libro' (2009a: 20).

[22] 'Miro esa cara, el agujero en la mejilla, el agujero más grande en la garganta, la boca quebrada y los ojos opacos donde se ha quedado flotando una sombra de muerte. Me siento insultado, como me sentí sin saberlo cuando oí aquel grito desgarrador detrás de la persiana' (2009a: 20).

the distinctive element of documentary narratives (in comparison with other realistic discourses) is something beyond language: the intention of truthfulness. Of course, this leaves the reader facing a choice of whether or not to believe in the authority of the narrator as a truth-teller, for it is rhetorically impossible to identify particular marks of truthfulness within the text itself, even when a literary critic might reflect upon aesthetic characteristics of the work, or a journalism scholar on the author's ethics on the use of sources. The complexity of documentary stories, therefore, lies on the level of strength in the pact of truthfulness established by the work with each reader and with communities of readership (editors, publishing houses, media, etc.).

In the private space of that first encounter between two flesh-and-blood individuals, Livraga is the storyteller and Walsh is the listener. In the public space of the text, first a newspaper and later a book, Walsh is the storyteller, Livraga a character and we, the readers, now listen to both Walsh and Livraga's accounts of themselves.

Operación Masacre narrates the true story of the clandestine detention and execution of a group of twelve male civilians by the Provincia de Buenos Aires police, on the night of 9 June 1956. The events occurred under the dictatorship of Pedro Eugenio Aramburu, who became self-proclaimed, de facto president after the military coup that deposed President Juan Domingo Perón in 1955. During this period, citizens thought to be sympathetic towards Peronism were fired from their jobs, or even detained. Radical Peronist groups, led by General Juan José Valle, had been secretly organizing a rebellion against the dictatorship, to begin on 9 June, after a revolutionary proclamation that would be broadcast over the radio, during the live coverage of a boxing match that started at 11:30 pm. One of the houses in which political meetings were held was that in which the victims were listening to the match that night, in a working-class neighbourhood in the municipality of Vicente Suárez. Some of these workers were actually involved in the Peronist rebellion, and therefore they were waiting for the radio's signal, while others were there just because of the match. By then, the conspiracy had been discovered by the government, and Aramburu had authorized martial law and signed a decree for the death penalty, so as to make the insurrection an exemplary case of repression. The law was expected to be executed as soon as it was announced over the radio. However, the detention of civilians accused of organizing the rebellion, as Walsh demonstrated later, occurred before martial law was announced. The victims were first taken to police offices, and then to a landfill in the locality of José León Suárez, where they were shot in cold blood. The execution, however, was not completely successful, for seven of the men survived and escaped. Although the execution was reported by the media, there was no public knowledge about the survivors until Rodolfo Walsh managed to interview them and publish their accounts.

In a testimonial style similar to that of Gabriel García Márquez's *Relato*, Walsh's work is also the product of interviews with the victims, and it is more polyphonic, for it is narrated from the perspective of the seven survivors. In contrast with García Marquez's story, however, *Operación Masacre* goes beyond the testimonial versions and includes textual evidence, in order to prove the irregularities of the judicial process. Because of its blend of materials obtained from Walsh's process of investigation, and the use of effective narrative strategies, the book has been considered 'the most authentic example of documentary narrative in Latin American fiction' (Foster 1984: 42).

Contrary to García Márquez, who wrote the sailor's story initially because it was his job as a journalist at a mainstream newspaper, Rodolfo Walsh used journalism as a way of denouncing a crime he could not discuss in any other format. I agree, therefore, with Roberto Ferro that in Walsh's investigation there is an ethics of rescuing an erased collective memory which takes priority over any aesthetic intention (1994: 145). Walsh stated his ethics of writing clearly: 'I wanted one of the multiple governments of this country to acknowledge that its justice system was wrong to kill those men, that they were killed for no good reason, out of stupidity and blindness. I know it doesn't matter to the dead. But there was a question of decency at hand, I don't know how else to say it' (35).[23]

Walsh was consciously aware of the powerful effect of narrative. An analysis of his work should therefore give appropriate space to his storytelling techniques, for style and ethics are thoroughly combined in Walsh's aim of bringing to light a story that needed to be believable. It was not by chance that Walsh was drawn to write about a 'true crime story', being already interested in writing crime fiction himself. He was already known in Argentinian literary circles by the time he began his 'campaña periodística' (journalistic campaign), as he used to call his series of publications on the executions. He started his career as a proofreader and translator. In 1953, he published the short story collection *Variaciones en rojo* (Red variations), which won the Municipal Prize for Literature. Editing the collections of short stories by Argentinian authors *Diez cuentos policiales argentinos* (Ten Argentinian Crime Short-Stories, 1954) and *Antología del cuento extraño* (Anthology of the Uncanny Short-Story, 1956) also showed his commitment to the promotion of crime fiction. His active role in the literary field might explain why Walsh's first intention was to publish the survivors' story in a book and not in the press. After his story was published in newspapers, he assumed his journalistic task with such an ethical commitment to the profession that he became an example to follow for later generations of journalists in Latin America.

Nevertheless, Walsh continued to write more crime fiction than journalism. He had important journalistic roles outside writing, for he was one of the founders of the Cuban news agency Prensa Latina in 1959, along with Gabriel García Márquez, and of the clandestine Argentine news agency Ancla; and he also worked as an editor of the popular Argentinian magazines *Primera Plana* and *Panorama*, where he was in charge of future names, such as Tomás Eloy Martínez and Martín Caparrós. Nevertheless, the story of the executions at José León Suárez was the main topic on which he wrote exhaustively as a journalist, with the exception of *Caso Satanowsky* (Satanowsky Case, 1958/1973) and *¿Quién mató a Rosendo?* (Who Killed Rosendo?, 1968), both also published originally in the press and later in books. Amar Sánchez (1992) analyses

---

[23] 'Pretendía que, a esos hombres que murieron, cualquier gobierno de este país les reconociera que la justicia de este país los mató por error, por estupidez, por ceguera, por lo que sea. Yo sé que a ellos no les importa, a los muertos. Pero había una cuestión de decencia, no sé cómo decirlo' (2009b: 311).

these three works within the genre of non-fiction or testimonials.[24] According to her, Walsh's whole narrative is the product of an intersection between the *novela policial* (crime novel) and journalism, that is, between two marginal textual genres, for they both emerged from mass culture.

If Walsh is an antecedent of a very particular trend in today's Latin American journalism, that which gives evidence to the failures of the state and argues for justice for its victims, it is precisely because of his (literary) construction as a narrator-journalist-detective in search of the truth. Ana María Amar Sánchez counts the prologues of all book versions of *Operación Masacre*, for instance, as evidence of the conscious construction of a textual subject, who is both Walsh-the-author and Walsh-the-narrator. A reading of Walsh's non-fiction, therefore, must consider the double nature of these texts, acting in two discursive spheres: the real and the literary.

In contrast with the American 'New Journalists', who, by similar narrative strategies, were able to become star reporters, Walsh was looking for an 'unbelievable' truth: the crime committed by the state (Amar Sánchez: 151). As opposed to crime fiction, in which justice can be obtained, Walsh's non-fiction demonstrates that, in contexts where the state is responsible for the crime, the only possible chance for justice comes through narrative. I agree with Amar Sánchez that Walsh's literary consciousness can be traced throughout his narrative, particularly in his self-representation; however, this reading must not exclude his newspaper production. Along with Roberto Ferro (2009), therefore, I argue that an interpretation of Walsh's *Operación Masacre* must take into account the whole process of investigation and writing as an open journalistic campaign. For it is true that the format – whether newspaper or book – changes the reading according to each genre's conventions. In the case of documentary narratives originally published as journalism, it is necessary to read each version as a part of the overall authorial process of investigation. Narrative, I believe, was used by Walsh as a tool to both disclose information about a fact not recognized as such by official accounts or mainstream media, and to offer protection to the victims through evidence.[25]

In order to construct a reading of *Operación Masacre* that considers the process of investigation and narration as a whole, I here follow Ferro's classification. He organizes Walsh's journalistic campaign into three phases, which show the transformation of Walsh from journalist to militant.

The first phase of the publication process includes the initial, unsigned texts, based mainly on interviews with the survivors and their families, published as Walsh was gathering evidence to support the position of the victims.[26] They are five pieces

---

[24] Despite the interesting defence that Amar Sánchez gives of the use of the term 'discourse' instead of 'genre' when reading Walsh's journalistic writing, and on which I agree, she continually refers to non-fiction as a genre.

[25] In order to narrate this event that did not have a place in the official records, Walsh had to create a name for it himself, and thus he called it 'Operación Masacre' (Ferro 2009).

[26] The first publication made on the massacre was a transcription of the complaint made by the first known survivor, Juan Carlos Livraga, denouncing the authorities for committing the crime. It was entitled 'Castigo a los culpables' and published on 25 December 1956, in *Propósitos*, a prestigious leftist newspaper, directed by Léonidas Barletta. According to Ferro, it was Walsh who convinced

published in *Revolución Nacional*, a weekly newspaper led by a Peronist syndicalist group outside the party: 'Yo también fui fusilado. El caso Livraga – Los hechos' (I also was one of the executed. The Livraga Case – The facts, January 1957); 'Habla la mujer del fusilado' (The wife of an executed man speaks, 29 January 1957); 'La verdad sobre los fusilados' (The truth about the executed, 19 February 1957); 'Nuevas informaciones sobre la masacre' (New information about the massacre, 26 February 1957); and '¿Fue una operación clandestina la masacre de José León Suárez?' (Was the José León Suárez massacre a clandestine operation?, 26 March 1957).[27]

The second phase consists of the eight parts of the reportage,[28] entitled 'La "Operación Masacre"', which was published from 27 May to 15 July 1957 in *Mayoría*, an ideologically Peronist illustrated weekly magazine.[29] This phase also includes an 'Obligado Apéndice' (Compulsory appendix, 31 July 1957); the first edition of the book *Operación Masacre – Un proceso que no ha sido clausurado* (Operation Massacre) – A Case that has not been closed, published by Ediciones Sigla in December 1957, which was followed by another 'Obligado Apéndice II' the same month in *Mayoría*; and 'La prueba decisiva de la Operación Masacre' (The decisive evidence of Operation Massacre, February 1958), a transcript of a declaration made by those responsible for the executions, published in *Azul y Blanco*, a major political outlet with nationalist ideology.

Until this stage, according to Ferro, Walsh still believed that the state institutions were adequate channels through which to pursue justice. An example of this was his journalistic strategy to withhold names or documents as he uncovered them, in cases where he believed that the evidence could damage the legal process. The publications covering the third phase, however, show how Walsh used journalism to collaborate with Montoneros, a leftist *guerrilla* group associated with Peronism – although Walsh always maintained a critical position towards them. The publications of this phase are '¡Aplausos, Teniente Coronel!' (Applauses, Lieutenant Colonel!, *Azul y Blanco*, March 1958); '¿Y ahora . . . Coronel?' (And now . . . Colonel?, *Azul y Blanco*, April 1958); and the following editions of the book, also printed in Buenos Aires: *Operación Masacre y el expediente Livraga con la prueba judicial que conmovió al país*

Barletta to get involved in the case. Because the text was unsigned, it has not been considered part of Walsh's journalistic campaign, although according to Ferro the brief introduction to this publication must have been Walsh's, as he admitted his initials were printed at the bottom. Walsh met Livraga the day after this publication and interviewed him for the first time. Although *Propósitos* continued to follow up the legal case, they did not want to publish Walsh's interview due to personal and political reasons, since it was considered a communist outlet and it was under constant threat of censorship.

[27] Before publishing the article dated 26 February, Walsh had already interviewed another survivor, Juan Carlos Torres, but instead of writing his testimony in the newspaper, he decided to write a report to the case's judge, so that he could assist in the legal investigation. This was part of Walsh's journalistic strategy, which consisted not of simply disclosing all the information he gathered, but of influencing the government's actions (Ferro 2009).

[28] As I stated in the Introduction, I am using the term *reportage* to refer to the major journalistic genre that aims to disclose a truth, using several sources and showing evidence. However, the pieces were announced by *Mayoría* as 'notas'. In Argentina, *reportaje* designates any kind of journalistic piece.

[29] Walsh was paid for his journalistic work, although it is not clear how much. He received $1,000 Argentine pesos as an advance payment for the series in *Mayoría* (Ferro 1994).

(Operation Massacre and the Livraga file with the judicial evidence that moved the country, Continental Service, 1964), *Operación Masacre* (Editorial J. Álvarez, 1969) and *Operación Masacre* (Ediciones de la Flor, 1972), which was the last one to be edited by the author.

Walsh's final text was 'Carta abierta de un escritor a la Junta Militar' (Open Letter from a Writer to the Military Junta), sent via post to members of the press on 24 March 1977.[30] By that time, following the military coup of 1976 that imposed the last Argentinian dictatorship (under the command of Jorge Rafael Videla), Walsh was living clandestinely, although he had been constantly in danger since his first publication on the executions:

> Now I won't think about anything else for almost a year; I'll leave my house and my job behind; I'll go by the name Francisco Freyre; I'll have a fake ID with that name on it; a friend will lend me his house in Tigre; I'll live on a frozen ranch in Merlo for two months; I'll carry a gun; and at every moment the characters of the story will come back to me obsessively. (46)[31]

On 25 March 1977, while walking through Buenos Aires city centre, trying to distribute more copies of his letter, Rodolfo Walsh was shot and kidnapped by members of the army, despite his attempts to defend himself. His body was never found, and therefore he is considered one of the disappeared, although there are accounts that claim that his corpse was seen in a government building.

Taking all of the cited publications as one extended work, *Operación Masacre* can be read as a complex and open palimpsest, for its content was constantly reworked and edited, and it was never to be finished. In the following sections, I will focus on two of the many layers of Walsh's palimpsest: the first series of texts signed by him in *Mayoría* and the last self-edited version of his book.

A story that never happened

In 1969, Walsh related his initial difficulties in finding a publisher, casting light upon the environment of censorship and fear felt throughout Argentina under the dictatorship:

> That's the story I write feverishly and in one sitting so that no one beats me to it, but that later gets more wrinkled every day in my pocket because I walk around all of Buenos Aires with it and hardly anyone wants to know about it, let alone publish it. You begin to believe in the crime novels you've read or

---

[30] A bilingual edition English/Spanish of this document was published online by the Argentinean government at http://www.jus.gob.ar/media/2940455/carta_rw_ingles-espa_ol_web.pdf.

[31] 'Ahora, durante casi un año no pensaré en otra cosa, abandonaré mi casa y mi trabajo, me llamaré Francisco Freyre, tendré una cédula falsa con ese nombre, un amigo me prestará una casa en el tigre, durante dos meses viviré en un helado rancho del Merlo, llevaré conmigo un revólver, y a cada momento las figuras del drama volverán obsesivamente' (2009a: 20).

written, and think that a story like this, with a talking dead man, is going to be fought over by the presses. You think you're running a race against time, that at any given moment a big newspaper is going to send out a dozen reporters and photographers, just like in the movies. But instead you find that no one wants anything to do with it.

It's funny, really, to read through all the newspapers twelve years later and see that this story doesn't exist and never did (47).[32]

In his account of the story behind the story, Walsh comes to realize that journalism is only possible in the fictional sphere of the movies, far away from the reality of Argentinian media under the dictatorship. Within an environment of fear, he notices that fiction and news become inverted, for it is only in novels where there is space for a story like his. It is understandable, then, that Walsh's book did not find a publisher, nor a space in a mainstream newspaper, but rather in the marginal *Revolución Nacional*:

So I wander into increasingly remote outskirts of journalism until finally I walk into a basement on Leandro Alem Avenue where they are putting out a union pamphlet, and I find a man who's willing to take the risk. He is trembling and sweating because he's no movie hero either, just a man who is willing to take the risk, and that's worth more than a movie hero. (47–8)[33]

Argentinian reality transforms him and his editor into fictional characters, heroes of a subversive movie. An anonymous writer then publishes, for an anonymous audience, details of an event that was erased from official media. Later that year, the story found a publisher, and Walsh's signature was going to be included in the weekly newspaper *Mayoría*. The text is called for the first time: 'La Operación Masacre', subtitled 'Un libro que no encuentra editor' (A book that does not find an editor) (see Figure 2.3). Ironically, the format of the publication transforms the story that was originally conceived of as a book into a journalistic piece, at the same time as Walsh was acknowledged as its author.

---

[32] 'Ésa es la historia que escribo en caliente y de un tirón, para que no me ganen de mano, pero que después se me va arrugando día a día en un bolsillo porque la paseo por todo Buenos Aires y nadie me la quiere publicar, y casi ni enterarse. Es que uno llega a creer en las novelas policiales que ha leído o escrito, y piensa que una historia así, con un muerto que habla, se la van a pelear en las redacciones, piensa que está corriendo una carrera contra el tiempo, que en cualquier momento un diario grande va a mandar una docena de reporteros y fotógrafos como en las películas. En cambio se encuentra con un multitudinario esquive de bulto.'
Es cosa de reírse, a doce años de distancia, porque se pueden revisar las colecciones de los diarios, y esta historia no existió ni existe' (2009a: 21).

[33] 'Así que ambulo por suburbios cada vez más remotos del periodismo, hasta que al fin recalo en un sótano de Leandro Alem donde se hace una hojita gremial, y encuentro un hombre que se anima. Temblando y sudando, porque él tampoco es un héroe de película, sino simplemente un hombre que se anima, y eso es más que un héroe de película' (21).

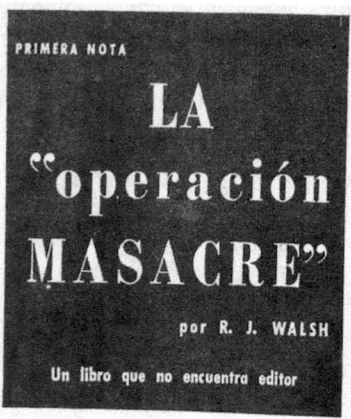

Figure 2.3 First page of Rodolfo Walsh's 'La Operación Masacre. Un libro que no encuentra editor' (Operation Massacre. A book that does not find an editor), Buenos Aires, 17 May 1955, p. 8.

It is interesting to note that in this first publication as a journalist, Walsh's authority is validated based on his prestige as a fiction writer. In the unsigned presentation that precedes Walsh's own introduction to his first 'nota', the editor comments:

> The reader will ask: is what is told here serious? Which is equivalent to: is the author serious? And, are the narrated events true? Regarding the author, Rodolfo J. Walsh is unanimously considered one of the two or three best writers of crime

short-stories of our language. . . . Regarding the second question, are the narrated events true? The reader must judge for himself through the irrefutable evidence attached to the story.[34]

The 'seriousness' of the writing task is here related in terms of fiction writing and not particularly associated with journalistic ethics, which are rather linked to the ability of the author to highlight the correct evidence.

Literature is thus blended with journalism in these publications, not merely because of the stylistic devices used by Walsh, but also through an overarching fictional worldview that impregnates the reportage. It is not insignificant that references to filmmaking were already present in his first text, as Walsh proposed the idea that reality is experienced like a movie in his prologue to the book version. The editor, for instance, declared in a style that emulates a narrator in film: 'and now, let's gamble for truth and justice. Let the events speak, with the authority of the evidence and the irresistible magic of the pen that, in a cinematographic rhythm, presents one and the other.'[35] Walsh himself confessed in his introduction that the story seemed cinematographic to him. He compares the story with the format of the *novela por entregas* (serial novel), although he does it in relation to the official accounts of the crime. From the outset, his introduction defends his story as a proper, journalistic piece because of his investigative method: he claims to have spoken with many witnesses, gathered material evidence and even obtained transcripts from secret government meetings (9).

Whereas the polyphony of testimonies makes the story trustworthy, it is the storytelling technique that transforms the fragmented oral and written evidence gathered by Walsh into a verifiable account. By the time Walsh started publishing the story in *Mayoría*, he had done most of the investigation. In contrast with the initial articles in *Revolución National*, these show a literary coherence and a self-awareness of the role that the journalist plays as a compiler of the story. This is shown particularly in the first-person introduction and the *costumbrista* chronicle style of the scenes in which he depicts, one by one, the everyday lives of the survivors that mark the formal beginning of his reportage and his book.[36] Style, however, is always dependent on ethics, for it is by means of the narrative, and not solely by revealing evidentiary

---

[34] 'El lector se preguntará: ¿Es serio lo que aquí se dice? Eso equivale a preguntar: ¿Es serio el autor? y ¿Son ciertos los hechos que se narran? En cuanto al autor, Rodolfo J. Walsh está considerado unánimemente uno de los dos o tres mejores escritores de relatos policiales de nuestra lengua. . . . En cuanto a la segunda pregunta, ¿Son ciertos los hechos que se narran? Juzgue el lector mismo a través de la irrebatible prueba anexa al relato. (1957: 8).

[35] 'Y, ahora, a jugarse por la verdad y la justicia. Que hablen los hechos, con la autoridad de las pruebas y la magia irresistible de la pluma que, en cinematográfico ritmo, va presentando unos y otras' (8).

[36] The *crónicas costumbristas* were published in Spanish American newspapers around the turn of the twentieth century by literary authors who belonged to the *Modernismo* movement, such as José Martí, Rubén Darío and José Enrique Rodó. They were 'brief articles on virtually any subject, written in a self-consciously literary style, that were meant to be entertaining as well as informative' (González 1993: 84). Authors used a variety of rhetorical strategies to persuade their audience of their own political or cultural agenda; while American journalism was moving on to a condensed, 'objective' style, they preferred the more interpretative, oratorical model from the French press. For more about the *modernista* chronicle style, see González 1983, Mahieux 2011 and Rotker 1992.

documents, that Walsh manages to convince the reader of the irregularities of the judicial case. For instance, the detailed chronological account of the night of the detentions is put there so as to explain the reasons why the executions were a crime and not a legal procedure. Another example is the use of metaphors to define a reality that was denied by officials. Just as García Márquez's story was termed 'an odyssey' in *El Espectador* newspaper, so Walsh used the same literary reference, calling the adventure of the Argentinian massacre's survivors a 'dramática odisea', while editing Livraga's 'Castigo a los culpables' (Punishment to the guilty ones, 2009c: 283). In a similarly sensationalist tone to that used for the sailor's story, one that was in fashion in the journalism of the time, the cover of *Mayoría* announces Walsh's reportage as a 'Historia vívida y completa de las víctimas inocentes de la matanza de José León Suárez y de los que salvaron milagrosamente su vida' (The vivid and complete story of the innocent victims of the José León Suárez slaughter that miraculously saved their lives) (see Figure 2.4).

Figure 2.4 Cover of *Mayoría* magazine, featuring Rodolfo Walsh's Operation Massacre. Buenos Aires, 17 May 1955.

Crafting the truth

Operación Masacre, along with all the texts included as part of Walsh's journalistic campaign, is written in mostly in the third person. It is possible to imagine that this decision is a rhetorical strategy, used to demonstrate a political consciousness, coming from an author who was clearly committed to writing from the position of the victims. One exception is the subtle use of the 'I' in the footnotes, where Walsh generally gives validation to, or discredits testimonies within the narrative. The other exceptions are the prologues, written for the various editions of the book, for as explained earlier, the author habitually included new information in each subsequent edition, as the investigation of the case advanced.

The 1972 edition of *Operación Masacre*, the last one edited by Walsh before he disappeared, divides the story into thirty-seven chapters and three sections: 'Las personas' (The people), 'Los hechos' (The events) and 'La evidencia' (The evidence). Most of the content of the book was published unchanged from the newspaper version, with the exception of the second part of the reportage, which he eventually substituted with Livraga's judicial file.

A literary approach to the prologues demonstrates that *Operación Masacre* was Walsh's *bildungsroman*. In a sense, it was his story of becoming a writer, from novelist to journalist, but also of becoming an active political agent.[37] Even when Walsh obscures himself throughout the story, presenting it in the third person apart from in footnotes, the reader cannot avoid the fact that the narrator is a real person, one who risked, and ultimately lost, his life in order to tell the truth he had discovered. In this paratextual reading of his work, Walsh's story would then be part of the plot. Walsh can only tell the story by displacing his body to the locations where the facts occurred, talking to people there and introducing himself as the witness of the invisible reality. This is evident when he narrates his first trip to the place of the executions, a landfill, in the company of his research assistant, the journalist Enriqueta Muñiz:

> So one afternoon we take the train to José León Suárez and bring a camera with us, along with a little map that Livraga has drawn up for us in pencil, a detailed bus driver's map. He has marked the roads and rail crossings for us, as well as a grove and an X where it all happened.... Enriqueta says 'It happened here,' and casually sits down on the ground so that I can take a picnic photo of her because, just at that moment, a tall sullen man with a big sullen dog walks by. I don't know why one notices these things. But this was where it happened, and Livraga's story feels more real now. (48–9)[38]

---

[37] In his press publications, Walsh declared that he was not a Peronist, and called active members of the party 'esos temibles seres' (1957: 9), stating that his work was not looking for a political aim. Nonetheless, he would later be linked with Montoneros, and his work as an agent of this *guerrilla* group is now publicly known.

[38] 'Así que una tarde tomamos el tren a José León Suárez, llevamos una cámara y un planito a lápiz que nos ha hecho Livraga, un minucioso plano de colectivero con las rutas y los pasos a nivel, una arboleda marcada y una (x), que es donde fue la cosa ... Enriqueta dice 'Aquí fue' y se sienta en la

As in the chess scene, Walsh evokes a context where fiction and reality are constantly in flux, contrasting the non-experienced memory of the executions with the vision of an empty space that could have been the site of a picnic, but was not. There may not be anything that can be used to prove the crime at that landfill; knowing what happened, however, transforms the experience of being there from a simple walk into a paranoid and fearful adventure. Walsh and his companion are not just walkers, after all – the picnic becomes a grim joke – and for them, as for the reader, every detail (such as the mysterious man with the dog) is a potential clue. This ironic depiction, or construction, of the story-space shows the constant merging of fiction and reality in such a repressed society.

The reader, however, will not be reminded of the self-represented narrator from this point onwards. After the prologue, the narrator does not have a strong presence in the story. Nevertheless, the 'I' is still used in the footnotes as a strategy to assure credibility. Footnotes are used, as in a scientific discourse, to compare details or to add more precise information (generally in the form of documents) to the oral testimonies, which are part of the story. These notes function as contradictions or validations of the informants' testimonies. For instance, in the second part there is an emphasis on Walsh's aim to check and confirm data by displaying documentary proof. This kind of information alerts the reader to different versions of the facts, a series of fragments lost and found by the journalist. By showing his research method, stating that he could only sit and write after having heard all the versions of primary witnesses, the author reinforces the pact of credibility with the reader. The last word, however, is the written one, for the legal document is the main evidence of truth, rather than oral testimony, as it is shown in one of the footnotes (2009c: 51).

I believe, however, that the muted presence of the 'I' in the book does not make the work less subjective in its perspective. One can identify the contrast between the representation of the self and the representation of others, whose difference from the narrator is indirectly emphasized. Written in a *costumbrista* style, which also echoes the style of an anthropological report, the descriptions of the space of the narration highlight aspects of the environment to indicate the working-class background of the victims: 'six blocks west of the train station lies the neighborhood where so many unexpected things are going to happen. It exhibits the violent contrasts common to areas in development, where the residential and the filthy meet, a recently constructed villa next to a wasteland of weeds and tin cans' (69).[39]

Although Walsh's intention is to narrate the particularities of each victim's life story, he ends up creating his own ethnographic picture of Argentinian working-class culture. In order to understand the motives behind the workers' actions, he needs to

---

tierra con naturalidad para que le saque una foto de picnic, porque en ese momento pasa por el camino un hombre alto y sombrío con un perro grande y sombrío. No sé por qué uno ve esas cosas. Pero aquí fue, y el relato de Livraga corre ahora con más fuerza' (2009a: 22).

[39] 'El barrio en que van a ocurrir tantas cosas imprevistas está a unas seis cuadras de la estación, yendo al oeste. Ofrece los violentos contrastes de las zonas en desarrollo, donde confluyen lo residencial y lo escuálido, el chalet recién terminado junto al baldío de yuyos y de latas' (32).

recreate the stage on which they are going to act. Overall, the portraits of the victims of the massacre are the most explicit example of the journalistic trend towards presenting stereotyped characters. Walsh focuses on a physical and psychological description of victims but he emphasizes the notion of a 'common people' to draw connections between them. Therefore, Mario Brión is described as 'a serious young man and a hard worker, the neighbours say. We gather that his has been a normal life, with no bright highlights or dazzling adventures' (94).[40] Similarly, Pedro Livraga is 'a thin man of average height and ordinary features. . . . His ideas are entirely commonplace and shared by other people in town: they are generally correct regarding concrete and tangible things, and more nebulous and random in other arenas' (98).[41] The descriptions are presented from the point of view of an omniscient narrator, one who already knows the characters' destiny and therefore relates every element of their personality to their final actions. Perhaps influenced by scientific discourse, Walsh depicts characters whose destiny is evidently marked by social determinism:

> He is a tower of a man, this Vicente Damián Rodríguez, a thirty-five-year-old man who loads cargo at the port and, heavy as he is, plays soccer, a man who retains something childlike in his loudness and his crankiness, who aspires to more than he is able to do, who has bad luck, who will end up chewing on the grass of a barren field, asking desperately for them to kill him, for them to finish killing him since the death that he is gulping down won't get done flooding him through the ridiculous holes that the Mauser bullets are leaving in him. . . . Nothing is as he imagined it would be. (102)[42]

Walsh's narrative exposes the problems inherent in representing reality through literary devices. As David Foster has noticed, there is an intrinsic risk in Walsh's aim to convince the reader with a 'highly fictionalised narrative' about a massacre that was never covered by official news. He judges that the success of the book relies on a reader who is aware of the corruption of the state rather than on Walsh's 'narrative talents' (Foster 1984: 43). In my view, what *Operación Masacre* relies on is that Walsh's intention to tell the truth will hold more weight for a reader, particularly one looking for information on silenced or ignored facts within a repressed society. That may be the reason why, even if the final version of the story can be read as an open defence of Peronist ideology, *Operación Masacre* is also an emblem for Latin American journalism

---

[40] 'Un muchacho serio y trabajador, dicen los vecinos. Una vida común, sin relieves brillantes, sin deslumbres de aventura, reconstruimos nosotros' (42).
[41] 'Flaco, de estatura mediana, tiene rasgos regulares. . . . Sus ideas son enteramente comunes, las ideas de la gente del pueblo, por lo general acertados con respecto a las cosas concretas y tangibles, nebulosas o arbitrarias en otros terrenos' (43).
[42] 'Es una torre de hombre este Vicente Damián Rodríguez, que tiene 35 años, que carga bolsas en el puerto, que pesado y todo como es juega al fútbol, que guarda algo de infantil en su humanidad gritona, y descontenta, que aspira a más de lo que puede, que tiene mala suerte, que terminará mordiendo el pasto de un potrero y pidiendo desesperado que lo maten, que terminen de matarlo, sorbiendo a grandes tragos la muerte que no acaba de inundarlo por los ridículos agujeros que le hacen las balas de los máuseres. . . . Nada es como él imaginaba' (45).

and other testimonial-based narratives. At the outset of his publishing adventure, Walsh criticized the mainstream media for remaining silent, 'For many months I have witnessed the voluntary silence of all the "great press" about this execrable slaughter and I have felt ashamed',[43] but after the second edition, the story had changed the author. As can be observed in other works analysed in this book, the journalist's experience of a revelation or a life-changing moment while investigating the story has become characteristic of many Latin American documentary narratives. In my view, this is due to disillusionment with the journalistic profession, once the author realizes it is not as glamourous as it might have been in modernist times or in countries with more robust protections for the freedom of speech. Walsh undergoes an interesting transformation in his notion of journalism, which is no longer the openly naïve one he expressed in his introduction to the *Mayoría* reportage, but one based on bitter experience:

> There is yet another failure. When I wrote this story, I was thirty years old. I had been a journalist for ten years. Suddenly I felt I understood that everything I had done before had nothing to do with a certain notion of journalism that had been taking shape in my mind, and this – investigating at all costs, gathering testimony of what is most hidden and most painful – this did have something do with it and fit into that notion. . . . So I asked myself if it was worth it, if what I was chasing was not a fantasy, if the society we live in really needs to hear about these things. I still don't have an answer. In any event, you can understand how I may have lost some faith – faith in justice, in compensation, in democracy, in all those words, and finally, in what was once, but is no longer, my trade. (338–9)[44]

This disenchanted view of journalism and his public renunciation of the craft was ultimately erased from the 1972 edition for unknown reasons. As Ferro states in his introduction to the critical edition of *Operación Masacre*, while reading a work produced under such disturbing circumstances, that was subjected to constant editing according to concrete changes in the social context of its reproduction, one can only offer 'speculative reflection' on Walsh's open-ended investigative and writing process (2009: 9–10). It is my speculation, then, that Walsh ended up experiencing a sense of what Polit has identified as a sense of 'betrayal of what is right' and the 'loneliness' of the journalist, resulting from a perceived moral failure of the state (2019: 55–8). For not only were Walsh's informants victims of state violence and impunity, but so was the

---

[43] 'Durante varios meses he presenciado el silencio voluntario de toda la "prensa grande" en torno a esta execrable matanza, y he sentido vergüenza' (1957: 9).
[44] 'Cuando escribí esta historia, yo tenía treinta años. Hacía diez que estaba en el periodismo. De golpe me pareció comprender que todo lo que había hecho antes no tenía nada que ver con una cierta idea del periodismo que me había ido forjando en todo ese tiempo, y que esto sí – esa búsqueda a todo riesgo, ese testimonio de lo más escondido y doloroso– tenía que ver, encajaba en esa idea. . . . Entonces me pregunté si valía la pena, si lo que yo perseguía no era una quimera, si la sociedad en que uno vive necesita realmente enterarse de cosas como éstas. Aún no tengo una respuesta. Se comprenderá, de todas maneras, que haya perdido algunas ilusiones, la ilusión en la justicia, en la reparación, en la democracia, en todas esas palabras, y finalmente en lo que una vez fue mi oficio, y ya no lo es' (2009b: 313–14).

author himself. By listening to and witnessing how others suffered, Walsh might have also experienced a traumatic effect of violence, which, according to Polit, is usually expressed by journalists through feelings of rage or guilt. Walsh's emotional declaration that he had lost hope in social values such as justice and democracy is unfortunately similar to the feelings expressed by contemporary journalists dealing with the stories of victims of human rights violations all over Latin America.

Nonetheless, Walsh's literary consciousness regarding the writing process did not fluctuate so drastically. His metafictional reference to the reader shows that the fiction writer remains present and in a dubitative fashion he closes his research questioning his own literary – or journalistic? – ability, 'I get annoyed thinking about how much better it would be if I wrote it now. *Would I write it now?*' (339).[45] As can be shown in Walsh's case, the preference for a grammatical 'I' is not necessarily the only indicator of a subjective, and deeply political worldview, but it is sometimes the only available response to social and individual trauma. The 'I' thus does not imply detachment from the word of the other, but another degree of involvement and caring for the other. Through the first-person narrator, a socially committed or politically engaged author can develop and strengthen his or her sense of belonging to a certain community, as will be shown at length in the following chapters.

---

[45] 'Pienso con fastidio que ahora la escribiría mejor. *¿La escribiría?*' (314).

Part II

Belonging

3

Out of place

In Elena Poniatowska's *Luz y luna, las lunitas* (Light and Moon, the Little Moons, 1994), there is a full-page monochrome photograph that captures, head to toe, two women holding arms (see Figure 3.1). Both women are standing still on bare soil, with a brick wall in the background on which birdcages are hanging. Despite their age, height and different skin tones, at first glance the women seem similar. They are smiling at the camera, both wearing floral summer dresses with pale-coloured cardigans and upswept hair. If one looks closely, however, the small, subtle differences in appearance become more evident. The woman on the left wears discoloured clothes, the seams of her dress are coming undone, and she has on old, broken shoes, whereas the woman on the right wears better-quality clothes, stylish black high heels, a watch and bracelet on one of her wrists, and her hair has been professionally styled. Although both are facing straight into the camera, the woman on the left has a half smile, displaying something of a challenging attitude, while the other one has a more controlled, open-mouthed smile, displaying the same charm as someone posing for the social section of a newspaper.

There is a caption at the bottom of the page quoting a phrase from the text that the image illustrates: 'You are a worthless *catrina*.'[1] If one knows that the woman on the left is Josefina Bórquez, and the one on the right, Elena Poniatowska, it becomes clear which woman is referred to as the *catrina*, and who is the one naming her thus.[2] The image taken by the photojournalist Héctor García is in the book as evidence of what the text 'Vida y muerte de Jesusa' (Life and Death of Jesusa) describes. In this chronicle, author Elena Poniatowska writes about the development of her friendship with Josefina Bórquez, who participated in the Mexican Revolution and later worked as a laundress in a poor neighbourhood in Mexico City. Under the name of Jesusa Palancares, Josefina became the protagonist of Poniatowska's most famous testimonial novel *Hasta no verte Jesús mío* (translated as *Here's to you, Jesusa*, 1969).

Elena's encounter with Josefina/Jesusa responds to a long-standing wish to belong that can be traced back to her autobiographical novel *La "Flor de Lis"*: 'blondie, blondie,

---

[1] 'Usted es una catrina que no sirve para nada'.
[2] In Mexico, *catrina* is used to refer to an elegantly dressed woman who belongs to the upper class or pretends to. It is also used in its masculine form, *catrín*.

Figure 3.1 Josefina Bórquez and Elena Poniatowska, photographed by Héctor García in Mexico City, February 1966.

it is so obvious that you are not one of us, you don't know about our traditions!'[3] Being *güerita* in Mexico, or 'a true blonde' as Carlos Fuentes once described Poniatowska, is a sign of foreignness. National identity, defined as a sense of belonging to the Mexican land and culture, would become a question for authors like Poniatowska to solve. The desire to belong is present throughout Poniatowska's work, and determines her self-representation:

- But you are not from Mexico, are you?
- Yes, I am.
- But you don't look like a Mexican.

---

[3] 'Güerita, güerita ¡cómo se ve que usted no es de los nuestros, no sabe nuestras costumbres!' (*The fleur-de-lis*, 1988a: 74).

– Oh really? What do I look like then?
– *Gringa*.
– Well, I am not a *gringa*, I am Mexican.
– You don't look like it.
...
– I am from Mexico because I want to be, it is my country.[4]

The image of Poniatowska getting her high heels dirty on the unpaved soil, the *catrina* against a half-constructed wall, provokes a sense of displacement. In Garcías's photograph, as in her own writing, there is a clear contrast between the author and her surroundings, including the representation of the others to whom she clings to, desperately trying to belong.

This sense of displacement is also present in the documentary narratives of Carlos Monsiváis, although from a medial perspective, rather than that of a complete outsider longing to belong. The cover of the first edition of Monsiváis's *Los rituales del caos* (The Rituals of Chaos, 1995) is illustrated by popular cartoonist Rafael Barajas 'El Fisgón' (see Figure 3.2). In the black-and-white cartoon, the idea of chaos takes the form of a terrible traffic jam in Mexico City. Among the cars, trucks and buses, and their angry drivers, there are crowds of all sorts occupying the street in order to protest, to celebrate or to pray, and there, also, is Carlos Monsiváis. Depicted as a reporter, notebook and pencil in hand, Monsiváis can pass unnoticed, for he is not at the centre of the drawing, but discreetly positioned in the right upper corner, his body lost among other characters and objects in the urban scene. He is observing from the same street where everything is happening, but at the same time he stands alone. From this strategic position, therefore, he sees the housewives, the peasants, the students, the workers, the young, the old, the children, the drunks, the priests, the vandals, the Virgin of Guadalupe, the Mexican flags, the political banners, a ball, a trumpet, a candlestick, all passing by in front of him – and he writes.

Poniatowska and Monsiváis are part of the long list of chroniclers of Mexico City. Since colonial times, the *cronistas de la ciudad* have documented the interactions between the urban public space and its inhabitants.[5] After independence from Spain, common practices, festivities and ceremonies gave a sense of '*lo nacional*' to Mexican

---

[4]   – Pero tú no eres de México, ¿verdad?
    – Sí soy.
    – Es que no pareces mexicana.
    – Ah sí, entonces ¿qué parezco?
    – Gringa.
    – Pues no soy gringa, soy mexicana.
    – No se te ve.
    ...
    – Soy de México porque quiero serlo, es mi país (73–4).

[5]   In 1926, historian Manuel Romero de Terreros published *Bibliografía de cronistas de la ciudad de Mexico*, in which he enlisted sixty-six urban chroniclers, including the friars Diego Durán, Bernal Díaz del Castillo, Bernardino de Sahagún, Gerónimo de Mendieta and the priest Francisco Javier Clavijero.

Figure 3.2 Book cover of Monsiváis's *Los rituales del caos* (The Rituals of Chaos), Mexico City: Era, 1995, illustrated by Rafael Barajas.

culture and transformed the city. As Monsiváis noted, based on writer Ignacio Manuel Altamirano's notion of national culture, Mexican literature would find a way of becoming 'national', by naming Mexican places, recognizing a new social space and creating the character of *el pueblo*.

The *cuadros de costumbres* were the texts in which the *modernista* chroniclers described Mexico City's everyday life in the newspapers of the turn of the twentieth century. Through these texts, the intellectuals would thus create their own version of the Mexican people, while simultaneously maintaining a distance from them. For example, writer and politician Ignacio Manuel Altamirano described the indigenous individual like this: 'We, the cause of all his ills, are ashamed of his presence, we believe that his misery accuses us and humiliates us in front of the foreigner; we view his joys with horror, and his brutal drunkenness generates weariness in us.'[6] This stereotype is not so different from anthropologist Roger Bartra's description of *el pelado* or *mestizo vulgar*, a marginalized urban figure with a peasant past which, for Bartra, represented the modern Mexican individual after the Revolution. Unlike the indigenous myth, *el pelado* is unable to adapt to contemporary urban life and therefore he becomes highly violent, he is neither a self-denigratory figure nor a product of nationalism, but an 'amphibian image' of Mexican modernity facing an existential crisis (Bartra 1987: 112).

Monsiváis agrees with Bartra that the national culture is a construction of the Mexican elite, coming from the intellectuals as well as from the institutions in power. However, while Bartra thinks that *el pelado* is the new man, as he is part of the mythology created by the political system to blur social differences, Monsiváis argues for his authenticity. For him, this new man is not a fictional character but a flesh-and-blood figure who can be found in the populace. Monsiváis contrasts the concept of national culture with that of popular culture, the latter being the one created by the people through a process involving the reappropriation and transformation of the former: 'What among us has been called "popular culture" is the product of both the dominant classes' will and the joyful and anarchic adaptations made by the masses to such a plan of domination.'[7]

From the 1920s to the 1940s, national culture was under construction from above, in an effort to legitimize each of its parts. Since the 1950s, however, the process of *desnacionalización* began to challenge tradition (Monsiváis 1978). As children of the second half of the twentieth century, it was possible for Poniatowska and Monsiváis to criticize chauvinism and, thus, to represent Mexico City's public space in a different way from previous urban chroniclers. This might be due to their approach to the public space, which resonates closely with Henri Lefebrvre's (1991) definition of it as the product of the interaction between subjects and the space – physical, mental and social – and the environment where they act.

Monsiváis and Poniatowska are conscious of their role as mediators between the dominant culture and the popular one. They use, therefore, mass media as a platform to give Mexican narrative a twist. In their texts, they deconstruct the stereotypes created by nationalism, and in that sense they act in opposition to those writers who, according to Bartra, are part of the hegemonic political system. As a response to what Bartra calls the upper classes' *desdén* (disdain) for the rural and urban masses, Monsiváis and Poniatowska attempt to represent Mexico's people and places from a dialogical and horizontal perspective rather than a vertical one. What surprises a contemporary reader is that in times where censorship was a common activity of the media, these

---

[6] 'Nosotros, causa de sus males, nos avergonzamos de su presencia, creemos que su miseria nos acusa y degrada frente al extranjero; sus regocijos los vemos con horror, y su brutal embriaguez nos produce hastío' (in Monsiváis 1978: 163).

[7] 'Lo que entre nosotros ha habido con ese nombre "cultura popular" es fruto de la voluntad de las clases dominantes y de las adaptaciones gozosas y anárquicas hechas por las masas a tal plan de dominio' (1978: 98).

authors managed to criticize the political system and still be part of the cultural elite.[8] It is my belief that baroque rhetorical techniques might have helped these authors to survive the political dangers, along with their own self-aware role-playing on the cultural field, but perhaps a more targeted sociohistorical approach would find other kinds of explanations.

In opposition to the institutional discourse that aimed to romanticize *mestizo* culture, these chroniclers try to contrast worlds in tension. When Monsiváis writes about popular culture in the sense of resistance and civil empowerment, he is referring to a certain type of middle class, that of educated young people, professionals and activists. These 'clases medias radicalizadas' (radicalized middle classes, 98) are the idealized audience to whom Monsiváis and Poniatowska address their books and newspaper texts.

In *Fuerte es el silencio* (Strong is the Silence, 1980), for instance, Poniatowska observes poor Mexican neighbourhoods from the perspective of an outsider, but uses indirect speech as a form through which to approach others, and to understand their situation based on a narration of their everyday life: 'Although for us a peasant hut, no matter how humble it is, seems better than a proletarian shack, those people who come from the countryside still believe in the kindness of the big city, that someday will give them what the land has not given.'[9]

That 'us' as opposed to 'them' represents two confrontational worldviews from which the city can be experienced. These confrontational worldviews are also exposed in Monsiváis's chronicles, although in a more sarcastic and humoristic style than that of Poniatowska. In 'La disidencia magisterial: los apóstoles se cansaron de serlo' (The magisterial dissent: the apostles got tired of being apostles), a piece from *Entrada libre* about a teachers' strike in Mexico City centre, Monsiváis reflects on the problems of the educational system via the stream of consciousness of an angry driver who is not able to circulate through the streets because of a march:

> The car driver is desperate. For an hour he has been stuck in that huge block of noises and haste turned into hysteria, and he is sick of paying for the democratic advance of society with this delay and his ire. What the hell does he care for the Oaxacan teachers, and what do they win by fucking up the traffic? All of you go to hell with your slogans and your local fights. And go teach your mother![10]

---

[8] Corona and Jörgensen explain how in Post-Revolutionary Mexico the political stability of the country was reflected in the 'continued coexistence between the government and the press' (2002: 7). Reporters could not write about certain topics, such as those listed by José Joaquín Blanco: 'Our Lady of Guadalupe, the president, the army, and the newspaper's major commercial sponsors'. The *cronistas*, on the contrary, were able to enjoy much more freedom of speech.

[9] 'Aunque a nosotros nos parezca mejor una choza campesina, por más humilde que sea, a un tugurio proletario, ellos, los que vienen del campo, siguen creyendo en la bondad de la gran ciudad que algún día les dará lo que no les ha dado la tierra' (23).

[10] 'El automovilista está desesperado. Desde hace una hora ha quedado varado en esa inmensa cuadra de ruidos y premuras vueltas histeria, y está harto de pagar con su retardo y su ira el avance democrático de la sociedad. ¿A él qué carajos le importan los maestros de Oaxaca, y qué ganan éstos

From a more ironic perspective, in his 1970s chronicle collection *Días de guardar*, Monsiváis shows another kind of other, the new bourgeoisie, while describing mass culture:

> Today is the premier of *Hair* in Acapulco. Outside the theatre, a compact absence of multitude prevents the popular reception, postpones the glorious irruption of The Beautiful People, who are arriving wrapped in that metaphysical pause that requires the admiration of others, and that used to be known as a delay. . . . The reporter – that is, the one who writes this and dreams of becoming such – highly regrets his ignorance of the Good Mexican Society and the Jet Set, which causes his indifference to the congregated Illustrious Last Names, which motivates him to review – in a failed attempt to hold styles – the varied lack of imagination that organises the outfit.[11]

In this piece, Monsiváis becomes an anti-chronicler. Unlike a conventional theatre critic, he does not focus on the play but on its audience. He parodies high society news by ignoring the important names of the theatregoers.

In line with García Márquez's (1996) later idea of considering journalism a literary genre, Monsiváis considered the chronicle and reportage to be of a different degree of importance than any other journalistic genre. Although both authors seem to be concerned with the higher prestige that literature has enjoyed over journalism in the Latin American cultural field, Monsiváis emphasizes the social importance of the themes addressed by *crónica* rather than the 'literary' strategies used. In his opinion, mass media does not have enough time and space, or even money, or freedom, to allow authors to publish texts in which social problems can be discussed in depth. Yet they are the forms in which the other can be represented:

> Chronicle and reportage are close to minorities and the majority of people without a place or representation in the mass media, to the indigenous groups, the undocumented people, the unemployed and underemployed ones, the organisers of independent syndicates, the farm day labourer, the immigrants, the peasants without land, the feminists, the homosexuals and the lesbians. To write about them in chronicles means to recognise their modes of expression, to oppose to the idea of news as merchandise, to exhibit the inquisitorial right wing politics, to question the prejudices and sectarian and male chauvinistic limitations of the left wing militancy, to specify the rescued elements of popular culture.[12]

---

con joder el tráfico? Váyanse a la chingada con sus lemas y sus pleitos locales. Y denle clases a su madre' (1987: 180–1).

[11] 'Hoy se estrena *Hair* en Acapulco. Afuera del teatro, una compacta ausencia de multitud evita la recepción popular, posterga la irrupción gloriosa de The Beautiful People, que va llegando envuelta en esa pausa metafísica que solicita la admiración ajena y que antes se conocía como tardanza. . . . El reportero – o sea, quien esto escribe y que así se sueña – lamenta muchísimo su ignorancia de la Buena Sociedad Mexicana y del Jet Set, lo que provoca su indiferencia ante los Ilustres Apellidos congregados lo que le impulsa a revisar – en un vano intento por retener estilos – la variada falta de imaginación que organiza la vestimenta' (Monsiváis 2010b: 20–1).

[12] 'La crónica y el reportaje se acercan a las minorías y mayorías sin cabida o representatividad en los medios masivos, a los grupos indígenas, los indocumentados, los desempleados y subempleados, los

It is clear from this passage that using the means of literature, and the platform of the press, journalists act as mediators between social organizations and state institutions. It is not surprising, then, that chroniclers in Latin America, and particularly in Mexico, became public intellectuals who represented public opinion.[13]

Elena Poniatowska: The lady behind the notebook

Hélène Elizabeth Louise Amélie Paula Dolores Poniatowska was born in Paris in 1932 to a French father with Polish and American origins, Prince Jean E. Poniatowski Sperry, and to Paula Amor de Ferreira Iturbe, a French-Mexican woman of Russian ancestry, whose family had left Mexico after the end of the Maximilian Empire (Schuessler 2007). Because of the Second World War, the family immigrated to Mexico with ten-year-old Elena. Poniatowska's first language was French, which she spoke at home, and she spoke English in the British-sponsored school she attended, the Windsor; meanwhile, she began to learn Spanish from the family maids. She was sent to the United States to study in a Catholic private school run by nuns at the Convent of the Sacred Heart in Philadelphia, after which she returned to Mexico City. As has been noted earlier, considering Poniatowska's upbringing in French and English-speaking cultures, her identification as Mexican as well as her identification with Latin America and the Spanish language are clearly deliberate choices (Chevigny 1985).

Poniatowska has developed an openly leftist political ideology that emerged in her works, especially in *La noche de Tlatelolco* (translated as *Tlatlelolco massacre*, 1971) and *Fuerte es el silencio* (Strong is the Silence, 1980). She has also publically demonstrated her political beliefs, as when she supported the first presidential campaign of Andrés Manuel López Obrador in 2006.[14]

Throughout Poniatowska's work, there is an ethical attitude towards the other. This attitude is marked through her identity (at least as it is represented in her writing): that of an educated and privileged woman, who in spite of her foreign background looks for her Mexican identity in those who are different from her. This section explores how Poniatowska's desire to belong defines her interest in Mexican popular culture. I perceive that this interest in popular culture oscillates between a cosmopolitan literary identity and a journalistic one, which is closely related to one of the essential aims of testimonial authors: that of looking for 'social justice' (Nance 2006).

---

organizadores de sindicatos independientes, los jornaleros agrícolas, los migrantes, los campesinos sin tierras, las feministas, los homosexuales y las lesbianas. Cronicarlos es reconocer sus modos expresivos, oponerse a la idea de la noticia como mercancía, exhibir la política inquisitorial de la derecha, cuestionar los prejuicios y las limitaciones sectarias y machistas de la izquierda militante, precisar los elementos recuperables de la cultura popular' (2010a [2006]: 126).

[13] Historically, the newspaper began to be a space for public opinion when literary journalism was introduced into its news pages (Habermas 1992).

[14] Her experiences as part of López Obrador's movement were published in *Amanecer en el Zócalo. Los 50 días que confrontaron a México* (2007).

Poniatowska began her journalistic and literary careers simultaneously. In 1954, she started working at *Excélsior* newspaper, interviewing politicians and artists. The same year, she published *Lilus Kikus*, a collection of twelve short stories. In the 1950s, in a journalistic sphere dominated by male authors, the interviews offered Poniatowska a way into the Mexican intellectual circuits of the time (Steele 1989: 90). In addition, her interviews with famous artists made her name visible in the national print media.

Poniatowska's individual form of journalistic practice was a novelty for the time in Mexico, and it has been compared with that of the American 'New journalists' (Young and Young 1983). Her freedom to experiment with genres beyond traditional 'objective' journalistic writing in the Mexican press might also be explained by the cultural and socio-economic system that supported her.[15] According to Jörgensen (1994), Poniatowska obtained her first job as a journalist at *Excélsior* through family connections. The newspaper was considered to be pro-American, and Poniatowska's first task was an interview with the new US Ambassador in Mexico. At the beginning of her career, she would write mostly about high society.[16]

If her male colleagues were self-taught as journalists, then Poniatowska was an equal in that regard. One could say that she had an advantage over the average journalist, male or female, because of her cultural capital, including her full command of at least three languages, and the intellectual environment in which she grew up.[17] It was this environment, in fact, which facilitated her approaches to people that she would otherwise not have been able to gain access to as a young woman who was just starting a journalistic career. Her first interviews can thus be analysed as representative of a process of (female) identity formation, for they had a direct referent in the real-life experience of the author, as she remembered in our interview:

> When I was young, I went crazy without knowing anything about anything, but when you are young, I think people like you, even if you don't know anything and ask pure idiotic questions. You are liked because of your youth. Besides, at the time I did journalism, there were few journalists, so you would arrive, and people would accept you. . . . I asked Diego Rivera if his teeth were made out of milk because I had never seen a painting by him, I came from a nuns' convent. I said to myself 'he is very tall, very big and his teeth [are] very small' and he said 'yes, they are of milk and with these teeth I eat the nosy little Polish girls' and then I had an

---

[15] For a complete analysis of Poniatowska's evolution as a 'privileged' women writer in Mexico, see Chevigny (1985), who states that 'the particular force of Poniatowska's work derives from the emptiness she found in her position as a woman of privilege and from her using that position to cultivate a readiness of imagination and spirit' (50).

[16] In the foreword to Schuessler's biography of Poniatowska, which uses her nickname 'La Poni', as its title, Carlos Fuentes remembers: 'I first met Elena at a ball held at Mexico City's Jockey Club. She was disguised as a charming kitty cat, all in white; a true blonde, she wore a mask that covered only the top part of her face, and very light-coloured jewels. She looked like some lovely and adorable creature dreamed up by Jean Cocteau' (ix). Two of the most recognizable contemporary Mexican authors did not meet in a literary workshop or at any artistic event but at a society ball.

[17] Rather than admire journalists, she admires fiction writers, such as Marguerite Yourcenar, Virginia Woolf, Elvira Lindo and Catherine Mansfield (see Interview 6).

interview. And I got an audience that used to say 'let's see what this silly girl [*esta babosa*] is going to ask'. (Interview 6)

There are certain characteristics of a personal identity that prevail as a stylistic mark of the author, particularly when she writes about intellectuals or artists. As in Rivera's case, her foreignness – starting with her last name, an uncommon one in Mexico – is a mark of distinction that generates peculiar conversations, and she has incorporated that into her worldview.

Although it is true that men held the professional field, the Mexican mass media was a less-competitive market than is the case today. There was no professional training for journalists, so the *oficio* (the trade) needed to be learned from the outset. In a country with high levels of illiteracy, it was hard to find either men or women whose cultivation and writing abilities were outstanding. In *Todo México* (All Mexico), a collection of interviews with celebrities made mostly in the 1970s and published in seven volumes (1991–2002), Poniatowska shows an awareness of her privileged status, particularly in her profile piece on Argentinean author Jorge Luis Borges. While the rest of reporters had to chase after any and all statements by Borges during his visit to Mexico City, she was able to see him for long and have private conversations. Poniatowska employs humour and irony as a way of exposing a rather mundane side of the intellectuals she interviews, as demonstrated in the last scene of her profile of Borges:

> – As it happens, I thought you must not have read my short-stories.
> – Why is that, *maestro*?
> – Because of the questions you are asking me.
> I feel ashamed.
> – Is it because I am not an erudite woman and I come unprepared?
> – No – he says sweetly– I prefer your freshness. You have an *awareness*; I can sense it.
> My notebook falls down. Oh, my God![18]

In this passage, the author depicts herself as a serious journalist, for she intends to pose important questions to her important interviewee. The interview, however, turns out to be almost impossible: the interviewee is cold. Poniatowska ends up looking for a solution to a very practical matter: she searches for a blanket to cover Borges's body instead of continuing the interview. She allows herself to be mocked in a hilarious situation that goes beyond the formal conventions of a professional interview, but only after she has revealed an interesting conversation with the author. This conversation

---

[18] – Es que pensé que usted no había leído mis cuentos.
– ¿Por qué, maestro?
– Por las preguntas que me hace.
Me avergüenzo.
– ¿Por qué no soy erudita ni vengo preparada?
– No – dice dulcemente – prefiero su frescura. Usted tiene una *awareness*, puedo percibirla.
Se me cae la libreta. Ay, Dios mío (1991: 149)

is in fact witty in tone and full of literary references, which was indeed far beyond the level of conversation being held by the group of journalists who were following Borges continuously but did not know what to ask to him. By the end of the interview, it is clear that Poniatowska was just pretending to be one of those shy reporters who know nothing about Borges's work.

As in this interview, Poniatowska's documentary narratives are written in the first person, through a self-referencing narrator. By representing herself as a naïve woman and inexperienced young reporter, Poniatowska engages with her ideal reader: a middle-class, modern, urban man or woman, who may be afraid of acting like her in a similar situation, but who recognizes in her a social equal. The 'I' in her texts, however, is rather elusive because the narrator becomes a hidden character. Poniatowska offers authority to the text by her mere silent presence. This is applicable even when she writes about her aunt, the poet Guadalupe 'Pita' Amor, or her husband, the astronomer Guillermo Haro. During my interview with Poniatowska, she declared that she intentionally tried to conceal herself when writing the chronicles:

> The day I have time or want to write my biography I will use the 'I', but when I am doing a chronicle of something that happens outside of me I don't see the need to insert myself, to talk about myself: whether my feet hurt or if I have been standing for 12 hours waiting, for example, in an earthquake or a tragedy, as in the many I have lived through. (Interview 6)

Based on this statement, it can be inferred that Poniatowska's conception of the chronicle excludes the author's own experience of approaching others. The ethics of her own writing led her to criticize the abuse of the first person by *cronistas*, who represent themselves in the action, or even as protagonists of their texts. It is also interesting how she defines the genre of *crónica* as opposed to autobiography. For Poniatowska, the chronicle is a well-defined genre, determined by its focus on otherness, the world beyond herself, for it is a genre in which she is not allowed to express the self, as she is able to in fiction.

Regardless of her reluctance to make the first-person narrator the protagonist of her stories, Poniatowska is evidently aware of the subjectivity of her task. When I asked her if she had thought of writing her memoirs, she said no, because 'in the interviews and chronicles there is a lot of my own life'.[19] Later during the conversation, she would recall my question on this topic, since she thinks that in her journalism the 'I' is not present at all:

> When you tell me that if I have not written my autobiography, I would say that in the books one writes, merely the fact of choosing certain events and leaving

---

[19] My interview with Poniatowska was conducted before she published her first volume of personal memoirs/fictional family biography called *El amante polaco*, using a self-referenced, first-person narrator (The Polish Lover, 2019).

aside certain others is already a way of speaking of oneself. Anyway, you talk about yourself, even doing an article, don't you? (Interview 6)

Poniatowska's writing style demonstrates that the act of editing can be a creative task. The creativity of editing is demonstrated by the selection of the information she collects from her journalistic investigation. The more outstanding examples of this are *La noche de Tlatelolco* and *Hasta no verte Jesús mío*, both of which experiment with the effect of transcribing the recorded voices of others into written discourse. What Poniatowska brings into discussion in her response to my question, however, is the link between life and writing, for she is usually so involved in the process of investigation that it becomes not only a professional activity but also a real-life experience that shapes her writing. The 'I' therefore expresses itself only through the exploration of the other, as dictated by the rules of the genre.

Despite her own statements on this matter, and based on a close reading of those texts with the self-referenced narrator, I argue that Poniatowksa uses the first-person narrator as an aesthetic solution to the problem of verisimilitude. She then constructs a witness-narrator in texts in which the informant, usually a marginal other, would not be considered a legitimate source of information for traditional journalism. Therefore, as the interviewer legitimates the importance of the witness by the mere act of listening to and recording his testimony, the reality she aims to show appears credible through the very presence of the author in the text. By explaining her own working process, the author demonstrates that the point of view of a surprised and rather naïve narrator is a conscious literary construction:

Liliana Chávez: I sense that your gaze in the chronicles of this period is a very surprised gaze at reality, as if you saw it for the first time, what were you experiencing?
Elena Poniatowska: I don't think I saw it as for the first time, but in order to write I had to give importance to what was happening. (Interview 6)

On the one hand, having positioned herself as a public intellectual, the topics she chooses become important because of her very decision to write about them. She is aware that she will be published and read. If Poniatowska's *crónicas* do not focus on the process, the difficulties or adventures experienced by the *cronista* in order to tell the story, as the writing of later generations usually does, it is because her narrative authority is not based upon the construction of a self-referenced character. Her authorial strength has already been established by her social background and the literary prestige of her signature.

On the other hand, against her own desire to give voice to the voiceless, there is still a strong presence of the self in a search for identity. By writing about others through the eyes of a fresh – and always surprised – first-person narrator, she is not hiding the difference of those who have been 'voiceless', but constructing a trustworthy witness with whom a bourgeois reader can relate. This reader will trust in her to be the Charon in their journey to another Mexico they could be discovering together, maybe for the first time.

Lilus, Mariana and other strange women

Before *El amante polaco* (The Polish Lover, 2019), *El universo o nada* (The Universe or Nothing, [2013] 2014) was the closest that Poniatowska's output came to autobiography. It is the biography of her husband, the astronomer Guillermo Haro, told by a self-referenced, first-person narrator. In this book, the narrator remembers herself as a devoted housewife, albeit quite absent-minded and unwilling to make strong decisions. In contrast with this self-representation of a scientist's wife who wishes to please her husband's political and social circles, Poniatowska has also written about other women with admiration for their independence, freedom, strength, courage and lack of care for social conventions. For example, in *Las siete cabritas* (The seven young female goats, 2000), a collection of seven profiles of Mexican women intellectuals, Poniatowska focuses on female identities that contrast variously with her own self-representation.[20]

There is a clear difference between these women and Poniatowska's self-referenced narrator in autobiographical-adjacent works. The author usually portrays herself as a childish or naïve woman who behaves 'properly', a good Catholic girl with a lack of self-esteem, who is insecure regarding her artistic capabilities. Female sexuality is explored by a narrator who is shocked, but aware that she is writing about what she considers to be exceptional lives. This is shown especially in 'Nahui Olin: la que hizo olas' (Nahui Olin: the one who made waves), a profile of a model, painter and poet. Olin's background is actually quite similar to Poniatowska's, for she also came from an upper-class French family that included intellectuals and writers. Nevertheless, the contrast between both female identities is evident, for the freedom and sensuality experienced by Olin cannot be compared with Poniatowska's established narrator: 'Her eyes are of a brutal eroticism, even violent. There is no man or woman now in Mexico nor in the early twenty-first century who dares write like that, feel like that, fall in love like that, paint like that.'[21] Poniatowska admires Olin, and tries to explain her behaviour and identity, although she describes her as if she came from another world. Olin's early erotic writings surprise the narrator, as there is no chance that Poniatowska's *alter egos*, Lilus and Mariana, would be able to write or act like Olin.

---

[20] The profiles are on Frida Kahlo, Pita Amor, Nahui Olin, María Izquierdo, Elena Garro, Rosario Castellanos and Nellie Campobello. Poniatowska declares in the introduction that it was her little daughter who suggested that title. In Mexico, the word *cabra* (goat) is used to refer to a person who acts in a crazy manner. The author, however, might be making a parodic reference to 'Los siete sabios' (The seven wise man). This was a cultural society founded in 1916 by male intellectuals who became powerful in Mexican politics (Krauze 1985).

[21] 'Sus ojos son de un erotismo brutal, hasta violento. No hay hombre o mujer ahorita en México y a principios del siglo XXI que se atreva a escribir así, a sentir así, a enamorarse así, a pintar así' (63).

Although all women are indeed portrayed as independent and strong in her writing, Poniatowska only explores the erotic while writing about intellectual or aristocratic women. While she depicts marginalized, uneducated women in relation to their household tasks and their poverty, in the case of the artists she explores their inner life in a deeper sense, describing their intelligence, as well as their sensuality. An outstanding example is *Tinísima* (1992), a biographical novel about the American-Italian photographer Tina Modotti which contains the most erotic prose of Poniatowska's work. If, in fiction, Elena Poniatowska barely writes on eroticism, she challenges herself by choosing to profile women whose biographies render the topic inevitable.

By choosing to write about these women, however, the author inscribes herself within a generation of women artists who were in confrontation with a patriarchal and conservative society. Yet her first-person narrator can only access this other world by means of irony and a self-conscious innocence. Their childlike perspective has become a signature feature of Poniatowska's narrators. For instance, in *Lilus Kikus*, a coming-of-age story of a rich girl in Mexico City, the protagonist criticizes the society she lives in through a heavy use of irony: 'Lilus heard people saying that silly women are the most charming in the world. Yes, the ones that know nothing, the ones that are childish and absent-minded.'[22]

Poniatowska's construction of a childish point of view is more complex in *La "Flor de Lis"*. This novel can be read as a continuation of Lilus Kikus's adventures, for the life of Mariana, the narrator, is quite similar to Lilus's, although she is already a teenager. Mariana's character is crafted through a mixture of religious taboos and an awareness of the significance of sexuality. She shows a fascination for the mother's body, and an obsessive but repressed desire to possess her. At a time when she discovers that the naked body must be hidden, her friendship with other women is most strongly rooted in her admiration for their physical beauty.

Faced with the impossibility of knowing the other completely, Poniatowska adopts the role of the silent observer. She embodies Virginia Woolf's description of the non-fiction writer as one who observes the lives of others through their windows (1929). Poniatowska's first-person narrators, however, are not revealed in one place for long, as they are in a state of continuous displacement. If the little girl, Lilus Kikus, observes the world from her house window, the young woman Mariana observes it from the moving window of a bus. In Poniatowska's autobiographical fictions, therefore, self-identity is represented as a process undergoing constant change, simultaneous to the ongoing process of discovering otherness:

> I like to sit on the sunshine in the middle of the crowd, that people, in my city, in the centre of my country, in the belly button of the world. . . . My country is this stone bench from which I look at the midday . . . my country is the

---

[22] 'Lilus oyó decir por allí que las tontas son las mujeres más encantadoras del mundo. Sí, las que no saben nada, las que son infantiles y ausentes' (1987 [1954]: 53).

tamale that I am bringing right now from Huichapan street number 17, from the FLEUR-DE-LIS. 'Make it green chilli', I will say: 'A green chilli tamale with chicken'.[23]

In Poniatowska's writing, the figure of the other – who could be another woman or the more abstract 'Mexican people' – is so closely intertwined by means of popular language with the figure of the narrator that the whole narrative is affected by the worldview of a self-referenced narrator who aims to become one with her characters/informants. As this technique is used by Poniatowska's narrators regardless of narrative genres, her journalistic writing cannot be analysed independently from her literature, but as a wide, life-long documentary project in which value rests in the intersection of the two cultural fields on which she has learned to play. Poniatowska has constructed a narrator with the ability to question a politician, engage in intellectual conversation, as well as the ability to ask for the street food she likes in the most common language of the area.

A guilty *catrina* goes out

During the Mexico City earthquake of 1985, Elena Poniatowska and Carlos Monsiváis were working side by side. They were both interested in telling stories of the catastrophe, but their methods were quite different, as Poniatowska remembered later:

> He [Carlos Monsiváis] used to tell me often 'why do you develop personal relationships? Just write and it is over'. I could not just write, but I would go looking for the wheelchair, for the bed, to the pantry for the rice so they had something to eat. These kinds of things tire you emotionally very much. To be able to write to get involved is terrible.[24]

Poniatowska's emotional commitment to the lowest social classes is represented in her writing, which shows her awareness of her role as a public intellectual in a country comprising dramatic contrasts. She has written on topics she feels are important, sometimes regardless of her own personal interests. For example, she does not like her books *Gaby Brimmer* (1979), about a girl with brain paralysis, and *Las mil y una . . . La herida de Paulina* (One thousand and one . . . Paulina's wound, 2000), about a girl who wanted to abort a child conceived by rape, but she wrote them as favours to friends

---

[23] 'Me gusta sentarme al sol en medio de la gente, esa gente, en mi ciudad, en el centro de mi país, en el ombligo del mundo. . . . Mi país es esta banca de piedra desde la cual miro el mediodía . . . mi país es el tamal que ahora mismo voy a ir a traer a la calle de Huichapan número 17, a la FLOR DE LIS. "De chile verde", diré: "Uno de chile verde con pollo"' (1988a: 261).

[24] 'Él [Carlos Monsiváis] me decía mucho "¿para qué estableces relaciones personales? Tú escribe y se acabó". No podía solo escribir, sino que iba por la silla de ruedas, por la cama, a la despensa por el arroz para que tuvieran qué comer. Este tipo de cosas te desgasta muchísimo emocionalmente. Para escribir es nefasto involucrarse' (Steele 1989: 104–105).

who are activists (see interview 6). Also, she frequently develops affective relationships with her informants, particularly with those whom she interviews over months or years. An outstanding case is her long friendship with Josefina Bórquez, known as Jesusa Palancares in *Hasta no verte Jesús mío*.

In *Luz y luna, las lunitas*, Poniatowska offers an image of the journalistic task as one where the journalist intrudes on the lives of other people. The informants are not usually part of the everyday life of the journalist, but Poniatowska shows how the encounter with the other can create affective relationships beyond the merely professional ones between an interviewer and the interviewees. This situation is exemplified in the author's *crónica* about her friendship with Josefina Bórquez, on whom her character Jesusa Palancares, the protagonist of her testimonial novel *Hasta no verte Jesús mío*, is based. In 'Vida y muerte de Jesusa' (Life and death of Jesusa), the reader is aware that for Jesusa to tell stories, as Poniatowska asks her to do, is not an important job compared to accomplishing the daily and difficult household tasks that allow her to survive:

> – Look, you have been coming here for two years, being a nuisance and you don't get anything. So we should stop this here.
> I went away with my notebook against my chest as a shield. In the car I thought: "What a nice old woman, my God! She does not have anyone in her life, the only person who visits her is me, and she is capable of sending me to hell".
> I was late the following Wednesday (it was the reborn unconscious) and I found her outside on the sidewalk.

She grumbled:

> – Well, what happened with you? Are you not getting it? At the time you leave I go to the barn for my milk, go out for my bread. You are a pest if you keep me here waiting.[25]

As a self-reflective narrative, this chronicle includes the thoughts of the journalist regarding her experience of the encounter with the informant. By inserting this dialogue, Poniatowska questions the ethics of the profession, the apparent right of the journalist to intrude on other's life. Jesusa may not be an 'important' character in

---

[25] – Mire, usted tiene dos años de venir y estar chingue y chingue y no entiende nada. Así de que mejor aquí le paramos.
Me fui con mi libreta contra el pecho a modo de escudo. En el coche pensé: '¡Qué padre vieja, Dios mío! No tiene a nadie en la vida, la única persona que la visita soy yo, y es capaz de mandarme al carajo'.
Al miércoles siguiente se me hizo tarde (fue el renacido inconsciente) y la encontré afuera en la banqueta.
Refunfuñó:
– Pues ¿qué le pasa? ¿No entiende? A la hora que usted se va, salgo por mi leche al establo, voy por mi pan. A mí me friega usted si me tiene aquí esperando.
Entonces la acompañé al establo (Poniatowska 1994: 42).

Mexican social or political life, but she is aware of her own right to tell or not to tell her story. From then on in the chronicle, Poniatowska tries another approach to Jesusa that indicates her own openness to a more intimate interaction, beyond the conventions that would guide a formal journalistic interview, where the journalist has the power or the right to shoot questions and the informant has to answer them. The informant then becomes Poniatowska's Charon, guiding her journey into an unknown world:

> Taken by the hand of Jesusa, I was in touching distance of poverty, true poverty, when the water that is picked up in buckets and is carried carefully so it is not spilled, when the washing is done on a metal sheet because there is no sink, when the electricity is stolen through '*diablillos*', when the hens lay eggs without shells, 'only the mere *tocata*', because the lack of sun does not allow them to calcify.[26]

Josefina Bórquez, aka Jesusa Palancares, and Elena Poniatowska, represent two faces of the same country. Poniatowska's physical displacement from a poor neighbourhood in the outskirts of Mexico City to an aristocratic house in the same city depicts the dialogue that continues in opposed worlds:

> On Wednesday afternoons I would go to see Jesusa and at night, when I arrived home, I would accompany my mother to some cocktail party at some embassy. I always pretended to keep the balance between the extreme poverty that I shared in Jesusa's neighbourhood, with the abundant lights, the pomp of the receptions. My socialism was lip service only.[27]

When, finally, Poniatowska invites Jesusa to her house, the latter does not end the friendship, as the author feared, as she says, 'I already knew that you were a *catrina*.'[28] By letting the reader know that Jesusa thought that she was an upper-class woman, a *catrina*, Poniatowska exhibits an important bias, for her encounters with informants are hardly ever equal. While interviewing elites, Elena reveals her embarrassment at not being professional, due to her inexperience and her lack of formal education. On the other hand, while talking with people from lower social classes, she experiences a sense of guilt, generated by the acknowledgement of an unequal situation she is not able to change through her writing. The awareness that her stories depend upon another's suffering leads her to question her privileges: 'For me, Jesusa was a fictional

---

[26] A *diablillo* is a home-made, illegal artefact designed to transfer electricity to a place in which the service was not hired. 'De la mano de Jesusa entré en contacto con la pobreza, la de a de veras, la del agua que se recoge en cubetas y se lleva cuidando de no tirarla, la de la lavada sobre la tableta de lámina porque no hay lavadero, la de la luz que se roba por medio de "diablillos", la de las gallinas que ponen huevos sin cascarón, "nomás la pura toccata", porque la falta de sol no permite que se calcifiquen' (42).
[27] 'En las tardes de los miércoles iba yo a ver a la Jesusa y en la noche, al llegar a la casa, acompañaba a mi mamá a algún coctel en alguna embajada. Siempre pretendí mantener el equilibrio entre la extremada pobreza que compartía en la vecindad de la Jesu, con el lucerío, el fasto de las recepciones. Mi socialismo era de dientes para afuera' (52).
[28] 'Yo ya sabía desde endosantes que usted era catrina' (52).

character, the best of all. Jesusa was right. I took advantage of her, as Lewis did with the Sánchez family . . . neither my current life nor the previous one has anything in common with Jesusa's. I continued being, after all, a woman in front of a typewriter'.[29]

Poniatowska's true stories are not obtained through a purely scientific methodology, such as she considers anthropologists like Oscar Lewis used.[30] As a woman of letters, Poniatowska finds, through language, a way of respecting the other's identity, for she tries to transcribe popular phrases in her chronicles. Language, however, is the undeniable distinguishing mark of the difference between the narrator and the marginalized other. Therefore, the text becomes the space in which the two different worldviews collide. The author confesses, for instance, that she had to look up some of Jesusa's words in the dictionary. As opposed to the interviews with intellectuals and artists, the encounters with marginalized others are not usually represented in Poniatowska's documentary narratives in the form of complete dialogue, but rather as carefully selected quotations. For if the dialogue is not between equals, the self should be almost erased in order to leave space for the complete experience of otherness, as if there were no mediation.

Even though differences of social class are an overarching obsession in Poniatowska's writing, they are not so evident in her documentary narratives as they are in her biographical fictions. In her journalistic works, social differences are not explicitly questioned by the narrator, for she prefers to merely transcribe the voices of others; rather, it is in fictional autobiographical texts, like *La "Flor de Lis"*, where the author's long-term concern is exposed in its great complexity:

> But, who are these people? Where are all these people coming from? Aunt Francisca asks, as if she had discovered a new human species.
> – Aunt, they are common people, everyday life people.
> – You have said it right, common people. There was not so much of that before. I have never seen such crowds of ugly people at the same time.[31]

By developing strong affective relations with her informants/characters, Poniatowska-as-journalist might be acting as if she wanted to respond to a mystical call from the strange priest of *La "Flor de Lis"*, the one who motivates Mariana to go outside her

---

[29] 'Para mí Jesusa fue un personaje, el mejor de todos. Jesusa tenía razón. Yo a ella le saqué raja, como Lewis se las sacó a los Sánchez . . . ni mi vida actual ni la pasada tienen que ver con la de Jesusa. Seguí siendo ante todo, una mujer frente a una máquina de escribir' (52).

[30] Poniatowska worked with the American anthropologist Oscar Lewis as a research assistant. She edited and corrected his interviews with Mexican peasants for the book *Pedro Martínez: A Mexican peasant and his family* (1964). After this job, she began a new stage in her career, focusing on those Mexicans who were most different from her: the poor, marginalized urban and rural men and women.

[31] Pero ¿quién es esa gente? ¿De dónde sale toda esa gente?, pregunta tía Francisca como si hubiera descubierto una nueva especie humana.
– Tía, es gente común y corriente, gente del diario.
– Lo has dicho bien, gente común. Antes no había tanta en el mundo. Nunca he visto tal multitud de gente fea a la vez (1988a: 80).

comfort zone to confront the unknown reality of her country: 'Dare to walk among the crowds, among the pelados, as you call them, encourage yourself, break the established order.'[32] Poniatowska, thus, seeks not only a dialogue with others, but a complete fusion.

Carlos Monsiváis: A protestant reporter in a Catholic country

When Carlos Monsiváis was still a child his family moved from La Merced – a poor neighbourhood in the city centre still known for its illegal activities – to Portales, a newer and quieter middle-class area, by then almost a suburb of the capital; 'La Portales' would be his residence until his death in 2010. In his autobiography, published at the age of twenty-eight, he narrates:

> Since the beginning, the petty bourgeoisie welcomed me into its bosom. I grew up enraptured in front of a 'Last Suppers' landscape; call-the-technician-because-the-washing-machine-is-broken; what-are-you-giving-to-your-mother-as-a-gift-on-May-10; your-grandmother-looks-very-much-like-Sara-García; let's-go-to-Cuernavaca-next-Sunday; and other symbols of the elegance and rise a social class.[33]

Later in the same text, which somehow echoes both the teenage confessional and the rebel perspective of J. D. Salinger's *The Catcher in the Rye* (1951), Monsiváis depicts himself as 'precocious, protestant and presumptuous.'[34] He offers as evidence an account of the everyday activities of a young urban man exposed to drugs and late-night parties, but also to the ideological influences of Sunday School and literature. Although this text does not attempt to present itself as a *crónica*, it is an early example of the descriptive style that Monsiváis would go on to employ in later works and that would distinguish his texts from more traditional journalistic productions.

As if he was already announcing a topic that would be present in his future work, Monsiváis chooses to start his own life story with a class-based definition of the self. In a few playful images, he exhibits the elements through which a new society was developing kitsch aesthetics, technology, consumerism, popular culture, film, leisure

---

[32] 'Atrévete a caminar en la multitud, entre los pelados como ustedes los llaman, aviéntate, rompe el orden establecido' (251).
[33] 'Desde el principio la pequeña burguesía me acogió en su seno. Fui creciendo extasiado ante un paisaje de "Últimas Cenas"; llama-al-técnico-porque-se-descompuso-la-lavadora; qué-le-vas-a-dar-a-tú-mamá-el-diez-de-mayo; cómo-se-parece-tu-abuelita-a-Sara-García; vámonos-el-domingo-a-Cuernavaca; y demás símbolos de la elegancia y el ascenso de una clase' (1966: 11). Published in 1966 with a prologue by Emanuel Carballo, *Autobiografía* is the only autobiographical work by Monsiváis, and it was never reprinted. In May 2008, *emeequis* magazine published a selection from the book under the title 'La biografía que Monsiváis quisiera sepultar' (The biography that Monsiváis would like to bury), although it was illustrated with photographs donated by Monsiváis himself. In the introduction to the text, the editor states that Monsiváis tried to erase any trace of the book (Vega 2008).
[34] 'Precoz, protestante y presuntuoso' (11).

and urban lifestyle. Monsiváis was born when the post-revolutionary social agitation was over and the Partido Revolucionario Institucional (PRI) had consolidated a strong nationalistic culture. This was the period when President Lázaro Cárdenas started a programme of import substitution in order to accelerate the country's own means of production. Monsiváis's family experienced the consequences of an economic stability that allowed social mobility and the rise of mass media and consumer society.

Monsiváis was known as a journalist, a fiction writer, a public intellectual, a historian, a radio presenter, an activist, an art collector, a bibliophile, a defender of animal and human rights, and also an actor.[35] During his prolific literary career, he published essays, journalistic articles, film and music reviews, translations, short stories, prologues and plays. It is not surprising that many of those genres can also be found in the five chronicle collections published while he was alive: *Días de guardar* (Rest Days, 1970), *Amor perdido* (Lost Love, 1977), *Entrada libre* (Free Access, 1987), *Escenas de pudor y liviandad* (Scenes of Modesty and Frivolity, of 1988) and *Los rituales del caos* (The Rituals of Chaos, 1995).[36]

The author initiated his career as a journalist by hosting a radio programme on cinema at Radio UNAM. During the 1970s and 1980s, when he was the director of *La cultura en México* (Culture in Mexico), the cultural supplement of *Siempre!* magazine, he started to obtain wider recognition. Throughout his writing career, he continued to publish in counter-culture, leftist and marginal publications as well as in mainstream media – even in those publications which were in competition with each other, or were ideologically opposed, such as the newspapers *Novedades, Excélsior, El Universal* and *La Jornada* and the magazines *Proceso, Nexos* and *Letras Libres*. His column, *Por mi madre bohemios* (I swear by my mother, bohemians!), was published in regional newspapers around the country, a fact that also brought him national recognition as a leader of public opinion far beyond the cultural elite of the capital. In *Crónica de la literatura reciente* (1982), José Joaquín Blanco included Monsiváis among other, then young, authors, such as Carlos Fuentes, Sergio Pitol and Elena Poniatowska. The critic considered Monsiváis to be the first 'free writer' of modern Mexico (1982: 85).

While Poniatowska's chronicles are rooted in the Latin American *testimonio* tradition, and adopt ethnographic techniques, Monsiváis looked more at American New Journalism as a stylistic model for his writing.[37] In fact, his *crónica* style might be compared – although it has not been thus far – to the essays of Susan Sontag and

---

[35] He is known in the film industry for *Los caifanes* (1967), *Fonqui* (1985) and *The Life and Times of Frida Kahlo* (2005). He was an actor in nine films, the writer of four, and he appears as himself in at least twenty-four documentaries, television series and movies <http://www.imdb.com/name/nm0598658> [accessed 28 April 2021].

[36] So far, the only English translations of Monsiváis' work are *Mexican Postcards* (1997), which includes *crónicas* and essays from a variety of books, selected and translated by John Kraniauskas, and *A New Catechism for Recalcitrant Indians* (2007), translated by Jeffrey Browitt and Nidia Esperanza Castrillón from the original 1982 work *Nuevo catecismo para indios remisos*.

[37] Monsiváis's personal library, open to the public after his death as part of the Biblioteca de México, contains a wide collection of the major New Journalists: Truman Capote, Norman Mailer and Tom Wolfe. He also owned first editions of the works of Pierre Bourdieu, Roland Barthes, Michel De Certeau and Susan Sontag. One could infer then that Monsiváis was aware of the literary, sociological

Joan Didion in the 1970s. He might also have been influenced by social theorists of his time. The style and theme of *Días de guardar*, for instance, resembles Roland Barthes's *Mythologies* (1957). If Poniatowska's pact of verisimilitude is based on a careful editing of her informant's voices, leading direct speech to the extreme, Monsiváis prefers the use of indirect speech and stream-of-consciousness writing to recreate otherness. This can only be attempted through the means of literary techniques: 'While he cannot fully overcome the unbridgeable gap between his own and the consciousness of those others, he carefully positions himself metajournalistically as "other" to all' (Egan 2001: 231).

Monsiváis's hybrid style and methodology allowed Octavio Paz to say, according to Blanco, that he was a symbol of the modern urban Mexican and represented a new literary genre in himself.[38] Regardless of his popularity in mass media, for he was himself a cultural referent in Mexico, Monsiváis did not achieve the same levels of prestige in local academic circles. Even though Monsiváis wrote exhaustively on Mexican culture and nationalism, he was barely quoted by social scientists publishing on national identity in the 1980s.[39] Monsiváis's creative way of describing and interpreting contemporary Mexican society might have been uncomfortable not only for the political sphere but for both traditional academic and journalistic circles. This is because it touched on issues of what might be described, in Bordieuan terms, as the battle on the Mexican cultural field between high-brow culture and popular culture. This was demonstrated with the Paz-Monsiváis controversy of 1976-7. Regardless of the admiration that the young Monsiváis had for Paz, and the positive comments Paz had already expressed regarding Monsiváis, they were involved in a public disagreement. They criticized each other's intellectual and political attitudes through a series of articles published in *Proceso* magazine. The controversy was interpreted as a generational struggle for cultural power and legitimacy rather than as an ideological discussion ('Polémica Carlos Monsiváis–Octavio Paz' 2004). During the dispute, Paz wrote: 'Monsiváis is not a man of ideas but of witticism. The accumulation of details is not a defect when writing a crónica; but it is in intellectual criticism and politics. Lightness becomes a tangle and there appear the three fatal "*fu*": [his writing is] confusing, profuse and diffuse.'[40] Paz's disdain for the *crónica* genre is evident in this quote, but it is my conviction that what was really at stake

and anthropological trends of the 1960s–80s, especially those studies centred on popular culture, film, photography and everyday life.

[38] The quote, however, does not appear in the book by Paz that is referenced, although the last phrase has also been quoted by José Emilio Pacheco in *Las alusiones perdidas* (2007).

[39] In *La jaula de la melancolía. Identidad y metamorfosis del mexicano* (The cage of melancholy. Identity and metamorphosis of the Mexican, 1987), for instance, Roger Bartra refers to six essays by Monsiváis in his bibliography but only quotes him in two footnotes. Also, Néstor García Canclini's *Culturas híbridas. Estrategias para entrar y salir de la modernidad* (Hybrid cultures. Strategies for entering and exiting modernity, 1989) strongly overlaps with Monsiváis's intellectual interests, but mentions only two of his papers.

[40] 'Monsiváis no es un hombre de ideas sino de ocurrencias. La acumulación de detalles no es un defecto cuando se escribe una crónica; sí lo es en la crítica intelectual y política. La ligereza se convierte en enredijo y aparecen las tres funestas fu: confuso, profuso y difuso' (*Proceso* 1977).

in this controversy was the dominance of two opposed worldviews and positions in Mexican society. Beyond the different textual genres of these authors, there are other questions regarding genre that might have been underlying the discussion: although by then, Paz represented the cultural and political elite of a solemn and heteronormative society, Monsiváis was proposing an ironic, postmodern way of looking into a society from its margins.

Nevertheless, the question of whether Monsiváis was a symbol of the counter-culture, specifically that of the 1980s in Mexico City, is debatable. It is true that Monsiváis published often about minorities and popular culture, topics that usually did not find space in academia or journalism. However, he wrote from the position of a public intellectual, working through the mainstream media. Socially, he was part of the underground circles of young artists, or at least he was known there, and visited cafés and bars frequented by gay and feminist activists, publishers of small magazines and avant-garde artists (Osorno 2014). One of the striking characteristics of his public persona is actually that he was friends with people holding both left- and right-wing ideologies, and he maintained a critical position regarding all parties in power.[41] Being critical of those in power from the inside, as Egan observes, made him a polemical character, but also gave him an exceptional position as both witness and mediator. After all, he was aware of the influential role of the journalist in his society:

> The journalist, that tenant of the vanities of Life, a being who mixes a romantic mood with cynicism, who gets excited about what is not published and gets bored about what is printed. What is there to do? He did not invent the System, it is not his fault that Mexicans are so careless, and one cannot live without eating.[42]

The centre of all margins

From a liminal position, as an insider and outsider at the same time, a new, modern Mexican figure, Carlos Monsiváis chooses to look to his immediate past and reflect on its contradictions. He is aware of the construction of a certain Mexican identity through the use of language, but also through the senses and through appearances. Reality is then the result of the people's appropriation of the official discourse, as when in *Amor perdido* (Lost love, 1977), he transcribes phrases used by the common people that apply the word 'Mexican' as an adjective:

---

[41] This and other information regarding Monsiváis's social and intellectual circles is based on my interview with his friend the editor and scholar Consuelo Sáizar (2016).
[42] 'El periodista, ese inquilino de las vanidades de la Vida, un ser que mezcla el ánimo romántico y el cinismo, que se entusiasma con lo que no se publica y se aburre con lo que sí se imprime. ¿Qué se le va a hacer? Él no inventó el Sistema, no tiene la culpa de que los mexicanos sean tan dejados, y no puede vivir sin comer' (Monsiváis 2010a: 110).

FRUSTRATED MEXICAN
- How Mexican you sound!
- Oh, how Mexican you are today!
- You look so Mexican!
The term 'Mexican' is used as a pejorative, and the strength of another stage of nationalism becomes clear, the parodic one. How proud we are to live in the worst country in the world!⁴³

Monsiváis's way of incorporating *el pueblo*, its problems, assumptions and beliefs, can be seen as a postmodern version of Juan Rulfo's stylization of popular language. In '¡¡¡Goool!!! Somos el desmadre' (Goooal! We are the riot), published in *Entrada libre. Crónicas de la sociedad que se organiza* (Free access. Chronicles of the organized society, 1987), a self-reflective first-person narrator describes football fans on their way to the stadium during the 1986 World Cup that was held in Mexico. Monsiváis depicts himself as the witness who only goes out of his home to quietly observe *el pueblo* (the people) and their messy, festive noise, *el relajo*, passing by: 'I contemplate for a long time the groups in Tlalpan avenue . . . The kids gather around a point, they catch and release cars as they wish, they dance over the tops and they shake those trapped, and before giving way they require cheers, vocal ecstasies at the feet of the new institution of triumphalism.'⁴⁴ In the next paragraph, he positions himself as a solitary man unable to share *el desmadre* of the streets, while still moving among it. When, in the middle of his chronicle, the narrator confesses to knowing nothing about football, the reader already knows that the story was less about the game than about the masses celebrating their own version of national identity. Proposing what is perhaps a postmodern, baroque, Mexican version of Bakhtin's concept of 'carnival', *el desmadre* for Monsiváis is inherent to urban culture. Beyond a rather existentialist critique of Mexican identity as an intricate game of masks that hide the 'true' self – as proposed by other intellectuals such as Paz and Bartra – Monsiváis's idea of the masquerade is more aligned with the colonial survival strategy that Bolívar Echeverría (2000) sees in what he calls *'ethos barroco'*. That is, a will within the form that refers to a degree of adaptation that is nevertheless resistant, that does not totally conform to the conqueror's plans of domination, and which might eventually lead to a rupture with the hegemonic powers, as symbolically represented by the *fiesta* and popular art. For Echeverría, the baroque strategy is a resistance against, but within, modernity; it is an everyday experience

---

⁴³ MEXICANOS FRUSTRADOS
– ¡Qué mexicano te oyes!
– ¡Ah, qué mexicanos vienen hoy!
– ¡Qué mexicano te ves!
El término 'mexicano' como peyorativo y ya se transparenta la fuerza de otra etapa nacionalista, la autoparódica. ¡Qué orgullo vivir en el peor país del mundo!
(Monsiváis 1977: 340).
⁴⁴ 'Contemplo largo rato a los grupos en la calzada de Tlalpan. . . . Los chavos se acumulan sobre un punto, apresan y sueltan automóviles a su antojo, bailan sobre los toldos y zarandean a los atrapados, y antes de conceder el paso demandan porras, éxtasis vocales a los pies de la nueva institución del triunfalismo' (Monsiváis 1994 [1987]: 216).

of disenchantment and rupture that comes back in periods of crisis, catastrophe or great social change (223). As a subversive strategy of resistance, which uses the carnival and other semiotics of the excess and the carnivalesque, the Latin American baroque narrative tradition can be related to the concept of 'camp'. They share a taste for the playful use of irony and wit (Sontag 1964), but, more importantly, they share the contemporary sense of political, critical resistance to hegemonic worldviews, even within mainstream media and popular culture, and against a normative view of gender (Cleto 1999, Shugart and Waggoner 2008).

The portrait of the modern chronicler as a public figure who mediates between lower and upper classes resembles the romantic figure of the *flâneur*, the *paseante* or stroller, who would walk the streets of Paris in the late nineteenth century. However, in the postmodern era, the chronicler is rather a nostalgic, anachronic dandy. Particularly in the case of Monsiváis, the self-constructed image of the *cronista*, by the means of rhetoric, represents – although only by attitude, lifestyle or point of view, rather than by fashion – the dandy's most modern version, drawn from camp aesthetics (Sontag 1964). That is: a self-made middle-class man interested in form and appearance, who is able to move from one social class to another.

Monsiváis would hardly represent himself more openly than in his only autobiographical book: 'I am passionate about my defects: exhibitionism, arbitrariness, uncertainty, snobbery, fatalism.'[45] Although the self is not so evidently depicted in his most popular chronicles, the sense of being out of place permeates his narrative. As Egan notes, he is 'a self-fashioned outsider who invades the home territory of Mexico's elite and popular sectors' (2001: 231).

In a Catholic and family-oriented country, he was raised by a divorced mother, Esther Monsiváis, who educated him in the Protestant faith. On the one hand, attending Protestant Sunday School influenced his worldview, as can be observed in the constant biblical references found in his narratives. On the other hand, official schooling immersed him in the complex mixture of nationalistic discourse and Catholic culture, which he would criticize through most of his writing. A true representative of an urban, middle-class man, Monsiváis used his intermediary position to be a critical observer of Mexican social life, of both the lower and upper classes.

Another important element in the formation of Monsiváis's public persona as an outsider in a conservative society must have been his homosexual identity. Although this was never referred to either in his writing or in his public life, it was common knowledge among his closest social circles (Lamas 2010).[46] For while Monsiváis supported LGBT causes both in his writing and in his life as public intellectual – he attended the Mexico City gay pride parade as guest of honour, for instance – it

---

[45] 'Me apasionan mis defectos: el exhibicionismo, la arbitrariedad, la incertidumbre, el snobismo, la condición azarosa' (Monsiváis 1966: 62).
[46] According to Marta Lamas, weeks before he died, Carlos Monsiváis was planning to write a prologue for *Que se abra esa puerta* (Let that door be opened, Monsiváis 2010c), which was published posthumously. What he would have written if he had the time one can never know, although the working title can be read as a request or a plea, and already suggests the image of 'getting out of the closet' associated with a public openness towards the homosexual self.

remains true that there is no evidence of the disclosure of his identity in interviews or public events, and he was not seen as a gay author in the collective imagination. It may be argued that if he had lived in a different society, the representation of the self in Monsiváis's writing could have taken another form to that which he adopted, of an elusive, baroque, or ironic narrator, who makes the reader feel his presence as witness, but at the same time says little about himself.

In contrast with Salvador Novo, who was the protagonist of his own chronicles, Monsiváis was never at the centre of his narration (Villoro 2007). It is possible to infer, however, that Monsiváis's intention might have been to follow his intellectual father in his literary techniques to represent a similar worldview. Monsiváis begins his biographical work, *Salvador Novo. Lo marginal en el centro* (Salvador Novo. The marginal at the centre, 2000b), with a reflection on Novo's homosexuality and the influence this identity had on his writing:

> Novo derives aesthetical practices, strategies for telling the truth, challenges of gesture and writing from his sexual orientation . . . he tries excessively to follow the refined and sagacious journey: the intellectual who decides to become a popular figure, the marginal man who obtains the acceptance of the society that, morally, despises him . . . the gay sensibility begins in an evident way with Novo.[47]

Even if there is not an evident homosexual identity represented in Monsiváis's literature, it is still possible to find a queer sensibility in his approach to reality. Like Novo, Monsiváis challenges traditional conceptions of identity through language. He questions not only national identity, as critics have noted, but also sexual identity. But, unlike Novo, Monsiváis could not obtain the social recognition of this part of his identity in life, even when he gave readers some clues: 'The intimacy of the author is always available to his readers.'[48]

Although in his autobiography the self is more obviously present than in his further *crónicas*, the position of the first-person narrator hardly changes in his documentary narratives. The narrator is always a middle-class public intellectual who is able to declare without guilt that: 'for me, the underdevelopment is the impossibility of seeing Bergman's The Silence or of contemplating Margot Fonteyn and Nureyev or enjoying a good musical comedy or to being updated in the Last Shouts and readings and existential turns. But overall, the underdevelopment has fewer cultural and more drastic implications.'[49]

---

[47] 'Novo desprende de su orientación sexual prácticas estéticas, estratagemas para decir la verdad, desafíos de gesto y escritura . . . intenta desmedidamente la refinada y sagaz travesía: el intelectual que se propone ser figura popular, el hombre marginal que obtiene el acatamiento de la sociedad que, moralmente, lo desprecia . . . con Novo empieza de modo ostensible la sensibilidad gay' (11–12).

[48] 'La intimidad de un autor está siempre a la disposición de sus lectores' (12).

[49] 'para mí, el subdesarrollo es la imposibilidad de ver El silencio de Bergman o de contemplar a Margot Fonteyn y Nureyev o de gozar una buena comedia musical o de estar al día en Últimos

Contrary to Poniatowska, Monsiváis did not always respect the speech of his others. He did not quote them verbatim (he might not have recorded them at all). His style is, however, coherent with the standing point from which he used to document reality. I believe he did not need to distinguish the otherness through direct quotations of their voices because he was acting not as a mediator but as an another other. There are moments, however, when Monsiváis chooses stream-of-consciousness narration in order to appropriate the voice of a collective other. This collective other becomes a symbol of national identity, as represented through a 'Monsiváian' lens: 'In everyday life I am a worthless motherfucker, on the top of being a worthless motherfucker, I discover that this is an assessment method as any other, because not giving a damn, lacking of the most elementary rights, among them that of a visible future for me and my family, does not stops me from having fun.'[50]

Published when journalistic writing in Mexico was still solemn and rigid, as was the official *priísta* discourse, Monsiváis's chronicles are outstanding for their sense of humour, irreverence and irony.[51] His style has been analysed through the lens of *neo-barroco* and the Bakhtinean idea of the 'carnivalesque' (Kraniauskas 1997; Egan 2001; Moraña and Sánchez 2007). The next section explores the concept of 'camp' as an overall influence on his narrative, for I think that in Monsiváis's *crónicas* there is a camp worldview from which he explores and (re)constructs the self and reality.

Mexico 'camp'

Carlos Monsiváis died in 2010, and his corpse was honoured in Palacio de Bellas Artes, Mexico's most important theatre. It was a two-day public funeral, organized by the Mexican government, under the presidency of the right-wing party PAN. Few media outlets reported in real time that during the ceremony a group of LGBT activists covered the coffin with a rainbow flag, which was later hidden by a larger Mexican flag.[52]

In Monsiváis's *crónicas* one can discern the influence of the Latin American baroque narrative tradition that was revitalized for the twentieth-century narrative by Alejo Carpentier, whom Monsiváis must have read. The presence of *heteroglossia* is also evident as a stylistic technique used by the author, for the collage of voices used to

---

Gritos y lecturas y giros existenciales. Pero en general el subdesarrollo tiene significados menos culturales, más drásticos' (56).

[50] 'En la vida diaria yo valgo madre, pero además de valer madre, descubro que éste es un método de evaluación como cualquier otro, porque valer madre, carecer de la mayoría de los derechos elementales, entre ellos el de un porvenir visible para mí y mi familia, no me impide divertirme' (2010a: 126).

[51] This similitude between journalism and official, political discourse may not be surprising since media content was controlled by the government, and reporters could be corrupted by institutions. Giving money to journalists in exchange for a favourable image or news piece was common practice (Monsiváis 2010a).

[52] Monsiváis wished to have a public funeral at Bellas Artes building, and he had it (Sáizar 2016).

represent a collective, massive otherness is obviously reminiscent of Bakhtin's findings in his theory of the novel and of Sarduy's Latin American reappropriation of the style in his own theory of the neobaroque narrative (1974, 2013). I argue, nevertheless, that a revision of Monsiváis's writing from the perspective of camp aesthetics can offer a deeper and more complex understanding of his poetics. After all, within a common postmodern context, both baroque and camp sensibilities display similar rhetorical qualities, such as parody, irony, performance, and a focus on aesthetics and resistance (Shugart and Waggoner: 29).

The concept of camp allows Monsiváis to uncover the elusive self in his writing, as well as to reflect on his own ethical and aesthetical positions towards the representation of otherness. In her essay 'Notes on "Camp"', Susan Sontag refers to the concept as a modern sensibility whose essence is artifice and exaggeration, or in other words, the unnatural. 'Camp' is applicable to people and objects, but it is a taste rather than a theory, and therefore it is hard to explore it from a perspective based on reason. In Sontag's definition, camp is an action upon the world, which aims to convince the audience of the benefits of an artificial, stylish world:

> To camp is a mode of seduction – one which employs flamboyant mannerisms susceptible of a double interpretation: gestures full of duplicity, with a witty meaning for cognoscenti and another, more impersonal, for outsiders … Behind the 'straight' public sense in which something can be taken, one has found a private zany experience of the thing. (2009 [1964]: 281)

Originally named only among 'small urban cliques', Sontag states that camp has a strong connection with the androgynous and the epicene, in the sense that it responds to exaggeration and artifice. Contemporary critique from media and gender studies coincides with Sontag's view on camp regarding its playful and melancholic nature as a sensibility or a taste that in the popular consciousness was associated with homosexual male communities, mostly from wealthy social backgrounds in Europe and the United States. In order to cope with the burden of social stigma, these communities would use irony and wit in language and cultural productions as a strategy for self-defence and for developing a sense of belonging (Shugart and Waggoner 2008: 25–6).

Going beyond a sterile discussion merely about his gender identity, I propose a reading of Monsiváis from a camp perspective based on textual analysis of his chronicles and the sociopolitical context of their production within the field of popular culture in Mexico at the end of twentieth century. In this way, I also believe that a broader definition as used by more recent theorists of camp would apply better to Monsiváis's narrative. Besides the traditional conceptualization of camp, where it is usually associated with an upper class, Anglo-Saxon gay male culture or with the subversion of gender conventions, for Shugart and Waggoner there are also two other important types of camp that have been invading contemporary media since the 1990s: 'pop camp' and 'resistive camp'. It is the latter kind of camp, with its potential for the disruption of conventions regarding both gender and genre, that I consider more apposite in describing Monsiváis's political position and rhetorical style.

On the one hand, Monsiváis manifested a preference for essay topics on Mexican popular culture and on works or individuals that expressed a melodramatic sentimentality, such as nationalist cinema, folklore, celebrities and soap operas. Although as a cultural critic and chronicler he maintained an ironic distance from his objects of study, as a collector he demonstrated a strong personal taste for popular culture, especially in objects from the nineteenth century (Chávez Díaz 2019). On the other hand, he maintained a subversive attitude towards social and state institutions. Monsiváis's intricate, often affected writing style easily bears relation to Sontag's definition of camp as something playful and witty, but it could never be considered apolitical, so therefore the author shows a critical, ironic distance from camp aesthetics. However, there is no doubt that he was interested in Sontag's work on the topic, although his position towards the employment of the term was rather ambiguous. In 'De las variedades de la experiencia homoerótica' (On the varieties of the homoerotic experience, 2010c [2007]), a late paper in his career, he criticizes the use of the term 'camp' to refer to questions of identity. Nevertheless, in 'El hastío es pavo real que se aburre de luz en la tarde (notas del camp en México)' (Boredom is a peacock that gets bored with light in the afternoon – notes on camp in Mexico), an earlier text published in *Días de guardar*, Monsiváis directly appropriated Sontag's discourse, translating her 'notes' without doing the proper referencing. I believe, however, that these two opposed interpretations of Sontag's essay can be read as an artifice, or the narrator's deliberate self-contradiction.

Just like Oscar Wilde – the camp writer par excellence and one of Monsiváis's favourite authors – the chronicler loved aphorisms. Monsiváis used to incorporate into his texts certain aphorisms from Mexican popular culture, as well as his own creations. The anti-solemn tone and the parody of the self and others, which are also characteristic of camp aesthetics, are part of Monsiváis's chronicle style. As in Sontag's essay, the use of jottings instead of the formal essay structure is usual in Monsiváis's texts.

Sontag makes a list of objects and people that can be considered camp, from Tiffany lamps and Swan Lake to Mozart and Wilde. After reading Sontag's essay, Monsiváis adds to this list an eccentric variety of Mexican figures and things, such as María Félix, Salvador Novo, Jorge Negrete, the Palacio de Bellas Artes, Amado Nervo's poems or Chapultepec Castle. Indeed, if one considers Monsiváis's broad interest in popular culture, the list of camp objects and people could be infinite. It is his own consciously camp perspective that makes a different view of Mexican reality possible through his texts: 'In a country that has suffered extensively about its politicians, its official man of letters . . . its spirit of seriousness and absolute solemnity, the Camp is a perspective of justice and vengeance.'[53]

Another example of Monsiváis's affinity with camp aesthetics is his activity as a collector. The author collected a huge number of paintings, toys, comics, postcards, print media and other heterogeneous objects. Most of these objects were acquired

---

[53] 'En un país que ha padecido vastamente a sus políticos, sus literatos oficiales . . . su espíritu de seriedad y su solemnidad absoluta, lo Camp es una perspectiva de justicia y venganza' (Monsiváis 2010b: 191).

in Mexico City flea markets, and they show the collector's camp taste, particularly embodying camp's nostalgic approach to the past and its close relationship with *kitsch* aesthetics.[54]

If camp is, thus, an 'epicene' looking into the world, Monsiváis used language to appropriate this style as a method of self-expression, but also to create his own version of Mexico through language. It is in this camp version of Mexico that Monsiváis's identity could be, perhaps, fully expressed. For life is not stylish, as Sontag says, 'to perceive Camp in objects and persons is to understand Being-as-Playing-a-Role. It is the farthest extension, in sensibility, of the metaphor of life as theater' (280). By the end of his autobiography, a young Monsiváis expresses his desire to dance and sing in the main square of Mexico City, the *Zócalo*, which is the symbolic centre of his country. It is through his writing that Monsiváis performs his ambiguous, ever-changing, role in Mexican society. If gender is a performance in which the self freely acts according to a social script (Butler 1988), a gendered, embodied chronicler is also a performer on a textual stage. The genre conventions might already be established, but he is free to innovate and to wear the mask that he feels will better enable him to resist or to transgress such conventions. If it is the case that not all chronicles relate to the camp in their exaggerated, ostentatious or outrageous mode of performing gender and genre conventions, there are definitely some authors who I see as being closer to a baroque stylization of reality and language. These authors utilize theatrical behaviour in their writing and in their self-fashioned public persona as a subversive response to the normative. It is certainly the case in Monsiváis's work, but also in the work of other urban chroniclers who might be termed 'performers', like Pedro Lemebel and María Moreno, and, more recently, Gabriela Wiener and Cristian Alarcón.

The chronicler meets the people

To walk the city is an act that chroniclers must make twice. Firstly, they experience the act physically, during their ethnographic-journalistic research, and then symbolically, by representing the experience in their writing. By the mere act of walking on the streets, the chroniclers are occupying the city. Therefore, space for these authors is a social place of performance, but also it becomes a place for knowledge through the art of writing it (Lefebvre: 33). Contrary to the *voyeur*, who according to De Certeau (1984) aims to pleasantly observe the crowds from a skyscraper, Monsiváis and Poniatowska are walkers in their city. They are not contemplative strangers but citizens as any other, immersed in the crowds that they describe.

In works such as Monsiváis's *Los rituales del caos* or Poniatowska's *Todo empezó en domingo* (Everything started on Sunday), which continues a *costumbrista* tradition, there is an exhibition of the polyphonic and multisensory possibilities

---

[54] Monsiváis's collection of popular culture is at the Museo del Estanquillo, founded in 2006 by the Mexico City government after his donation. For an analysis of his collection and its relationship with Mexican popular culture, see Chávez Díaz (2019).

of representation, where the city is a space of interaction between social classes, memories and experiences. For these authors, Mexico City can only be described by an endless accumulation of spatial references. The city is understood as an experience of the senses, that is, by means of the body occupying and sharing a space with others. In the introduction to the 1997 reprint of *Todo empezó en domingo*, Poniatowska describes the city as follows: 'Infinite city, Mexico is all the cities; it is Paris and New York, Berlin and Madrid, Warsaw and Prague. It has all ages, it is pre-Hispanic and modern. It is horrible and fascinating. It is cruel and unruly, it gives knife stabs and thundering kisses. Sordid and homicidal, it is disgusting and it is a girl having her first communion.'[55]

Poniatowska uses personification as a technique to describe the city. Through language, the city is then transformed in an ageless, cruel and fascinating woman who can be loved and hated at once. She also presents a close contact between the reader and the city by evoking the sound of kisses, the feel of stab wounds, the taste of tacos, corn, sweet potatoes and coffee and the smell of carrion.

Emphasizing the visual over any other sensorial approach to the city, Monsiváis begins *Los rituales del caos* by asking the reader what kind of photos he would take of the 'endless city'. From the perspective of an observer who tries both to experience and to find the appropriate distance to reflect upon that experience, he describes the space as if it could only be fully meaningful when it is crowded, occupied by its habitants:

> Visually, Mexico City signifies above all else the superabundance of people. You could, of course, turn away from this most palpable of facts towards abstraction, and photograph desolate dawns, or foreground the aesthetic dimension of walls and squares, even rediscover the perfection of solitude. But in the capital, the multitude that accosts the multitude imposes itself like a permanent obsession. (Monsiváis 1997: 31)[56]

Following Lafebvre in the idea of space as a social construction, Monsiváis focuses on the people's use of space to approach the meaning of spatial practices. Squares and murals can be beautiful, but if one looks at them alone, they are not saying all they have to say. By insisting on the multitude as protagonist, Monsiváis is making evident the 'illusion of transparency' that Lafebvre considers to be part of what a public space conceals. According to these ideas, observing the empty city is not experiencing it at all, for it is the mass as character that shapes the city's identity. The chronicler then chooses to create images that connect the mass with the public space in specific

---

[55] 'Ciudad infinita, México es todas las ciudades; es París y Nueva York, Berlín y Madrid, Varsovia y Praga. Tiene todas las edades, es prehispánica y es moderna. Es horrible y es fascinante. Es cruel y es díscola, da puñaladas traperas y besos tronados. Sórdida y homicida es asquerosa y es niña de primera comunión' (14).

[56] 'En el terreno visual, la Ciudad de México es, sobre todo, la demasiada gente. Se puede hacer abstracción del asunto, ver o fotografiar amaneceres desolados, gozar el poderío estético de muros y plazuelas, redescubrir la perfección del aislamiento. Pero en el Distrito Federal la obsesión permanente (el tema insoslayable) es la multitud que rodea a la multitud' (17).

circumstances: 'Multitudes on the Underground (where almost six million travellers a day are crammed, making space for the very idea of space' (Monsiváis 1997: 31).[57]

City and citizens become, therefore, the same object of study, for they are that 'identidad acumulativa' (accumulative identity), the sum of all places and subjectivities. As Egan notes, the Mexican contemporary chronicle 'thrusts its opinions, emotions, criticisms and other personal stances upon the public, engaging the reader in a dialogue that may co-opt, conspire or challenge' (93). This is shown particularly in the chronicles on the 1985 Mexico City earthquake. Rather than placing the attention of the narrative on specific individuals, Poniatowska and Monsiváis focus on the mass. For Poniatowska, the mass becomes a synonym for civil society. The mass is the protagonist: 'A multitude throws itself out onto the street, a frightened mob stops in front of the buildings. Several volunteers are detached from that multitude. They enter the hand chain, they climb to the rubble, they ask for a pick, for a spade.'[58] What matters for Monsiváis, on the other hand, is the discovery of the mass as a collective force: 'The social rearrangement is unexpected. The neighbours cordon off ruined sites and the housewives prepare food, but there are the young ones who take the weight of the action.... They don't consider themselves heroes, but they feel part of the heroism of the tribe, of the neighbourhood, of the gang, of the group spontaneously created, of the different city.'[59]

In both cases, chroniclers are taking to the streets and therefore appropriating and constructing public space, along with the citizens they are writing about. Contemporary Mexican chronicles represent the consciousness of the other and sensorial imagery in order to force the reader to participate in the construction of the discourse (Egan 2001). In *Luz y luna, las lunitas*, for instance, Poniatowska seems to take the reader by the hand, walking with them from her middle- and upper-middle-class neighbourhoods to the poor ones in which her informants live. The chronicler thus identifies with a reader who, like herself, might have never walked through the outskirts of the city. She describes the space as an outsider might experience it, always in comparison with a more comfortable side of the same city.

According to De Certeau, the sense of being in a space that has disappeared also contributes to the notion of space as a source for memory. In *Todo empezó en domingo*, Poniatowska uses the first-person plural to include herself in a new urban society (1997: 14). The chronicler writes to preserve the memory of those spaces that have already changed. At the same time, she opens a dialogue with a reader who can also remember details of that recent past, proposing a collective reconstruction of the original space.

---

[57] 'En el Metro (casi seis millones de usuarios al día) se comprimen para cederle espacio a la idea misma de espacio' (17).
[58] 'Una multitud se echa a la calle, una turba espantada se detiene frente a los edificios. De esa multitud se desprenden muchos voluntarios. Entran a la cadena de manos, suben a los escombros, piden un pico, una pala' (1988b: 21).
[59] 'El reordenamiento social es inesperado. Los vecinos acordonan los sitios en ruinas y las amas de casa preparan comida, pero son los jóvenes quienes llevan el peso de la acción.... No se consideran héroes, pero se sienten incorporados al heroísmo de la tribu, del barrio, de la banda, del grupo espontáneamente formado, de la ciudad distinta' (2006: 78).

Monsiváis also describes lost spaces in 'Los días del terremoto' (The earthquake days), published in *Entrada libre*. In this text, the narrator names a building that has been destroyed, while he recalls the experience of a group of dressmakers during the 1985 earthquake in Mexico City (1994 [1987]: 91–2). Although Monsiváis uses a third-person narrator, referring to himself as *reportero*, he becomes the storyteller who appropriates the speech of others in order to preserve collective memory (Benjamin 1999). Monsiváis narrates the experience of the earthquake in indirect style, but he chooses direct speech to highlight the faith of the informant in God and the 'Virgen de Guadalupe', including in the story another element of cultural identity. In a style that resembles John Hersey's *Hiroshima* (1946), this passage positions the transformation of the space at the centre of the narrative. But it is the destroyed space in relation to its occupants that gives dramatic tension to the story. This is why the chronicle is not about the destruction of a building but the story of the people who died in it and of those who survived to give their testimony.

The lost place represented in the texts does not need a real or immediate referent, for it is an abstraction of the memory (Lefebvre 1991). Nevertheless, the *crónica* becomes a representational space by relating to both objects and people. Chroniclers, thus, as anthropologists, ethnologists and psychoanalysts, consider representational spaces to be complex and dynamic entities. By depicting public spaces as meaningful products of their societies, and not as isolated landmarks of national culture, the urban chroniclers are also constructing an alternative space for social interaction. These *cronistas* demonstrate that Mexico City can only be experienced from multiple and diverse points of view.

Although they adopt different positions regarding the self, both Poniatowska and Monsiváis explore their confrontations with all kind of others in the public space. In their narratives, the masses are formed of the poor, the female, the homosexual, the indigenous, the peasant, the student. These others are not passive but active citizens who move, talk and express themselves in the streets, squares, parks, schools, stadiums and public transport of the city. Chronicle, as conceived by these authors, is a discursive mode to represent public space, and 'the society that organises itself', in Monsiváis's words. Beyond this conception, the chronicle is also a public space itself, one in which the *cronistas* position themselves as public intellectuals.

Considering the history of censorship that media and journalists have suffered in Latin American societies, it is understandable that the hybrid discourse of the *crónica* has been the place for public discussions that could not be presented in other journalistic discourses. Therefore, the chronicles of Poniatowska and Monsiváis can be considered a public space as defined by Jürgen Habermas (1992), that is, as a space in which the democratic actions of citizenship are encouraged. By documenting and interpreting social interactions, both chroniclers are able to show the ways in which Mexican society has produced its own public space. They, thus, offer to their readers an aesthetic experience and, at the same time, reveal new knowledge.

Since Independence, art, at least in the form of high-brow culture, has been a privileged space for Mexican elites, a practice isolated from popular culture and the collective construction of national identity. Between literature and journalism, the *crónica* is a hybrid, transcultural space in which intellectuals encounter other citizens, a space in which a public conversation becomes possible. As a hybrid genre, between high-brow and popular cultures, I argue that this kind of urban *crónica* proposes a Mexican form of 'camp', one that mixes its playfulness with a long-standing 'tropicalised' tradition of the Bakhtinean 'carnival' as a strategy of subversion and survival in a morally and politically restricted society. If, for Sontag, this humorous, critical detachment is only possible for an affluent elite, Monsiváis's baroque, campy, stylized texts demonstrate that subversive laughs and pleasures can also come from the popular classes in the form of a *relajo* or *desmadre*, which may be the only way in which Mexico City and its inhabitants can be captured in text.

Living and writing in a city that is constantly reshaping itself, Poniatowska and Monsiváis use documentary strategies to perform their desired roles in Mexican society, to strengthen a sense of belonging while they express their nostalgia for other ways of being. For, as was the case with their predecessors, the urban chroniclers from the 1920s and 1930s, Poniatowska and Monsiváis are also 'accessible intellectuals' (Mahieux: 6) who look for an identification with their ideal reader who is also an inhabitant of the same public space in which they move and perform their role as chroniclers. Mediating between the elites and the people, they share with them the everyday life in the city, its dramas and aspirations. Insiders and outsiders at the same time, they position themselves between the literary and journalistic spheres with a narrative authority based on a performed critical distance. Through humour and irony, they get involved, they are part of that new organized society, still from a position of privilege, of course, but they are able to put their feet on the mud, to protest and be part of the masses. Unlike the newspaper chroniclers from the first decades of the twentieth century, however, they cannot avoid holding a disenchanted view of modernity, even an apocalyptic one in the case of Monsiváis. They go and meet the people they are interested in writing about, as an ethnographer would do; and in doing so, they open a transitional path for a new turn in contemporary *crónica*, which eventually go on to leave the newspapers to find literary prestige (and personal safety) in the book format. From a different point of the compass, Tomás Eloy Martínez is another contributor to this transition, connecting the Latin American tradition of *crónica* to global literary journalism. The following chapter thus explores another kind of narrative performance, that of the investigative journalist in search for the truth.

4

A certain effect of truth

During the Peronist era, many newspapers and magazines were shut down, and journalists disappeared.[1] It is not surprising then that for Argentinian intellectuals, fiction was the most popular form through which to write about reality. In the context of censorship and political instability, literature maintained a complex relationship with Peronism (Mayer 1994). To write about Peronism, fiction writers used metaphors and allegories rather than referring directly to facts and real names.[2] Nevertheless, it was difficult, if not impossible, to publish an objective account of the regime from inside the country. The study of Peronism was conducted by foreign historians, particularly in the United States, who were free of the regime's censorship.[3]

After Juan Domingo Perón's death, Robert Alexander published *Juan Domingo Perón: A History* (1979). In this work, the American historian mentions that after several attempts he interviewed Perón in Madrid, on 1 September 1960. Alexander was disappointed by the falsehoods in Perón's speech. He did not use these impressions, nor his interview notes – seemingly, he did not record the conversation – as part of his historical narration at all, but left them as an appendix.

---

[1] My examples here concern only events from Juan Domingo Perón's lifetime (Páez de la Torre 2002; Gambini 1999). He was president of Argentina during two periods: 1946–1955, and 1973–1974. Peronist ideology, represented by the Partido Justicialista, had a contemporary revival during the presidencies of 1989 (Menem), 1995 (Menem), 2003 (Kirchner), 2007 (Fernández de Kirchner) and 2011 (Fernández de Kirchner).

[2] From this period, one can find short stories like Julio Cortázar's 'Casa tomada' (Taken house, 1946), Jorge Luis Borges's and Adolfo Bioy Casares's 'La fiesta del monstruo' (The monster party, 1955), David Viñas's 'La señora muerta' (The death woman, *Las malas costumbres* 1963), Ricardo Piglia's 'Mata–Hari 55' (*La invasión* 1967); poems like Leónidas Lamborghini's 'El letrista proscripto' (The banned song writer, *Las patas en las fuentes* 1965) and 'Eva Perón en la hoguera' (Eva Perón in the bonfire, *Partitas* 1972), Néstor Perlongher's 'El cadáver' (The corpse, *Austria–Hungría* 1980); and novels such as Ernesto Sábato's *Sobre héroes y tumbas* (*On Heroes and Tombs*, 1961), Beatriz Guido's *El incendio y las vísperas* (The fire and the eve, 1964), and Leopoldo Marechal's *Megafón o la guerra* (Megafón or the war, 1970). See Davies (2007) for more information.

[3] Argentinian historians like Hugo Gambini and Horacio Verbitsky wrote some articles under the regime, but only started to publish books after Perón's death, and after democracy were restored in 1983. Martínez himself waited until 1985 to publish *La novela de Perón*, and even longer to publish the complete transcriptions of his interview in *Las memorias del General* (1996). Exceptional cases are the authors with explicit sympathy for the regime, like Enrique Pavón Pereyra, who claimed to be Perón's official biographer.

Another American historian, Joseph Page, published what remains one of the most relevant and complete biographies on Perón in 1983. Although Page states that his intention is to tell the truth, he admits in the introduction to his work:

> Juan Perón presents formidable obstacles to the biographer. He left behind relatively few reliable records of his long public career, perhaps under the conviction that he would fare better in the eyes of posterity if judgments about him did not rest upon hard fact. His many books, pamphlets, articles, speeches, letters and taped conversations are so permeated with contradiction, exaggeration and misstatement that they must be used with extreme caution. (1983: ix)

Page continues his introduction by narrating his surprise while he found out that the personal archives of both Perón's first and his second presidencies were being eaten by rats in an abandoned government storage facility. He also mentions the difficulties associated with obtaining other reliable material for his research: the correspondence was locked in Madrid, either saved by his secretary or lost. Publications from the time were hard to find, and people who knew Perón closely refused to give their testimony.

Contrary to the motivations of these researchers, Argentinean journalist and novelist Tomás Eloy Martínez (San Miguel de Tucumán 1934–Buenos Aires 2010) decided to interview Perón for a popular magazine. The author, however, was to agree with the academics regarding the difficulties of distinguishing fact from fiction in Perón's own accounts of his life. What was left in the margins or appendices of the history books form the centre of Martínez's narratives.

In this chapter, I focus on the displacement of authorship of the Peróns' story, from Perón himself to Martínez's multiple versions of it. Therefore, I propose a reading of 'Las memorias de Juan Perón' (*Panorama* 1970) and 'Las memorias de Puerta de Hierro' (*Las memorias del General* 1996/*Las vidas del General* 2004) as paratextual discourses accompanying the novels *La novela de Perón* (The Perón Novel, 1985) and *Santa Evita* (1995).[4] I believe these works published as 'novels' are defined by an original documentary intention. The evidence for this can be traced through some earlier letters of Martínez's and through interviews that I found in the author's private archives at the Fundación Tomás Eloy Martínez in Buenos Aires. To analyse the chosen texts in relation to the novel, I use Gérard Genette's metaphor of the palimpsest, focusing particularly on paratexts (1997).[5]

---

[4] *Las vidas del General* was the author's last edition of *Las memorias del General*. Both editions have the same content, including 'Las memorias de Puerta de Hierro', except for the exclusion of a text originally published in *Panorama* magazine, and the addition of two more texts in *Las vidas del General*. In 2009, Alfaguara publishing house reprinted the book as part of their collection, Biblioteca Tomás Eloy Martínez. Quotes given from 'Las memorias de Puerta de Hierro' follow this latest edition.

[5] According to Genette, paratexts, or the texts that accompany the literary work within or outside the book itself, influence the reception and consumption of that literary work. He proposed the existence of a dialogical condition in certain texts that he calls 'hypertextuality'. Thus, if a given text can present a direct or indirect interaction with other texts, this hypertextuality functions as a

I suggest that Martínez is able to change the meaning of Perón's discourse through a game of palimpsests: he reworks the same piece of information (his interview with Perón) into diverse literary and journalistic genres. Following Genette's taxonomy,[6] the epitext of all these works concerning Perón is the conversation between Tomás Eloy Martínez and Juan Domingo Perón.[7]

Tomás Eloy Martínez and the Peronist palimpsest

Tomás Eloy Martínez's career is an example of how history, literature and politics are intertwined and influence Latin American documentary narratives.[8] Better known for his novel *Santa Evita* – which was inspired by the former first lady of Argentina, Eva Perón, and is one of the most translated Argentinian novels of all time – Martínez is also recognized within the Latin American journalistic elite for being a founder of newspapers, a media consultant, editor and workshop instructor.[9] He also had an academic career as professor of Spanish literature, mostly at the University of Maryland and Rutgers in the United States.

His journalistic career started at *La Gaceta de Tucumán*. During this time, Martínez also studied for a bachelor of arts degree in Spanish and Latin American Literature at Universidad Nacional de Tucumán. He moved to Buenos Aires in 1957 to work as a film critic for *La Nación* newspaper. In 1962, journalist Jacobo Timerman founded *Primera Plana*, where Martínez started to work initially as a film and literary critic and later as chief editor.[10] Martínez used to publish book reviews and interviews with

---

palimpsest in which other texts can also be discovered. Once these texts are discovered, however, the interpretation of the given work is modified.

[6] Genette defines epitext as 'any paratextual element not materially appended to the text within the same volume but circulating, as it were, freely, in a virtually limitless physical and social space' (1997: 344). He mentions newspapers and all kinds of media production, including interviews, as examples of epitexts.

[7] The recording was edited posthumously by Fundación Tomás Eloy Martínez under the title of *Tomás Eloy Martínez: Juan Domingo Perón: Encuentro en Puerta de Hierro* (Tomás Eloy Martínez: Juan Domingo Perón: Encounter in Puerta de Hierro, 2014). Designed as an art-object, the work contains heavily edited fragments of the conversations in a CD-ROM format. It also includes a booklet with quotes from Martínez and Perón, along with photographs.

[8] Unless other sources are quoted, the biographical information on Martínez is based on a copy of his 'Curriculum Vitae', obtained in the archive of *La Gaceta* newspaper, information available from the author's official website at <fundaciontem.org>, as well as on Martínez-Richter (1997), Roffé (2003) and Fickelscherer (2003).

[9] Martínez was editor-in-chief of the *Abril* magazines in 1971, and he founded the newspapers *El diario de Caracas* in Venezuela in 1978 and *Siglo 21* in Guadalajara, México, in tandem with Jorge Zepeda Patterson in 1990. The next year, he created the literary supplement *Primer Plano* for the *Página/12* newspaper in Buenos Aires, which he was director of until 1996. He also participated as an assessor in the creation of García Márquez's journalism foundation, FNPI, in Colombia. Martínez taught workshops on narrative techniques and editing for this foundation, and was one of its most active promoters.

[10] This weekly publication represented the modernization of Argentinian media after Perón's dictatorship, passing from intellectual, elitist magazines such as *Sur* to publications directed at a broader audience, based on the democratic ideals of the Cuban Revolution and mass culture

authors who in several cases were also his friends, such as Carlos Fuentes, Augusto Roa Bastos, Mario Vargas Llosa and Adolfo Bioy Casares. Furthermore, Martínez was one of the first editors to publish reviews of Gabriel García Marquez's *Cien años de soledad* (*One Hundred Years of Solitude*, 1967), and he welcomed the Colombian author when he visited Buenos Aires for the first time (Martínez 1998).

Although Martínez was younger than the Boom writers, he shared the literary and publishing environment of their time. His idea to write about Perón might have been influenced by the day he first met Carlos Fuentes and heard about his project on the novels of dictatorships (Martínez 1994: 12–13). During this time, he met Francisco Porrúa, editor of *Sudamericana*, the publishing house behind Martínez's first novel, *Sagrado* (Sacred, 1969). By then, Martínez was also working in television, conducting the news programme *Telenoche* at Canal 13, and his journalistic work was beginning to earn him recognition and prizes.

In 1970, Martínez moved to France in order to study for a master's degree in literature at Université Paris Diderot.[11] During his stay in Europe, Martínez was also a correspondent for the Argentinian publishing house *Abril*, which owned the magazines *Siete Días*, *Siete Días Internacional*, *Semana Gráfica* and *Panorama*. It was in this period, and as a job assignment for *Panorama*, that Martínez interviewed Juan Domingo Perón, who was by then an exile in Madrid.

Martínez returned to Buenos Aires in 1971 as editor-in-chief of the *Abril* magazines. In *Panorama*, he published the news of the execution of sixteen people, members of Peronist and leftist organizations, in the city of Trelew. Four days after this, Martínez was fired from the magazine. The author, however, travelled to Trelew as a freelancer in order to interview witnesses of the event. As a result of his investigation, Martínez published *La pasión según Trelew* (The Passion According to Trelew, [1973] 2007).[12]

The Trelew story changed his life; the fifth edition, produced just three months after the first one, was prohibited by the local government at the beginning of Perón's last term as president (Martínez 1997). Perón died in 1974, and was succeeded by his widow, Isabel Martínez de Perón, who had also been his vice president. During this time, Martínez received threats from the Triple A, a terrorist group led by José López Rega, who had formerly been Juan Domingo Perón's personal secretary. As a consequence, the author went into exile in Venezuela in 1975. Eventually the author moved to the United States; from there, he published journalistic articles for *La Nación*, *El País* and *The New York Times Syndicate*. This period was Martínez's most prolific: he published *Santa Evita* (1995), followed by the non-fiction work, *Las memorias del General* (The Memoirs of the General, 1996), the collections of chronicles and articles,

---

(Quattrocchi–Woisson 2003). Evoking *Time* magazine, and inspired by the style of American New Journalism, it is not surprising that the magazine's products, aimed at a middle-class reader, circulated in the international market (Mudrovcic 1999).

[11] Under the supervision of the Russian theorist Tzvetan Todorov, he wrote a dissertation on Jorge Luis Borges and fantastic literature.

[12] By then, Martínez was working at *La Opinión* newspaper. As director of its literary supplement, *La Opinión Cultural*, Martínez was in contact with authors such as Osvaldo Soriano, Ricardo Piglia, Juan Gelman and Rodolfo Walsh.

El sueño argentino (The Argentine Dream, 1999) and *Ficciones verdaderas* (True Fictions, 2000), and the novels *El vuelo de la reina* (The Flight of the Queen, Premio Alfaguara 2000) and *El cantor de tango* (The Tango Singer, Premio Konex 2004) and his final novel, *Purgatorio* (Purgatory, 2008). In 2009, he won the Premio Ortega y Gasset de Periodismo, the most prestigious prize for a journalist in the Spanish-speaking world. The same year, he became a member of the National Academy of Journalism, and he was declared a Distinguished Citizen of Buenos Aires. By then suffering from brain cancer, he returned to Buenos Aires, where he died on 31 January 2010.

Memories and news

'Las memorias de Juan Perón' (The memoirs of Perón) is the result of real encounters between Juan Domingo Perón and Tomás Eloy Martínez that took place at Perón's house in Madrid, Puerta de Hierro. From 26 to 29 March 1970, Martínez recorded Perón reading his memoirs, which had previously been dictated to Perón's secretary, López Rega. The recordings were transcribed and edited by Martínez, and, after the approval of Perón, they were published over the next month in three parts in *Panorama*, a weekly magazine based in Buenos Aires.

The first part of Perón's authorized memoirs featured on the cover of issue 155, which appeared in the week beginning 14 April 1970 (see Figure 4.1). The headline announces, in big white letters, 'Las memorias de Juan Perón' as an exclusive document. It shows a full-colour photograph of an elderly Juan Domingo Perón outside his Spanish country house. He is wearing a brown suit, blue-and-red-striped tie, and golden ring and watch. Unlike the iconic images of Perón from his presidential terms, in this one he is holding one of his dogs in his arms while looking at it, smiling. The text covers pages twenty to twenty-five, under a section called 'Documentos', which highlights its historical rather than journalistic nature (see Figure 4.2). Nevertheless, the presence of a stand-first, written in the third person, calls attention to the journalistic procedures used to obtain the information. A stand-first is used in editorial design to set the tone, contextualize and sell the story. It tells the reader of the story's intention, and acts as the bridge or link, both textually and visually, between the headline and the body copy (Zapaterra 2007). In this case, however, it was also used to mention that Perón was in dialogue with the journalist Tomás Eloy Martínez (*Panorama* 20). The stand-first thus legitimates the truthfulness of the story, for it tells the readers that there was a reliable witness, while at the same time it gives prestige to the magazine by showing that their journalists are able to organize an encounter with such an important figure.

The body copy is written in the first person and published in three columns. Its subheadings clearly mark the topics of each section and indicate the text structure: 'El padre y la madre' (The father and the mother), 'Llegada a Buenos Aires' (Arrival in Buenos Aires), 'El hermano' (The brother), 'La vocación' (Vocation), 'La milicia' (The militia), 'Teoría de los valores' (Theory of values), 'Años de preparación' (Preparation years) and 'Años de realización' (Realization years). Additionally, the document is illustrated with eight black-and-white pictures showing Perón in different periods of

Figure 4.1 Cover of *Panorama* magazine, issue 155, 14 April 1970.

Figure 4.2 First page of Juan Domingo Perón's memoirs by Tomás Eloy Martínez, in *Panorama* magazine, issue 155, 14 April 1970.

his private and public life. Whether he is giving a speech, riding a horse or practising sports, Perón is represented as a strong, active and self-confident man. Of course, this may simply reflect Perón's narcissistic aims, since he supervised the publication. It is also possible that it was due to the editor's quest for profit, since it is known that a cover with a celebrity sells more magazines (Zapaterra 2007).

It is important to note that the text is not signed at all, although an editor usually writes the stand-first. Following a common practice of the time, *Panorama* was not particularly keen to give authorship to all its texts. A signature, however, would have been expected for a text based on an interview. One can only guess that it was Martínez himself who wrote the introduction in the third person, or his editor Norberto Firpo. The restricted conditions under which this publication appeared – with Perón acting as editor – and the general censorship of the press during that time in Argentina, does not allow one to think of the question of authorship as a mere issue of the conventions of journalistic genres. On the other hand, in *Las memorias del General*, Martínez stated that he disagreed with the final version of the magazine's text. This might be another reason why he did not sign it. Nevertheless, if declining to print his name after this text was a subtle way of protesting its unreliability, his most successful way of highlighting the untruthful nature of Perón's account would be by endlessly reworking the content of this original text.

There is no doubt that this is a text of deliberately blurred authorship, and, therefore, the question of its genre becomes unclear. If one considers a reading that takes into account the practice of journalism, it is clear that the text, as with any other mass media product, was collectively constructed by the informant, the reporter, the editors and even the designers. Although each of the participants would have had their own purpose in communicating a message through this text, one cannot forget that it is ultimately a commercial product. The magazine, then, is selling the supposedly true story of Perón.

Yet it is surprising that in later texts Martínez would refer to the encounter as 'entrevista' (interview), and the text that came out of it as 'autobiografía' (autobiography), 'historia de vida' (life story) and 'memorias' (memoirs). From a journalistic point of view, Martínez/Perón's text could easily fit into the category of news. For Teun van Dijk (1988), news is a kind of discourse that gives new information about recent events. The interview is a 'newsgathering encounter' (97), in which the source, text and conversation are transformed into news discourse. In this sense, the encounter between Perón and Martínez can be considered a newsworthy interview.

There is no doubt that news is constructed through dialogue, particularly in interviews. Nevertheless, the nature of the journalistic dialogue, as opposed to an everyday one, is rather complex. Genette considers, following Philippe Lejeune, that the interview is a false dialogue. Contrary to a conversation, an interview is a dialogue mediated by someone 'whose job it is to ask him (the interviewee) questions and record and transmit his answers' (356). It is 'a dialogue [that is] generally short and conducted by a professional journalist' (358). From this more critical perspective, 'Las memorias de Juan Perón' can be read as the product of a dialogue, a journalistic one maybe, but with no other purpose that to record information given by the interviewee. Reading interviews as carefully constructed, (false) dialogues can allow us to question, therefore, the ethics of some journalistic practices and their expressed aspiration to truth.

By declaring that he decided to make a *verbatim* transcription of Perón's speech during their conversations, Martínez demonstrates one of the major ethical and rhetorical problems of the journalistic practice: that of finding the balance between the voices of the self and the other. Although he tries to confront Perón's version with others, as any good journalist would do, young Martínez cannot escape his position as a powerless reporter, 'I was only the compiler, the mediator of the autobiography'.[13] When he met Perón, Martínez was at one end of a complex news system that aimed to legitimate the politician's discourse as trustworthy by publishing it as a journalistic discourse.

A parody of journalism

Martínez's *La novela de Perón* (The Perón Novel, 1985)[14] can be read as a rather late representative of what Hutcheon called 'historiographical metafictions' (1984),[15] and

---

[13] 'Yo era solo el compilador, el mediador de la autobiografía' (2009b: 154).
[14] The novel was firstly translated into English by Asa Zatz, published by Pantheon Books in 1988. However, here I quote the Helen Lane's translation from 1991, as reprinted in 1998 by Vintage Books.
[15] With this term, Hutcheon refers to a particular literary form of novel that appeared in the 1970s.

this has even been the point of departure for critiques of Martínez's novels on Peronism. Metafiction in the novel is generally used in the representation of Perón writing his memoirs. Perón, and not the autodiegetic narrator, is the most self-conscious character in the novel. He is the one capable of manipulating the story. Besides, still within the context of postmodernism thinking, the author's awareness of the complex relationship between literary and historical discourses was certainly influenced by Hayden White's reflections on historiography (1978).[16]

White's proposal to analyse history writing as a discursive construction is reinterpreted by Martínez in order to incorporate journalistic writing under this view, while considering the possibilities of finding fiction in social discourses. This is particularly evident in Martínez's rewriting of his conversations with Perón, in which he shows the shortcomings of the interview as a genre that represents two worldviews constantly colliding with each other. In this section, I focus on the role that some literary devices that have been considered characteristics of the postmodern novel, such as intertextuality and parody, play in *La novela de Perón* in order to expose the fictional nature of journalistic discourse.

The novel develops three stories with protagonists whose lives overlap on a single day: 20 June 1973. This is the date of Perón's return to Argentina after eighteen years of exile, when he sought to become president for a third time. Two of Martínez's stories are about writers. In the first one, Perón is writing his memoirs for a book, with the help of his secretary López (José López Rega). In the other one, Zamora the reporter is writing Perón's counter-memoirs for a magazine. The third story is about readers, for it is about a couple of radical Peronist leaders who are reading Zamora's reportage while preparing a march to welcome Perón at Ezeiza airport.

La novela de Perón cannot be analysed in isolation from Martínez's later work, which was also part of his Peronist cycle: *Las vidas del General*. In this documentary work, Martínez confesses that the encounter with the ex-president was not a properly journalistic interview. His assignment was to record a text read by Perón that had already been written by his secretary José López Rega. However, this recorded story was constantly changing before his eyes: 'Sometimes, Perón included digressions to the story and he was filling the gaps of what López was reading. At other times, the butler would correct Perón's memories or he embellished them with unbelievable comments.'[17] Perón's manipulation of the material during their actual encounter must have inspired Martínez, for he was not an innocent listener. As the quotation demonstrates, Martínez experiences the encounter from the perspective of a fiction writer. By describing his personal experience during the encounter, Martínez shows how reality and fiction are mixed.

La novela de Perón is Martínez's creative response to a reality that could not be represented through the conventions of a mimetic discourse. Because of Perón's

---

[16] It is possible that Martínez had these critical references in mind while writing *La novela de Perón* during his residence at the Wilson Center in 1983.

[17] 'A veces, Perón incorporaba digresiones al relato e iba llenando los vacíos de lo que López leía. Otras veces, el mayordomo corregía los recuerdos de Perón o los aderezaba con comentarios insólitos' (17).

censorship, the author could not publish the text as he wished to in the magazine. Nevertheless, he would rewrite the information and find – in the form of the novel – the freedom to tell the truth. The reference to Perón's authorized memoirs in the novel thus questions the validity of journalistic discourse, particularly that based on testimonials. This is shown when Martínez appears as a character in the novel. Intertextuality is used, for example, to show the fictional meaning given by López and Perón to the supposedly autobiographical text given to Martínez (2004a: 254). This also highlights the degree of malleability that information can have, for the existence of a recording is not proof that the story being told is totally true.

Later, in chapter 14 (entitled 'Primera persona', first person), Martínez appears in conversation with Zamora, discussing the use of the first person in journalism. Choosing a first-person narrator is a way of questioning the apparent objectivity of journalism, which usually employs the third person and does not refer to the journalist's personal experience (346). If Martínez-as-a-character is a well-known journalist who once interviewed Perón and has much more information on the topic that any other source, then Zamora is represented as a mediocre reporter.

There is a parodical representation of journalism throughout the story of Zamora writing the counter-memoirs of Perón, as ordered by his boss. This is particularly evident when the editor of the magazine decides to organize a welcoming party for Perón and his old friends and family (47–8). This passage portrays journalism as an activity motivated by sensationalist and economic concerns rather than by an ethical commitment to uncovering truth. Although Zamora does not agree with his editor's idea, he follows his instructions and writes a new profile of Perón based on the memories of a group of old people who are somehow related to Perón's hidden life. Therefore, rather than a metafictional discourse, one might say that there is metajournalism in this part of the novel. By reflecting the process of the journalistic investigation, this narrative technique solves practical matters concerning the use of the information gathered and the ways of telling it in a truthful manner.

Through the use of parody, the author demonstrates how reality can be constructed through media. The seven people who shared their memories and personal documents with Zamora in order to tell the truth about Perón's formative years are used primarily as informants for the cover story of the magazine, and then treated as decoration for the welcoming event that has been prepared in Ezeiza, and they are eventually abandoned (432).

After Perón has decided what to do with his past and present, there is no room for these other memories, even though they have also been published. The discourses of history (Perón's memoirs) as well as journalism (Zamora's counter-memoirs) are no longer enough to tell the truth. Therefore, it makes sense that the novel makes a parody of these discourses, for the technique shows the 'literary inadequacies of a certain convention' (Hutcheon 1988: 50). It is not through journalism, but through the novel that Martínez finds a creative response, free of others' control, for the telling of his true story.

History and the fictions of Evita

A year before her death, Eva Perón published *La razón de mi vida* (The Reason of my Life, 1951), in which she defines herself in relation to her husband, the president of Argentina, Juan Domingo Perón: 'I was nothing but a humble woman . . . a sparrow in a huge flock of sparrows . . . and he was and is the giant condor that flies high and safe among the summits and close to God. If he had not descended towards me and taught me to fly in another way'.[18]

Eva Perón's awareness of her identity as a public figure who people talk and write about continues throughout the text. The following year, in the United States, historian Robert Alexander published *The Peron Era*, based on his research and impressions following his travels to Argentina. He describes Eva's appearance and personality as the result of careful construction:

> 'Evita' Perón, as she is familiarly called in Argentina, is about five feet five, but appears taller because she wears her hair artfully arranged in an 'upsweep'. She has dark brown eyes, blonde hair with reddish tints, and a startlingly white skin (partly natural and partly the result of the skilful use of make-up). Milton Bracker has commented that she 'can be equally impressive in a strapless evening gown, a two-piece light print or floppy slacks'. Friends and enemies are in agreement that Eva Perón is a woman of great personal fascination. (1951: 102)

This description can hardly be compared with Eva Perón's self-portrait. Rather than focusing on her participation in the social discourse or her political power, the historian highlights the fake elements of the look upon which she based her public image: the hairstyle, the make-up and the clothes. Appearance was important in the construction of Eva's identity.

By analysing several images of Eva's short career as an actress in relation to contemporary women's fashion, Sarlo (2003) shows the process by which she constructed the public appearance of her body. Sarlo confirms the impression that Juan Domingo Perón's biographer Joseph Page had of Eva: 'Though she was not beautiful, sexy or particularly talented, Eva Duarte (Evita to her friends) was blazed with a tenacity that had lifted her from an obscure, small provincial town to a career in theatre, radio and film' (Page 1983: 4). For Sarlo, the uniqueness of Eva – what she calls her *excepcionabilidad* – is indeed her capability to shift from one place to another, and, in consequence, to be out of place.

The exceptional nature of Eva, however, was not rooted in her social background, but in her performative ability. Although her acting qualities were not enough for the artistic scene, she managed to use them in a place where they were not the norm: the political scene. With a kind of beauty that was out of fashion for the actresses

---

[18] 'Yo no era ni soy nada más que una humilde mujer . . . un gorrión en una inmensa bandada de gorriones. . . . Y él era y es el cóndor gigante que vuela alto y seguro entre las cumbres y cerca de Dios. Si no fuese por él que descendió hasta mí y me enseñó a volar de otra manera' (13).

of the time, Sarlo demonstrates that Eva was recognized as a beautiful woman only after she became the president's wife. It is perhaps not surprising that Eva insisted that her life actually started with Perón. The idea of Eva as an artistic construction, and as a malleable body, became a central axis in Martínez's fictional works on Peronism, but particularly in *Santa Evita*. Nevertheless, the first-hand source of information that the author has about Eva Duarte's transition into 'Evita' is his interview with Juan Domingo Perón. During that conversation, Perón confesses: 'Eva Perón was my product. I prepared her so she could do what she did.'[19] The story of the first encounter with Eva, which Perón narrates to Martínez in this interview, was published in 1970 in *Panorama* magazine as part of the series of Perón's memoirs. The document was to be used later as a source by historian Joseph Page in his biography of Juan Domingo Perón, while Martínez himself would use it for his novel.

Deconstructing the myth

Evita died in 1952 and her corpse was embalmed and put on public display. Three years later, the rule of Juan Domingo Perón was overthrown by a military coup, and he went into exile in Spain. Eva Perón's corpse was kept hidden by the new government, and it was only returned to her widower in 1971. *Santa Evita* narrates the story of this corpse.[20]

In other texts from his Peronist cycle, such as *La novela de Perón* and *Las memorias del General*, Martínez relies exhaustively on his personal account of the real-life encounter with Perón as a primary source. Nonetheless, in *Santa Evita* the author cannot rely on his own memory as witness to a particular moment, since he did not personally meet Eva Perón. In consequence, the use of other sources of information is essential to his representation of her in the novel.

While Page and other writers succeeding him would go on to use Martínez's journalistic texts to approach a more vivid, first-hand view of Juan Domingo Perón, Martínez himself looked for different kinds of audiovisual material such as films, photographs and radio recordings to create his portrait of Eva. This is not only relevant to the construction of Eva as literary character but it also suffuses the novel with a sense of what Martínez described as 'a certain effect of truth'.[21]

Martínez looks for alternative sources of information to deconstruct Eva, and in doing so he creates his own documentary material. During the research for his novel, he conducted interviews with marginal informants, whose testimonies may not have been considered by historians. It is particularly interesting to note that the two main testimonies through which the documentary effect of the novel is sustained are the men responsible for Eva's public identity at certain points: the hairdresser Julio Alcaraz,

---

[19] 'Eva Perón es un producto mío. Yo la preparé para que hiciera lo que hizo' (2009c: 57).
[20] The English translations from this novel are taken from the 1997 Doubleday edition, translated by Helen Lane.
[21] 'un cierto efecto de verdad' (1988: 49).

who was the guardian of her body in life, for he was in charge of her daily physical appearance; and the soldier Héctor Eduardo Cabanillas (renamed Tulio Ricardo Corominas in the novel), who was the guardian of Eva's dead body, since he directed the strategy to hide the corpse and get it out of Argentina.

Until now, *Santa Evita* has been read as an intersection of multiple discourses inspired by other authors, and thus it is considered to be written in a style evocative of citation (López Badano 2010; Davies 2010). What I propose, however, is to emphasize the investigative process at the core of Martínez's narrative. By doing so, I wish to demonstrate that through the use of the research techniques and discursive genres of journalism – particularly the interview – the author finds a way to erase the opposition between information and narration.

The author creates a metafictional narrator, also named Tomás Eloy Martínez, who is represented as a journalist obsessed with the truth, conducting exhaustive research involving broadly differing sources of information, regardless of how difficult it might be to talk to people or to find certain documents. Therefore, one could say that the author is speaking through his narrator, using strategies of self-representation to reinforce his narrative authority.

As the plot becomes more incredible, details of the narrator's process of investigation help to construct the pact of credibility with the reader. Throughout the novel, the narrator constantly notifies the reader that he has the documents that verify the story he is narrating. However, since the reader cannot actually access those documents, the story's credibility is based on the word of the narrator. The game of doubt and trust thus includes the reader, for just as the author-narrator needs to believe in his informants, so the reader needs to take a position on how to read a story that never seeks to define itself.

Reality is represented through documents, recordings and photographs, the content of which is not reliable: 'The sources on which this novel is based are not altogether reliable, but only in the sense that this is true of reality and language as well: lapses of memory and imperfect truths have found their way into them' (1997: 126).[22] While, on one hand, the narrator can assure the reader that there is plenty of documentation, he cannot, on the other hand, admit his own trust in the information provided by those documents.

Strange as it may seem, some of the magical-realistic elements of the novel are in fact real, in the sense that they did not come out of the author's imagination, but were included as a result of witness testimonies. For example, the interview transcripts show that all the informants actually told Martínez that they saw flowers and candles every time the corpse was moved to a new secret place; they also insisted upon the truth of the curse that surrounded everyone involved with the care of the corpse. Ironically, the most strongly fictional element in *Santa Evita* is the representation of the self-referential narrator, who at the same time is, and is not, Tomás Eloy Martínez. In his

---

[22] 'Las fuentes sobre las que se basa esta novela son de confianza dudosa, pero solo en el sentido en que también lo son la realidad y el lenguaje: se han infiltrado en ellas deslices de la memoria y verdades impuras' (Martínez 2002: 153).

aim to give voice to all the marginal protagonists of Eva's story, the author ends up recreating himself in such a way that he becomes the protagonist of the novel.

It is only at the close of the novel that the narrator gathers together his three main informants for the story he has undertaken to tell: Tulio Ricardo Corominas, Jorge Rojas Silveyra and Carlo Maggi. This is certainly a nod to the author's interviewees. More importantly, the representation of this interview is an ambiguity because it functions as a literary device that paradoxically reinforces and destabilizes the credibility pact with the reader. There is no doubt that the author is questioning the borders between reality and fiction:

> 'I came because there was a story,' I reminded them. 'Tell it to me and I'll be off.'
> 'We read that novel of yours about Perón,' Corominas explained. 'It's not true that the body of that person was in Bonn.'
> 'What person?' I asked cagily. I wanted to find out what name he called her by.
> 'Her,' he answered. 'Eva.' He raised his hands to his imposing, drooping double chin, and immediately corrected himself: 'Eva Perón.'
> 'As you said, it's a novel,' I explained. 'In novels, what is true is also false. Authors rebuild at night the same myths they've destroyed in the morning.'
> 'Those are just words,' Corominas said emphatically. 'They don't convince me. The only thing that means anything are facts, and a novel, after all, is a fact' (367).[23]

There is evidence that Martínez really interviewed the men these characters are based on more than once and across different years, although in the novel they are depicted as having a single, long night of conversation in a café in Buenos Aires. Metafiction is a useful strategy for the demonstration of a documentary effect in the representation of Martínez and the others. This leaves it down to the reader to decide whether or not they believe that the story is real. Even if one does not check this episode against the real interviews, it is still hard to believe that these men would have initiated a conversation on poetics, discussing Martínez's *La novela de Perón*. What the reader is 'listening' to in this secret conversation is the voice of the author, and what he chooses to represent of others.

As a journalistic palimpsest, *Santa Evita* disobeys Virginia Woolf's advice regarding biography, since, for her, the truth of real life and the truth of fiction can never mix, 'let them meet and they destroy each other' (1967: 234). Martínez's original intention was not to mix both kinds of truth, but rather to focus on the 'real life' truth, if one attends to the evidence of his working process. In a 1989 script called 'Evita rest in

---

[23] – Vine porque había una historia – les recordé – Cuéntenmela y me voy.
– Leímos la novela suya sobre Perón – aclaró Corominas – No es verdad que el cuerpo de esa persona estuvo en Bonn. [...]
– Como usted dijo, es una novela – expliqué – En las novelas, lo que es verdad es también mentira. Los autores construyen a la noche los mismos mitos que han destruido por la mañana.
– Ésas son palabras – insistió Corominas – A mí no me convencen. Lo único que vale son los hechos y una novela es, después de todo, un hecho (421).

peace' (which was never filmed), Martínez advised the potential filmmakers: 'All the information in this story is based on original documents and recordings which belong to the author. Due to the secrecy that still protects these materials, I beg to the editors to maintain the utmost discretion regarding its content.'[24] The author refers to the plot as 'a non-fiction story',[25] although he introduces his characters as a novelist would do. By making this statement, however, the author is trying to sell his idea. It is based on the value that a story with some documentary evidence would have to the filmmakers, and ultimately to the audience. He gives himself credibility by the possession of documents. Nevertheless, while he affirms that he owns that material, he asks readers simultaneously to be careful with the content. Martínez owns the documents, but what is important is to maintain the privacy of the accounts written there. He knows he is only the keeper of the confidences entrusted to him in an interview, or found in an archive during his research. In a certain way, he is not the creator of the story but the custodian of its evidence. This awareness of the potential legal conflicts when relying on others' discourses is also shown in a similar film project from 1989, 'La historia de Evita' (The story of Eva), in which Martínez advises that all the characters are historical, and thus it is convenient to change their names so as to avoid legal problems (1989c).

For Genette, plagiarism can be seen as a form of intertextuality, although it is not so explicit as other types of palimpsests; it is an 'undeclared, but still literal borrowing' (2). But what may be a stylistic decision for writers of fiction becomes an ethical question for those who work with the material of real lives. Although a novelist himself, Martínez makes his position clear regarding the undeclared use of others' words in a non-fictional work.

The biographer, says Woolf, is not an artist but a craftsman; 'his work is not a work of art, but something betwixt and between' (227). Walter Benjamin uses the same analogy for the work of the storyteller, as a figure also distinct from the writer of fiction. However, there are differences in their approach to this craftsman. For Woolf, this type of writer requires direct contact with facts and so worries about obtaining the most accurate and varied amount of information regarding real people. For Benjamin, the craftsman, or storyteller, is precisely the opposite of those who seek information. Thus, storytelling is the resistance of narrative against information, which is considered by the critic to be a new way of communicating reality that defines our era. When using journalistic material for his documentary projects, Martínez could be represented both as Woolf's 'biographer' or Benjamin's 'storyteller', for he is carefully selecting and editing the words of others to fit into the form he wishes to create for his/their stories.

Santa Evita has been characterized variously as a representative novel of the Latin American Post-Boom, or of postmodern aesthetics, or as a product of the turn-of-the century discourses that suffused the Western world and are encapsulated by New Historicism (Davies 2010; López Badano 2010). Nevertheless, one could argue that the

---

[24] 'Todos los datos de esta historia están respaldados por documentos originales y grabaciones que pertenecen al autor. Debido al secreto que aún protege a estos materiales, se ruega a los editores mantener la mayor reserva posible sobre el contenido' (1).

[25] 'Relato de no ficción'.

decision to shift from a pure documentary or journalistic discourse to a fictional one may have had an ethical or legal basis rather than simply an aesthetic one.

The novel does preserve a documentary effect due to the journalistic nature of the sources, which exist in playful interconnection with each other within the text. This effect, however, is also indebted to the postmodern context of its production, as much as it is due to the author's intentions to relate unknown facts about Eva Perón's life. In any case, this information – obtained by the author through an investigative process – is at the same time represented through literary devices and therefore is open to being invested with more complex meanings.

If, in his other works on Peronism, Tomás Eloy Martínez was, like Woolf's ideal biographer, interested in exposing the facts of real life with obsessive detail, it is only in *Santa Evita* that he seems to find the most effective format to portray his own version of Eva, and, through her, his interpretation of Peronist Argentina:

> Was Santa Evita going to be a novel? I didn't know and I didn't care. Story lines, fixed points of view, the laws of space and times, slipped through my fingers. The characters sometimes spoke in their own voices and sometimes in other people's, merely to explain to me that what is history is not always historical, that the truth is never what it appears to be. It took me months and months to tame the chaos. Certain characters resisted. They came onstage for a few pages and then left the book forever: the same thing happened in the text as happens in life. But when they went off, Evita was no longer the same: the pollen of other people's wishes and memories had rained down on her. Transfigured into myth, Evita was millions. (54)[26]

In her research on life-writing and the forms in which fictional and non-fictional biography try to obtain knowledge of 'the real, other person', Ina Schabert (1990: 13) argues that, in order to avoid moulds and to draw a complete profile of another human being, the writer should study not only the historical setting of the person but also this uniqueness, assuming his free will and analysing his singularity through psychoanalytic methods.[27]

In reference to Jean-Paul Sartre's biography of Gustave Flaubert, *L'Idiot de la famille*, Schabert describes comprehension as a method for getting to know the other

---

[26] '¿Santa Evita iba a ser una novela? No lo sabía y tampoco me importaba. Se me escurrían las tramas, las fijezas de los puntos de vista, las leyes del espacio y de los tiempos. Los personajes conversaban con su voz propia a veces y otras con voz ajena, sólo para explicarme que lo histórico no es siempre histórico, que la verdad nunca es como parece. Tardé meses y meses en amansar el caos. Algunos personajes se resistieron. Entraban en escena durante pocas páginas y luego se retiraban del libro para siempre: sucedía en el texto lo mismo que en la vida. Pero cuando se iban, Evita no era ya la misma: se había llovido el polen de los deseos y recuerdos ajenos. Transfigurada en mito, Evita era millones' (68).

[27] Although in Sarlo's *La pasión y la excepción* (mentioned earlier), there are no signals for an exhaustive biographical work on Eva Perón, it is interesting to note that her aim to find the 'exceptionality' of Evita as a public figure reflects Sartre's methods of acquiring knowledge of others' lives, as described by Schabert.

completely that implies emotional distance, as opposed to sympathy. Therefore, rather than an achievement, comprehension is defined as praxis or 'a way of living'. Based on the analysis of intertextual and paratextual material written by Tomás Eloy Martínez before *Santa Evita* was published, there is no doubt that for the author, Juan Domingo and Eva Perón were part of his experience, for his interest in every detail of their lives became an obsession. Nevertheless, after an exhaustive process of research and production of texts on the topic that lasted for decades, Martínez, through the self-described narrator, confesses his helpless confusion at the end of *Santa Evita*: 'I don't know where in the story I am. In the middle, I believe. I've been here in the middle for a long time. Now I must write again' (369).[28]

Searching for a magical-realist corpse

Around four months after the publication of 'Las memorias de Juan Perón' in *Panorama* magazine, Tomás Eloy Martínez initiated an interesting epistolary exchange with Norberto Firpo, his editor at *Siete Días* in Buenos Aires.[29] It was 1970, and Martínez was living in Paris. These three letters, two written by Martínez and one by Firpo, can be read as an intriguing pre-text to *Santa Evita* as well, as they shed new light on the interpretation of this novel that is based on historical characters.

Besides an attempt to pursue the truth of an important national matter – the disappearance of the embalmed corpse of Eva Perón – Martínez writes these letters to convince a magazine to buy into his promising but as yet non-existent product. Although he starts the first letter by describing himself as a journalist with more luck than talent (1970b: par. 1) through the actions he narrates, Martínez is represented as an enthusiastic, proactive and self-confident reporter. At the same time, his editor appears to perceive him as a clever, trustworthy and experienced journalist.

Firpo's letter also emphasizes the commercial intentions inherent in dealing with the subject of Peronism, particularly when he asks Martínez to look for an interview with Juan Domingo Perón to talk about what is going to happen after he dies.[30] The editor is aware of the sensitive task he is asking Martínez to undertake, but he is also aware of Martínez's ability to succeed:

> It is possible that Perón will not be very happy to talk about this topic, but maybe yes: he would have the opportunity to speak out on the survival of Peronism, a charming topic. Nevertheless, one must not confront him with this question at the

---

[28] 'No sé en qué punto del relato estoy. Creo que en el medio. Sigo, desde hace mucho, en el medio. Ahora tengo que escribir otra vez' (423).
[29] These letters are not published, but are part of the author's archive held by the Fundación Tomás Eloy Martínez in Buenos Aires, where I was able to consult the originals.
[30] The response from Martínez to Firpo's letter is not in the archives, and there is no evidence that this interview actually happened. This would have been the second conversation between Martínez and Perón in Madrid, after the one that was published that year in *Panorama*.

beginning of the conversation, but guide him to it little by little, and for that we are counting on your astuteness.³¹

The three letters thus offer an insight into the journalistic environment of the time, that is, how reality was being constructed by the mainstream media in Argentina. Another example of this is demonstrated in Firpo's letter, when he asks Martínez to convince Perón to become a political columnist for *Siete Días*:

> This is about making him to commit to writing five or ten columns for us, as a political columnist, without jargon or old stories. It would be a success for us. SD is winning we sell around 70,000 copies per week in the capital city, and all this suggests that the rise in the price did not affect anything, and that by the end of the year we will get to the blessed 200,000 copies that Don César wants.³²

It is obvious that what matters here is magazine sales. Firpo must persuade Martínez, and Martínez in turn must persuade Perón, in order for a certain story to be told, and for it to become available to the magazine's readers as news. There is no evidence that prior to his first conversation with Perón, Martínez was interested in the topic, either in his journalistic or fictional writing. Therefore, it can be inferred that this interest in Peronism, particularly in Eva Perón, was also an economic one. Martínez was working as a foreign correspondent, and in order to earn his salary he needed to write interesting stories. By the end of his second letter, Martínez confesses to Firpo that Eva's story may be his last work for the magazine because he is tired of not knowing if he will continue working in Paris or if he might return to Buenos Aires (apparently, he was waiting for the director's decision).

Nevertheless, a reading of these letters as a private epitext also allows a different approach to Martínez's literary work. The letters demonstrate the documentary intentions of the author at the outset of his writing on Eva Perón. At the same time, they offer insights into the contemporary journalistic field, and, in doing so, show how the media contribute to the construction of reality. Although it cannot be denied that the hidden adventures of Eva Perón's corpse could easily be the plot of a fictional story, these letters from the 1970s show the intentions of a journalist who was following some hints of a story he believed in, trying to discover a truth that would be revealed just one year later, when Eva's corpse was finally returned to the widower, Juan Domingo Perón.

---

³¹ 'Es posible que a Perón no le haga mucha gracia hablar de este tema, pero tal vez sí: tendría oportunidad de declamar sobre la sobrevivencia del peronismo, un tópico encantador. Por otra parte, no habría que enfrentarlo a este interrogante, de entrada, sino – y para ello contamos con tu astucia – ir metiéndolo de a poco' (Firpo: par. 2).

³² 'Se trata de comprometerlo a que nos escriba 5 ó 10 columnas a la manera de un columnista político, sin caer en la arenga o en la historia vieja. Sería un golazo para nosotros. SD está en ganadora: vendemos alrededor de 70.000 ejemplares por semana en la Capital y todo hace suponer que el aumento de precio no incidió para nada, que a fin de año llegaremos a los benditos 200.000 ejemplares que quiere don César' (par. 2).

Regarding the documentary intentions of the author in writing *Santa Evita*, the letters demonstrate that the novel cannot be read as a historical one. This is because the author was himself a part of an unfinished chapter of Argentina's history: he was actually an actor in his own still unfinished plot. For a twenty-first-century reader, who is engaging with the novel years after the deaths of Juan Domingo and Eva Perón, the work may be viewed as predominantly about historical figures within a particular period of Argentina's history. But what the letters bring to our attention is that, from the beginning of his research, Tomás Eloy Martínez did not approach the topic as an historian or even as a fiction writer, but as an investigative journalist. This can also be demonstrated by the way in which he represents himself in his writing. Primarily, he is concerned with discovering the 'real' story of a highly relevant topic, which was a newsworthy one for the Argentinian media, and, secondarily, he is aware of the importance of the format, and how best to deliver the story in an interesting way to his readers. Martínez found that a journalistic investigation was the only possible method of finding the truth about the corpse – at least for him, as he was at that time better known as a reporter. The only way of publishing the story, however, would be as fiction and not as a report or journalistic text in a popular magazine.

Of course, the preference for a literary genre over a journalistic one was not only an artistic decision, but a reaction to the censored and dangerous environment for writers in Argentina. The topic itself was being treated as fiction even in the letters that dealt with a potential journalistic story: Martínez was very careful not to mention the name of Eva Perón, and he referred to her as 'Yoko Lennon', and to the city where her corpse may have been concealed, as 'Ono', humorously comparing Eva's influence over Argentina to that of Yoko Ono in the separation of The Beatles. He was so aware of the power of fiction to communicate truth in a censored environment that he reinforced his theory of Eva's corpse being buried somewhere in Europe by reminding Firpo of Rodolfo Walsh's 'Esa mujer', a short story that first appeared in press in 1965, which is interpreted by Martínez as reportage full of clues:

> As you know, Rodolfo Walsh was the only man who worked seriously on the question of the corpse. He had a long interview with a colonel whose name I don't have in mind right now (but who is the protagonist of the short-story 'Esa mujer'), in whose SIDE office, over a closet, there was Yoko's little coffin for a pair of years. In the middle of a bout of drunkenness, this colonel confessed to Rodolfo (he told me the story in detail) that he buried Yoko himself, 'standing, in a place where it rains a lot'.[33]

---

[33] 'Como sabés, Rodolfo Walsh fue el único tipo que trabajó seriamente en el asunto del cuerpo. Él tuvo una larga entrevista con un coronel cuyo nombre se me escapa ahora (pero que es el protagonista del cuento "Esa mujer"), en cuya oficina de la SIDE, sobre un armario, estuvo el cajoncito de Yoko un par de años. En plena borrachera, este coronel le confió a Rodolfo (él me narró minuciosamente esa historia) que él mismo había enterrado a Yoko "parada, en un lugar donde llueve mucho"' (Martínez 1970b: par. 4).

By stating that Walsh worked seriously on the topic because Martínez heard directly from him that the anecdote was true, Martínez offers his own vision of fiction as a valid and reliable format through which to transmit information. This applied particularly during a period when it was not possible to do so through journalism. In *Santa Evita*, Martínez mentions Walsh's short story again, based on his own 1991 interview with Moori Koenig's widow and daughter in Buenos Aires (2002: 59). As the author does in real life, the narrator in *Santa Evita* needs to know, to verify, that there were real people behind the characters. When the narrator of *Santa Evita* tells the women about Walsh's story, the reader – even if they are not familiar with 'Esa mujer' (That Woman) – is made aware of the contrast between the intertext and the environment and characters described in the passage. Besides, whether or not the interview between Walsh and Koenig really happened is never clear in the novel. It is possible then, that Martínez-the-author no longer believed that the encounter actually occurred. According to the transcripts in the author's private archives, by the time he approached the widow, his other main informant, Héctor Cabaillas, had already told the author that Koenig did not know what happened with the corpse in the end, nor did he know the place where it was resting.

Martínez's obsession with discovering what really happened to the corpse might have motivated him to keep trying to verify the truthfulness of Walsh's fictional story. At some point, it became a game in which Martínez, if he had to publish a journalistic text, would have to decide who was he going to believe, for all had told him their version: Walsh, Cabanillas and Koenig's widow. What is important to highlight here is that by inserting the reference to Walsh's 'Esa mujer' in his novel, Martínez is showing us that his intentions are more literary than journalistic. In the same passage, Martínez also refers to Borges's 'La muerte y la brújula' (Death and the compass) as another example of fiction representing reality during the Perón era. Intertextuality, therefore, plays a significant role in the novel; it is the form by which Martínez gives reality a transcendental meaning, that which, according to his own poetics, can only be displayed when facts are represented through fiction.

Instead of questioning the truthfulness of Walsh's story – which he refers to as a 'reportaje' in his letters to Firpo – in *Santa Evita* Martínez-as-narrator leaves the decision of whether or not to believe it to the reader. Nevertheless, by the end of the chapter, the widow declares that Walsh's story was not a short story, a 'cuento', but something that really happened: '"It really happened. I was listening to them as they spoke. My husband recorded the conversation on a Geloso and left me the tapes. It's the only thing he left me." The eldest daughter opened a sideboard and showed me the tapes: there were two of them, inside transparent plastic envelopes' (1997: 47).[34]

Although Martínez did interview the widow as part of his research for the novel, at least according to the transcripts that are conserved in his archive, there is no evidence in those transcripts of any question or reference to Walsh's story. Describing a narrator observing the evidence – the recordings of that interview – does not make the story

---

[34] 'Yo estuve oyéndolos mientras hablaban. Mi marido registró la conversación en un grabador Geloso y me dejó los carretes. Es lo único que me ha dejado. La hija mayor abrió un aparador y mostró las cintas: eran dos, y estaban dentro de sobres transparentes, de plástico' (60).

more or less real, but it does add the patina of reality to his novel. It is interesting, then, that what the author chooses to invent in this half-real scene in the novel is precisely the mention of Walsh, as if he still wanted to defend his colleague's short story as reportage.

Reality becomes fiction again when Rodolfo Walsh is introduced as a character in dialogue with the narrator. The narrator – who is a self-insert, also named Tomás Eloy Martínez – remembers an encounter with Walsh in a café in Paris. The encounter is a literary recreation of an apparently real meeting, since the conversation was mentioned in Martínez's letter to Firpo. In the novel, the narrator tells Walsh about a recent conversation he had with a secretary, who told him about the expensive and unnecessary construction of a coal bunker replacing the garden at the Argentinian Embassy in Bonn. This is said to have occurred ten years before the scene as it is described. After listening to the secretary's story, Walsh – who by then had already published 'Esa mujer' – confesses that although he always supposed that Bonn was the city were the corpse was buried, he was never sure about it until now:

'Evita is in that garden. So that's where they're keeping her.'
'Eva Perón?' I asked, believing I'd misunderstood.
'The corpse.' He nodded. 'So they took it to Bonn, then. I always presumed so, and now I know' (283).[35]

At the same time, the narrator can confirm – to himself and his readers – that the short story actually represents a real dialogue, since the colonel in the short story really existed. And so the narrator of *Santa Evita* insists: 'Everything in his account was true, but it had been published as fiction, and we readers also wanted to believe that it was fiction. We thought that in Argentina, which prided itself on being Cartesian and European, there was no place for any delirious notions of reality' (284).[36]

Following Martínez's investigation, one is able to see Walsh's documentary intentions, although he, too, wrote his narrative as fiction. The interview with Moori Koenig could have been real, but Martínez finally discovers that – despite his own desire to believe Walsh's story – the facts, the information that the interviewee gave to Walsh, were not. The problem of credibility, however, was not that of Rodolfo Walsh himself, but affected the informant, Carlos Eugenio de Moori Koenig, in whom he trusted. Eventually, Martínez discovered that Moori Koenig had his own reasons to lie, although they were more complex than they seemed to Walsh.

Both Walsh and Martínez wanted to write the 'truth' about the case of the disappeared corpse, and they both found their own ways of doing so through fiction. They employ different methods in their approaches to this 'real story'. Walsh acts more

---

[35] – En ese jardín está Evita. Entonces, es ahí donde la tienen.
 – ¿Eva Perón? – repetí, creyendo que había entendido mal.
 – El cadáver – asintió – Se lo llevaron a Bonn, entonces. Siempre lo supuse, ahora lo sé (328).
[36] 'Todo lo que el cuento decía era verdadero, pero había sido publicado como ficción, y los lectores queríamos creer también que era ficción. Pensábamos que ningún desvarío de la realidad podía tener cabida en la Argentina, que se vanagloriaba de ser cartesiana y europea' (329).

like a storyteller: he listens to the story of another person, someone who he apparently trusts, and he rewrites the story in a way that allows him to safeguard the identity of his informant. On the other hand, Martínez conducts a long, journalistic investigation, cross-checking different sources and double-checking information.[37]

Evidently, although both of them were respected journalists by the time they were writing their narratives, the two authors found different solutions to the problems of representing this real story. Their opposing worldviews are shown in *Santa Evita* in the same encounter at the Parisian café:

> 'Let's go look for the body,' I heard myself say. 'Let's leave for Bonn tonight.'
> 'Not me,' Walsh said. 'When I wrote "That Woman" I put myself outside of history. I've already written the story. And that's the end of it for me.'
> . . .
> 'Maybe I'll load it into the trunk of the car and bring it here,' I said. 'Maybe I'll take it to Madrid and hand it over to Perón. I don't know if he wants it. I don't know if he ever wanted that body.'
> Walsh contemplated me inquisitively from far behind his opaque glasses. I sensed that my obstinacy took him by surprise. (285–6)[38]

The clearest contrast that Martínez's writing draws between them is evident in the way they conceive of writing about facts. Both authors have chosen to use fiction in order to represent reality, but Walsh limits his task to the production of a short story, where real names are not mentioned and the composition can be read as a work of fiction regardless of its reference points in Argentina's history. For Walsh, his task as writer ended when he finished writing what he wanted, for what he wanted was merely to write a story. In contrast, Martínez cannot conceive of telling a story crafted out of a single anecdote from a single informant: he needs to be a part of the story in order to write about it. However, the fictional devices in Martínez's writing are used to represent the self. The metanarrative allows the author to construct a self-referenced narrator in the first person, who is even more impulsive and enthusiastic than the author himself. Unlike the journalist that Martínez is shown to be in his exchange with Firpo, who prepared the trip to search for the corpse based on rational arguments and who waits

---

[37] According to Ezequiel Martínez (2014) – the author's son, and director of Fundación TEM – Tomás Eloy Martínez had an obsession with what he used to call 'las zanjas de la historia': that part of the story where there was a lack of information or particular uncertainty regarding the facts. The author used to go to the place where the event had taken place to interview all witnesses left.

[38] – Vayamos a buscar el cuerpo – me oí decir – Salgamos para Bonn esta noche.
   – Yo no – dijo Walsh – Cuando escribí 'Esa mujer' me puse fuera de la historia. Ya escribí el cuento. Con eso he terminado.
   . . .
   – Tal vez lo cargue en el baúl del auto y lo traiga – dije – Tal vez lo lleve a Madrid y se lo entregue a Perón. No sé si él lo quiere. No sé si él quiso ese cuerpo alguna vez.
   Walsh me contempló con curiosidad desde la lejanía de sus anteojos opacos. Sentí que mi obstinación lo tomaba por sorpresa (331).

for, or at least looks for, the approval of his editor, the narrator of *Santa Evita* decides to engage in the adventure as soon as possible.

Martínez's journalistic interpretation of a story that could be sold, as opposed to the rather romantic perspective of Walsh – which expresses the impossibility of finding or telling the truth – is made evident by the end of the scene in the Parisian café. Walsh shows Martínez a photograph of Eva's corpse taken by Moori Koenig, who gave it to him. Aware of the value of the object, the narrator laments that his friend did not sell the photograph, but Walsh only responds, 'That woman isn't mine' (287).[39]

Martínez consciously raises the topic of Eva's corpse as a symbol of the social and political situation in Argentina. For fifteen years, no one in Argentina admitted to knowing where it was. However, the question of the appropriation of a corpse – and not just any corpse, but that of Eva Perón – is more than a national metaphor here. Beyond the metaphorical appropriation, the narrator actually expresses to Walsh his desire to search for the corpse and to exhume it himself. The episode in the novel in which both authors meet also brings into question Walsh and Martínez's opposing conceptions of the representation of reality within fiction. Walsh refuses to make commercial use of his treasure, while the narrator simultaneously considers selling the first-hand testimony he is listening to. The relationship between the aesthetic solutions posed by Martínez's work and the ethical questions those solutions pose in turn can be analysed in contrast with the author's archive. There is evidence that Martínez actually intended to find the corpse in order to tell his, ultimately journalistic, story. In the 1970 letters, Martínez tries to convince Norberto Firpo to go beyond journalism and act as protagonist of the news he aims to construct:

> Wherever Yoko might be, the affair is of such importance that the only way of getting ahead of it is not taking photographs or telling the story, but by transferring the corpse. Imagine if Siete Días declares that the corpse is – for example – in Torres, Brasil; the FAP, the SIDE, the CIA and all the acronyms of the world will know it while the corpse remains on the road in an L.N. Alem-Taller. On the publication day of the magazine, the corpse would not be where we said it was anymore. There are so many interests in play.[40]

That same aim of searching for some breaking news – a story that could be sold successfully, and not just form part of a collection of short stories – had led Martínez to propose to his editor a plan to look for the corpse, as if they were part of a detective novel. Despite the fantastic tone of the proposal, Martínez lays out his plan in rational language. Once again, the question of Eva's corpse as an object that can be – albeit not

---

[39] 'Esa mujer no es mía' (332).
[40] 'Cualquiera fuere el lugar donde esté Yoko, el affaire es de tal gravedad que la única manera de salir adelante con él no es tomando fotos ni contando la historia, sino trasladando el cuerpo. Imaginate, si Siete Días sale diciendo que el cuerpo está – por ejemplo – en Torres, Brasil, la FAP, la SIDE, la CIA y todas las siglas del mundo se encargarán de saberlo en el trayecto L. N. Alem–taller. El día de la salida de la revista, el cuerpo ya no estará donde decíamos que estaba. Hay demasiados intereses en juego' (Martínez 1970b: par. 8).

easily – manipulated and appropriated is in the air. Martínez knows that finding Eva's corpse will lead the magazine, and himself of course, to journalistic success. History is malleable and can be changed – and sold.

Martínez's suggestion to his editor may seem naïve. Nonetheless, by considering that a search for the body was actually a possibility, he demonstrates an awareness of the media processes through which news is constructed. The author knows that news cannot be fiction, for he is not suggesting invention or lies, but still he is able to make an impact on reality so it can be made newsworthy. Full of excitement and ambition, Martínez's letters to Firpo can be read as *crónicas* in their own right, particularly the one dated 28 August 1970, in which Martínez narrates in detail his research trip to Bonn and failure to prove that Eva's corpse was buried in the Argentinian Embassy there. Faithful to the ethics of the journalistic craft – since the idea of writing the story without verifying it was never entertained – Martínez never published the reportage he proposed to his editor in any other medium, but continued to conduct research, until his findings were later transformed into the novel *Santa Evita*.

The documentary intention of *Santa Evita* is, nevertheless, evident through a closer look at the process of the novel's production, as has been demonstrated. This is precisely because Martínez was careful to protect his informants when it was still dangerous to talk about the topics he was researching. One can infer that, in order to maintain the realism of the story as far as possible, Martínez acted primarily as a journalist rather than as a fiction writer, but he found in the novel the most ethical and aesthetically appropriate solution for the representational problems he faced. For instance, Tomás Eloy Martínez wanted *Santa Evita* to be labelled as a novel on the cover precisely so that he would not face problems from people who would read it as non-fiction (Ezequiel Martínez 2014).

In addition, it is important to highlight the detail that during Martínez's research into the background of the story, he interviewed three military men who were responsible for the operation to move Eva's corpse from Argentina to a cemetery in Italy. They gave Martínez original documents as evidence that their testimony was true, as the transcripts of those interviews demonstrate. However, Martínez did not represent these men in the novel in direct relationship with those particular documents; nor did he even mention their real names. That also proves that Martínez acted as a professional journalist would in his investigation, and this is reinforced by the transcripts of the interview held with Cabanillas and Rojas Silveyra:

> TEM: Maybe you have a curse as well, one must be very careful with the information because one never knows what the fanatics are capable of. One never knows with Peronists.
>
> CAB: Of course. I tell you, Martínez, that I have done this in all confidence, with all honesty telling you the truth, although there are things that obviously can't be published.
>
> TEM: You have told me those things clearly: 'Don't say this, this neither, Soralla's name should remain ...'

CAB: No, of course, it is dangerous. Besides, I have children, grandchildren.[41]

Empathy and trust were the basis upon which the sources gave Martínez their information. A similar situation arose when, in his letters to Firpo, he stated that he managed to get into the Argentinian Embassy. Martínez reports that he had met people who were willing to give him information.[42] The author's technique of developing empathy with others in order to obtain information is clearly evident in the way he led Cabanillas, Sorolla and Koenig's widow to talk about a possible case of necrophilia. Martínez raises the topic in different ways depending on each informant and the relationship they had with the man accused of the act, Moori Koenig. When he talked with Cabanillas, for example, he asked him directly about the topic:

> TEM: But, pardon me. There are the three or four months in which Moori Koenig is in charge of the corpse. The important thing – because there are a lot of legends here – is to look at what really happened. What I have heard and read about this issue is that there were practices of necrophilia performed on the corpse, to tell you in a vulgar language, the corpse was fucked. I am sorry to use this hard language, but we are among men.[43]

By pointing out that they are among men only, the interviewer tries to position himself as an equal in an intimate conversation, preparing an appropriate environment for the confession. The conversation continues without any direct response – apparently due to Cabanillas's struggle to find the words to describe the episode in question – but Martínez maintains a gentler, although quite misogynistic tone in his interview, until he obtains the evidence he sought:

> TEM: Pardon me, coronel. Pardon me because I am coming back to a story that is alien to you. Did people drink on the corpse? Was the corpse used as a table ...?

---

[41] 'TEM: Igual tiene esa especie de maldición detrás, hay que tener mucho cuidado con la información, porque nunca se sabe lo que pueden hacer los fanáticos Peronistas, nunca se sabe.
CAB: Por supuesto. Yo le digo, Martínez que yo me he prestado a esto con toda confianza, con toda honradez diciéndole la verdad, aunque hay cosas que evidentemente no pueden publicarse.
TEM: Usted me las ha dicho, claramente: 'Esto no lo diga, esto tampoco, el nombre de Sorolla hay que mantenerlo ...'.
CAB: No, por supuesto, es peligroso. Aparte yo tengo hijos, nietos'
('Cabanillas2': 11–12).

[42] Regarding Martínez's relationship with his informants, his son Ezequiel Martínez pointed out, as he was witness to some of his father's interviews, that he was very charming, and he made people feel very comfortable quickly; he could talk with any person and make them feel as if they were talking with an equal (personal interview, 19 November 2014).

[43] 'TEM: Pero, discúlpeme. Ahí quedan los tres meses o cuatro que Moori Koening está a cargo del cadáver. Lo importante es – porque ahí hay mucha leyenda – ver exactamente qué es lo que pasó. De lo que yo he oído y he leído en todo este asunto es que hubo episodios necrofílicos con el cadáver, para decírselo en lenguaje vulgar, que se lo cogieron al cadáver. Disculpe que use este lenguaje crudo, pero estamos entre hombres' (1989a: 2).

CAB: I can't testify to that, I heard that it happened. Obviously one of the causes for Moori Koenig's replacement was that Osorio Arana heard comments about Moori's sacrileges with the corpse, that there were ceremonies around the corpse, parties, and that people were shouting and throwing wine on the corpse and all that.[44]

On the contrary, when the author interviews Moori Koenig's widow, he does not seem to have asked direct questions about the rumours of necrophilia. He listened to her side of the story, even if in his notes on the conversation he shows himself to be aware of a different version. In the transcript of the interview, Martínez quite literally underlines the fact that the widow gives him another version of the story (1991: 2).

There is an obsession with the truth that can be perceived throughout the transcripts. Questions to verify dates, details of how the corpse was hidden, descriptions of places and people are constantly repeated to each informant, as if Martínez was looking for contradictions, and also for a part of story that had not been discovered yet. As the characters are moved by an obsession to possess Eva through the manipulation of her dead body, Martínez is also obsessed with possessing her through information, as his fictional self remembers in *Santa Evita*:

> I remembered the time when I went looking for the shades of her shadow, I, too, in search of her lost body (as is recounted in several chapters of *The Perón Novel*), and the summers I spent gathering documentation for a biography that I was planning to write and that was to be called, as was predictable, The Lost Woman. Led by that thirst, I spoke with her mother, the steward of the presidential residence, her hairdresser, her film director, her manicurist, two actresses from her theatrical company, the comic musician who got her work in Buenos Aires. I spoke with marginal figures, and not with the ministers or fawning admirers of her court, because they were not like her: they couldn't see the razor's edge or the narrow lines along which Evita had always walked. (52–3)[45]

---

[44] 'TEM: Discúlpeme, coronel. Perdóneme que vuelva sobre una historia que le es ajena a usted. ¿Se había bebido arriba del cadáver, se había hecho mesa . . . ?

CAB: Personalmente no me consta, a mí me llegaron comentarios de que sí. Evidentemente una de las causas justamente del relevo de Moori Koening, es que le habrían llegado a Osorio Arana versiones de que estaba evidentemente cometiendo un sacrilegio con ese cadáver, que se estaban hacienda ceremonias al lado del cadáver, festejos, y gritaban y tiraban vino encima y todo lo demás' (3).

[45] 'Recordé el tiempo en que anduve tras las sobras de su sombra, yo también en busca de su cuerpo perdido . . . hablé con la madre, el mayordomo de la casa presidencial, el peluquero, su director de cine, la manicure, las modistas, dos actrices de su compañía de teatro, el músico bufo que le consiguió trabajo en Buenos Aires. Hablé con las figuras marginales y no con los ministros ni aduladores de su corte porque no eran como Ella: no podían verle el filo ni los bordes por los que Evita siempre había caminado' (66). Among the documents I discovered in Tomás Eloy Martínez's private archive, there were transcripts of interviews with different sorts of informants who witnessed a part of Perón's or Eva's life, for example Elvira Barilatti, a school teacher who was a friend of Perón's aunt, and Luis Ratto, a lawyer who was Perón's college classmate. These transcripts also contain notes or brief physical descriptions of the interviewees and the location of the encounter. The questions focus on descriptive details about places where Perón lived or used to visit. The archives also contain copies of documents such as CIA reports on Perón and Perón's letters (Buenos Aires, Archivo TEM).

As opposed to a historian's utilization of his research, Martínez will not give any conclusive or complete story about what happened to the corpse. By playing with the borders of literary genres and their conventions, Martínez is actually questioning the nature of a real story. Therefore, his novels offer not only a critique of social and political issues in Argentina, but also a critique of the ways in which reality is narrated.

Finally, this chapter has explored the investigative process of a journalist in a context of state and media censorship and the ways in which storytelling can be used through diverse genres of fiction and non-fiction in order to reconstruct historical events. In doing so, however, the limits between information and narration are blurred, and its effects go beyond the rhetorical problem of genre hybridity. I believe that a paratextual reading of Martínez's Peronist novels complements and certainly challenges the traditional interpretation of these texts as fiction. It is evident that Martínez deliberately experimented with diverse modes of documentary narration to represent his encounters with Juan Domingo Perón. It can be presumed that this was because of the author's aim to show that the discursive mode, even in journalism, can actually change the way in which reality is perceived. As an experienced journalist, Martínez was aware of the power of media in the construction of reality. As a novelist, Martínez shows how the practicalities of the journalistic trade constantly redefine the meanings of truth in contemporary, mass media–driven societies, 'The medium would replace reality; the medium was the reality.'[46] Analysing the material conditions of the news craft offers a more comprehensive view of the conditions of journalistic investigation in Latin America and thus of its particular forms of storytelling; this is most evident in the correspondence between Martínez and his editor but also in contemporary metajournalistic narratives such as the ones I analyse in the following chapters.

---

[46] 'El medio sustituía a la realidad; el medio era la realidad' (2009b: 150).

Part III

Listening

5

Local conversations in globalized times

Martín Caparrós (Buenos Aires 1957) and Juan Villoro (Mexico City 1958) are considered two of the best chroniclers in contemporary Latin America. Apart from their careers as fiction authors, they are both part of the group Nuevos Cronistas de Indias and teachers at the Fundación para un Nuevo Periodismo Iberoamericano. They also share a passion for football, as is revealed in their famous football *crónicas* and their co-authored book *Ida y vuelta: una correspondencia sobre fútbol* (Round trip: a correspondence about soccer, 2012). In this chapter, however, I focus on two texts that are not actually acknowledged by their creators as proper *crónicas*, for they were not planned as such and, according to the authors, were rather written by chance: Caparrós's *Una luna. Diario de hiperviaje* (A moon. A hypertravel diary, 2009) and Villoro's *8.8 El miedo en el espejo. Una crónica del terremoto en Chile* (8.8 The fear in the mirror. A chronicle of the earthquake in Chile, 2010). In these works, discourse hybridity goes beyond the traditional and quite prescriptive definition of the genre of *crónica*, as Caparrós emphatically advises the reader: 'this is not a chronicle: it is only a diary of hypertravel.'[1]

The objective of this chapter is to explore the research procedures as well as the literary devices employed by Villoro and Caparrós in the aforementioned works. I believe that these authors exhibit the contradictions between local and global realities by representing the encounter with the other from the perspective of a professional journalist and cosmopolitan, cultivated middle-class man who travels freely around the world. I thus look into how conversations with strangers that appear in Villoro's *El miedo* and Caparrós's *Una luna* expose an alternative method through which contemporary social and environmental problems can be approached.

Contrary to their other travel writing, the self-reflective narrators are travellers exposed here to otherness in a foreign country.[2] Neither journey was undertaken for

---

[1] 'Esto no es una crónica: es sólo un diario de hiperviaje' (2009: 62). According to what Caparrós said during our interview, the word *crónica* was hardly used by journalists in Argentina, for it referred to the most marginal position on the journalistic scale: the young apprentice who went out into the streets in order to gather the information that a more experienced journalist required in order to write the news. Neither Caparrós or Villoro have been this kind of journalist, or at least not for long. After a period in the newsrooms, they have worked mostly as freelance writers.

[2] There are other travel books that received wider acknowledgement from the critics: Caparrós's *El interior* (The Interior, 2006), which is a travelogue of the author's adventures while driving through the northern provinces of Argentina, and Villoro's *Palmeras de la brisa rápida: un viaje a Yucatán*

happy reasons, and the narrators are confronted by existential and moral questions. By depicting themselves as explorers in unexpected lands or situations, Villoro and Caparrós follow the tradition of the so-called '*crónicas de conquista*' (chronicles of conquest) initiated by European writers, regularly missionaries or military men, travelling to the Americas during the Spanish and Portuguese colonization. They are, however, aware of the anachronistic task of a traditional chronicler in today's world. Based on their physical and intellectual experience of approaching others in a globalized era, they create not only a particular style and point of view – closer to postmodern aesthetics than to conventional journalism – but they also raise questions of ethics and communication. Therefore, both authors deal with what Thea Pitman (2008) has identified as a trend towards a type of postcolonial travel writing in Latin American literature, particularly in Mexico, since the late 1990s.

These chroniclers embrace a postmodern worldview and innovative narrative style in contrast with their Latin American predecessors, particularly in their configuration of a self-aware metafictional narrator. However, I believe that their main difference from the tradition of travel writing in the region is Villoro's and Caparrós's mediatory role, for they travel through their countries, or other regions of the developing world, as insiders with respect to culture but as outsiders in social class. This duality makes their self-representation highly problematic, particularly in the encounters with their informants.

The journalist as protagonist

Una luna and *El miedo* cannot be read as traditional chronicles, but as a broader type of documentary narrative. In their aim to give meaning to a personal and collective experience, they use a variety of testimonial-based genres (e.g. diaries, letters, electronic messages, notes, press articles and interviews/conversations), intersected by fictional modes (such as poems, novels). These books seem to propose that traditional methods of documenting reality are no longer adequate to narrate the experiences of a globalized citizen moving through chaotic times and spaces.

Neither book was originally conceived as a literary-journalistic project. The life stories or journalistic profiles of young migrants included in *Una luna* were published one year before in a shorter, edited version as part of a UN report, *Jóvenes en movimiento* (Young people in movement, 2007). 'El sabor de la muerte' (The taste of death), a section of *8.8 El miedo en el espejo*, was originally published in *La Nación* newspaper, a week after the 2010 earthquake in Chile, which was experienced by Villoro while he was attending a conference on children's literature.

Although *Una luna* actually contains chronicles, for Caparrós the book is rather a travel diary, which was never supposed to be a book:

(Fast breeze palm trees, 1989), an account of Villoro's own experience while travelling to his grandmother's land as part of a commission for a Mexican collection of travel books.

Until today – until now, seated in this bar in Amsterdam, with such cold temperatures outside, and inside a slight loneliness – I hadn't thought this could take the guise of a book. I just had to put together my stories about young immigrants. But since I went out I've been taking notes, because I still haven't learnt to travel any other way. I try and I try, but I can't. And now (a strong cigarette, a Belgian beer, three friends shouting on the next table) when I look at the notes that have begun building up I imagine that perhaps they make some sense – and I think about publishing them because I still haven't learnt to write into silence. I try, I try so hard, but I can't – yet.[3]

The narrator thus emphasizes the private origins of his writing. For him, *Una luna* is the product of his travel notes, which were written on the road, to freely express his thoughts and feelings while he was working for the UN project. Unlike his travel notes, the UN texts had to be precise and impersonal.

Written originally as a personal side project, *Una luna* then becomes the subversive response of an author who cannot conceal his voice within that of a third-person narrator. It is important, however, to consider Caparrós's decision to configure a self-insert narrator as a business traveller. As opposed to those who travel for pleasure or in search of adventure, as the old *cronistas de Indias* did, or who travel out of necessity, like his own informants for the UN report, this narrator travels in order to work. He depicts himself as a modern globalized traveller, flying from one side of the world to another in hours.

On the contrary, in *El miedo*, Villoro approaches a narrative drawn from personal memory as a self-conscious decision to make public a private and unexpected experience of the fear of death. The narrator here is also a writer travelling because of work, for he is to be a speaker in a conference.

Both books are born of private writing, of personal experiences that were not intended to become public. Writing their testimony freely, without the limitations of any institutional report or a newspaper assignment, becomes a way to escape from reality for Caparrós and Villoro, and at the same time to make sense of it in a deeper manner. According to his own account, Caparrós did not conceive of *Una luna* as a publishable book, since it was intended to be a present for the guests of his birthday party, and was based on personal notes made during his travels (see Interview 2). Similarly, Villoro configures a narrator who decides to write a book about the earthquake he lived through in Chile only after his hands stopped trembling, as he narrates in *El miedo*:

---

[3] 'Hasta hoy – hasta ahora, sentado en este bar de Amsterdam, con tanto frío afuera y adentro leve soledad – no había pensado que esto pudiera disfrazarse de libro. Yo sólo tenía que armar mis historias sobre inmigrantes jóvenes. Pero desde que salí que estoy tomando notas – porque todavía no aprendí a viajar de otra manera. Lo intento, lo intento, pero no. Y ahora – un cigarrillo fuerte, una cerveza belga, tres amigos que gritan en la mesa de al lado – cuando miro las notas que se han ido acumulando imagino que quizá tengan algún sentido – y pienso en publicarlas porque todavía no aprendí a escribir para el silencio. Lo intento – fuertemente lo intento – pero no todavía' (2009: 62)'

'Are you going to write about the earthquake?' a journalist colleague asked me as soon as I landed in Mexico City airport.

'When my hands stop trembling,' I answered. Some days passed before that was possible. In Santiago I had taken some notes, without the slightest concentration.[4]

Villoro's attempt to make sense of his traumatic experience is represented textually by independent paragraphs. This unconventional fragmentation of the text symbolizes the flow of thoughts that can be registered in a notebook, jumping from one idea to another without a logical transition.

Both narrators show a consciousness of the chaotic and non-linear process of writing through a journey in which dramatic experiences are encountered. Registering their accounts is not a way of preserving facts anymore, but a way of trying to understand what is going on. However, the notes based on feelings and thoughts as they apparently appear within the author's mind – a sort of real stream of consciousness – are not transcribed word for word to conform with the format of the book, but are mixed with remembrances. The narrators are, furthermore, aware of the lack of reliability in this approach to reality, as Caparrós demonstrates when he narrates his observations on men in a bar in Lusaka, who he thinks are drinking milk. On the next page, however, he describes the joy of the experienced and bored traveller who finally finds an authentic local experience. The anecdote of the men drinking milk in a bar is demystified by the encounter with other people:

The traveller doesn't know shit. He supposes, searches, thinks, affirms – and quite often he carries on supposing. The boys from Stanley Bar didn't drink milk [. . .] there was a type of chicha, an alcoholic drink made out of fermented corn that they call chibuku round here. They tell me that now, on my way to the airport, and I am able to make the correction. But it was pure chance: the more logical thing would have been never to realise. Until what point should we continue checking – or, in other words, at what point should we start suspecting?[5]

These reflections on the limits of the observer to interpret other cultures leads the reader to question the unreliable nature of the text itself and therefore of the documentary genres as a way of representing reality. By choosing to present the experience as it supposedly happened, Caparrós risks his credibility as a narrator of

---

[4] ' – ¿Vas a escribir del terremoto? – me preguntó un colega periodista apenas aterricé en el aeropuerto del D.F.
    – Cuando me dejen de temblar las manos – contesté. Pasaron unos días antes de que eso fuera posible. En Santiago había tomado algunos apuntes, ajenos a todo sentido de la concentración' (2010a: 21).
[5] 'El viajero no sabe una mierda. Supone, busca, piensa, afirma – y muchas veces sigue suponiendo. Los muchachos del Stanley Bar no tomaban leche: en esos tetras blancos tan lechosos, con letras que decían shake shake, de donde salía un líquido tan leche, había una chicha, una bebida alcohólica de maíz fermentado que aquí llaman chibuku. Me lo dicen ahora, camino al aeropuerto, y puedo corregirlo. Pero fue un azar: lo más lógico habría sido no enterarme nunca. ¿Hasta qué punto hay que seguir averiguando o, dicho de otro modo, desde qué punto desconfiar?' (Caparrós 2009: 162).

real stories. Nevertheless, this procedure allows him to demonstrate the impossibility of observation and interpretation as reliable methods of research. In a similar tone, Villoro echoes Giorgio Agamben's idea of the 'integral witness' – one who can relate the complete experience – in order to reflect on the function of the chronicle as a way of approaching what cannot be uttered (2010a: 24).

Within the fragmented textual structure, digressions and flashbacks are used to relate current experiences to past experiences. These techniques allow the authors to develop their literary motives, beyond their particular documentary intention. Experiencing the 2010 earthquake in Santiago de Chile by chance, Villoro remembers the 1985 Mexico City earthquake, and thus the fear of death becomes a motif in his writing. In the case of Caparrós, interviewing young migrants in places where he has lived before reminds him of his own youth, and a tone of nostalgia permeates the book.

The narrators observe and interpret reality through the lens of their own past experiences, their literary and cultural references, and through national and individual identities. Caparrós-as-narrator is a white heterosexual Western man travelling to poor areas of the world, as Villoro depicts himself as a Mexican author stuck in Chile unexpectedly. Their expectations, observations and feelings during the travels are influenced by their represented identity. They are aware of their own perspectives and are willing to show their position to the readers. By doing so, both authors become critical of the social order they represent, too. For instance, Caparrós questions not only the globalized nature of contemporary travel, but also the role of the humanitarian institutions claiming to save the world while travelling first class:

> The desert down there is beautiful and Moroccan, riddled with colours. The chardonnay is Chilean, the sauvignon is New Zealand, the foie gras is French, the salmon is Canadian; the man on my left is American, the one on my right is Senegalese, but the three of us are NGO people reading reports about poverty and social emergencies in the West of Africa. This is class Men, of course: well-understood solidarity begins with oneself.[6]

The authors, however, construct their narration from the perspective of someone for whom the journey was imposed by others. Having positioned themselves as men of letters, writing becomes their way of making sense of the forced travelling experience, so whatever happens outside their home can only be interpreted by the means of language.

Villoro's and Caparrós's documentary narratives might not be reliable as pieces of traditional journalism, but they claim to be honest with their own human experiences in encountering otherness. The narrators are aware of the limits of the journalistic

---

[6] 'El desierto allá abajo es bellísimo y marrueco, plagado de colores. El chardonnay es chileno, el sauvignon neozelandés, francés el foie, el salmón canadiense; el señor de mi izquierda es norteamericano, el de mi derecha senegalés, pero los tres somos oenegeros leyendo reportes sobre miseria y emergencias sociales en el oeste de África. Es clase Hombres, por supuesto: la solidaridad bien entendida empieza por sí mismo' (35).

genre in the representation of reality, as when Caparrós-as-narrator tells the story of an African businessman under a tree and he doubts about how to write about him:

> What should I do then? Should I begin by telling the story, following the canons of the good old New Journalism, and then go on with my reflections? Should I ignore the story since it seems too purposeful, almost fabricated? Should I try to lend it credibility with some fact or detail that makes it unique, complements it? Or should I put together a little discussion about what to do with it, so that no one can doubt that the story was real, and my intentions were all for the best?[7]

Metafiction or, more accurately, metajournalism, is used by Caparrós to control, to an extent, the interpretation of the facts. This is a stylistic device frequently used by (meta)documentary narratives, particularly in the depiction of scenes in which the journalist-narrator is writing in real time about his surroundings. From a table in a Parisian café, for instance, Caparrós tries to remember an interview that he conducted in El Salvador a month before (88). Similarly, Villoro's account of the earthquake can only be interpreted when he is back home.

There is thus a sense of dislocation, for the place of writing is hardly ever the same as the one where the experience occurred. The narrator in *El miedo* informs the reader that he has made notes while he was waiting for a flight to return to his own country. It is improbable, however, that during the moment of the earthquake, he was taking notes. This is why the most sensitive narrative episode in his book, the narration of his own experience while dealing with the possibility of his own death, could only have been written from memory:

> When the movement finally stopped, there was a feeling of unreality.... After a few seconds, the screams that the building had suffocated with its creaks became audible. I opened the door and I saw a thick cloud. I thought it was smoke and that the building was on fire. It was dust. I felt a burning heat in the throat.[8]

Villoro's account of the earthquake is influenced by his own aesthetic aspirations. If the text were purely a journalistic one, he would not care, or have the space in the newspaper, for comments of a philosophical nature. In this scene, however, Villoro is not only narrating the event as it happened, but also depicting himself as an obsessive

---

[7] '¿Qué hago entonces? ¿Empiezo por contarla, como mandan los cánones del buen viejo nuevo periodismo, y después sigo con mi reflexión? ¿La ignoro porque parece demasiado a propósito, casi inventada? ¿Trato de darle verosimilitud con algún dato o detalle que la singularice y complemente? ¿O me armo una pequeña discusión sobre qué hacer y así ya nadie duda de que la historia era real y mis intenciones las mejores?' (Caparrós 2009: 159).

[8] 'Cuando el movimiento cesó por fin, sobrevino una sensación de irrealidad.... Al cabo de unos segundos, los gritos que el edificio había sofocado con sus crujidos se volvieron audibles. Abrí la puerta y vi una nube espesa. Pensé que se trataba de humo y que el edificio se incendiaba. Era polvo. Sentí un ardor en la garganta' (61–2).

man who was willing to risk his life rather than exit the building without his valuable possessions or his shoes well tied.

In their documentary narratives, Caparrós and Villoro confront themselves with natural and social phenomena which they cannot control, such as earthquakes, poverty, globalization and death. Their metadocumentary narratives go beyond the journalistic aim of registering an event, and even beyond the parodic intention to show the construction of reality by the media, in the style of authors such as Tomás Eloy Martínez. Citizens of a globalized society, Caparrós and Villoro abandoned any attempt at control, and their writings show the impossibility of shaping reality into a unified, coherent narrative.

Martín Caparrós around the world

When researching his stories on migration for the UN, Caparrós worked under specific circumstances. He had to act as an anthropologist and journalist, yet he had very little time to get to know the places he visited,to learn their customs or languages or to understand what it was to live as a local. The result was an informative institutional report which, besides the collected life stories, included quantitative data, such as statistics, maps, photographs and historical and sociological information. The life stories that Caparrós and other authors recorded were considered by the editors to be emotional and evocative (Laski and Schellekens 2007: ii).

As I have already mentioned, Caparrós's travel notes were later turned into the book *Una luna*. The book incorporates the migrants' testimonies from the report, and even more. The greatest difference is the change in the narrator's voice. In the report, the stories are presented in the form of journalistic profiles or in a biographical style, using a third-person narrator to describe facts, with direct quotations from the interviewees. On the contrary, the stories in *Una luna* are narrated in the first person, by a self-reflective narrator who takes time to give detailed descriptions of the context of the encounter with the interviewees, and even of the problems he had in reaching them.

Another outstanding difference is the question of authorship. The UN stories are anonymous, for Caparrós's name appears in the credits of the booklet as part of the editorial team, as editor-in-chief and under 'Periodistas/Autores de las Historias de Vida' (Journalists/Authors of Life Stories), but not as author of any specific story. On the contrary, in Caparrós's *Una luna*, there is the strong presence of a self-represented narrator.

Whereas in the report, credibility is given to the testimonies by the supporting data and by institutional reliability, in *Una luna* this credibility is sustained through the authority of the narrator as witness. The narrator in the book is depicted as a participant-observer, in whose experience and knowledge the reader should trust. If this rather subjective story that frames the multiple life stories of others can then offer a sense of reality, it is also because of its form. *Una luna* is not presented as a memoir but as a diary written on the road, a type of text that might resemble an anthropologist's field journal. In the book, subjective information, such as perceptions, feelings, thoughts and interpretations of the stories told, is as reliable as the statistics are for the report. This is due to the narrative effect of the discourse chosen to frame the testimonies.

Although the facts of the stories of the young migrants in a globalized world are barely modified in the report version, Caparrós nevertheless eliminates the dialogue. The speech that in *Una luna* is represented as a conversation, a fragment of a real, recorded, interview, in the report it is limited to the isolated declarations of the informants. Stylistically, the disappearance of the narrator-interviewer from the text can be interpreted as a way of giving voice to the other, as has been the case regarding testimonial literature. This disappearance of the authorial voice, however, restricts the plurality of meaning that the text can offer as well, as it makes a debate on the ethical implications of the encounter between the journalist and his interviewees more difficult. An example is the story of Natalia, a young woman from Moldova who was sold by her husband to a human trafficker. The story in the report begins with Natalia's impoverished childhood, while in the book Caparrós first narrates his own journey to meet her.

Another modification of the testimony lies in its descriptions of places and people. In the report, the testimony appears out of context, and the circumstances leading to it are not problematized. In *Una luna*, Caparrós lets the reader know who is the writer of that testimony: someone who is able to enjoy a Parisian delicatessen before travelling to an impoverished former member of the Soviet Union, who is aware of the historical, political and aesthetic differences between the world he has travelled from and the one he is travelling to. The narrator does not conceal his perceptions of the place, nor his own ideology or preferences.

By representing himself in the interview situation, Caparrós shows the conversation to the reader from behind the scenes and, therefore, transforms the testimony into a dialogical space for both real and literary encounters. The report ends Natalia's story as follows:

> 'Why do you talk to us?
> Well, initially I wanted to hide my story, because here when they know, they don't treat you like a victim but as guilty. But now I know I have to tell it: if not, I will spend all my life thinking about those months. Telling it is a way of letting it go and helping other young women like me, so it won't happen to them.
> What do you hope from the future?
> Natalia becomes silent, thinks, tries to smile.
> What a difficult question.
> She says'
> ('Natalia. Moldova, victim of human trafficking': 2007: 28).[9]

---

[9] ¿Por qué hablas con nosotros?
 Bueno, yo primero quería ocultar mi historia, porque acá cuando se enteran no te tratan como víctima sino como culpable. Pero ahora sé que tengo que contarlo: si no, me voy a pasar toda la vida pensando en esos meses. Contarlo es la manera de dejarlo atrás y de ayudar a que no le pase a otras chicas como yo.

In *Una luna*, the same part of the story is narrated as follows (words in bold highlight the parts that are not in the report):

'– Why do you **talk** with us and not with your family?
– **Because they would never understand me**. Initially I wanted to hide my story, because **here in my country** when they know, **they discriminate against you** . . . Natalia tells us, but she does not want her face looking clear in the photographs
. . .
– What do you **hope** for the future?
Natalia becomes silent, thinks, tries to smile, **she rubs her false eye with a finger. It is snowing outside. The good thing about snow is that it flows in the air** . . .
– What a difficult question.
She says, **after having answered so many impossible questions**'.[10]

Although some of the stories in the report do include questions, these are presented in bold, separated from the rest of the text – without the use of hyphens, as in a script or a novelistic dialogue – and there is no identification of their speaker, as if the interviewer were hidden or did not exist at all. In the book, on the contrary, the reader can recognize the Argentinian identity of the interviewer by noticing the accent mark on 'hablás' (to speak) and 'esperás' (to hope). Additionally, the description and perception of Natalia's reactions to the questions, passages which do not appear in the report, offer a subjective dimension to the story, one told from the point of view of a concrete narrator. The representation of Natalia in the book reveals someone shy, frightened and embarrassed by the interview. The report does not include either Caparrós's reflections on Moldova, or his final comment interpreting Natalia's attitude during the conversation, which shows his awareness and recognition that she has answered many difficult questions.

In the book, details of the environment, such as the note on the snow and the narrator's effort to relate the weather to the story, are also important, for they provide the stage on which the encounter between the self and the other occurs. In contrast with the report, Natalia continues to act as a character in *Una luna*, but only as seen through the eyes of the one who registers her movements and attitudes:

¿Qué esperas del futuro?
Natalia se calla, piensa, intenta una sonrisa.
Qué pregunta difícil.
Dice
('Natalia. Moldova, víctima del tráfico de personas': 28).

[10] –¿Por qué **hablás** con nosotros y no con tu familia?
– **Porque ellos nunca me entenderían**. Yo primero quería ocultar mi historia, porque acá **en mi país** cuando se enteran **te discriminan** . . .
Dice Natalia, pero no quiere que su cara se vea clara en las fotos . . .
– ¿Qué **esperás** del futuro?
Natalia se calla, piensa, intenta una sonrisa, **se restriega con un dedo el ojo falso. Afuera nieva. Lo bueno de la nieve es que vaga en el aire** . . .
– Qué pregunta difícil.
Dice, **tras haber contestado tantas preguntas imposibles** (27–8).

Natalia and I were seated side by side, but we were looking at Alexandrina, who was translating from Moldovan into English. I have just spent five hours listening to a young woman with an eye made of glass and such a hard life that her husband gave her to a human trafficker, even when she was pregnant, and all the rest. There are things that cannot be heard with impunity.[11]

As one can see from the aforementioned fragment, the conditions of the dialogue are problematic not only because of the social and cultural differences between the interviewer and the interviewee, but also because of the language barrier. As opposed to the transparent testimony offered in the report, in *Una luna* the reader is invited to look behind the stage and see what happens when the public dialogue is over. Furthermore, Natalia will continue to be present in the book through the narrator's own assimilation of her testimony. Some pages later, Caparrós's recalls her when he is looking at the prostitutes in the windows of the red-light district in Amsterdam (64–5). The narrator's travelling experience was influenced by Natalia's story, to the extent that he is no longer able to look for sexual services as he used to. It is also surprising that a physical feature that shocks the narrator, the fact that Natalia only has one eye, is not something important in the report but becomes a symbolic element used to depict Natalia as character in the book. The narrator confesses another fact that goes untold in the report: Natalia asked him for money in order to relate her life story to him. If Natalia's life has been part of a business in which she has been the victim, then by exposing this fact the narrator gives narrative (and some economic) power to the marginal other. Natalia is the owner of her own story, able to negotiate the value of her words with the interviewer. In choosing to write about his own interactions with the informants, Caparrós generates another reading of their testimonies, one with a strong emotional impact.

The stories heard, recorded and transcribed first as isolated testimonies in an institutional and conventional report become the raw material for the author's travel palimpsest. This new product goes beyond the mere aim to be informative in order to show the story that unites all the other stories: the story of the researcher doing his fieldwork.

As in the case of Tomás Eloy Martínez, editing becomes the main narrative strategy employed by Caparrós to appropriate the voices of his informants. Caparrós resignifies the testimonies by describing the circumstances of the production of his research. Through the format of the book, the author is then able to offer an additional aesthetic dimension to what would otherwise have remained a handful of dramatic stories published in a conventional report. Furthermore, when the book leaves the realm of the personal birthday gift from a man to his friends and is published by Anagrama, one of the major publishing houses in the Spanish language today, the work unavoidably

---

[11] 'Natalia y yo estábamos sentados uno al lado del otro pero los dos mirábamos a Alexandrina, que traducía del moldavo al inglés, del inglés al moldavo. Acabo de pasarme cinco horas escuchando a una chica con un ojo de vidrio y una vida tan dura que su marido la entregó, embarazada de él, a un traficante – y todo el resto. Hay cosas que no se pueden escuchar impunemente' (28).

also becomes a commodity.[12] After all, this is the work of an author who is not used to not putting his name to his writing.

Juan Villoro's aftershock stories

On 6 March 2010, Villoro published 'El sabor de la muerte' (The taste of death) in the Argentinian newspaper *La Nación*, which he would later incorporate in a longer form to *El miedo*. The newspaper version was the first of Villoro's attempts to represent his life-changing experience through writing (see Figure 5.1).

As in the case of Caparrós's works, Villoro's first-published version of this text does not differ too much from the book's in content and style, but the differences are still highly significant in terms of genre, authorial intentions and reader expectations. Some parts of Juan Villoro's *El miedo* are also written in the style of a field journal. The self-referential narrator is also a writer, and he was not able to put down his pen and paper, even during the catastrophic days he recounts. Nor was this book originally thought of as a text to be published.

Analysing the process of editing allows us to better comprehend the author's conception of the journalistic and literary genres, since by making minimal changes – for example, adding or reducing phrases in paragraphs, changing elements of the structure and choosing what to highlight – Villoro demonstrates his awareness of the conventions of each field of production, even if it is only so that he may challenge them.

Of course, there is a political contrast in the two spaces of discourse. Whereas 'El sabor de la muerte' was published in a traditional, conservative newspaper in Argentina, it was a small, independent publishing house in Mexico, Almadía, that published *El miedo*. A different type of analysis will be necessary to compare the texts in terms of the ideology of their respective media and the influence that this might have had on the editing of the content. In general terms, there are no obvious marks of political censorship in the newspaper version. Nevertheless, I do consider that the contrast between the two different print media demonstrates the author's preferences for the book format over the mass media. It seems that, for contemporary chroniclers, the book is becoming a preferable alternative medium to express their own relationship to facts, and even to inform their audiences in a wider and more complex way of the realities around them.

Moreover, the conventions and the intentions of the publishing spaces and the genres of discourse they display are what modify the production of meaning regarding the events and their factual representation. The first narrative that Villoro had published on the earthquake can be read thus as a journalistic text, formally a *crónica*, although defined by the newspaper as *opinión*. On the contrary, the extended or unabridged version of the text included in *El miedo* cannot be considered a

---

[12] One of those friends to whom he gave the original publication of the book happened to be Jorge Herralde, founding director of Anagrama publishing house (see Interview 2).

Figure 5.1 Newspaper cover of Juan Villoro's 'El sabor de la muerte' (The taste of death). Buenos Aires: *La Nación*, 2010.

conventional *crónica*. Because it has been incorporated into the book, this second version has become another layer of Villoro's literary account of the earthquake. In order to narrate a collective experience of the event, *El miedo* therefore blends the first journalistic text with other registers, like the essays, testimonies and electronic text messages.

The newspaper text appeared on page 4 of *La Nación*, in the section for international news called '*Exterior*', and as part of the special reporting that the media was doing under the label of *Tragedia en Chile*. The dramatic tone employed to present the news is evident in this title, which alludes to suffering and pain by using the word 'tragedy'. This tone is also obvious in the topic of all the texts on the page. Two texts focus on the feelings of people affected by the earthquake: Villoro's 'opinion' piece and a reporter's interviews with Chilean marines whose families were in Chile. The other two international news items on the page cover the popular protests on the economic crisis in Greece – including a full-colour photograph of the police attacking citizens – and China's attempts to decrease social inequality.

The main section of the page, however, is formed by the two texts on the earthquake. The text of reporter Diana Salinas Plaza is the *nota principal*, since it is placed at the top of the page, illustrated with two big colour photographs. Nevertheless, Villoro's text has more words. Both texts focus on personal experiences, illustrated by photographs that also show people being affected by the accompanying stories. The testimonies of witnesses, therefore, are significant to the newspaper's coverage of the catastrophe.

The great difference between these texts is the mode of representation, which demonstrates the hierarchy of authorship. The newspaper reporter, Salinas Plaza, reproduces other people's testimonies as obtained through interviews. The veracity, or sense of truthfulness, which defines the journalistic value of her text, is based on the experiences recounted by others and not on her own opinions. This sense of truthfulness is also reinforced by style, because the text is published in a conventional documentary genre, that of news writing. Veracity is also strengthened by the photographs that illustrate the piece, which show the interviewed subjects and therefore reinforce the nature of the referent. Textual testimonies are more real because the subjects were recorded and photographed.

Conversely, Villoro's text is considered to be a journalistic narrative mainly because of his signature. The veracity – or verisimilitude, if we consider this a hybrid discourse between literature and journalism – depends on the author's own words, and his prestige as a *cronista*. He does not need to quote anyone else in order to validate his account, nor did the section editor have to add any photographic evidence. By publishing Villoro, *La Nación* demonstrates itself to be a space for the 'real', but also for high-quality writing.

There are other signs of the editors' intentions to highlight the value of the author, as distinct from how a reporter is usually presented. For example, under Villoro's signature, the phrase 'para *La Nación*' (for *La Nación*) is followed by the indication of place: 'SANTIAGO, Chile'. This makes it clear that the author has written the text specially for the newspaper, even if he is not on its regular payroll. It also shows that Villoro is acting as a correspondent. Sending the text from the place of the catastrophe adds more value and truthfulness to the work. Besides, while Salinas Plaza's text does not give any information about her, Villoro is advertised as an important witness.

Despite Villoro's prestige as a literary author and intellectual, his chronicle is a conventional, journalistic one. It responds to the reader's expectations of the genre since it is an individual account of the earthquake. Of course, in terms of style, his text is remarkably different from that of traditional news reporting and writing, but still, I maintain, he follows the conventions of the journalistic discourse, the overall aim of which is to offer news.

To begin the text with a numerical account of the facts – provided in just ten lines – is not solely a stylistic decision. This is a question of genre conventions, for in journalistic writing the first paragraph is expected to be an abstract of the text, and it must include the main facts. This famously described 'inverted-pyramid' structure serves to justify the newsworthy nature of the story. If by any chance Villoro was not aware of this, his editors certainly would have been. Villoro was, therefore, expected to narrate his own experience, although of course with a minimal reference to the, by then well-known, objective facts.

For the newspaper, Villoro's testimony is important because of the cultural value the author's name adds to its pages: the text deserves a wider space because he is a public intellectual who also happens to be at the site of the event at the 'right' moment. This is particularly relevant if one contrasts the longer version in the book, in which anecdotes provided by other people and interpretations or opinions of the earthquake are an important part of the text. The newspaper version, on the contrary, only focuses on his testimony. The journalistic text does not include references to the other people in the hotel, with whom Villoro experienced the earthquake, or their conversations. Yet these other testimonies are a central part of the author's narrative in *El miedo*. The testimonies represent the catastrophe as an apocalyptic experience – and not only for one individual. The newspaper version also ignores details of Villoro's anecdotes about the airlines, which are told in the book in a tone that is critical of the Mexican government and the globalized economy. Additionally, in the book, Villoro remembers the 1985 earthquake in Mexico and offers many references that he draws from his own national culture.

The text in *La Nación* focuses on Villoro's detailed, sensory description of the first minutes following the catastrophe, as well as on his broad brush strokes depicting the devastated city. For example, the headline 'El sabor de la muerte' (The taste of death) and the subheadline 'Pillaje y rating' (Sacking and rating) provide a more impressionistic depiction of the facts, unlike the reflective tone of the book.

The extracts from the text that are highlighted in the page design, marked with a change in typography, also show the media's intention to highlight the most dramatic side of the text: 'When the movement stopped, there was a feeling of unreality. I stood up. It was not normal to be alive' / 'Our life had stopped and we did not know when our afterlife would begin. We were in limbo'.[13] The emphasis on the self and his direct

---

[13] 'Cuando el movimiento cesó, sobrevino una sensación de irrealidad. Me puse de pie. No era normal estar vivo' / 'Nuestra vida se había detenido y no sabíamos cuándo comenzaría nuestra sobrevida. Estábamos en el limbo' (idem).

proximity to death is evident here as a discursive technique to catch the attention of the reader, and also to make the narrative a newsworthy one. Within the limited space and genre constraints of the newspaper, Villoro nevertheless manages to hold a critical position regarding the representation of the catastrophe in the media:

> Rumours replaced news. A town that feared an invasion by other town was mentioned. The fragmented story of the media was showing quarrels of tribes and it was repeating a governor's statement asking the army to use their weapons.[14]

Although this passage can be found in the book almost verbatim, the meaning cannot be the same, since it is presented within another discursive context, framed by a more complex representation of the facts. It is surprising to find this critical statement published in an outlet of the mass media that simultaneously acts just as Villoro describes. However, the critique here may be considered light, if one compares the book version, which has a few additional and more critical comments (highlighted in bold by myself):

> Rumours replaced news. **There was talk** about a town that feared an invasion by another town, **with which it had an ancestral rivalry. The vigilance of the ONEMI, the organisation of the army that must give alerts in the case of a tsunami, and that confused the tidal signal with the lighter of rough water, was questioned.** . . . The fragmented story of the media was showing quarrels of tribes.[15]

In a style reminiscent of the *modernista* chronicle for its use of intertextuality, Villoro ends his newspaper text with a reference to Neruda's poetry. Of course, in the book version the dialogue with the poet is more significant, for three of Neruda's poems are quoted as epigraphs: 'Oda a la tormenta' (Ode to the storm), 'Oda al edificio' (Ode to the building) and 'Entrada a la madera' (Entrance to the wood).

One of the main differences between the newspaper text and the book is that in the latter format the author uses intertextuality to mediate the representation of his personal experience. Multiple voices are present in the book, through direct and indirect references to poems, novels, mobile text messages, blog entries, emails, mass media narratives, the author's own writing and his recollections of conversations. Villoro's references to others' texts demonstrate the highly intellectualized testimony of the narrator, but also allows the author to reconstruct reality from multiple perspectives, demonstrating that reality is more complex than the version constructed by the media.

---

[14] 'Los rumores sustituyeron a las noticias. Se mencionó a un pueblo que temía ser invadido por otro. El relato fragmentario de los medios mostraba rencillas de tribus y repetía las declaraciones de una gobernadora que pedía que el ejército usara sus armas' (idem).
[15] 'Los rumores sustituyeron a las noticias. **Se habló de** un pueblo que temía ser invadido por otro, **con el que tenía rivalidad ancestral. Se cuestionó la vigilancia de la ONEMI, la organización de la armada que debe dar alerta en casos de tsunami y que confundió la señal de maremoto con la más leve de marejada.** . . . El relato fragmentario de los medios mostraba rencillas de tribus' (2010a: 73).

On another level, some chapters recall John Hersey's *Hiroshima*.[16] Like Hersey, Villoro narrates the catastrophe as experienced by some of its victims, focusing on their memories, both before and after the event. Villoro also focuses on the victims' experiences, but a narrative of a catastrophe lived under different conditions inevitably has to be aware of changes in modes of representation. Unlike Hersey, who focused on the pain of the victims, with detailed descriptions of the experienced horror, Villoro constructs a narrative in which the narrator and his characters are conscious of their privileges, so that the joy of being alive somehow emerges:

> On the same day, February 27, Antonio Skármeta and Esteban Cabezas came to the hotel to make sure we did not need anything. Other colleagues sent text messages offering dishes, sea food and wines. We felt like we were on a revised version of the Titanic: we were adrift, but the service was splendid.[17]

This rather humoristic and ironic tone marks a distance from the experience itself but also from the traditional chronicle. The narrator compares his experience with other famous catastrophes, but also with fictional scenarios. He shows that an earthquake in the twenty-first century cannot be perceived, or narrated, as if it were the same as other catastrophes in the past. The true story of this earthquake, although dramatic in its own way, was experienced from a hotel, and the narrator was using technology that connected him to the rest of the world.

In contrast with the experience of the 1985 earthquake in Mexico, in which thousands of people died, the 2010 earthquake in Chile is, for the author, if not a happier memory, at least a less painful one. While chroniclers of the 1985 earthquake, such as Elena Poniatowska and Carlos Monsiváis, centred their narratives on their observations of devastated streets and buildings and on interviews with the victims, Juan Villoro concentrates on isolated non-places, such as the hotel or airport. He also relies on the testimonies of others, particularly those from his own community of artists and intellectuals.

The impossibility of getting out of this nightmarish, post-apocalyptic scenario is also compared with being a character in *Lost*, an American television series that narrates how the survivors of an airplane accident must wait on an island to be rescued (68). Besides the references to contemporary popular culture, references to canonical literature are mixed with those to other, less well-known titles, such as a novel by German author Heinrich von Kleist, translated as *El terremoto en Chile* (The Earthquake in Chile, 1808). This intertext is explored by Villoro in a rather academic style, as if by analysing others' writing on earthquakes, he could illuminate his own insights on the

---

[16] Hersey's book also influenced texts by Carlos Monsiváis and Tomás Eloy Martínez.
[17] 'El mismo 27 de febrero, Antonio Skármeta y Esteban Cabezas se presentaron en el hotel para cerciorarse de que no nos faltara nada. Otros colegas mandaron mensajes de texto ofreciendo platillos, mariscos y vinos. Nos sentimos en una versión revisada del Titanic: estábamos a la deriva, pero la atención era espléndida' (2010a: 72).

matter. Nevertheless, for Villoro's purposes, the only possible comparison to his task of narrating the experience of the Chilean earthquake is the experience of being in a reality show:

> The cancellation of flights and the occasional failure of telephone, Internet, electricity and water services were the visible signals of the catastrophe in Santiago. It was like being in a reality show: our life was similar to the controlled reality of a television studio; on the contrary, what was outside turned out to be terrible and almost fictitious: the cameras depicted a savage reality in the South of Chile.[18]

From the narrator's perspective, the real earthquake cannot be found in his account, nor in those of his friends, but it is also not to be found in the testimonies shown by the news. The others' experiences, as represented by the media, are fictional because they present an extreme reality (75). In comparison to that one, the privileged experience of Villoro and his friends in the hotel seems as unreal as a reality show can be: an in-between space in which reality and fiction meet.

In the book, Villoro acts as a reporter, offering information from all kinds of sources and representing a collective experience from multiple perspectives. Ironically, in the newspaper version, Villoro is introduced as a literary author. Yet clearly, the book format offers him a richer space to tell his story.

The literariness of *El miedo* thus is not based on its fictional elements, but on the interpretation of real-life experiences through the use of stylistic devices and the incorporation of different genres. Following Hutcheon's differentiation between *event* (a historically situated phenomenon) and *facts* (those events that have been chosen to be included in a narrative), Villoro's narratives on the 2010 earthquake in Chile can be read as two facts concerning the same event, or two diverse forms that each give meaning to individual and collective experience.[19]

El miedo is thus a palimpsest that includes the newspaper chronicle as one of the diverse discourses through which Villoro expresses his real-life experience. Whereas for media purposes – that is, for an immediate account of the catastrophe – Villoro-as-journalist published a testimonial and informative text as soon as possible, Villoro-as-literary-writer needed more time, and space, to translate the experience into multiple layers of meaning. Only through a hybrid discourse, a meta documentary narrative, is the author able to assimilate experience, understand events and transform this into knowledge.

---

[18] 'La suspensión de vuelos y la ocasional falta de teléfonos, Internet, suministro de electricidad y agua fueron las señas visibles de la catástrofe en Santiago. Era como estar en un reality show: nuestra vida se asemejaba a la realidad controlada de un estudio de televisión; en cambio, lo que estaba afuera resultaba temible y casi ficticio: las cámaras retrataban una realidad salvaje al sur de Chile' (74–5).

[19] For Hutcheon, 'neither form of representation can separate "facts" from the acts of interpretation and narration that constitute them, for facts (though not events) are created in and by those acts' (1989: 72).

Approaching strangers: A dialogic method

As I have demonstrated so far, Caparrós's *Una luna* and Villoro's *El miedo* both display the problem of genre hybridity, as well as the authorial struggle with reader expectations. It seems, also, that the representation of reality becomes a more complex question when the narrator is depicted in a foreign environment or unexpected situation. These selected works, therefore, are exemplary of the responses of contemporary Latin American authors to both questions of storytelling and documentation.

In order to complement the textual analysis with the authors' own conceptualization of their working process and documentary intentionality, I interviewed Caparrós and Villoro. What follows is an interpretation of my conversation with them, through which I compare their responses and connect them with my own research objectives.[20]

Responding to similar questions on their research methods and writing processes, both authors showed an awareness of the differences in the production of non-fictional work in comparison with fiction writing, although they focused on different aspects of the process. Villoro's responses focused more on the post-research process, particularly on selecting and editing the raw material and on matters of self-representation. Caparrós commented more on fieldwork, especially in response to questions regarding the social and political relevance of the topic chosen and the ethics of the representation of otherness.

Both agree on the idea that *crónica* is quite a well-defined genre, one whose value resides mainly in its ethics more than its aesthetics: there is an awareness of a certain responsibility or commitment to telling the truth to their readers, or at least to relate what they have witnessed or empirically interpreted from their own investigation. There is, nevertheless, a clear contrast in the conceptualization of their individual work as chroniclers. For Villoro, the creative element of the process of writing seems to be more relevant, whereas Caparrós is primarily moved by ideological motivations. Whereas Villoro is located towards the more moderate left wing of politics, Caparrós constantly refers to his writing as political and has made clear his commitment to left-wing thought: 'I believe in that, a chronicle that I care about has to be political, in different ways: in its form and possibly also in the issues it deals with' (interview 2). On the contrary, Villoro's chronicles are usually based on his own reflections rather than on exhaustive, ethnographically inspired research.

The authors share important concerns relating to the problem of finding a balance between telling a story and imparting information. During the interviews, they both constantly highlighted these concerns through descriptions of their own process of research or writing, through personal anecdotes, or with examples from their literary and journalistic references.

What I found most striking, however, were their responses on the use of the first person, because they demonstrate a rather prescriptive concept of *crónica*. According

---

[20] For full transcripts, see the appendix. All following quotes referring to my interview with Caparrós are from Interview 2 and those referring to Villoro's are from Interview 7.

to them, this genre denies or devalues the role of the journalist as protagonist of the chronicle. Ironically, this idea clearly contrasts with their own writing, as I have demonstrated, because they do create a metafictional narrator with a strong authoritative voice. Furthermore, most of the time this narrator has a determinant presence in the story, beyond his mere role as a witness or observer.

The intention to document facts enters into conflict with questions of self-representation, as both authors constantly observe, since the mere definition of *crónica* depends on a pact of credibility with the reader. Therefore, whether to include or exclude the 'I' does matter ethically, and it seems to be an unsolved problem in their writing, especially for Villoro. It is interesting that while Villoro directly disagrees with the use of the chronicler as protagonist, he usually employs the first person in his own *crónicas*, as we have seen in this chapter. During our interview, Villoro expressed on two different occasions his dislike for the personal, narcissistic type of chronicle, in which the protagonist is the chronicler himself:

> There are chroniclers of high narcissism who consider themselves to be more important than the news and sometimes these are people with such a colorful personality that you appreciate that they are in the foreground, but in general I distrust this procedure and I think it is better for one to accompany the facts. Of course, I am very present, especially in metaphors, in comparisons, in quotations, that is, in the way things are told. I think I do have a very personal style, but not so much regarding interpretation, [it is not like] I do things, I open a door, I find a treasure. (Interview 8)

In contrast, Caparrós does recognize his active role in the stories, although it has to be thoroughly justified: 'It is weird when I am not there, I don't remember, probably when my participation does not add anything. If someone is telling his story, he is telling it by himself; on the contrary, sometimes a story does not progress if the interpellation is not there' (Interview 2).

Additionally, there is an unstable treatment of the *testimonio* as an inevitable part of a documentary discourse, for credibility is also based on the ability of the chronicler to display a multiplicity of discourses. However, displaying a variety of voices in the text is a great challenge for the writer, because the misuse of the technique can pose a risk to the narrative. The words of others are in constant negotiation with the author's. Beyond the theoretical implications that testimony as a genre presents, this is also a practical matter, embedded in the materiality of the information, as Caparrós demonstrates when discussing editing:

> when I am in a situation I am editing. When I am listening to someone, I see what phrase serves [a purpose], what does not. In general, it allows me to understand what things I need, what things I am missing – what I have can come from just before or after what I am getting at that time. Of course, then, when I finally sit down, new things appear, relationships appear that I had not seen before and so on. (Interview 2)

The chronicler-as-editor is then as essential to the plot as his informants are. Against the idea of imagining the chronicler as an insatiable explorer, explains Caparrós, he likes to acknowledge that sometimes the chronicler is bored, desperate or mad. There is thus an intention to create a narrator who can be closer in experience to any other contemporary traveller and to whom otherness will not be a preconceived, sometimes idealistic, reality but a subjectively perceived one.

As in other first-person genres, there is a narcissistic dimension that must be acknowledged in documentary narratives, as derived from a conscious, creative writing process. The use of the first person in documentary narratives is nevertheless particularly problematic in terms of ethics, as the concerns of the authors interviewed demonstrate. Both Villoro and Caparrós consider self-representation in *crónica* to be valid only when the story somehow justifies the strong presence of the chronicler as witness. This justification, however, is ultimately an authorial decision that can only be legitimized by means of language. If the chronicler wants to be part of the plot, he has to convince, to impose his view on the reader, by deploying all his literary ability.

The 'being there' strategy, which depicts the chronicler as a traveller doing fieldwork and then reporting faithfully on his findings, actually influences not only the interpretation of facts but also the plot. Similar to the conscious process of framing or setting the scene, there is also a clear self-consciousness regarding the creative process involved in representing the self and others. Indeed, Caparrós uses the concept of character to refer to his informants: 'In their life they will be anything, but in my book, they are characters' (Interview 2). Similarly, Villoro expresses his process of selecting informants as an artistic task:

> A chronicle must seem like something concrete, it should not seem like a piece of interrupted life, but it must have a symbolic unity and it is often complex to find this symbolic unity. Then you have to look for a secondary character that appears at the beginning of the chronicle and contributes to the outcome. You have to look for some emotional gesture that gives you a sense of closure. (Interview 8)

It is interesting to note that both authors refer to their informants as literary characters and to the chronicler's task of interviewing them as a performative act. For they are aware of the important role that empathy plays in their interaction with the interviewees; artifice becomes inevitable in order to obtain information. The chronicler, according to Villoro, is like an actor whose preparation is sometimes more interesting than the topic of the chronicle itself to read about. Similarly, Caparrós reflects on his investigative techniques, showing his awareness of the task of a professional listener:

> One of the weird things that always happens to me and I am glad, and I don't know why they happen, is that people feel like telling me things; it is a privilege. Maybe because I know how to show them that I am listening to them, maybe I learned to show that I listen, to make the right comment at a certain time that makes the other feel somehow understood and then want to go on. (Interview 2)

Listening is actually a highly valued skill in chroniclers, although the dialogue is still difficult for a self that is almost never similar to the other, and when there are mutual prejudices interfering with communication. Caparrós's self-referenced narrator usually depicts these uneasy dialogic situations. Independently of the authors' intentions to consider themselves professional listeners, within the narrative the scenes in which the journalist narrates his dialogues with the informants is a resource of verisimilitude that functions as legal protection for both social actors. Through storytelling, therefore, the journalist publicly depicts himself as a witness, and his act of listening becomes part of the evidence that the event narrated really happened.

In his responses, Caparrós displayed the assumption that he had mastered this ability, and his references to the importance of his role as listener emerged several times in our conversation. However, when he relates the act of listening to that of editing, he frames his experience of encountering the other, choosing the informant and his words only for what they can offer his authorial interests.

Another aspect of performativity is then also shown in the dialogue, which is an essential source of information. Caparrós's empirical reflections on fieldwork demonstrate the collective dimension of the chronicle as a product constructed by the self and the other in dialogue. This dialogue is never an equal one, and even the memory of it cannot be preserved from unintentional bias. In this regard, it is particularly interesting that Caparrós decided to explain the complexity of interpreting others' reality with an anecdote:

> Thinking of something that had to be in the book of *El hambre*, a lady in Niger told me how she made a millet ball, which is what they eat every day. She was the first one to tell me how she made that ball, and I said, 'and do you eat that every day?', from the perspective of this Western myth of food diversity, and she says 'yes, whenever we can', talking from that other side. (Interview 2)

This encounter might have been particularly meaningful for the author, since the scene is first referred to in *Contra el cambio* (Against Change, 2010) but represented in detail as the starting point of *El hambre* (Hunger, 2014: 9).[21] The recurring scenes of the encounter between the journalist and his informants, in the texts and during interview, opens a debate on the limits of the dialogue as a tool for approaching otherness. Although Caparrós tries to be empathetic and to adapt himself to any situation, this is not possible all the time. However, the author perceives himself as a mediator, someone who comes from an in-between region. This position, a consequence of coming from a *mestizo* culture, he said, allows him to approach many problems more intimately. Nevertheless, the encounter is not always equal: because of his appearance he is sometimes considered to be a typical European or American white man, and that affects the first impression of the other towards him.

---

[21] This is the only work by Caparrós published in English so far; translated by Katherine Silver in 2017 and distributed by Penguin Random House.

In these narratives, the other enters the text not as a protagonist but as a secondary character. This is, I suspect, because in contemporary metadocumentary narratives, the centre of the story is the theme. The voices of others are no longer the element that leads the story, as in *testimonio* literature. These voices have become a malleable piece of information that can be cut, edited and modified in order to serve the authors' purposes. This shift from the individual testimony focus to an almost scientific aim to analyse reality configures, if not a new other, at least a new representation of otherness. This might explain why the authors prefer to call their informants characters rather than *personas*.

For Caparrós, today's *crónica* must have a sharper focus on problems that transcend the context of individual life stories, which has traditionally been the focus of *testimonio* narratives. This new focus offers the possibility of moving beyond what he pejoratively calls '*crónica caniche*' (poodle chronicle). Caparrós then criticizes the recent boom in a sensationalist and frivolous type of chronicle. Caparrós's critique of a more commercial type of chronicle is somewhat striking as he is obviously aware of the need within the genre to attract the attention of editors and readers, at least when it is written with a view to be sold, whereas this is in a popular magazine or in a book. When I asked him about what he considers a successful or useful interview to be, for example, he declared that it has to do with finding words that are worthy of being quoted. As in the case of Poniatowska, Monsiváis and Martínez, Villoro and Caparrós perform a leading position in the Latin American cultural field, especially one gained through publishing *crónicas*. This privileged position offers them the moral authority to be mediators between the state and *el pueblo*, and to define what is worthy of being publicly exposed about those not-so-visible others, who trust their life stories to them. Of course, the other's truth-telling, in the case of documentary narratives, is usually a free act of trust, a desire for narration that he or she shares with the journalist listener, in contrast to a compulsory confession to a judge, a priest or a medical doctor. However, there is still a degree of power, in the sense that Foucault used the term, held over the informants when they have not the same political accountability or authority as the journalist-narrator does, as in the case of Caparrós's testimonies, gathered originally when he worked as a UN reporter. Based on Foucault's questioning of truth-telling as a 'truthful' enterprise, Butler considers it to be the case that when a subject tells the truth, they are not only communicating that truth, nor are they only bringing the weight of their power over others, but they are also conveying what is true for the self: 'my speaking is also a kind of doing, an action that takes place within the field of power that also constitutes an act of power' (2005: 125).

Travelling nevertheless remains necessary for Caparrós and Villoro to consolidate the credibility pact with the reader and to bring a certain sense of legitimacy to their work as documentarists. 'Being there' becomes another rhetorical strategy, and so does the representation of the self as an observer. This might explain why there is a contradiction between the authors' intentions to write from the perspective of mere observers of others' lives and their active role as narrators. Villoro, for instance, considers the role of the chronicler to be one which offers an interpretation of the testimonies, and therefore the author must be aware of the risks of reproducing too many testimonies: 'The overabundance of testimonies could lead to an absence of the most important thing, which is the interpretation of the testimonies, because literature gives you not only data about reality but the emotional meaning of reality' (Interview 8). According to Villoro, the difference between a testimonial-like text and a discourse which seeks appreciation because of its 'literary' quality and its knowledge is based on the interpretative task of the author, rather than on the stories of others. Based on Caparrós's and Villoro's documentary narratives, it does seem that in times where readers are overwhelmed by data, with testimonies and news published every minute by mass media everywhere, chroniclers are still looking for narratives that can help make sense of the contemporary world.

If the contemporary chronicler is moved by *'problemas'* and not by *'situaciones o historias'* (events, stories), then he would be proposing an alternative kind of literary journalism which is not based on news, and that could be researched using the methods of a social scientist, thus resembling something like an academic research project. These narratives would also be different from testimonial literature, since individual life stories are no longer at the centre. The selection of the informants, who will be transformed into characters, is no longer based on an individual's heroic or distinguished features, but on their suitability to represent certain social groups affected by specific global or local problems. This explains why Caparrós is able to say that his motivation for travelling to a remote and small town is because that is the most obvious environment in which he can find out more about the problem of hunger in the world. The physical displacement of contemporary chroniclers in search of encounters with otherness, therefore, is much more conditioned by the identification of evidence that supports their own thesis, and much less by the potential for adventure or fantastic discoveries, which motivated the old *cronistas de Indias*. Nonetheless, I don't consider this change in their thematic interests or research methods to be a sign that the authors are always moving beyond a documentary intention, or beyond the *crónica*. Rather I take it as a sign of their aim to differentiate themselves from common newspaper reporters, while at the same time, they claim to be part of a Spanish American literary tradition that goes back to colonial times and that in Latin America has been much more prestigious than the journalistic one. Innovation is an important value for contemporary documentary authors who wish to stand out against an excessive data flow within the media. Their search for novelty in form and in content might be driven by their own artistic aspirations and evolution as authors, from a medieval or *modernista* chronicle style to more postmodern or baroque trends, but also by the commercial objectives of the platforms and markets across which their work is disseminated and valued. One must not forget that documentary narratives are also, and sometimes essentially, information as a commodity, crafted for and circulating in a globalized, cosmopolitan market. In any case, metadocumentary narratives, such as the ones analysed in this chapter, reveal to what extent the reflexivity of the self is provoked by another and how. For the act of storytelling is a collective practice in which the informants' stories as told to the journalists, the journalists' own reappropriation of these stories, and even my own story in this book, compiled after reading and listening to their stories, are endlessly intertwined. Self-reflection, as Butler notes, is not always reached in a rational way, but as a result of an external demand or imposition. In the case of documentary narratives based on journalistic interviews, it is my view that sharing an account of oneself becomes a 'form of seduction' (Butler 2005: 125). It is this particular form of incitement to truth-telling that I address in the next chapter, by examining the encounters between the self and others depicted by a younger generation of authors.

6

Being there

In one of the final scenes of Cristian Alarcón's *Cuando me muera quiero que me toquen cumbia. Vidas de pibes chorros* (2003),[1] the journalist is in a poor neighbourhood of Buenos Aires, visiting Sabina, one of his sources, when a shooting occurs. The male neighbours take their guns and run out to the street, encouraged by the women to defend their *villa*. Crouching behind the curtains, spying from the window, the journalist observes that, except for a child, he is the only one who remains in the house, 'hiding like a sissy'.[2]

There is a double notion of 'field' in this image of the journalist at work. Alarcón's self-representation in this scene illustrates the medial position of the documentary author across two fields in which the 'other' is encountered. First, there is the physical space of the encounter with the informant, whose background differs from that of the narrator. Alarcón marks this difference, and thus his outsider position, by representing a surprised narrator – hiding, cowardly – while his source experiences the shooting as an almost natural event. Second, there is the imaginary space of writing, in which the encounter with the reader takes place. The author is writing for an ideal reader. This ideal reader, it can be assumed, is from a much more privileged social background: closer to the journalist's own than to that of his informant. The exhibition of the journalist's feeling of fear or insecurity in such environments is a narrative technique used to form a connection with the reader on an emotional level. As neither the author nor the reader belongs to the informant's context, the reader would hardly be in a position to experience for himself a scenario like the one he reads about. Therefore, the narrator acts as a mediator between both 'others': the informant and the reader.

According to the authors analysed in this chapter, one of the most exciting things about journalistic investigation is the possibility of getting out of one's comfort zone in order to meet people and to be in places that one would not usually experience, as Cristian Alarcón expressed in our interview: 'I love the idea of going in and out of that particular world, I love the idea of not staying imprisoned in my own world.' (Interview 1)

Towards the end of the twentieth century and the beginning of the twenty-first, there has been a trend among Latin American testimonial authors to narrate the

---

[1] Translated as *Dance for me when I die* (2019), this is currently the only work of Alarcón's available in English. The translated quotations from this book, however, are here my own translations.
[2] 'Amariconadamente escondido' (112).

stories of others, emphasizing the subjective perspective of the journalist as a first-person narrator. This trend might be seen as dated in comparison with other, similar narrative practices around the world, particularly in the United States. For example, while American New Journalism has its basis in the subjective perspective and representation of the journalist as a character (Wolfe 1973), the use of the first person still causes polemical debates in Latin American literary journalism.[3]

In this chapter, I explore the conditions that make the use of metafiction possible, or even necessary, as a recurrent narrative technique used by the latest generation of Latin American authors who are working on testimonial-based stories. In order to do so, I analyse four books published in the 2000s that are based on true stories of violence and mourning from Latin America: *Cuando me muera quiero que me toquen cumbia* (2003) by Cristian Alarcón (La Unión, Chile, 1975),[4] *Los suicidas del fin del mundo. Crónica de un pueblo patagónico* (The suicidal ones at the end of the world. Chronicle of a Patagonian Town, 2005)[5] by Leila Guerriero (Junín, Argentina, 1967), *La cuarta espada. La historia de Abimael Guzmán y Sendero Luminoso* (The Fourth Sword. The Story of Abimael Guzmán and The Shining Path, 2007)[6] by Santiago Roncagliolo

---

[3] A reading of reflections on *crónica* by the most popular authors of the genre today gives us an idea of the importance that the discussion surrounding the first-person narrator has in the Latin American journalistic field. See Jaramillo Agudelo (2011) and Angulo Egea (2014).

[4] *Cuando me muera* tells the story of Víctor Manuel 'El Frente Vital', a thief who became an urban legend after being killed by the police in 1999, at the age of seventeen. It is set in a shantytown (*villa miseria*) on the outskirts of Buenos Aires, in which the narrator – a journalist also living in the Argentinian capital – becomes immersed in order to interview friends and family of the victim. It is the result of three years of journalistic investigation, and for it Alarcón won the Samuel Chavkin Prize for Integrity in Latin American Journalism, awarded by the North American Congress. The book is considered by the Latin American journalistic scene to be an example of *crónica* or non-fiction narrative, but it has barely been studied by literary critics. Carmen Perilli (2010) considers the book to be a novel and relates its style to the format of traditional realism and melodrama, as well as to what Jean Franco (2013) has called 'globalized *costumbrismo*'.

[5] *Los suicidas* is about young people who committed suicide between 1997 and 1999 in Las Heras, a small town in Patagonia. The first-person narrator, Leila Guerriero, tries to uncover reasons for the wave of suicides by staying in the town for a while and talking with its inhabitants. Although the narrator is not able to solve the case, the book shows the complex and depressing environment of a province that is some distance from the capital city, and in which young people have no hope for the future. Guerriero was originally working on this story to publish it as a report in the Argentinian edition of *Rolling Stone*. When the magazine ran out of money to support her investigation, she decided to continue it as a personal project, which eventually became her first book (see Interview 5).

[6] *La cuarta espada* is a lengthy profile of Abimael Guzmán, a former philosophy lecturer at Universidad de Huamanga, in Ayacucho, who became the leader of the subversive terrorist organization, Partido Comunista del Perú, also known as Sendero Luminoso (Shining Path). The group, which began its operations in rural areas of the country, claimed to be inspired by Marxist-Leninist-Maoist ideology, and was one of the players in the armed struggle conducted in Peru between 1980 and 2000. According to the Comisión de la Verdad y Reconciliación, 69,280 people died during this period, which is thought to be the longest and most violent one in the history of Perú. *La cuarta espada* can be read as a continuation of Roncagliolo's interest in this time, which began with the writing of *Abril rojo*. Roncagliolo interviews the family, friends and enemies of Guzmán, most notably Elena Ipanaguirre, aka Camarada Miriam, Guzmán's long-term partner, and an important member of the movement. Roncagliolo reconstructs the life of Guzmán, giving details of his childhood, relationships and education. As he narrates the process of the investigation, coming back to his country as a correspondent for a foreign newspaper, Roncagliolo also remembers his personal experience, growing up in the middle of a civil war he could not understand. The author's

(Lima, 1975) and *La vida doble* (2010)[7] by Arturo Fontaine Talavera (Santiago de Chile, 1952). The works by Fontaine and Rocangliolo are set in the context of civil and state violence during oppressive regimes in Chile and Perú in the 1970s and 1980s, whereas the others concern young, marginalized people in the context of the Argentinian crisis of the 1990s. Except for Arturo Fontaine's *La vida doble*, which has been explicitly described as a novel, all texts considered for this analysis are difficult to define under a fixed category, and thus I will refer to them as metadocumentary narratives.

It was my hypothesis in critically approaching the selected works that self-referentiality and other metafictional devices were a consciously crafted rhetorical strategy used by the authors to strengthen their relationship with fiction, to go beyond the realm of the factual and to insert themselves into a more 'literary', and thus prestigious, genealogy of storytellers. However, my interviews with them gave me another experience to take into consideration in this meta-analysis on investigative procedures, since the methodological phenomenon itself revealed other complex dimensions that are embedded in the interview as a confessional genre, that is, 'as a way of making the self appear for another' (Butler 2005: 113). It follows that any account of oneself is always addressed to another and thus neither their informants' accounts nor their own accounts can avoid the two-way bias provoked by the listener who is involved in the telling of their story.

Based on her own interpretation of Foucault's accounts in interviews, Butler states that the truth-teller is inevitably influenced by the communicative situation in which he feels compelled to give his account, whether this be a confession to a priest, a judge, a journalist or any person with their own agenda of research interests. His confession is a reaction to the presuppositions of a specific interlocutor, who in this case was a female doctoral student of Spanish literature, coming from Cambridge to ask them

---

research for this book started while he was working on the journalistic piece 'La cuarta espada del comunismo' (The Fourth Sword of Communism, 2005). This text gives a general overview of the personal and political life of Guzmán, and it was published in Madrid in *El País* newspaper on 11 October 2005, just after Guzmán's third trial had begun. *La cuarta espada* has been read as a biography, *crónica* and novel. Although it has not drawn very much academic attention, the book was a bestseller and caused polemical reactions in the media.

[7] The work was translated into English by Megan McDowell, appearing under the title *La vida doble: A novel*, and published by Yale University Press. It narrates the life of Irene/Lorena, a former French teacher who gets involved with a left-wing political group during Augusto Pinochet's dictatorship in Chile. After being tortured by the police, she becomes a secret agent of the government, and has to infiltrate her former group, betraying her friends. The novel is written from the perspective of the victim, who is telling her life story to a writer while in exile in Stockholm. The period of the narrative oscillates between the time of the dictatorship, when Lorena remembers her time as a guerrilla in Chile and Cuba, and her peaceful, everyday life as an old woman in Sweden. There, she had adopted a new identity; not even her daughter knew about her past. Fontaine based his protagonist on the life stories of the real ex-militants Luz Arce, Marcia Alejandra Merino and Carmen Castillo, who had already published their own testimonial books. The author said he had had long conversations with one of them, and with former secret agents, whose identities he has kept anonymous (see Interview 3). The author also obtained information from testimonies and documents made public by the Comisión Nacional de Verdad y Reconciliación, established in 1990 to investigate the crimes committed under Pinochet's dictatorship. In 2011, the novel was awarded the Premio Las Américas in Puerto Rico and Premio José Nuez in Chile. Although it has not been fully analysed in academic journals, it was largely and positively reviewed in media outlets.

specific questions about their work as journalists and authors. I interviewed them to be able to compare their declared documentary intentions with their investigative and creative production, but in doing so, I was able to reverse their role in an interview, from listeners to speakers. Although in their works they represent themselves as empathetic listeners to other's testimonies, it was out of a performative, social situation that their account of themselves (concerning other accounts of other selves) was possible. Therefore, their self-critique should be considered within the limits of the concrete public performance, which in fact conforms to the only context possible for self-examination as noted by Butler, and not as a straightforward, unquestionable account of who they are when outside this situation.

The interview phenomenon highlights another problem regarding textual representations of the self. If the account of oneself is only possible as a response to the other, who demands it and listens to the self, then there is a relationship of power between the social actors involved, in which truth-telling comes at a cost (Butler 2005, Foucault 2012). Although I agree there is an unequal position of power between the interviewee and the interviewer, I think this is much more evident in acts of confession involving a subject who is legally or spiritually obligated to give his account. If all forms of questioning imply a sense of responsibility and care towards the other, as Butler concludes, following Levinas, it is my view that in the case of the journalistic interview, and more subtly in the psychoanalytical one, the accountable self offers his unique story as a free act of trust and love to the listener, who subsequently is able to reverse his role, to share his own story, even if both accounts are fragmented and heterogenous. According to Adriana Cavarero's theory of the 'narratable self' (2000), the relational nature of the storytelling act inevitably passes through a phase of seduction and it is based on a mutual desire for narration that may go beyond genre and sociohistorical conventions. Through telling his life story as he pleases to other who cares to hear it, the self seeks an ideal unity, that is impossible to achieve outside the narrative realm.

As performative acts in the constant reshaping and renegotiation of power and desire, both self-identity and genre are intertwined, for there is no way to get to know the self outside a communicative, performative relationship with the other, and this relationship is always shaped by genre conventions. In what follows, I explore metadocumentary narratives as performative acts, focusing on scenes of verbal and embodied 'truthful' accounts given by the self and others in interaction. I follow Butler and Foucault's studies on confession and truth-telling in order to demonstrate the implications of self-representation in storytelling.

Who are you?

Exhausted after telling her life story, Lorena shouts desperately at her interlocutor, the self-referenced narrator of Fontaine's *La vida doble*: 'Stop, ok? Let's leave this here. I don't want to go on. It is too much. I don't like your inquisitive look, I don't like the corners of your mouth, there is a hint of obscenity there. I feel that I humiliate myself and get dirty when I confide in you. It is useless. You don't understand anything.

You never could.'[8] Before sitting down to write, Fontaine did archival research and interviewed women in exile who were victims of government violence during Augusto Pinochet's dictatorship in Chile. Instead of a journalistic book, he decided to use the information he had gathered to write a novel. In his opinion, there was no way other than fiction to make sense of the stories of the victims: 'the conversation stimulated my imagination a lot, because there were thousands of things that could not be resolved in that conversation' (Interview 3). The conversation was the author's way of approaching the source in order to understand her suffering. Nevertheless, it is precisely through this conversation that he realizes the impossibility of such a task. The information gathered from testimonies is not enough to help the writer tell the story he had imagined.

In the work of documentary writers, there is a risk of failure, or disruption, in their communication with others. This is particularly evident in situations in which the interviewee has suffered traumatic experiences that the listener cannot totally relate to. Peter Berger and Thomas Luckman (1967) describe it as 'unsuccessful socialization', that is, a discrepancy between identity and the representation of objective reality. The absence of a shared objective reality, according to Berger and Luckman, is common in societies in which the role of each individual is not clear. This may explain why, at least in Latin America, violence – rather than dialogue – is a more common response when the diverse realities of each individual are confronted.

Lorena's character in the novel *La vida doble* is an outstanding literary reflection on the loss of social roles in a broken society. Although Fontaine and his interviewees belong to the same generation of Chileans citizens, their lives under Pinochet's regime were so different that they cannot share the same idea of reality. It is understandable, thus, that in violent contexts the encounter between self and other may cause a disturbance in each individual's sense of reality, as is depicted in the dialogues between the narrator and Lorena in Fontaine's novel. Yet it is dialogue that is the essential condition for documentary narratives to exist, as their authors' main purpose is getting to know another. It is my view that while studying this kind of work, rather than focusing on narrative and investigation techniques only, a deeper connection with ethics should be explored by relating literary and 'documentary' representations of the selves involved in the stories to contemporary phenomenological and political thinking. As hybrid discourses, playing with literary conventions as well as those of the social sciences, documentary narratives are in alignment with the performative turn in contemporary philosophy.

Conceiving of identity as a relational, performative practice, Cavarero (2000) has pointed out the importance of considering the listener while writing life stories. According to the feminist Italian philosopher, the first question that we should ask one another is, 'who are you?'. Reading Cavarero, Judith Butler postulates that this question provides an opportunity to recognize the other in his uniqueness: 'This question assumes that there is an other before us whom we do not know and cannot

---

[8] 'Basta, ¿no? Dejemos esto aquí. No quiero seguir. Es demasiado. No me gusta tu mirada curiosa, las comisuras de tu boca no me gustan, un dejo obsceno. Siento que me humillo y ensucio mientras te cuento. Y es inútil. No entiendes nada. Nunca podrías' (24).

fully apprehend, one whose uniqueness and nonsubstitutability set a limit to the model of reciprocal recognition offered within the Hegelian scheme and to the possibility of knowing another more generally' (2005: 31). Asking 'who are you?' opens the space for dialogue. Therefore, the other will become known by his responses to the one who takes time to listen to him.

'Who are you?' is in fact the initial question that the narrator seeks to address in any story based on testimonies. In their dialogues with the writer, sources exhibit the vulnerable position of those who are expected to answer. In *La vida doble*, Lorena tells the truth about her hidden past because she is being asked to speak by someone with more power than her. For Cavarero and Butler, the vulnerability of the other is exposed as an aspect of social interaction: 'In stark contrast to the Nietzchean view that life is essentially bound up with destruction and suffering, Cavarero argues that we are beings who are, of necessity, exposed to one another in our vulnerability and singularity, and that our political situation consists in part in learning how best to handle – and to honour – this constant and necessary exposure' (Butler 31–2). This may explain why stories of mourning and violence are particularly difficult to tell. The exposure of the other, who trusts his story to someone else, requires an ethical response from those who listen. Butler draws attention to the role that the real experience of encountering others has in constructing subjectivities, for it is through 'proximate and living exchanges' that individuals address the question, 'who are you?', and relate to each other (30).

Documentary narratives show that this question is asked by both social actors involved in the conversation: the journalist and the source. Therefore, the self is also exposed and can eventually take the place of an other by choosing to respond to the questions of his interviewee. Contemporary writers, as I will explain later in this chapter, do let the others speak. They do this, however, not by reproducing a full transcription of their testimony, as their colleagues from other generations tended to do, but by allowing them to interrupt their own authoritarian speech. And, in the best intentioned cases, this might be a gesture of what Mexican author Cristina Rivera Garza has called *comunalidad*, that is, a collective sense of cultural production (2013).

Considering the role of those who listen, therefore, this philosophical approach to true stories might provide clues towards an understanding of the value of mediated testimonies in contemporary societies. Regardless of the claim that subaltern subjects now have more freedom and tools for expressing themselves individually, there is a new boom in testimonial narratives mediated by a professional writer. I believe that this way of dealing with real-life stories remains an option because of the intrinsically confessional nature of the *testimonio*, especially with regard to stories about violence and mourning.

If vulnerability is an inevitable consequence of human interaction (Butler 2005; Cavarero 2000), it is natural that it can be revealed in books that aim to reproduce real encounters between individuals. Therefore, vulnerability is also a condition of the creation of journalistic stories. Journalism, I believe, consciously exposes both the journalist and his or her sources, particularly in the genre of interview. Of course, one must be aware that the journalistic interview differs from other types of interviews: if not in the techniques of interrogation, or in the choice of topics, then in its intentions.

According to Janet Malcolm (2012), while the legal, psychoanalytic, medical or social sciences conduct interviews intended to help the interviewees somehow, the journalistic ones have no direct effect on them. Journalists are aware of their professional role while in the field, listening to others, as Guerriero recognizes: 'I also take into account that this is not an exchange of favors, this is journalism: if you want to tell me your story, I will tell it, but do not wait in return for me to publish you a letter in the paper, or to help you solve your life or transform myself into your friend' (Interview 5).

As opposed to a fiction writer who can construct characters' identities as his imagination wishes, the documentary author is destined to fail in giving a complete account of his characters' lives. No matter how long the conversations with the other are, the response to 'who are you?' remains incomplete.

Empathic listeners, unreliable narrators

Trust is an essential requirement for a successful relationship between the journalist and their sources, and sometimes it is the only way to obtain the desired information. It is not surprising then that documentary books start or end with acknowledgements dedicated to their informants: 'To all the people in Las Heras, who generously told me their stories'; 'To all the characters in this book for lending me their voices'.[9]

As a condition of earning this trust, the authors referred to in this chapter insisted on the importance of being empathetic. While talking about his first approach to his sources, Roncagliolo emphasized his conscious intention to be pleasant so people can confide in him (Interview 7). If, for Roncagliolo, earning the informants' trust is a matter of strategy, for Guerriero it is a natural consequence of being someone discreet: 'for some reason I think people feel they can trust me to tell me a story they would not tell anyone else' (Interview 5).

The author–informant relationship also depends on the conventions and expectations they each have of the genre in which the testimony will be told. Fontaine, for example, highlights the difference it makes for victims of Augusto Pinochet's dictatorship to talk with a novelist rather than to a journalist: 'they knew I was a fiction writer and that made them not so on guard and we drank, we talked; there was humour and time. I was interested in the details; I did not care about anything in particular' (Interview 3). He emphasized that he did not formally interview them, but rather shared conversations. Nevertheless, in methodological terms, the process of research for Fontaine's novel does not seem to differ much from that of more journalistic books,

---

[9] 'A todas las personas de Las Heras, que generosamente me contaron sus historias' (Guerriero 2006: n.p); 'A todos los personajes de este libro por prestarme su voz' (Roncagliolo 2007: n.p).

in which their authors also refer to the encounters with others as conversations, rather than formal, structured interviews.

All authors focus on the importance of avoiding judgements, because this attitude is for them the key to building up empathy during fieldwork. Regardless of the authors' declared intentions, it is worth noting that in their writing they are constantly judging their characters. There is, then, a contradiction between their attitude towards fieldwork and what they ultimately do with the informants' stories in their books. I believe this can be explained by the role of documentary authors as creators of, as well as actors within, social frames.[10] In order to give meaning to what they witness, documentary authors need to set some limits, to frame the naturally chaotic experience that reality presents. They do so by selecting certain information from the others' lives, and from their own encounters with them.

Nonetheless, during the process of investigation, authors relate differently to their informants. When I asked about his method for approaching informants for the first time, Alarcón explained that he is extremely clear about who he is and the purposes of his investigation: 'I am not allowed to lie, I don't get to play an imposter. I am too transparent, and people can tell everything about me, and as they can tell everything I don't make great efforts to avoid my amphibious condition in any way' (Interview 1). Like Alarcón, Guerriero prefers to be 'herself' and behave in the most honest way possible:

> When people are really different and belong to a world that has nothing to do with my world, I have an attitude just as discreet, very humble, very cautious, I would tell you, because I do not want to be a demagogic person and chameleonize and become part of that person's world when I am not; and I also don't want to be offensive and contravene any of the little codes that are in people's lives and that one still fails to comprehend. (Interview 5)

For Guerriero, there is no difference between the *persona* and the journalist-narrator. However, there was a contradiction in Guerriero's interview responses regarding the question of self-representation. While she intends to represent her real self in her texts, she recognizes the fact that she would never meet certain people or go to certain places if she were not a journalist:

> Journalism is the best excuse to get anywhere, so journalists are usually curious, fearless people, etcetera, etcetera. Having the chance to get into the gang world in El Salvador with the perfect trade is also very attractive, isn't it? (Interview 5)

Guerriero's self-portrait of the intrepid reporter is recurrent in other *cronistas*; it is actually a role some journalists like to play. Roncagliolo's emphasis on the exciting

---

[10] According to Erving Goffman (1974), a social frame is a selection of flesh-and-blood activities in which the individuals are exposed.

variety of roles that journalism offers does not differ much from Guerriero's explanation of the advantages of the profession: mainly getting into other people's business. This is illustrated by Roncagliolo's response in our interview regarding the first-person narrator of *La cuarta espada*: 'I think the narrator is the person I was at the time. Normally I am not that political, I usually try to be rather more frivolous than the man who writes that book, because I think your life is better that way, but when you do a journalistic investigation you become someone else, you have to become someone else' (Interview 7).

Self-defined as a journalist and not a literary writer, Guerriero emphasizes being herself because in doing so she reinforces the pact of truthfulness with the reader. It is not surprising then that the authors who are more able to describe the role of the journalist as an actor are the ones who also write fiction. As opposed to Guerriero's view, Roncagliolo showed no shame in declaring that he transforms himself in order to obtain the information he wants:

> I become a different person for each book, because I have to move in a different medium, gather information from different people and those people have to be shown that you understand their language, that you speak their language and that you are interested in what they are telling you. That is what I like the most. In fiction you live the life you want in a lonely and personal way, but in journalism... you become the person who could have understood the protagonist. (Interview 7)

Aligned with Caparrós and Villoro, Roncagliolo views the journalistic investigation as a process of characterization. In order to obtain the desired information for his story, the author needs to transform himself. If, as Goffman states, the self is not a well-defined entity, but 'a changeable formula of managing oneself' (573), then it might be true that Guerriero is being herself when she is reporting in the field, just as much as all the other authors are themselves, although they do so in a more cynical way. The self that they will expose to readers later, when they come back home to write, is another story.

The potter's hand

In *La cuarta espada*, Roncagliolo seems to transcribe his conversation with Elena Ipaguirre, the partner of Sendero Luminoso leader Abimael Guzmán. It takes place in a Peruvian prison, and the self-referenced narrator displays curiosity about Guzmán's opinion of his latest novel, *Abril rojo*:

– Mr. Guzmán has read your novel.
– Really? You are allowed to see him?
– Only in the trial sessions. In one of them he asked me for your novel, and I sent it to him.

I did not know how to respond. As usual in these cases, I said the most stupid thing that came to mind:

> – I hope he liked it.
> – He appreciates that, for the first time, an author talks about us without insulting us. But he considers it to be too neutral. On this topic you have to identify yourself, you have to take a side.
> – I see.[11]

By this point in the book, the reader knows that the narrator has a cynical perspective on leftist ideology, or indeed on any ideology: 'I am a satisfied bourgeois, and I've left behind my university years. . . . I will finish the investigation, I will immerse myself in another thing and this will be concluded.'[12] Roncagliolo-as-narrator, however, hides this aspect of himself from the informant, isolating it so that it remains for the reader's knowledge only.

The author is aware of the importance of listening rather than talking during the process of investigation. Listening empathetically, thus, is a journalistic strategy. In our interview, Roncagliolo expressed his awareness of the importance of this strategy. If Roncagliolo feels that the trust that people give to him is highly valuable, this is only to the extent that trust is essential to obtain the information for his story. The author remains silent during the interview, but the narrator speaks for both in the book. Storytelling becomes, thus, the interviewer's space for full expression.

Transcribing the other's speech onto paper is certainly part of a journalist's task, and, therefore, it is professionally justified. From the authors' perspective, in doing so they are practising journalism. Nevertheless, making public a private, intimate conversation can be highly problematic in terms of ethics, for representations of real encounters usually reveal more information than the mere interpretation of events.

For Benjamin, information and storytelling in modern times are two clearly differentiated modes of communication which have competed with one another:

> The replacement of the older narration by information, of information by sensation, reflects the increasing atrophy of experience. In turn, there is a contrast between all these forms and the story, which is one of the oldest forms of communication. It is not the object of the story to convey a happening *per se*, which is the purpose

---

[11] – El señor Guzmán ha leído su novela.
   – ¿En serio? ¿A usted le permiten verlo?
   – Sólo en las sesiones del juicio. En una de ellas me pidió su novela, y yo se la hice llegar.
   No supe qué responder. Como es habitual en estos casos, dije lo más estúpido que me vino a la mente:
   – Espero que le haya gustado.
   – Aprecia que, por primera vez, un autor hable de nosotros sin insultarnos. Pero considera que es demasiado neutral. En este tema hay que definirse, hay que tomar posición.
   – Ya (230).

[12] 'Soy un burgués satisfecho, y dejé atrás la edad universitaria. . . . Terminaré la investigación, me sumergiré en otra cosa y esto habrá terminado' (190).

of information; rather, it embeds it in the life of the storyteller in order to pass it on as experience to those listening. It thus bears the marks of the storyteller much as the earthen vessel bears the marks of the potter's hand. (1999: 113)

By the end of the twentieth century, however, the distinction between information and storytelling was no longer as clear. Documentary narratives, at least in the case of Latin America, demonstrate the blurred boundaries between literature and journalism not only at a stylistic level but at an ethical one. This is shown particularly in scenes in which the journalist-narrator feels uncertain of the success of his or her investigation. Self-reflections concerning the purpose and nature of the job are common in this kind of narrative. For example, in Guerriero's *Los suicidas*, the journalist finds herself alone in a hotel room with no television signal, questioning the reasons for her travel to a windy, dusty town in Patagonia: 'What did I go there to look for? I don't know what I saw. What was I looking for?'[13]

Today's documentary narrators are situated in a medial position in the cultural field, because they are a blend of two figures: the storyteller and the professional listener to the truths of others. The former comes from the literary tradition, while the latter emerges from the journalistic one. Additionally, one must take into account the technological changes that are modifying Latin American journalistic institutions, for, as Polit notes, contemporary journalists feel the need to be considered authors in order for their work to be recognized and legitimized in the literary field, because they believe in their work as a form of art, although it is clear that their signature is not valued equally everywhere (2019: 16–17). In my view, the new models of transmedia that allow any citizen with a camera and internet access to have a much more active role in the public sphere are also transforming not only the conventions of the journalistic genre but the very definition of journalism.

Rather than a mere literary or media-based analysis, I believe that a transdisciplinary approach is much useful in the case of hybrid texts such as the ones that form my corpus. In considering documentary narratives as a cultural phenomenon, we must encompass a reading that accounts for the narrative voice or, in Benjamin's terms, the traces of that potter's hand on the vessel. According to Benjamin, the storyteller works not only with his voice, but also with his body, since he has to displace or relocate himself in order to observe and listen to other people's stories. The storyteller comes back to his community to retell those stories, but the stories he tells are marked by the traces of his own experience.

By conceiving of the act of storytelling as a craft, we thus acknowledge the creative element in any kind of narrative (Benjamin: 107). It seems, however, that the documentary writer is more reluctant than most types of author to accept that their narrator is a literary construction. In fact, some *cronistas* strongly defend the idea that the narrator is a faithful representation of the real person who interviews people, taking notes and strolling around.

---

[13] 'Qué fui a buscar ahí. No sé qué vi. Qué estaba buscando' (26).

The representation of the journalist within the text depends, however, on how each author conceives of the profession and of his or her role in the cultural field. Some authors do agree that the narrator in a documentary narrative is the product of a consciously constructed process. It seems, thus, that for literary journalists the decision to write in the first person is primarily a matter of ethics. If they cannot invent the story they are telling, then neither are they able to imagine a narrator other than themselves. The writers interviewed were very reluctant to regard the narrator as a fictional character, as Caparrós ironically said, 'If the narrator is a character, he is a character that looks very much like me' (Interview 2). In the same line of thought, Guerriero said: 'I am not very different from what is in the texts.... There is always a narrator that is a bit of a construction, but it is an edited version of yourself rather. It is what the story needs, but it is not an invention' (Interview 5).

There is then a strong defence of the first-person narrator as a faithful representation of the author, as opposed to a literary character. I believe this attitude is related to the question of authority in the text, for the authors are well aware of the importance of their role as witnesses. Roncagliolo, for instance, thinks that in *La cuarta espada* he represents just another source of information. During our conversation, Roncagliolo was in fact annoyed when I rephrased the question to emphasize the effect that the narrator has on a sceptical reader:

> Liliana Chávez: I am talking about a 'narrator' because as a reader I don't know if you are him or not...
> Santiago Roncagliolo: It is me! It is me! There is no ambiguity: that gentleman is me, everything he tells is true, everything he says is what happened to me.
> (Interview 7)

Of course, admitting that the first-person, self-referenced narrator is not the flesh-and-blood author, is, to these authors, equal to admitting that the text is not reliable as a true story. Nonetheless, and despite their journalistic intentionality in telling real-life stories, the authors are playing with the rules of narrative. Both fiction and non-fiction stories aspire to verisimilitude in order to make sense of reality beyond a mere account of the facts. Verisimilitude, therefore, is a literary effect that the authors must consciously construct (Riffaterre 1990), and so I argue that the narrator in a literary-journalistic text is still a fictional construct.

The construction of the first-person narrator is, therefore, the key element of literariness in this kind of narrative. Nonetheless, this literary effect goes against the authors' declared intentions in representing themselves. According to the authors interviewed, the choice of a first-person narrator is driven by ethical concerns regarding the other's word and not, apparently, by aesthetic choices. Leila Guerriero claims that dialogues are a strategy used in the portrayal of the interviewee's identity, but not in her own: 'Whenever I show up it is for the question to reflect something of the interviewee, not of me' (Interview 5). Guerriero points to the limited space she gives to her own voice, in contrast with the interviewee's testimony, as evidence of her aim to erase the marks of the potter's hand from the vessel. Although in our interview she did not recognize dialogue as an important part of her own narrative, I consider it to be in the dialogues precisely that the narrator exposes more about herself than about the other.

Certainly, these authors claim that they show reality by representing real conversations, as when Guerriero declared in our interview 'when these small dialogues appear, of course they happened in reality' (Interview 5). With this attitude, they may be underestimating the powerful literary effect of dialogue as a narrative technique, while defending their position as reliable storytellers.

The vulnerable 'I'

In *Los suicidas*, Carolina, the young sister of a teenager who committed suicide, interrupts the narrator in her role as interviewer. For a moment, Carolina takes the position of the journalist, for she stops answering the journalist's questions in order to ask the interviewer about her life in the city:

> And you have security in your house in Buenos Aires? Because here they say you have to live behind bars.
> – It is not so bad.
> – That is what people say on TV. Is the hotel where you're staying luxurious?
> – No.
> – They say that the rooms are luxurious. Do you want to know my dream?
> – Go for it.
> – Eh. . . . It will not come true.
> – Why?
> – Well, no, because it will not come true. That my sister comes back again – that having been said, there was a heavy silence.[14]

The contrast between the two participants in this dialogue is another example of how impossible it is to have an equal encounter with the other. First, what is a necessity for the foreign reporter – a hotel room – is a luxury for the interviewee. Second, whereas it is not difficult for the young interviewee to talk about the feeling of loss, for the

---

[14] ¿Vos tenés seguridad en tu casa en Buenos Aires? Porque acá dicen que tenés que vivir atrás de una reja.
   – No es para tanto.
   – Dicen en la tele. ¿El hotel donde vos estás parando es muy lujoso?
   – No.
   – Dicen que las habitaciones son un lujo. ¿Querés saber mi sueño?
   – Dale.
   – Eh. . . . no se va a cumplir.
   – ¿Por qué?
   – Y, no, porque no se va a cumplir. Que vuelva otra vez mi hermana – dijo, y se hizo un silencio pesado (88).

interviewer this is almost impossible. When there is nothing else to say, silence ends the conversation, for silence is the only way to express the emotions of both characters.

This passage demonstrates that, even in a guided conversation, the roles of the participants can suddenly change, and the one being questioned can become the inquisitor. In consequence, there is an inevitable exchange both of identities and vulnerabilities. This exchange echoes Butler's reading of 'narrations of the I', as accounts that are always interrupted by others, and thus begin *in media res*. I believe that the reproduction of situations in which the interviewer becomes the interviewee shows a fracture, an interruption of the perpetually unequal dialogue. By representing this exchange of roles, therefore, documentary narratives display the limits of approaching the other, as well as of representing oneself.

The limits of getting to know oneself, as Butler states, makes it possible to approach the other by recognizing a mutual vulnerability. For although it is true that *Los suicidas* cannot be read as a truly autobiographical presentation of Guerriero, it can still be read as the experience of a female journalist from a capital city travelling to a small town in Patagonia in order to understand why young people there commit suicide: 'How might it be, I thought, not to see yourself reflected in the news, not to have a place in the weather forecast, in statistics, not to have anything to do with the rest of a whole country. I imagined a life like that: one which no one care about.'[15]

Guerriero uses self-reflection here as a narrative technique to communicate her interpretation of the contrasting experiences between an urban woman and rural people. The book, therefore, is the result of a process of framing (Goffman 1974; Brunner 1990), and it shows the journalist's aim: to make sense of the chaotic situation she is witnessing. In fact, Guerriero said that she used the first-person narrative as a way of contrasting points of view, alluding to the gulf between her own and her ideal readers' worldview and the protagonist of her story: 'these people for whom the brutal was the only thing that was part of everyday life' (Interview 5).

Regardless of the social differences that these narratives constantly and consciously remark upon, it is interesting to note how the authors try to erase traces of inequality, both in their fieldwork and in their writing. From the perspective of journalistic practice, authors are aware of the dialogical nature of the task they are performing. In consequence, they can share their own stories with the informants who ask in reciprocity, as Alarcón says: 'I am willing to give information of myself and my own world to the other, I do not protect myself and then the way is much more direct. I am not afraid' (Interview 1). Guerriero also recognizes that she is exposed, and that she must share part of her own life story with informants, even if this exchange of information may not be the norm among journalists: 'I will be repository of a story that for them is the story of their life. I don't think it is a bad thing that they want to know who I am' (Interview 5).

---

[15] 'Cómo será, pensé, no verse reflejado en las noticias, no entrar nunca en el pronóstico del tiempo, en la estadística, no tener nada que ver con el resto de todo un país. Imaginé una vida así: sin que a nadie le importe' (149).

What is striking is that, in order to tell the story, authors try to avoid the dominant presence of the 'I'. According to my interviewees, this is because they do not wish to interrupt the other's testimony by becoming protagonists in the story. However, I believe that it is not the trace of the author's self that interrupts the other's story, but the other who interrupts the journalist's account of himself. The problem is not in the use of the first-person narrator but in the reading of testimonial-like narratives as straightforward accounts of the lives of others. I think that this kind of narrative is rather a collective product, in the sense that it is an account of all the selves involved in the encounters represented.

A reading of these narratives as a type of narrative of the self, as I see it, changes the position of the other in relation to his or her storyteller. It is in fact the other who interrupts the narrative of the self. This can be noted in Guerriero's *Los suicidas*, for the interviewees' responses frequently interrupt the narrator's reflections. However, she decides to hide what she really thinks during the conversations with her sources, saving her thoughts for her readers. This kind of situation, in which the author confesses to the reader what he or she cannot say face to face with the informant, is common in the narratives of other authors, such as Alarcón and Roncagliolo. Rather than the ethical considerations that they claim to be inspired by, the use of self-representation is a textual strategy. It is in their texts that authors transform themselves from professional listeners to authoritative speakers.

Following her aim to understand contemporary social problems, Guerriero, like all the documentary journalists studied so far, approaches her informants in a different manner to her readers. Guerriero constructs a self-reflective narrator who is able to relate to her readers and guide them through another reality. I argue, therefore, that framing or schematizing is the author's creative and ethical response to an incomprehensible, chaotic reality (Brunner 1990).

Guerriero's descriptions of space are quite apocalyptic in theme and romantic in style, particularly when she reveals the narrator's solitary reflections to the reader: 'I looked out the window. Dust, wind and torn apart trees. Somewhere – in Buenos Aires – there were places with lights, open-windowed houses, cinemas, magazines. Telephones. But all that was in a non-existent place. The North. The distant North.'[16] In contrast to Guerriero's intentions of writing a journalistic book based on recent events, *Los suicidas* also evokes the trope of civilization versus barbarism, which has been present in Argentinian literature since Domingo Faustino Sarmiento's *Facundo: civilización y barbarie* (Facundo: Civilization and Barbarism, 1845).[17]

Another case of 'necessary' contrast between self and other happens with Roncagliolo's *La cuarta espada*. In our interview, the author explained that he did not opt for a first-person narrator as a mere narrative strategy. From his perspective,

---

[16] 'Miré por la ventana. Polvo, viento y árboles desgarrados. En alguna parte – en Buenos Aires – había sitios con luces, casas con las ventanas abiertas, cines, revistas. Teléfonos. Pero todo eso quedaba en un lugar inexistente. El norte. Lejano norte' (109).

[17] Tomás Eloy Martínez referred to *Facundo* as a '*crónica magistral*' (2004b: 11). Calvi (2019) considers Sarmiento's work to be the origin of Latin American non-fiction.

metafiction is a literary device in his book, but only because that was a way to connect his own life story with that of the ideal reader, as he explained:

> If it were a stylistic resource it would be justified too, but I think it has to do with personal things, with my process with the book, with trying to understand my own story within this book and at the same time with the need to make a book that was readable outside Peru, that could have translations, that could be published in several countries, that could serve to make understandable what had happened there, and that meant not assuming there was a Peruvian reader who already knows everything that has happened there. How do you tell things without them being boring? Well, by telling my own story. (Interview 7)

In this response, the author expresses a cosmopolitan desire, in Siskind's terms, to connect with humans from all cultures, beyond Peruvian borders. He also demonstrates awareness of the two assumptions made by other documentary writers, that might influence their style more than they normally acknowledge. First, that some strategies are led by the book market, and, second, that real-life stories must not be boring. Roncagliolo's narrative solution is to construct a first-person narrator. This narrator is depicted as a global journalist who knows the context in which both his informants and his readers live, and therefore is able to inhabit both worlds. There is a discrepancy, however, in the representation of the self within the text and the self-perception of the author in the face-to-face conversation with the informants.

The medial position in which documentary writers move allows them to explore other worlds, but also to come back home to recount their stories. The narrative of that (failed) expedition, however, constitutes the trace of a desire for otherness that language still seeks to fulfil. For it is the existence of that desire that maintains the hope in storytelling as a space for the exchange of human experiences, even if the other remains a mystery.

Exposure thus is a leitmotif that opens new possibilities for the exploration of the representation of reality. But exposure can also be, as many Latin American journalists know, a dangerous endeavour; it is an actual mode of self-making, of reshaping the self while aiming to reshape the world, and there is always a price that must be paid for this, by all narratable selves who are implicated in each true story. The irony of this might be that it is not out of a narcissistic aim that some of these narratives expose the self in the form of a first-person narrator; it might also be because the author feels compelled to give an account of what he has witnessed, a response that aims for social justice towards the vulnerable other, for the author surrenders to another's demand for truth that transforms him, even if that comes with a price (Foucault, in Butler 2005: 126). Thus, storytelling allows for, or even demands, the exposure of both the informant and the journalist. For the narrator, the latter occurs particularly when they confront unexpected situations with their informants. In Roncagliolo's *La cuarta espada*, the journalist-narrator visits a women's prison in Lima to investigate the life of Abimael Guzmán for a Spanish newspaper, and finds himself overwhelmed by the compliments and flirtations directed at him:

> There are three female prisoners sitting at that table. Far from the military ideology that I expected, the three of them have gigantic smiles. They bombard me with questions. They want to know who I am, who I am visiting, where I come from, if Spain is pretty, if it is very far away, what I do for living. I have never been welcomed with such enthusiasm. I imagine they get bored. Especially the ones that have been fifteen or twenty years there. Any new face excites them. It is only when I say that I am a journalist that I notice a change of attitude.[18]

A similar scene is depicted in *Los suicidas*, when one of Guerriero's informants, Cecilia, an ex-prostitute-turned evangelist, comes to her hotel room unexpectedly to give her a farewell present: 'I was about to close the door when she said that, if she was a lesbian, she would be in love with me and she would like to make love to me. I said thanks. I did not know what to say.'[19]

A confrontation with otherness may leave the interviewers with no words in the moment, but the representation of this type of scene highlights the self-awareness of the narrator. However, Alarcón is perhaps the most exposed narrator, when he compares the journalist's search for an interviewee with the search for a lover:

> I tried so many times to be received by Mauro that I arrived, at what I had decided would be the last chance, full of that modesty generated by an insistence that becomes almost a begging or an annoying meddling. It had been more than a year since my first attempt through the call of Sabina Sotello, I feared that a new showing-up in his house would mean violence or the cruel mockery that the unrequited lover can suffer. I thought about the old rule of the trade that says that when an interview stops being a proposal that the other accepts or rejects, and becomes instead a long seduction and negotiation, it is evident that in the meanness of those words the secrets are hidden.[20]

It is clear from the aforementioned quotation that the search for an informant sometimes becomes a game of seduction. This is comprehensible if one considers that

---

[18] 'Hay tres internas sentadas en esa mesa. Lejos de la marcialidad ideológica que esperaba, las tres tienen una sonrisa gigantesca. Me ametrallan a preguntas. Quieren saber quién soy, a quién visito, de dónde vengo, si España es bonita, si está muy lejos, a qué me dedico. Nunca me habían recibido con tanto entusiasmo. Imagino que se aburren. Sobre todo las que llevan quince o veinte años. Cualquier cara nueva les hace ilusión. Sólo cuando digo que soy periodista, noto un cambio de actitud' (174–5).

[19] 'Estaba por cerrar la puerta cuando me dijo que, si ella fuera lesbiana, se enamoraría de mí y querría hacer el amor conmigo. Le dije gracias. No supe qué decir' (182).

[20] 'Tantas veces intenté que me recibiera Mauro que llegué, a lo que yo mismo había decidido sería la última oportunidad, lleno del pudor que provoca la insistencia rayana en el ruego o en la molesta intromisión. Pasado más de un año desde mi primer intento a través del llamado de Sabina Sotello, temía que una nueva aparición en su casa me significara la violencia o la sorna cruel que puede padecer el amante que se siente no correspondido. Pensaba en la vieja norma del oficio que indica que cuando una entrevista deja de ser una propuesta que el otro acepta o rechaza, y se transforma en una larga seducción y negociación, resulta evidente que en la mezquindad de esas palabras se esconden los secretos' (2003: 137).

any true story, published as part of a journalistic investigation, can only be known if the source agrees to share it freely. Alarcón's self-reflective narrator reminds one again of the notion of the journalist becoming an actor in order to obtain his desired reward: the other's story. Furthermore, Alarcón overacts in the game of seduction that he plays in order to interview gangsters in a poor neighbourhood of Buenos Aires. To earn the trust of his informants, it is not enough to say that he is a journalist, he needs to pretend he is the type of journalist the other expects him to be. The limits between the professional and personal are blurred, and the exposition of this fact becomes part of the plot.

Scenes such as this highlight the performative nature of the encounter with the other, but rather than debating about the limits of verisimilitude, I think this literary strategy invites us to rethink the procedures of self-reflecting based on genre and gender conventions. Although all the works analysed here appear to follow the basic conventions of the journalistic investigation, I argue that it is precisely their ambiguity regarding their literariness that allows these narratives to go beyond generic conventions in both fields. Furthermore, this literariness opens a creative space for self-fashioning and stylization. Like gender itself, at least in the performative way that Butler (1988) proposes defining it, metadocumentary narratives, and particularly the ones that self-define as *crónicas*, are malleable and in constant change, some even in resistance to, or looking for ruptures within the social conventions. Particularly in cases such as Alarcón's work, the reader witnesses a process of self-transformation, both of the narrator and of the informants, through descriptions of their bodies in action, performing a role. Their identities are depicted as fragmented – for a single, full, satisfactory response to the question 'who are you?' turns out to be impossible. Both gender and genre embody possibilities of self-making through a theatrical representation, and in this literature surely plays its role. These narratives are biographical in the sense that they show the traces of fragmented life stories; they are a reciprocal, collective, way of relating to others, to the world, while also redefining the self. For even when it is only through dialogue with others that the self can be realized, it remains the author who has the last word.

Conclusion

Throughout this book I have explored what happens when an author decides to give an account of himself or herself based the personal, embodied experience of listening to others. These accounts are relayed through written modes of truth-telling that I have here referred to as 'documentary' narratives, that take place within a concrete geographical and cultural context. These texts are expected to be truthful because they are legitimized by the conventions of the discourses and platforms through which they are disseminated and because they are the product of a confession from a specific individual who trusted his story to another. But they are also truthful because this 'another' happens to be an author and feels responsible for what he has witnessed, for the other's account, that is, he assumes the cost of this truth-telling, that through his public writing becomes part of his own account. So, there are in my view two properties of non-fiction narratives based on journalistic investigation that are important to consider if one wishes to address the problem of the representation of the truth (of reality, of the self, and others) in storytelling: the rhetorical, under which their literary value can be assessed, and the ethical, which considers the intentions regarding truth-telling and its consequences.

On the one hand, regarding the rhetorical property, it is important to consider the conventions of non-fiction within its concrete social context of production and of ideal circulation, that is, who and how the genre is validated – and valued – as a genre for truth-telling. In documentary narratives, therefore, there is a plurality of selves or egos that to diverse degrees struggle for the power to speak their truth. Nevertheless, one must not forget that the final version of the story is constructed by an author, whose proper name cannot function as a common one. The 'author-function', as Foucault calls it (1969), oscillates between the flesh-and-blood individual who signs the book and the narrator (1969). As opposed to its function in fictional texts, I would argue that the authorial function in documentary narratives should instead be considered as similar to that of scientific discourses generating knowledge from a subjective perspective. In these kinds of discourses, Foucault states, there is not a fictional, essential 'I', but a 'simultaneous dispersion' of egos without a fixed identity (309); the author is then only a part of what an individual is referring to, that can be outside the text.

While focusing on authors who are also considered part of the cultural elite, public intellectuals and such like, it is necessary to revisit Foucault's proposal of a re-examination of the 'privileges of the subject', regarding the authors' transdiscursive position and function in their texts and in the field they exercise authority in (314). In the case of the authors studied in this book, I believe that they could be considered as 'initiators of discursive practices' (310), and this is why it is particularly relevant to analyse their own views on '*el oficio*' (the trade), both the literary and the journalistic one. For the kind of documentary narratives they are producing now – irrespective of what they call them – differ from what others have understood to be *crónica* or testimonial literature, or similar, in the past. It is not by chance, I note, that these authors have been questioning their own procedures though metafictional devices; it is a time where a renewal of the Latin American *crónica* seems to coincide with great debates regarding journalistic practices in the region. There is no doubt that online media is dramatically changing the rules of the game, and documentary narratives and their means of production are being transformed into more technologically complex collective, transmedia projects. I believe, however, that some authors' responses to or ruptures with the generic conventions go beyond the realm of aesthetics and concern the second dimension of documentary narratives: the ethical intention to tell the truth.

To the extent that documentary narratives are a product of the interaction between at least two selves, usually many more, the narrator gives a responsible account in the name of himself and others. In contexts where the journalists are at risk because of what they published, it is important to continue the investigations about how truth-telling is produced, negotiated and disseminated under violent and authoritarian regimes. What is the cost, in today's Latin America, for the self to tell the truth? I hope this book can contribute to the search for some answers to this question. Although we cannot be naïve regarding the privileged status that the literary institution has in Latin American societies in comparison with journalism, as a literary scholar I feel committed to defending the use of the literary as a tool for resistance and freedom. Literature, especially those hybrid genres that are closer to the social discourses, has demonstrated itself to be a form of self-defence when truth-telling is not a power but a burden upon the author. I thus believe that the adjective 'literary', when it modifies the craft of journalism, is not only a description of a text of such outstanding quality that it goes beyond the 'mere informative'. Because living in a 'post-truth' world in which it has, nonetheless, been proven that truthful accounts still matter, literature is not solely a rhetorical device but a subversive strategy of survival for those who opt for the first-person narrative as a sign of moral commitment towards the other, rather than as a narcissistic pose.

In uncertain circumstances when the price of truth-telling might be death, the account of an author, who tells the story and describes why it matters, comes with both risk and a responsibility. Nevertheless, telling a true story is still a creative and ethical response to the human desire to be narrated, even if the act of telling and listening will not save us from our situation. In the following and final part of this conclusion, I will develop a proposed reading of documentary narratives that takes into account their confessional nature in the characters' extreme, symbolical and physical relationship with one and other. Because if it is in the act of confession itself that the self is performed, I propose that it is by means of the story he shares with a specific other, that individuals can really get to know one another and to strengthen their bonds with a community.

An erotics of testimony

In contemporary metadocumentary narratives, the act of exchanging stories with one another becomes more meaningful than the information offered by the stories.

These situations show that the differences between the self and the other may be mitigated by dialogue, and through writing. I think, following Doris Sommer (1990), that in societies in which there are huge differences between groups of citizens, the only possibility for a harmonious encounter among individuals can occur through narrative. Due to the specificities of the Latin American context, it can be useful to approach metadocumentary narrative as akin to what Sommer called 'an erotics of politics', when analysing the role of sex and politics in the foundational fiction of the region.

If romantic novels served the ends of the nation-building process in the nineteenth century, documentary narratives at the turn of the twentieth-first century likewise serve a collective desire to make sense of a chaotic reality, one that goes beyond the literary imagination. In these narratives, I believe, dialogue is eroticized in order to show the difficulties inherent in approaching others in times of fear and uncertainty.

During the process of investigating a true story, as I have mentioned, it is important for the authors to earn the trust of their sources. In building up a trusting environment, empathy and seduction play an essential role. Today's Latin American testimonial authors are more interested in seducing the other than in just letting him speak. This might be due to the change in the position of the subaltern in contemporary Latin America, even if his identity remains the same. This 'new' other gives his or her testimony in a context in which freedom of speech is more widespread – at least in comparison with the dictatorial periods – and access to new communication technologies has created more democratic platforms of expression, particularly through the internet. The other is thus more aware of his right to choose to whom he can tell his story, and how. The environment in which the encounter between the self and the other takes place is now one of negotiation, rather than a simple interrogation.

Metadocumentary narratives must involve the representation of the journalist, but his presence in the story is not due to a narcissistic trend in self-narration, as Hutcheon (1984) has claimed, but because every testimonial narrative enters the game of storytelling. This game, according to Cavarero (2000: 91) acknowledges the existence of the uniqueness of the other and his or her 'desire for narration'. This acknowledgement, however, is normally mixed up with the recognition of the meaning of one's own self, particularly when the story is about suffering and misery. For Cavarero, lovers exchanging their life stories are the model of the close relationship between Eros and narration. It is through love, Cavarero argues, that the self can recognize the uniqueness of the other:

> Similar to feminine friendships, love is indeed often characterized by a spontaneous narrative reciprocity. The reciprocal desire of a narratable self into a suitable narrator of her story is of course part of the narrative. In love, the expositive and relational character of uniqueness plays out one of its most obvious scenes. On the stage of love, the questions 'who am I?' and 'who are you?' form the beat of body language and the language of storytelling, which maintain a secret rhythm. (109)

In real-life stories that are the product of a conversation, it is interesting to identify whether the protagonists really present a desire for narrative as evident as that identified by Cavarero in a loving relationship. The books of Alarcón, Roncagliolo, Fontaine and Guerriero show that there is a process of seduction involving the telling of real-life stories, and it is normally initiated by the journalist. However, in places where giving a true account of the facts involves so many risks, telling one's own story to an other whom one barely knows may not be as easy or as pleasant as in Cavarero's example.

The process of approaching others can be a long one, and requires patience and creativity from the investigator. It is not surprising then that some of the authors interviewed referred to their relationships with certain of their informants as obsessions. Roncagliolo, for instance, mentioned that interviews are the last stage in his investigative process and that he must think about the informants' desires, dreams and phobias in order to bond with them. In a more passionate tone, Alarcón suggests that the process of 'finding the character' is not a conscious one, but a desire attempting to be realized. This shows that during the writing process authors do not make a distinction between fiction and reality, for they treat the real story and its protagonists as they would treat literary characters.

One of the revelations to emerge from looking at the authors' processes of production is that their motivation often has less to do with the ideals of investigative journalism – that is, getting to know the truth about certain events – and more to do with their desire to get to know the other. The interviewer, therefore, lovingly anticipates an encounter with the other. Before this encounter, the other is a desire, but after the investigation is done, he or she will be treated like any other source of information, or like a character waiting to be written. What is left in between is the dialogue, which becomes the space where reality and fiction meet.

The acknowledged desire to know the other, which is never accomplished through writing alone, can be fulfilled to a deeper extent in an actual encounter with the informants. In the dialogue with the informant, what Cavarero describes as 'the comfort of similarity' emerges. Looking for similarities may be a more effective way of approaching an unfamiliar other, rather than pointing out the differences. Besides, in the real conversations, the writer's *persona* is as vulnerable as the other. This is because his desire to be empathetic wins out over the desire to exert authority, which must later be recovered through writing. The uniqueness of the other, thus, is only shown in the process of writing, and not in the face-to-face interactions.

Through writing, nonetheless, the author initiates another game of seduction. This time, the game is played with the reader, as Lorena tells her interviewer in *La vida doble*:

> And the reader gets dizzy and nothing seems either real or unreal and he gets imprisoned in your abysses and inventions, he cannot escape. . . . This is what you are if you are a writer: a deceiver who disabuses so he can deceive again. It is power, mon chéri, the ungrateful power that always shows itself masked. Isn't it?[1]

---

[1] 'Y el lector se marea y nada le parece ni real ni irreal y queda apresado en tus abismos e invenciones, no tiene escapatoria. . . . Esto eres si es que eres escritor: un engañador que desengaña para engañar

Recognizing the uniqueness of the other implies that the other will always be 'another' (Riffaterre 1990), even if the desire that motivates the writing is that of getting a response to the question, 'who are you?'. This was precisely the question Fontaine was looking to answer when writing his novel, according to his own reflections in our interview: 'what kept me writing was nothing more than that question: who is this woman? Who is Lorena? What makes her the way she is? And I was really seduced by this, for years I have been trying to understand who this woman is' (Interview 3).

If the act of reading is a desire, as much as writing is the representation of desire, the desire to represent reality is never accomplished through language. That desire positions the writer in a more emotional state in their search for a truth, as opposed to conventional researchers in the social sciences. Guerriero refers to it as a perpetually unsatiated curiosity:

> There is always something that moves my curiosity, there is always a dark spot or blind spot that although one can read many news stories about those people, still generates curiosity, intrigue, and I cannot answer who that person is, what happened to that person. I think that is it: there is an unsatiated curiosity. (Interview 5)

To satisfy their desire, or curiosity for the other, the writer may exploit the other's own desires. According to Foucault (2012), people tell their stories because of the desire to be heard. Cavarero and Butler take Foucault's idea further, proposing that beyond that desire to be heard, there is also, maybe, a stronger desire to be narrated. Guerriero's *Los suicidas* can certainly be read from this perspective, particularly when the narrator exposes the 'behind the scenes' of an interview with a woman who works in prostitution:

> – How old were you when you came here?
> – Twenty-one [she whispers]. Eh . . . are you not going to record me?
> – If you want.
> – Yes, yes, I want [she jumps with exaggerated enthusiasm.
> I turn on the voice recorder].
> – Ready.
> – Do you have questions?
> – In my mind.
> – Ah. You don't have them written [she says with disappointment.
> Then she makes hectic gestures, pointing out the voice recorder, and I turn it off].
> – No, no, don't turn it off. Hide it behind the bread basket because it makes me anxious. And say that my name is Cecilia, and clarify that the name is changed to protect the identity.

This is, thus, the story of Cecilia. The story that Cecilia wanted to tell.[2]

---

una vez más. Es el poder, mon chéri, el ingrato poder que siempre se muestra enmascarado. ¿O no?' (129).

[2] – ¿Cuántos años tenías cuando viniste?
– Veintiún años – susurró – Eh . . . ¿no me vas a grabar?
– Si querés.

If Guerriero had wished to write a conventional report, the reader would not have needed to know about this dialogue, for it does not offer relevant information to explain why young people were committing suicide in Patagonia. What this passage offers, however, is two identities in dialogue, negotiating the terms of a story. Just by showing both women in conversation, this story is already covering more than one individual's account of the facts.

Beyond a technical discussion of the limits of genres and discourses, I have tried to show here how documentary narratives put real people and events into dialogue. By doing so, these narratives are confronting and renegotiating the rights of individuals to tell the story they want to tell. For it is true that Cecilia's story will be the one Guerriero chooses to divulge, at the same time as that particular story, her story, can only be told via the narrator.

The value of these narratives goes beyond the telling of news in a more comprehensible, entertaining or more 'literary' way. Real stories, told in a metafictional format, are indeed a ludic speech act that crosses the limits of conventional media. They are also, nonetheless, a blend of voices that is able to represent an erotics of testimony, rather than merely a utilitarian way of reproducing reality.

If the account of oneself is always an account given to a specific other, the game of telling and listening depends on the peculiarities of each actor involved and the particular relationship they construct during their encounters. Although this is hardly accepted by the journalistic authors I interviewed, it is certainly a concern expressed in Fontaine's novel when Lorena tells her interviewer: 'I order this material of oneiric horror, which is blurred for you, for myself. I have been keeping this for years and years, working inside me. I did not want to talk about this. I did not want to present the obscenity of the detailed description that humbles everything.'[3] It is clear in this example that the genre of the novel offers a more critical position from which to analyse the ethical implications of the encounters with (real) others.

Journalists such as Guerriero and Alarcón listen to testimonies in order to make sense of certain (newsworthy) events; the individual stories are alternative sources of information for the narrative. Unlike them, Fontaine's narrative is focused on the protagonist's testimony itself, which is the result of a long process of healing undergone by the victim. By deciding to tell her story to the novelist, the victim expresses her

    – Sí, sí, quiero – saltó con entusiasmo exagerado.
    Encendí el grabador.
    – Listo.
    – ¿Tenés preguntas?
    – Pensadas.
    – Ah. No las tenés escritas – dijo con desilusión.
    Entonces hizo gestos frenéticos señalando el grabador y lo apagué.
    – No, no, no lo apagues. Escondélo atrás de la panera que me pone nerviosa. Y poné que me llamo Cecilia, y aclará que el nombre está cambiado para proteger la identidad.
    Esta es, entonces, la historia de Cecilia. La historia que Cecilia quiso contar (152).

[3] 'Ordeno este material de horror onírico y borroso para ti, para mí. Llevo años y años con esto guardado y trabajándome por dentro. No quería hablar de esto. No quería la obscenidad de la descripción detallada que todo lo rebaja' (21).

desire to be heard, and for her experiences to be narrated by someone who recognizes value in her unique life story. In all cases analysed here, however, an equal dialogue between the self and the other remains impossible. The approach to the other can be the most empathetic or intimate one, but the storyteller still maintains a foreign perspective on them. I believe this foreign perspective is a distinctive mark employed by the author to legitimate himself or herself as a reliable storyteller.

By the end of his investigation, Alarcón is so engaged with the everyday life of his informants that he is able to pray, cry and eat with them during a funeral, as if he were part of the neighbourhood:

> I accompanied Sabina, Frente's brothers and Manuel to the thief's tomb, which had first brought me to the shantytown so long ago. We stood up in front of his black and white picture, in front of the intact offerings of the boys, in front of the Pronto Shake bottles that decorated it. Each of them kissed the picture. So did I. They crossed themselves. I did it too. And then we all went silent for a while. We cried until Sabina said that we should leave. We came back to villa La Esperanza. We ate together.[4]

The aim of connecting with others is represented in the narrator's use of the first-person plural, so as to indicate that he himself belongs within the community. However, the last line of the book pictures him leaving the *villa*: 'Then, at sunset, I walked away [*me alejé*] towards the station.'[5] The narrator does not just go away, for then he could use the verb *partir*; instead, he uses the reflexive *alejar*: he removes himself from the scene as if he were finally escaping, or recovering his initial distance from that poor neighbourhood.

Is there a new other?

In these times, where the other has access to more technologies that allow him to speak for himself, mediated testimonials are still necessary, whether this is because of the still unstable state of freedom of speech in Latin America's fragile democracies, or even if only to prove that someone else is still there, listening. Nonetheless, the representation of the performance of both self and other, through narrative techniques such as dialogue, indirect free speech and monologue, influences the construction of facts. Echoing Hayden White's ideas regarding historiography, I believe that information and

---

[4] 'Yo acompañé a Sabina, a los hermanos del Frente, y a Manuel, hasta la tumba del ladrón que me había hecho llegar hacía tanto tiempo ya, a la villa. Nos paramos frente a su foto en blanco y negro, ante las ofrendas de los chicos todavía intactas, ante las botellas de Pronto Shake que la decoraban. Cada uno besó la foto. Yo también. Cada uno se persignó. También lo hice. Y luego todos nos quedamos callados durante un buen rato. Lloramos hasta que Sabina nos dijo que partiéramos. Volvimos a la villa La Esperanza. Comimos juntos' (170–1).
[5] 'Luego, al atardecer, me alejé hacia la estación' (171).

narrative technique cannot be mixed without putting the transparency of a true story in doubt. In certain contexts of censorship and violence, the journalist's job cannot be seen only as that of a professional who listens to others and transmits a truth in their name (as the task of a journalist is usually defined). It is not surprising then that the authors studied here are more concerned with the ethics of representation than the technical methods for transmitting what they hear word by word. The narrator thus becomes a blend of storyteller and professional investigator, attempting to diminish the risk inherent in the transmission of the truths of others. The product of this mix of techniques – that I refer to as documentary narrative – can be studied either as another form of journalism, or an alternative way of telling the truth in response to particularly dangerous circumstances. In either case, they represent forms of knowledge, even if their unorthodox methods have not yet been legitimized, as has happened in the case of other factual discourses.

It is difficult to situate these texts in a concrete position within the chronology of a Latin American literary history. Yet I think they can be read as works by dislocated modern writers in a postmodern world, already anachronistic in their postmodernism. This is why I find it useful to return to Sarduy's reflections on *lo neobarroco* to describe their style: as a form concerned with superabundance and waste, the baroque opposes information (1975). I propose then to define documentary narratives as baroque, eccentric products of literary journalism.

While literary journalists transgress the utilitarian function of information in the press, they also subvert both literary and journalistic fields, transforming into an alternative vehicle through which to tell the truth (or certain truths). Nevertheless, it seems that uncovering the truth is no longer the sole aim of documentary authors; they also seek to know the other. They are situated on a threshold. As modern writers, they assume their role in the construction of Latin American reality, contributing to the completion of a total narrative. They use irony and analogy as modern writers do, in order to confront otherness.[6] Thus, these narratives prove that approaching the other – these strange people, as Kapuściński notoriously defined them – is still possible. The encounter, however, is never equal.

As my analysis of narrative dialogues is intended to demonstrate, there is an unresolved tension between the speech of the self and that of the other. The other becomes a narrative strategy used by the journalist to document fragments of collective memory. Recording and translating their voice onto paper is an act of care for their identities, but it is also a creative activity, for editing the other's testimony displaces the experience of the real encounter into the realm of the author's aesthetical aims. Therefore, I conclude that Latin American documentary narratives no longer focus on the representation of the other, but on the self and his or her transformation after having approached the other. Confronted with terrible facts, this narrator is still able to break from the paralysis of shock in order to describe what he witnesses, for he is a

---

[6] According to Octavio Paz (1974), if irony marks the differences with the other, exposing '*lo bizarro*' (the bizarre), then analogy finds similarities through '*lo bello*' (the beautiful).

mediator between the world of the other and his reader. Each true story becomes an individual creation, based on a real moment, an encounter with otherness.

Literary analysis assumes that, when reading a narrative, one must separate the real self in action from that of the narrator. This assumption is difficult to apply to hybrid texts such as the ones analysed here, because in practice the documentarists do not actually separate their real self from the one on the page. They defend the use of the first person to show to the readers their supposedly fair, trust-based relationship with their informants. In spite of that, I note that these authors play diverse roles, depending on the field in which they are performing and how they perceive their two interlocutors: the informant and the reader. During fieldwork, authors act as professional listeners. They try to adapt to the informants' expectations and look for similarities with them in order to develop empathy. Afterwards, in their writing, they try to connect with the reader, by stressing the differences between themselves and their informants. Whether the author depicts himself or herself as an outsider, or someone who manages to infiltrate others' worlds, what the reader gets to know is indeed a literary construction of the self, reliable or otherwise.

While the other is at risk of devolving into stereotype – a character in an edited version of their lives – the author's self becomes the most literary element. The fictional devices employed by non-fiction texts are found not in their 'literary' use of language, but in the construction of a self-reflective narrator. As opposed to other narrative genres, however, the nature of this type of narrator has to be traced throughout all the non-fiction works of each author, for it evolves through time as the real self does. Nevertheless, this stylistic decision, of including the self in the narratives of others, does not diminish the collective, dialogical nature of these texts, for they are striking examples of multiple selves exposing their desires for narration.

I consider documentary narratives to be both forms of cultural discourse and acts of truth-telling. Rather than judging them by their literary quality, I have sought to understand how their literariness contributes to, and departs from, specific forms of culture grounded in Latin America. In a region that still has lower-than-average literacy and generalized access to higher education, it is understandable that forms trying to preserve and to understand a rather archaic oral culture through the written word emerge. This element offers an additional cultural significance in comparison with audiovisual documentary forms, like documentary films or photojournalism. Although they are not emblems of popular culture per se, I claim that these narratives are situated at the intersection not only between diverse social and economic contexts, but between the diverse worldviews that are constantly colliding in the everyday encounters of the inhabitants of Latin America. For these reasons, this concrete documentary form can be considered truly Latin American, although similar forms exist in other regions where inequality, instability and uncertainty affect society. Finally, I have not sought to legitimize or delegitimize these authors or their works, but to illustrate through their work a broader phenomenon that comprises far more names than those I was able to study in full. I hope I have broadened the scope for the recognition of the diversity of worldviews, styles and identities exposed through the Spanish language.

Appendix interviews

The following transcripts are edited and translated versions of recorded interviews which were conducted in Spanish. All the translations are mine. Each transcript respects the order of the conversation, as it happened. The mark . . . at the end of a phrase symbolizes an interruption by the other speaker, the mark [. . .] denotes deviations from the topic which were omitted, and the mark *** acknowledges any radical change in topics, or the end of each session. Except for Leila Guerriero's, all interviews were conducted face to face, on dates and in places chosen by each interviewee. The length and number of sessions was determined by the availability and preferences of each author.

Interview 1

Cristian Alarcón (La Unión, Chile, 1970)

This interview was conducted in Alarcón's office in Puerto Madero neighbourhood, in Buenos Aires, on 19 November 2014.

What was your introduction to journalism and literature?

In my case, I believe that first it was literature and then journalism, that is, I was first a feverish reader of literature. I was a very lonely child, I focused on reading adventure novels and then I was a teenager, in the middle of a Patagonia that was very hostile, who sought in literature, especially Latin American literature, the traces left by exile. I was looking for a way back to Chile, let's say in the classics of Chilean literature, and then in my university years I searched for a more universal, less regional literature. When I came to university to study Journalism, I was conscious that what I wanted, in short, was to write books.

What year are we talking about?

I was born in 1970, my family and I went into exile in 1975, I arrived [in Argentina] when I was in junior high school, at the age of thirteen. My readings changed when Argentine democracy began in 1983. I graduated from junior high school in 1988 and entered the Universidad de la Plata in 1989. [...]

At the time, had you already heard of *crónica* or non-fiction in Latin America?

No.

What kind of readings on that genre were you able to find in that time?

I think Walsh was present, although he was not being read so much. Walsh was not widely read at the time. *Operation Massacre* was a canonical text, but nor was the centrality of the body of what we might call 'non-fiction'.

Was Walsh not read in Journalism School either?

No, I did not have a corpus which included Latin American narratives, it was not of any importance. There was very theoretical information, from the point of view of social sciences and communications, and there were writing courses in which we practised writing, but we went beyond school to look for literary training outside. We did so in writing workshops and in some peer groups with other young readers; we exchanged materials and books. There was a poetry workshop that was important to me, guided by an Argentine poet, Vicente Zito Lema, who forced us to read mostly the 'cursed poets'. We were quite fed with Argentine and also French authors.

Could you say that at the time the career of someone planning to become a journalist was similar to that of one who planned to write novels?

No, there was no crisscrossing, nor was there the idea that if you studied Literature you would become a writer. I don't know what other paths my contemporaries were following; we desired more than anything to have literary lives rather than to become writers. I think for a long time we thought we were Henry Miller or June (me more June than Henry Miller) or Verlaine or Rimbaud. We were inhabited by the idea that the intensity of our lives could not be that of an everyday, normal being. We had a habitus of the petty bourgeois, in which we gave ourselves to academic training: we were going to do something predictable with ourselves. At the same time as the organization *Hijos* (Sons) was founded (my partner at the time was the daughter of disappeared people), we discovered our open and profane sexualities; we experimented with writing, and we went into the media to try to live on writing, not because journalism seemed exceptionally interesting to us, but we thought we had to live from what one could write.

[. . .]

When did you discover that there were other modes for narrating the real, such as the chronicle? Which book left its mark on you?

Tomás Eloy Martínez's *Santa Evita* was important [. . .] In the graduate course I took to obtain the scholarship [at the newspaper] *Clarín*, they gave us that book and made us criticize it. I read [Martínez's] *Lugar común la muerte* [Common Place Death], then Martín Caparrós's chronicles in *Larga distancia* [Long Distance] and I understood that I had taken a long path to a literature that I had not taken into account, which later led me to be very voracious in the consumption of other important texts, such as the discovery of the New Journalism of Tom Wolfe and Gay Talese, the journalistic work of Gabriel García Márquez and later the canonical authors of the nineteenth century.

There are those who believe that the Latin American chronicle owes nothing to American journalism or that it comes from another tradition, what is your opinion about it?

I think it is a misunderstanding that has lent an important stylistic backwardness to many young storytellers: the belief that we came from what happened in New York, San Francisco and Los Angeles in 1960, that we were born with *In Cold Blood* or *Operation Massacre*. That is due to an enormous ignorance regarding the significance of Martí, Gutierrez Nájera, Amado Nervo, Rubén Darío, Sarmiento, Lugones.

Do you feel that you are more closely related to the tradition of the modernist chroniclers?

Hmm. . . . I am much closer to them, because of the construction of a gaze and the political significance they had in giving an account of the new world. Their texts were essential in shaping a new idea of nation.

As for your contemporaries, do you feel more part of a literary generation or of a journalistic one?

I identify more with the literature of Mariana Enríquez and Gabriela Cabezón Cámara, and recently with the productions of Emmanuel Carrére, Pedro Lemebel in Chile, Gabriela Wiener in Spain or Peru, let's say, that tradition of the Latin American chronicle that is more interested simply in good stories. I have a critical view of the centrality that the genre of chronicle has taken on in Latin America, because I think we can say that there is a liberal chronicle and a purist chronicle. I believe that there is a liberal chronicle that is obsessed with the rituality of style, that attempts to claim it is ultra-literary or supra literary, abandoning the political roles of the non-fiction or documentary text, which gives an account not only of universal themes, but also of axes that are important today and that will continue to be so in a hundred years for this continent. The quests of many chroniclers are stranded in this literary aspiration: a liberal ambition of singularity, without any commitment to the idea of deep inquiry and research, where the first subject of investigation is the chronicler, the self itself. This is not due to the appearance of an emphatic first person who overshadows everything with his prominence, but because of the self-awareness that a chronicler has to have to make sense of the story about others.

Do you think that political awareness or intention is the difference between a journalistic chronicle and a text that could be called fiction?

No, because there are fictional texts that have the same political radicality. It is not a difference between fiction and non-fiction; it is a difference about the place the author builds.

Could we talk about differences between fiction and non-fiction, beyond their intention of verisimilitude or authenticity?

The difference is the reading pact. I think at this point we have crossed the boundaries between fiction and non-fiction so many times that our readers are no longer as interested. Someone who finishes reading *Limonov* and wonders if everything Carrére says is true does not deserve my utmost respect.

How do you personally describe what you do?

I don't have a personal name for it. I define myself as a chronicler, in the terms in which the modernists [chroniclers] defined themselves. We are storytellers of the real, we consider that the real is a construction and not reality.

About this idea of constructing 'reality', why do you choose certain themes to build that reality and not others? Why do you think there are certain topics more attractive than others to write about in Latin America?

[. . .] I follow the obsessions that my unconscious provides me with. My motivation is not based on a strategic decision in order to account for an area of reality because it has not been inhabited or discovered. Of course, I try to be original in the choice of characters. I think one knows that one has a great story not because the story itself is good but because there is a character that is worthy and that will be memorable [. . .].

Why do you choose to tell a story through a non-fiction or documentary narrative over a fiction genre?

[. . .] The truth is that, to honor the real beings I have interviewed, I don't need to use fiction [. . .]

Is non-fiction a limitation in your writing?

Not at all because in *Si me querés*, for example, I made my characters transform into voices. These voices don't come from transcripts, they are voices created by the author; they give an account of the real because nothing they narrate is unreal or fictional. [. . .]

Does the idea that it is a book based on real facts mean it sells more?

I don't know, based on what my editors told me when I made the contract for the last book, it seems so. I must think they prefer the book to be non-fiction.

Why do you think there is a boom in non-fiction or chronicle in Latin America?

[. . .] Not everything that is written in non-fiction has the quality to be recognized as such [. . .] but there have been investments in it: from the García Márquez foundation to us, the chroniclers that have circulated tirelessly throughout Latin America giving workshops, conferences, motivating excitement about the genre in young people. 'Workshopism': it makes it possible for many to participate in the various workshops that made them authors, it is the awareness of young people that they can become authors, and it is an idea of the reader that is no longer that of a passive reader, who only aims to consume texts that will nourish them, but one that we are discovering in *Anfibia* magazine and that we call 'the reader-author'. They are the thousands and thousands of young people who have access to education in a world that is somewhat less unfair than we had ten or fifteen years ago, and who understand that information, communication, journalism are not only accumulation of data but a search for meaning.

Therefore, when they discover that they have the ability to narrate and give an account of the world in a singular form, they do not resign themselves to being readers; they also want to write, to belong, to be recognized, to be observed and be loved. [. . .]

What is your method when working on texts based on real facts?

At the beginning, I think I am closer to the ethnographers' snowball than anything else.

Do you have a defined method? Is your research mostly based on methods from the social sciences?

No, but I could consider myself an ethnographer. This is clear in the case of *Si me querés*, because I stay with the other without the intention of obtaining an interview. Observation and permanence. [. . .]

What does dialogue mean to you?

Maybe it is more about sharing time and space than using language to label intimacy.

Could you not be the narrator you represent?

The first thing I was aware of when I wrote *Cuando me muera* was of the procedure of building the voice of the chronicler and the chronicler as a character. [. . .]

What are your limits while writing a non-fiction text?

Dignity is the main limit: the dignity of the other, the dignity of oneself. Honour and respect the pacts of co-existence that one made with those others. The non-misrepresentation of the plots: the location of the plots must be exactly what it was. [. . .]

Maybe you would be telling another story. . .

Yes, everything changes direction. There is a respect for that, for the plot, for the place of the characters in the plot. I think that there is a respect for the way of speaking, that is, for the forms of language, and nor are they mechanical reproductions. It is certainly a more polished language, more accessible, but in which the work is that of the ear, that of being able to respect the melodies that in the end are essential to the discourses, and they are key for the existence of the other.

Even if the word being said is not accurate?

Oh no, the word is what has the least value. If he said 'shit' or 'poop', well, I don't know if I care that much [. . .] It seems to me that when one delves into a character, as the other opens up to one, one is playing themes; the character is accompanied by an investigation in which what appear are themes and conflicts, and those themes and conflicts are the truth.

How do you approach to people?

First with extreme clarity about who I am and what I want to do. I am not allowed to lie; I don't get to play an imposter. I am too transparent, and people can tell everything about me, and as they can tell everything, I don't make great efforts to avoid my amphibious condition in any way [*laughs*]. I explain where I come from, where I am going, what I am doing, why I want to do it. I try to be clear with my method: 'I am going to be with you many times, I will be unbearable at times, you will think I am unhealthily obsessed, it is not that, don't be afraid if I insist.' I am willing to give information of myself and my own world to the other, I do not protect myself and then the way is much more direct. I am not afraid.

Don't you maintain any distance between the author and the other?

No.

Have you had any difficulty with an interviewee due to a misunderstanding, because of so much difference between you?

Incredibly with what I am telling you, no. Neither the evilest *narco* nor the one that kills the most people, as in my last book, has been angry at me.

What is your relationship with people after you finish your research?

None.

Don't you see them again?

No.

Is that something you clarify to them?

No [. . .] if I feel like seeing them, I see them; for example, once a year or every six months I see the mother of El Frente Vital, but no more than that: they live far away, and I have very little time for my own personal relationships. I was closer, I had a hard time achieving this distance later on. Even Alcira, with whom I should have a more regular relationship because I am basically finishing raising her son, is someone I have a very sporadic dialogue with.

How different is your world from that other world?

It is very different, very different, but I like the difference. I love the idea of getting in and out of that world; I love the idea of not staying doomed to my own world. I am happy when I get away from my own world. I don't know if what I am looking for is something about them or something of mine. I sense it is more about me than about them.

What role does the reader play? Do you think about a specific reader?

No, except in *Cuando me muera*, because out of a book that was somewhat more baroque and queerer, and blurry and pretentious and literary, direct, in vain, I decided to make a book that was to be read by young people, who might be like the protagonists of the book; it was a decision. In *Transa*, I did not have such a concern anymore, and I think I am going to have it less now.
[. . .]

Do you still see these texts as a form of journalism anyway?

Yes, because I don't see it a contradiction to use literature in journalism. I make a very strong defence of journalism, shall we say.

How do you define journalism?

Journalism is a state. Rather, it should be a state of extreme sensitivity to contemporary issues, events, conflicts and tensions.

Interview 2

Martin Caparrós (Buenos Aires, Argentina, 1957)

This interview was conducted in Barcelona, during three sessions on 7 July, 16 July and 24 August 2014. The meetings took place in two cafés in the El Borne neighbourhood, where the author was living.

How did you get started in journalism and literature?

I started doing journalism very young, when I was sixteen, it was almost unintentionally. It was by chance, I wanted to be a photographer; I was working as what in Argentina is called a *cadete* – the guy who brings the coffees, the papers, in the writing of a newspaper – while waiting for the moment when I was going to start training as a photographer. And very much by chance, on a summer afternoon when there was no one there, a journalist asked me if I could give him a hand and write a few *notitas* [short news pieces] and I said yes, I liked to write – I was a teenager and I accumulated poems in a notebook – and that is how I started writing in the paper. That lasted a couple of years, but then I had to leave Argentina in 1976. I went to Paris, studied history, did other things. I felt vaguely like a journalist, but I did not work too much and actually what I did start doing was writing novels. Before returning to full-time journalism, I had already written three novels. I always felt much more like a writer doing journalism, among other things, not like a journalist trying to write a novel from time to time; I don't recognize myself at all in that definition.

Did you do the work of a newspaper reporter?

Yes, in that first newspaper I worked in the crime section, I went out on the street and all that, but very rarely did I work as a reporter in a newsroom. [. . .] When I returned to Argentina in 1984, I started doing journalism again, but in a cultural supplement: I commented on books, interviewed writers, then did a radio show, then ran a magazine, a television show. I was not in the newsroom as a reporter. I went back to reporting in an unexpected way, when I started doing chronicles in 1991 and I had to go out to the street.

What led you to the chronicle when you came from fiction and history?

I was interested in mass media. What I almost never did was newspaper journalism, that of daily battle, but I was always interested in the form of narrative journalism, shall we say. I did it a little bit in some media, in a magazine called *El Porteño*, around 1987. When I started doing chronicles, it was by chance [...] in 1991 my son was born, and I decided that I had to become a man of means: to have a fixed job, those things that parents have. I went to see a friend from a newspaper, I proposed something else, but he said to me, 'why that?' Why did not I make long-form journalism? And there, I did have to go out on the street, as you [Mexican journalists] say *reportear* [to cover]. We [Argentinean journalists] don't have a word; we say, 'to go out on the street', 'to do journalism'. [...]

Was there a role model?

[...] I started by rereading four books: *Operation Massacre* by Rodolfo Walsh – Walsh had been my first boss in the first newspaper where I worked, but before that I respected him very much because I had read it with great enthusiasm – *Lugar común la muerte* by Tomás Eloy [Martínez], which seems to me to be one of the great books of non-fiction that have been published in Latin America [...] One called 'Autumn daguerreotypes', something 'Autumn', by Manuel Vicent, a Spaniard who has for my taste one of the best, most musical styles in the Spanish language, I wanted to steal some of that music; and *Music for Chameleons* by Capote.[1] I reread those four books and tried to build myself a stylistic basis: like so, I started.

Was there not much written about the chronicle, like there is now?

Not only was there nothing written about *crónica*, but the word *crónica* was not in use. I have just been writing for this book *[Lacrónica]*, I am trying to reflect on why I came up with the idea of naming this series that I started doing in this magazine 'chronicles of the end of the century'. The word '*crónica*' was not in use, in Argentina even less so.

---

[1] Caparrós's reference on Vicent's work actually blends two book titles: *Inventario de otoño* (Autum Inventary, 1983) and *Daguerrotipos* (Daguerreotypes, 1984).

In Argentina, the chronicler is the lowest step in the scale of the journalistic trade; he is the new one, the young boy who has to go out on the street to get the information, but he does not write it; he takes it to the editor. [. . .] So it was almost a joke to say 'chronicler', it was to claim to be the lowest, unlike now, where it is to take a seat and put on a 'prose face'. There had been very good narrative journalism in Latin America in the 1960s, 1970s, but in the 1980s there was not [. . .] [Elena] Poniatowska, [Gabriel] García Márquez, Tomás [Eloy Martínez], [Rodolfo] Walsh and several others [published chronicles], but later, in the 1980s, it was no longer a very common practice, rather quite the opposite, and only from there began to relaunch. [. . .] I have read little of the American New Journalism; in general, I am not interested. There are two or three that I find absolutely overrated. I find Gay Talese illegible, or not illegible, but not interesting at all, just as Mailer appeals to me because he has a kind of uneasy ambition, which I always like. Talese does not interest me, I get bored, what do I know? [Tom] Wolfe seems to me to be a kind of assortment of onomatopoeias; there comes a time that he stops interesting me. I like Capote; I think he is a great writer [. . .] I started reading them out of curiosity when I had already published three or four books of chronicles, they had nothing to do with my training, they are not for me an important source. My inspiration was much more reading people like Tomás [Eloy Martínez], like [Rodolfo] Walsh, or periodicals in Argentina from the 1960s. A magazine called *Primera Plana*, where Tomás was editor-in-chief and wrote much content; I read the magazine when I was eight, nine, ten years old, and it fascinated me; there were very well-told stories. I learned from that, not at all from the American New Journalism.

Was Rodolfo Walsh your mentor as well as your boss?

No, as a boss he was not a mentor; he did not care very much.

What do you remember about him?

He was super kind, very shy; he was very focused on his texts; he was much less an editor than a journalist. What interested him was doing his journalism. Since he was boss, he had to take over a little bit, but he was not interested; sometimes he would make a comment: 'look at such a thing', but he did not check and correct. What I do remember impressing me was that he had a very deep knowledge of the Argentine police. [. . .]

Do you think your work as a journalist influenced your fiction?

I suppose so, but I don't know how. I suppose so out of a matter of principle: I tend to believe that everything that happens to me in life influences me, but not because I believe that journalism somehow informs my fiction; I don't really believe it. In fact, in my novels journalism is not present much. [. . .]

Is there a difference in your method while working for a journalistic piece in comparison with writing fiction?

There is a basic resemblance that has to do with prose. I try to play somehow with the same kind of prose in a fictional text as in a non-fiction text. I am not interested in making stylistic differences based on whether a text is fiction or non-fiction; on the contrary, I don't want to make those differences. It does not seem to me that non-fiction needs a different, more personal style, at all [. . .] obviously in a non-fiction text before I start writing I have to work hard: talk to people, find out things, think about issues, read a lot of material, etcetera, etcetera, and only after, at some point when all that starts to fall into place, can I finally write the book. In fiction, on the other hand, it is quite the opposite: there is an idea, I take a couple of quick notes and start writing. So, in that sense the processes are very different.

Either way, is there a creative element also in non-fiction?

Yes, of course, because it is writing work, in the strongest sense of the expression: it is the work of discovering what one did not expect, I mean, it still amazes me how at the time of being in front of the screen things appear that one did not know, even though in a case like that of a non-fiction text, one has previously worked on this matter for months and years. [. . .]

How do you start the research on a topic based on real events? Is there a particular method you have developed?

I am working more on themes than on real events. My last three non-fiction books, or all four in the last ten years, were more about themes [. . .] In that sense I think lately I am unsuccessfully looking for a name for this, because I don't know if it is a chronicle, what I am doing. I do not know if *Contra el cambio* is a chronicle, if *El hambre* is a chronicle; I say it is a chronicle-essay, a chronicle that thinks, an essay that tells, but I would like to find a synthesis, I still have not found it.

Has your writing evolved?

Yes, clearly. I think there has been a political development, too; an evolution that has to do with me regaining the idea that what I want to do has a very strong political substrate, and then that is why I am more interested in certain problems, in order to think of them as problems and not as narrative matter.

To what extent would a writer who relies on real events must have this commitment to society?

No one must have anything, but what I call the *crónica caniche* (poodle chronicle) bores me more and more: it is like those little dogs, all manicured, hairy, who are like an ornament of old ladies who serve nothing but for the ladies to put them on their lap, in the bag and walk with them. There is as a tendency to the poodle chronicle, to a kind of mannerism of the chronicle. [. . .] A certain nice format has been established, which looks good and then what some people do is to look for the freakiest freak and to tell a weird story in that flirtatious way. This is a formula applied to irrelevant things: that is what I call the poodle chronicle; and indeed, what interests me is that the chronicle is political. I believe in that, a chronicle that I care about has to be political, in different ways: in its form and possibly also in the issues it deals with. If others want to do something else, it is their business; I am not interested in doing it.

[. . .] There is always a very personal way of looking [in your work], you do not try to hide it, while in the 1970s the narrative voice was ceded to those who had no voice. . .

[. . .] it is in the last three pages of *El hambre*, where I say you have to do these things, look for solutions, out of selfishness, not out of supposed dedication; because you feel like a piece of junk if you don't, not because I have to give myself to others, sacrifice myself, but because I feel like crap if I don't. So, to feel good, what I want to do is try to think about these problems.

Or is it a symbol of these times perhaps: to relate to each other in another way?

[. . .] It seems to me that some of us are returning to thinking that we need to find ways of political intervention again, we just don't know which ones. Thirty years ago, it was very clear what kind of forms they were; if you wanted to change the social system, you already knew where to go, what bell you had to ring and where you had to sign up. Not now; now there is a confusing search, and in that confusing search there are different possibilities [. . .]

Do you consider such texts to be an alternative to traditional media? Could they be a new medium, a new kind of journalism?

Traditional media don't know what to do. Print media is lost in a situation where most of the news they post is old news, so they are looking for a format that saves them from that problem. What do traditional media do? Right now, they do not know, nor do we, it is a moment of transition, when one of the options that some are thinking of would be a more analytical [kind of] journalism, which would perhaps include more narrative journalism, because it is clear that the information is no longer given by the newspapers. [...]

What do you think of journalism in Latin America? Does it help us understand reality?

In general, it is quite bad, not to say lousy, but there is one aspect of it that is working, but that is the only aspect, which is journalism on social justice. Journalism has taken the place of the judicial institutions of several of our countries, and is dedicated to finding and exposing criminal acts, in general, of those who govern. I was going to tell you 'of those who have power', but in general it is about those who have political power, not economic power. In the rest they are doing very little other than repeating old material, from yesterday, or creating a stupid world made of footballers and busty women.

In this context, what do you consider to be the role of chronicles or non-fiction texts not published in the media but as books or anthologies?

Well, they are just not in the media. A couple of years ago, when these anthologies came out, I was called by a journalist from *El Mercurio* for a piece he was writing. He was asking a lot of questions, and I asked him, 'how long will this [piece] be?', 'like twelve thousand characters', and I say, 'look, what happens to the chronicle in Latin America right now is that your boss is much more likely to commission you a twelve-thousand-character note about the chronicle than a twelve-thousand-character chronicle'. This seems to me to be the exact synthesis of what is going on. It is a great success, but no one publishes it, no one uses it and that is why the best chronicles appear in magazines that no one reads, very commendable magazines, such as *Gatopardo, Etiqueta Negra*, etcetera, etcetera, with a very limited circulation, or in books. The place par excellence of narrative journalism at the moment is the book, which also has a fairly limited circulation. The interesting thing would be to see how it is done so that this journalism can circulate in electronic media, on the internet [...]

Do you think the audience is changing too?

I have no idea. I never know who the audience is for anything, and, in principle, I try not to know. It seems to me that taking an interest in the public is the worst thing a writer can do; a writer has to write as if there were no audiences. The audience is just a bad excuse for bad writers who are not able to deal with themselves and then find a kind of invented reference, of course, an outsider to justify what they do or what they don't do. I think the writer has to write against himself, not in favour of the public.

How do you select the people who can be part of your books?

It depends on each case. In a book like *El hambre* – about seven countries with different hunger-related problems – I needed people to tell me stories. It is a little random: I go to Niger with Doctors Without Borders; they make it easier for me to access a clinic for malnutrition, and I try to talk to whoever I can. Of the ten I talk to, there will be two to serve me and eight who don't, but there is no previous selection, what there is it is an attempt to go there and listen to them. I record everything; I don't believe in memory, especially since I think the way they tell you something is as important as what they tell you. In these cases, there is an unwanted intermediation that is translation, but I still like to think that something is maintained that way through tradition.

How much does the journalist who is there differ from the one who writes? Do you represent yourself differently?

I am currently writing about the construction of the chronicler, in fact, but I have not come to an interesting conclusion yet, I have to work more. I have been writing about it; I did not get to anything interesting. Someone who is written is always a character; the issue is the extent to which one lends him certain traits to produce a character that has such or such a characteristic.

Is it easier to represent others than yourself?

Yes [*long silence*], I have to think about it more, I still don't have an answer.

Have you had any particular difficulties with an interviewee? For example, the dialogue has not flowed well because of the differences between the two of you, that you have felt that he or she is very different from you. . .

Yes, it happens a lot, not because the other is very different, that they are very different doesn't matter; I think I can more or less adapt. Sometimes I screwed up by saying things I should not have said. Thinking of something that had to be in the book of *El hambre*, a lady in Niger told me how she made a millet ball, which is what they eat every day. She was the first one to tell me how she made that ball, and I said, 'and do you eat that every day?', from the perspective of this Western myth of food diversity, and she says, 'yes, whenever we can', talking from that other side. Such lags occur because one comes from such different cultural situations, and, when they occur, then I adapt; but overall, I think I can adapt, and I can listen. One of the weird things that always happens to me, and I am glad, and I don't know why they happen, is that people feel like telling me things; it is a privilege. Maybe because I know how to show them that I am listening to them, maybe I learned to show that I listen, to make the right comment at a certain time that makes the other feel somehow understood and then want to go on. People usually tell me a lot of things.

How do you define a successful or useful dialogue?

Well, it is actually very utilitarian, beyond the moment that excites me [...] most of all 'success', as you put it, has to do with extracting a sentence, words worth being quoted [...]

Janet Malcolm said there is no moral reason for a journalist to interview, like there is for a doctor or a psychologist...

Yes, to avoid that discomfort you can always say that for the person you are interviewing it will be good that his or her story is known, but it is an excuse like any other.

Do you make your own interview transcripts?

Yes, in general I transcribe; those recordings are too imperfect to be given to someone to transcribe them. Whenever I can, I give someone the tape to transcribe it. I consider that the only serious class difference in journalism is between those who transcribe and those who make others transcribe. I hate to transcribe, but there are many times when I have to do it, because the people who transcribe are bad, I don't know why they think they can change things, and another because in these messy talks, with interpreters and things like that, it is very complicated. Many times, I transcribe, and then I have a text from which I will extract four or five quotes.

How do you decide when to insert the dialogue, that is to insert yourself in dialogue with others?

It is weird when I am not there, I don't remember, probably when my participation does not add anything. If someone is telling his story, he is telling it by himself; on the contrary, sometimes a story does not progress if the interpellation is not there.

What characteristics does an informant have to have to be interesting to you?

I insist on rejecting the word 'informant', because informant seems as if he were someone who gives me information that I will then use in some way.

How do you refer to them then?

I call them 'characters'; they are the characters in my books. They are a character in the book. In their life they will be anything, but in my book, they are characters; they are not informants for the book, they are someone who shows up there, they can be less or more delineated, but they are characters. [. . .] There is no single [selection] criterion, it depends in each case what I am looking for; basically, what makes it worthwhile is to get some trait that will help me advance the general story [. . .]

Do you have an ethical guideline about this information you collect, any rules you follow for verisimilitude?

There are two issues. One is not to fuck people up. I remember a particularly harsh situation in that regard: I went to Burma; they would not let people talk. On the one hand, there were people who wanted to talk to me and I tried to look for them; and, on the other hand, somehow, I was worried about making them talk. I was risking little, if they were able to discover that I was a journalist and they could deport me, but they [the people I was talking to] could be put in jail; I was pushing them into something that could be very damaging to them. It was very awkward there. I could easily justify it to myself: they want to talk, and yet I was upset and worried. And, on the other hand, the subject of plausibility you say. I don't say, 'when she does not eat, she faints three times a day'; I say, 'she says that when she does not eat she faints three times a day'; I did not see her faint, I don't have any witnesses, to say that I would have to be sure, I don't affirm it, what I affirm is that she told me.

How much does the pact with the reader, in that everything he is reading is true, influence your writing?

[. . .] I think it is a complicated discussion, in which what I do not believe in is the notarial obligation, in the sense that if I say that in this bar there were blue roses someone comes and says, 'the flowers were orange', I don't give a damn, but there are people who do: the fact checkers of the great American media need to find out if the flowers were blue or not.

Do you use fact checkers?

No, I think it is disrespectful to use a fact checker. I think if you send a reporter to find out something, you have to believe him; if you don't, then don't hire him. [...]

How would you define journalism?

Do we have to define it? I never really set out to define journalism. The intention to tell the immediate of the world in which we live. I think it is an intention; then it works or does not work.

* * *

How was *Una luna* created?

It was a coincidence; I did not plan to write it; it just occurred to me one day that with that material I could put together a book. What I think connects it [to the latest books] is that global ambition, not to focus on a story but on a problem, and to deal with that problem in different parts of the world. That is the change that appears in *Una luna*, almost unintentionally, and then in *Contra el cambio* and in *El hambre* I deliberately do the same.

Una luna and *Contra el cambio* depart from the work you were doing for the UN, was there a conflict with the organization because you were doing alternative work?

They never told me anything. I did not plan on making a book with this [material]. I went on a trip because I had arranged to make these texts and I started taking notes on other things, because I always take notes on other things, because I like to. And just at one point in the trip, I thought I would tell it in the book. One night in Amsterdam I was having a beer in a bar, a little bored, and I realized that I could make a booklet coordinating those notes I was taking and the texts I was writing for the Population Fund. Just then, already in the middle of the writing, I thought that would be a book. Until then I was making life stories on the one hand, because that is what I was travelling, and I was taking notes without a particular purpose. From that moment on I started taking notes more deliberately because I thought it was going to be a book. But the book was so unexpected, unplanned, that what I thought that night was that I did not want it to be a classic book, in the sense that it would be presented as such in the publishing circuit, expecting to be published, to be sold. I did not see it as a book; it was something that was entertaining me. I thought about putting together a little book, but I would not have public circulation, I would do it just to give it to my friends on my fiftieth birthday.

But did you somehow like what you wrote?

Of course. I am not going to give something to my friends that I don't like [...] It was almost my birthday, and in Argentina there is this habit of giving gifts to children when they come to birthday parties. When the children leave, they give a candy to the guests, in Argentina this is called 'cotillón' [...] well, I said, I am going to make this book the cotillón of my party. So, I did an edition that never had any circulation. It was 200 copies, not because I had many friends, fifty people came to my party, but because it is very difficult to print less, the minimum was 200 [...] A couple of years later, [Jorge] Herralde proposed that I publish it, and I gave in to temptation, instead of resisting, as I should have done. [...]

It seemed to me that, unlike other chronicles of yours, the narrator in *Una luna* is set up more freely, with a free flow of consciousness.

Yes, I usually think it is one of my most intimate books in that sense, because they were indeed notes I took for myself and that is why I took care to say it is not a chronicle, that is why it is called a diary; the subtitle is 'hypertravel diary', or something like that [...] I say that the chronicles have to be written in the first person, but not about the first person, and this is very focused on the first person, so I say it is not a chronicle. [...]

Have you thought about the construction of the narrator? Do you think there was an intention in this book to create a narrator?

Not in that sense. Maybe he is the least fictional narrator of every narrator in my books, because, as I was saying, they were very personal notes that were not meant to construct a narrator, they were my notes.

Still, I think there is a connection between this narrator and the others in your books...

Well, because it is still me. If the narrator is a character, he is a character that looks very much like me.
[...]

Is there an ethical decision regarding the construction of the narrator? [. . .] to what extent is there a construction, a decision to show a certain facet of the self?

There is always a construction. It is a text, it is not a photocopy of a gentleman, and, therefore, there is a construction of every character that appears there. I don't see how there might not be that construction. When one writes, one is all the time more or less consciously deciding how each character appears. I suppose what you do understand is the fact that there should be no forgeries: I should not say 'I comb my braid in the mornings', but it is impossible to exclude construction because that is what writing is all about.

Do you think there is a difference between saying 'memoir', 'diary' or 'chronicle'?

Yes, clearly, that is why I put 'diary' [in the subtitle of *Una luna*], because a chronicle, for my taste, should not be about the first person, despite being written in the first person. The important thing about a chronicle is not that first person. As it is in this case, that is why I was careful to use the subtitle *diario*, so that there would not be the possibility of assuming that this is a chronicle, because it goes against my ideas of what a chronicle should be.

I see *Una luna* as being more like an intimate journey, while *Contra el cambio* is the journey outwards, confronting the self with what is outside. . .

Yes, I do think *Contra el cambio* is a chronicle, if there is such a thing, but I also think it is a chronicle of another kind to the extent that it is much more essayistic [in style] than what is generally understood as *crónica*. There is a genre problem that I still cannot solve, I don't know if I told you the other day. . .

I am more interested in this idea of the chronicle-essay, because it seems to me that in *Contra el cambio*, the narrator takes more of a political stance, an opinion towards what he sees, he does not only tell the story, the testimony. . .

Yes, it is not like I assume a more political stance, I think it makes it more explicit [. . .] In *Contra el cambio*, and then with *El hambre*, I decided that I wanted to explain this position much more, among other things because, as I told you before, they are books about problems, not about situations or stories, so when I raise a problem, I need that essayistic approach much more, that allows me to make sense of all that.

Do you think the chronicle genre is no longer enough in that regard?

No, it can be enough for me. I preferred not to, I preferred to do something else, which is what I am telling you. On the one hand, there is all this: whether or not the political position is made explicit; and, on the other hand, there is the problem of getting out of the strict narrative that chronicles tend to have, to move to these much more essayistic fields. When it comes to trying to put a certain problem – climate change, global warming, on the one hand, or hunger on the other – it could obviously be limited to a story in the style of the more traditional chronicle, but that did not satisfy me. So that is where I say I have not resolved the issue of genre yet. It seems to me that these [books], both *Contra el cambio* and *El hambre*, are not chronicles in the sense other books were. Even *El interior* is not a chronicle at all, but much more so than *Contra el cambio* or *El hambre*, to the extent that it is not about a problem but a journey. I have not found a generic definition yet; I would like to find a word or a concept that encompasses it.

Yes, me too.

Yes, that is a mess, isn't it? I used this idea of 'an essay that tells, a chronicle that thinks' or the 'chronicle-essay', but they are very imperfect forms, they are very difficult forms. There should be a word that would account for all this.
[. . .]

Do you ever experience self-censorship?

No, that is not my problem. [. . .]

Why is an Argentine interested in knowing about Africa or other countries?

I don't think of myself as an Argentinian. I think of myself as a person. For one thing, I am totally against nationalities. I think they are a sinister invention [. . .] I still consider myself an internationalist, in the sense that countries are instruments of control, oppression, damage, so I am not interested in thinking of things as an Argentinian.

However, in these books there is a sort of Argentinian gaze, as if they were winks to a culture behind it, a comparison...

They are not winks, it is me, it is who I am, I would be an idiot to try to pretend I am a Martian. I was born there, I lived there for much of my life, I lived in many other places too, my cultural training has a lot to do with Argentina, although it allows me to see what nationalism, patriotism, all that stupidity means; but I am still from there, and I don't want to pretend I am not. In fact, I wondered when I was doing *El hambre* what verbal techniques to use to translate dialogues that had, in most cases, been in other languages. So, all those dialogues are written in Argentinian; they say '*vos querés*', they don't say '*tú quieres*', because that is my language. If I translate from English, French, I translate into my language [. . .] So yes, I am absolutely Argentinian, but at the same time I understand how limited that is, and I try to think in other terms.

In certain parts of *Contra el cambio*, you state that the form in which you can identify with others comes from a marginal place, which is not the First World. Traditionally, as [Edward] Said has studied, for example, 'the other' is defined from the point of view of the European who travels and conquers; in your chronicles the self could also be the 'other', an other who is meeting another 'other'. Have you come up with any concept of otherness when confronting your characters?

Yes, in my first book of chronicles, in *Larga distancia* (Long distance), there are some paragraphs that talk about this, how being Argentinian allows me to look without the default gaze of a Frenchman, an Englishman or an American, probably with a slightly greater range, to the extent that it is an indeterminate way of looking; I mean, I do not look as French Cartesians would, nor as the British old lost empire or with an American patron of the world, etcetera, etcetera, but I look from a very mixed culture, very mixed, hybrid, and that allows me, it seems, a slightly greater approach to a number of problems. Of course, sometimes I have to clarify, because when, in a village in Zambia, I have to sit down and talk to someone, their first assumption is that I am part of the hegemonic, European-American gaze, let's say, because of my looks and all that, and sometimes I make it clear that I don't come from those places.

And that changes the relationship with them?

Maybe it changes it. I am hoping it does not change it. Some people understand this more than others because, say, the geopolitical knowledge that there is usually in

Zambian villages is not always very extensive, but sometimes there are people who understand that it is not the same to look at them from a European capital as from Latin America.

[...]

Mostly in *Contra el cambio*, but also in some of your other books, there are times when the narrator says that he does not know what he is doing there, that he is lost, [expresses] the idea of being alone. Is there always this existential crisis in the modern traveller?

I don't know what it is going to be like for the modern traveller. It happens to me often to say 'what am I doing here?', but this happens to me also in my house here, two blocks away; there are afternoons when I think, 'what am I doing?' I don't think that is any different depending on whether I am at my house in El Borne or in Antananarivo. What happens is that, because getting to Antananarivo requires a much greater effort, then being there [and] not knowing what you are doing seems more serious to you, because you have gone there, then there should be a stronger justification [...] facing the possibility of imagining the '*Cronista*', with capital C, as a kind of tireless explorer who enters the tempestuous jungles of the world, I also like from time to time to mention that the chronicler also gets bored, despairs, gets upset.

[...]

* * *

Do you have a particular method of selecting and editing the information when you sit down and write?

I don't just do that when I sit down to write, but I do it all the time. I am editing all the time; that is, on the one hand, when I take notes in the field, those notes are text, they are not annotations for later writing, they are very similar to the final text. I write, I don't take notes. And, on the other hand, also when I am in a situation I am editing. When I am listening to someone, I see what phrase serves [a purpose], what does not. In general, it allows me to understand what things I need, what things I am missing – what I have can come from just before or after what I am getting at that time. Of course, then, when I finally sit down, new things appear, relationships appear that I had not seen before and so on. [...] In fact, in many cases I am doing it as a script, while I am working in one place or on a situation. In general, what I try to do is that every day I check the script, depending on what I got that day, to see where the things I got lead, what I need to look for.

Do you think that journalistic work, its method of investigation, has more influence on this type of text than on fiction?

Well, what you do when you are on the ground, in a situation, is journalism: it is going and looking and asking. The problem is how you write it, that is where the whole difference is; but the work on the ground is absolutely journalistic, of a good journalist, that is someone who knows how to look, who knows how to think, who knows how to search. But probably good journalists can do totally different things with that, where there is no such textual work.

Interview 3

Arturo Fontaine (Santiago de Chile, 1952)

The interview was conducted in two sessions in Santiago de Chile. The first session took place at the author's house in Providencia neighbourhood, on 13 November 2014, and the second one was conducted the next day in a coffee shop close by.

Why did you choose to write a novel [*La vida doble*] and not a chronicle or testimony?

Because what a novelist always does, not only in this type of literature, is to interpret the facts, to go beyond the facts [...]

Although in this case the facts you tell are facts that for many people could be almost taboo [...] thinking about your novel, among all the criticism you received, did you receive any in reference to writing on a subject that not everyone talks about [in Chile]?

Yes, that was a risk, on both sides [the clandestine guerrilla groups and the Pinochet regime]. If you look at the figure of the male or female traitor, it is a character who annoys [those] on both sides of the conflict. In that sense, [the protagonist of the novel] is a politically incorrect character, in any of the places you put her. For me there was a risk there, especially from political criticism, but on the other hand, that was the challenge. On the one hand, capturing that woman's spirit, imagining that spirit and, on the other hand, touching on a universal theme that is betrayal [...] obviously I knew there were three of them, I transformed them into one. I met one of them, [whose identity] is the only thing that is not made explicit as a source in the book, I promised never to reveal who she is.

But did you interview her?

For a long time, and she agreed to do the interview because she had read previous novels of mine; she already knew how I worked [. . .] So a lot of things she told me she would never have told me if I was with a tape recorder, in a formal interview [. . .]

Do you consider fiction, in this case, to be a better medium, or an alternative form of reporting?

Yes, I believe that there is a liberation that allows one to reach areas of the soul that are blocked and that through the path of fiction can be opened. I also find that fiction reveals to you a kind of scab that covers the events when we get used to them [. . .] when I read all these documents in the Museo de la Memoria (Museum of Memory) – I am on the board and I was its founder – I saw something so dry, so impersonal and so repetitive from one case to another, [I saw] that that same accumulation is dulling your sensibility. You cannot feel anything.
[. . .]

Does it also have to do with privileged access to certain information?

No, no, I had information that anyone could get hold of. Yes, for obvious, ethical reasons, I was interested in the subject, so that I spent hours in the vicarage [*Vicaría de la Solidaridad*], for example, studying cases, studying folders, seeing how the documentation was assembled, following the thread to some cases. But first I read the documents and then looked for the testimonies: people I knew, and everything that is there, that I have read, but it is not that I have had privileged access to information, except what I told you about these interviews with one of these three women.

Do you have the recordings?

No, it was without recording, I never used a recorder, that was part of the rules of the game, except once. And then I interviewed some agents, I wanted them to tell me about these women, how they saw them.

Did you find agents who had worked with them?

At that time, they had worked with them, only they came from the Escuela de Inteligencia (intelligence school), they were professionals from there. [They told me] how they interact with these women who were on the other side, how they see them, how they treat them. [...]

How did you construct Lorena [the protagonist of *La vida doble*]?

[...] Speaking for a novel and to a novelist created between her and me an atmosphere of impunity, liberation, freedom, which allowed her to give an account. She cried a lot, she told me a lot of things, and some of that marked the final form of the novel. In the end, the shape of the novel, which I had a hard time finding, is the simplest and reproduces that situation a lot.

There is much of the representation of the dialogue between you and her...

[...] I intervened little, but I asked her a few questions and that atmosphere was created a little, where she would tell me, 'that look of yours tells me that you don't believe me', things like that. All of that later found a place in the novel. Now let me tell you why... you want another tea? [*the interview is interrupted while he is making tea*] [...] I think what I have done is pretty classic: it is taking a pre-existing story – who hasn't done that? – and build from it a story, a fiction.

Maybe the subject is the different thing...

Of course, the subject is special and, hopefully, the language in which it is narrated, in which the experience is given [...] what kept me writing was nothing more than that question: Who is this woman? Who is Lorena? What makes her the way she is? And I was really seduced by this, for years I have been trying to understand who this woman is.
   [...]

Did you have any experience doing this kind of text as a journalist?

No, and that was a great advantage, because they knew I was a fiction writer and that made them not so on guard and we drank, we talked; there was humour and time. I was interested in the details; I did not care about anything in particular [...].

I would like you to talk more about the conversations you had with this female informant [Lorena], what was the dialogue like?

Look, it was. . . first of all, it was not an interrogation, it was a conversation.

Wouldn't you call it an interview?

No. It was a conversation with long silences, with anecdotes, with stories of other people [. . .] I felt what I put in the novel: that freedom is the face of responsibility, of the impunity generated by fiction, in which I do not have a way of checking whether or not what you are telling me is like that or not.
[. . .]

Did these conversations transform you in any way?

I would say that it was a very impressive issue [talking to the anonymous female informant] and that it still affects me inside [. . .] When I talked to this woman, I had already done a lot of research, I already had a lot of writing, and I guess this had already allowed me to shape it. I already felt like I had everything I needed, and besides the conversation stimulated my imagination a lot, because there were thousands of things that could not be resolved in that conversation, which always happens, right? [. . .]

Why do you decide to represent yourself or create this character as a journalist? I don't know if the narrator is a journalist, I imagined it that way at least.

No, the narrator is a novelist [. . .]

Could you say that the novelist-narrator is you?

Well, yes, it is very close to who I am, that novelist who talks there, within that structure. Of course, the only difference is that there, for a game – that is a purely aesthetic decision – the novelist never speaks.
[. . .]

Were you inspired by or did you rely on any work in particular to find this structure?

[...] I read things, for example, some stories of agents, not crime novels but testimonies of real agents [...] I read a book by Marguerite Duras, *La Douleur*, where there is a very powerful torture scene.

The torture scenes in the novel are very powerful...

But if you see what Marguerite Duras did is very different from what I did, regarding the point of view, but it was something that interested me [...] Agents are not monsters, I did not meet monsters, I met very common people, with an excellent relationship with their son, with an excellent relationship with his second wife, another one with his mother or with his friends; guys I have no doubt who are very supportive as friends. The thing is, nobody is a criminal twenty-four hours a day, it is only at one time of the day; and no one is a criminal with everyone around him, only with [the person] whom was his victim. [...]

This is similar to what [Hannah] Arendt say about the trials against Nazis.

I read that, but Hannah Arendt's theory of the banality of evil seems to me to apply to a certain kind of character, not everyone. I did not get the impression that the characters I was with were bureaucrats like the ones she depicts. [...]

Does it have to do with gender? Does being a woman make all the difference?

I had not thought about it, but it is possible. Above all, it has to do with her culture, it seems to me, with her sensibility, because I built a character who has culture: who has studied French literature, who has read Fanon, who has read Nietzsche, right? not only Marx, of course, but who has read Rimbaud, Baudelaire [...]

I find this other vision of the lives of left-wing groups interesting. Do you think that the issue has been addressed from a distant perspective or without so much emotional involvement?

[...] There is a gradual development of a more distant gaze from what that really was like. One writer who I think has done an interesting job on this specific subject is

Horacio Castellanos Moya, a Salvadoran writer [...] I would say that there is a parallel in the sense that we are both studying documents, but not in general, rather in relation to the guerrillas, [which is] something more demarcated. This is something that, for example, [Pedro] Lemebel does not do, except in *Tengo miedo torero* (I'm afraid, bullfighter), but that is a novel and Lemebel is not involved in the guerrilla world, he does a very free thing [...] [Martín] Caparrós and [Eduardo] Anguita's *La voluntad*, which I quoted, also helped me a lot in exploring the guerrilla world. That book is very good. He [Caparrós] is a great chronicler. It is the best thing that has been done as a testimony of guerrilla life, it is three volumes, a very conscientious thing [...] I do not know much about what the chronicle is, but that book is certainly a documentary record on this topic, and it was very useful for me [...] besides, I talked exhaustively with him, with Martín [Caparrós] [...]

Something must be understood as *testimonio*, and that idea influences how people tell their own lives or experiences...

The point is that, when working on the format of a well-defined interview, or of a well-defined testimonial, a well-defined memory, you immediately establish a number of restrictions, and whoever speaks in that setting has a number of taboos [...] when you are an informant for a work of fiction, as in my case, there is a kind of bubble of freedom, where those repressions decrease greatly, if there is trust, of course, that I will not reveal their name [...] you can tell a testimony to a psychiatrist, to the confessor, to the priest, they can gather this kind of conversation. That is the equivalent.

Although in this case the testimony is known to be public in some way, that is a bit problematic.

Of course, it might be that the person doesn't tell you some things because he or she is cautious.

But even so the dialogue format generates this intimacy...

That is my advantage. Now, the advantage is that with the psychiatrist and the priest the person can say everything, but the downside is that they [the psychiatrist or priest] cannot say anything, that remains in the private registry, you lose it [the testimony]. So this format that we are analysing in the case of this novel is very unique. There is a pact of trust [...]

So what would you call what is going on in your novel?

A transmutation of the experience, of the data, of the testimony offered to you by the informant. [. . .]

* * *

Do you think that your work at the Museum of Memory or as director of the CEP [Centre for Public Studies] has influenced your interest in these forms of storytelling?

I think they have influenced me. Public issues have influenced my literature; my novels always address public themes and somehow both written testimony and personal testimony have certainly snuck into my literature everywhere [. . .]

Your literary beginnings coincide with a time when there was a work to recover oral sources, testimonies, within historical studies. . .

Yes, I think all of that influenced me and is also a pendular thing: the feeling that there had been too much magical realism. I was educated at school reading [Gabriel] García Márquez, [Julio] Cortázar, [Jorge Luis] Borges. I was writing Cortázian short stories at fourteen, like everybody else. Trying [to write] a story or a novel of that kind again, it was to me like chewing gum that had already been chewed. [. . .]

Do you recognize yourself in this tradition, even if you consider it something different now?

Well, what happens is what Harold Bloom describes in that old book called *The Anxiety of Influence*, I think one is formed as a writer a little against the father. I think there is something about finding your own language that makes you recognize yourself, reinvent yourself a little bit. Therefore, to continue working on that Rioplatense vein (Borges, Bioy) seemed a little barren to me and life, apart from that, was buzzing everywhere. I saw everything that was going on, all the feeling of life. Borges is a man who creates a very withdrawn life, and my life is the opposite of something like that. I was very immersed in the world, I felt like the world was telling me stories all the time. [. . .]

For people who writes *crónica*, the New American journalism is a great reference, is it the same for you?

Of course, I read Tom Wolfe, that whole group of New Journalism, which is obviously an interesting and very refreshing project and which has had a huge influence [. . .]

Why do you choose these themes? Do you relate to a personal experience or to any interest beyond a historical or general interest?

If you want to ask me if I was tortured or if I was imprisoned, no, I was not tortured or imprisoned.

But is there any personal motivation that will move you to write about these topics?

Well, I would say that what happens is that it was my generation's turn to live a time of very great political intensity [. . .] what could had been a sort of confrontation of political ideas becomes a fierce dictatorship, and obviously there you touch on ethical themes that for a writer are very difficult to ignore, and that give you very varied human material, because the human condition under extreme pressure is shown differently.

Interview 4

Francisco Goldman (Boston, United States, 1954)

The interview was held in Mexico City, on 9 January 2015, in a café in the Colonia Roma neighbourhood.

How did you get interested in literature and journalism? Did it happen at the same time?

It was not at the same time. I did pure literature, but when I was very young, I started reading people like Gabriel García Marquez, Graham Greene, all those writers who were so important in my training, in my teenage years. I noticed they were all journalists. Obviously in the United States we have examples; not only [Ernest] Hemingway, but Mark Twain, etcetera, but it was no longer very common for novelists to practise journalism, it was very rare, it was almost stigmatized [. . .] I felt very influenced by Latin Americans; being someone of Latin American roots growing in the United States, this offered me a huge bridge. Not only did they open new territory in literature, they obviously did, but also in my own personal life: it was a way out of a situation where I felt very uncomfortable, I did not know what to do on my own path. I did not feel very *gringo*; it was impossible for me to write like an Anglo-Saxon. For example, with the family I had, I felt like a fish out of water. So, the way García Márquez and others had to live their lives, to combine journalism and literature, was for me exemplary, not only their literature [. . .] I knew that in my life it was going to be very important to get out of the provincialism of a *gringo* grown in the Southeastern United States, in the suburbs. I had to connect with that part of the world that was my maternal family, and it was also a time when the relationship between the United States and Central America was defined by war, open, fierce war, in the 1970s, 1980s [. . .]

Was there a book that influenced your writing?

I don't think so; it was a combination of books. García Márquez's novels did influence me a little: the reporter-narrator in *Chronicle of a Death Foretold* has a bit of the novelist researcher [to him]. I really liked the role of journalism in *Conversation in the Cathedral*; that novel was very important to me at the time. And sometimes it was not about any particular work; overall it was about how writers like Mario Vargas Llosa, Gabriel García Márquez, [V. S.] Naipaul, Graham Greene, used journalism to nurture their novels. [. . .]

I find it very interesting how you chose to take the tools of journalism and bring them to literature; it could be the other way around. What was your idea of journalism?

I think it is the opposite. I was always more attracted to the aesthetic side, absorbing those issues of journalism into an aesthetic world. I think I am still a little like this: when I do pure journalism, I am not so worried about aesthetics. I am surprised when people say, 'this is very well written', because I am not thinking about it [. . .] I understand the difference: for me there is a great responsibility in journalism to be very ethical, not to invent anything, not to hide anything, of not being biased; if something comes that challenges your argument, you have to include it.

But do you prefer writing fiction to writing texts like *The Art of Political Murder*?

I prefer fiction. That is pure non-fiction, it was a commitment. I always separate them. [. . .]

Have you developed a special working method to be able to collect the information before writing your works or is it different for each one?

Yes, for each one it is different. I think I feel a little slow now, I don't know what is wrong with me. In *The Divine Husband*, I was so disciplined, making notes, and I looked at files and real data. And the truth is that the most heroic thing about *The Art of Political Murder* was not the writing, but the investigation, it was about how to keep all that data in your head. [. . .]

Did *The Art of Political Murder* become an obsession?

It became a horrible obsession; I never want to have such an obsession in my life again. One had to handle so many details, so many legal cases, so much evidence, so many legal statements, so many views, so many facts. They were like individual bricks that were used to build the narrative. I am amazed I did it.

[. . .]

Was it a commission or something you wanted to do?

It started with an article in the *New Yorker*. So I got obsessed, it was such a fascinating case. I did an article about the trial, and from there I felt very committed to that story and very committed to the people who were at the heart of that story. They are people who really needed someone to tell the truth, at least of their story, because there was so much lying, so much propaganda [. . .].

Did you have any censorship issues during the investigation?

Not about censorship, because my public was from the United States, but there was a lot of danger always in that case. There are still things happening in that case.

And after the book publication?

For a long time [there were issues]. I won enemies there forever [. . .] but I felt that these kids needed someone to tell the truth; I was the only one who was in a position to do it, and I felt very compelled to do so. It was also a fascinating story.

Do you consider that there are particularities of Latin American non-fiction that makes it different from the American New Journalism style or the non-fiction from other countries?

The chronicle is different, indeed. There is not much practice of *crónica* in the United States. Perhaps at some point there was: Joseph Mitchell, the old *New Yorker*. Now the *New Yorker* publishes few non-fiction items as literary works; overall you are there to be a journalist, to do well-written journalism, narrative journalism perhaps [. . .].

What do you think are the characteristics or differences between the journalism of the 1970s and 1980s and what is called *crónica* or literary journalism today?

In the 1970s and 1980s, everything had more political pressure. Those were times when no one could evade or ignore those pressures; it was a world very saturated with ideology.

Did you have to take a stand?

More or less. And I always refused to do that as much as I could, and it was a lot of fun because sometimes I criticized the left, sometimes I criticized the right. When that happened, I felt good, that I had achieved what I wanted. I never liked being so Manichean, being so simplistic, I was always at the side of victims. I have always said I have no ideology; I have always been someone who is mainly pro-human rights, someone who supposedly has no ideology.

Do you think your border position, between two cultures, and the way your education differs from a journalist trained in Latin America have influenced your work?

There is no doubt about it, but I have never had much sympathy for the *gringo* point of view, neither then nor now, but it is another way [of doing journalism], you are more detached. I am always aware that I am not writing about Mexico right now as a Mexican would, I keep a distant position.
[. . .]

Do you think that the 'I' should not be in the text?

As little as possible. That is one thing that sometimes frustrates me with novels. For example, the novel I am writing right now is so I-I-I, and sometimes I would like it not to be like that, but it is like that for now, it is a very personal novel. [. . .]

Interview 5

Leila Guerriero (Junín, Argentina, 1967)

This interview was conducted in a single online session through Skype, on 6 October 2015.

When we talk about chronicle or non-fiction in Latin America, we mostly talk about two influences: one is the tradition of testimony, the *crónica de Indias*, the oral history by anthropologists such as Ricardo Pozas in Mexico; and another tradition is the one of the American New Journalism. Do you recognize yourself in any of these traditions?

[. . .] One suddenly finds a narrative technique or a way of looking and believes that it is super original, and it turns out that that had already been done by Álvar Núñez Cabeza de Vaca or Mr Rodolfo Walsh, or Tomás Eloy Martínez or [Guillermo] Prieto or [Carlos] Monsiváis or one of the Spanish-speaking chroniclers [. . .] I was always a very bookish person, and I also read journalism; within journalism I had been dazzled by some things, some things that were done here in Buenos Aires; I lived in a province but had studied in Buenos Aires. At home, there were a lot of magazines of all kinds, of comics, cultural [material], a lot of newspapers; at home, six journals were received per day [. . .]. One of these journalists who caught my eye, say, perhaps the one that mostly did, was Martín Caparrós; another of these journalists was Rodrigo Fresán. These journalists were working at *Página 12* newspaper and *Página 30*, which was a magazine that was published in those years [. . .] what dazzled me with them was like, 'ah, you can write journalism in this way!', it was a more casual style, much less a 'suit and tie' writing style [. . .] now it seems that [Ryszard] Kapuściński and Gay Talese were like the distant cousins of the family; these people were born glued to a book! Well, in those years in Argentina, for me and for the journalists of my generation – I am forty-eight years old – they were complete strangers. We knew the classics: Truman Capote, Tom Wolfe and those of our own countries: Rodolfo Walsh, Tomás Eloy Martínez, Caparrós, but we were distant from other traditions, what do I know? From the American side we knew the obvious: Tom Wolfe, Truman Capote; I don't think anyone was reading Joan Didion, Gay Talese, Janet Malcolm in those years [. . .] to answer your question, I would say that I recognize myself as part of the tradition of that Argentine journalism. I feel a little arrogant saying this, because if I had to think about where I would like to go or which journalists are here in this great ocean that is journalism, that I belong to, I believe that I swim, or try to swim in waters similar to that stream of Walsh, Caparrós, of all these people, shall we say. Of course, later one begins to broaden the spectrum and discovers that there are also other Latin American chroniclers who had an aesthetic conception of journalism, such as José Martí, César Vallejo when he did journalism, etcetera, etcetera, or Juan José de Sousa, Enrique Raab. I feel more part of that current from the Southern Cone.

As for the literary field, what did you read that might have had an influence on your style?

My style changes a lot. I think the style I have now is radically different from the one I had fifteen years ago and that was very different from the style I had when I started writing. I used to be much more baroque; clearly, this baroque style came from readings that I respect very much and that I love that I did [read them], which are prose that I now enjoy as a reader, but that do not resemble my voice, like [Ray] Bradbury or the Boom writers: García Marquez, or post-Boom: Bryce Echenique, for example, is an author I find endearing; but when I was a girl, the truth is that what I used to read was very frugal literature: Horacio Quiroga, well, Bradbury in his own way has his frugal style, what do I know? [Robert Louis] Stevenson. It seems to me that I read the typical things that a boy reads when he starts in reading, like Horacio Quiroga [. . .] Then when I was more a teenager, I threw myself on the classics, it was like a formation, I was self-educated [. . .] I read the cultural supplements. One book was taking you to another. Then you discovered a guy named [Arthur] Rimbaud, that Rimbaud took you to [Paul] Verlaine and that one to [Gustave] Flaubert, and after Flaubert you ended up in [Vladimir] Nabokov. [Julio] Cortázar was like a more intense reading for me, but I think the style is formed with many layers of things. I also went to the cinema a lot, read a lot of comics, graphic novels [. . .] in the last ten years, it has been radical to have discovered an American author named Lorrie Moore. I think that woman influenced my style more, in my way of seeing things, than many of my previous readings. [. . .]

How do you define your writing?

I am a journalist. I don't write fiction [. . .]

Do you think that the book is now the place to do good journalism or more creative journalism?

Yes, of course, the book is a good place [for this]. The place within books is somewhere the nature of which is common to this type of journalism: it is a more restful place, with more space, the prose is careful, there is more editing work, etcetera, but one must also think that many of these books that are published are anthologies of chronicles that have been published in the media before, so it would be unfair to the media to say, 'the natural place of these things is the books'. I think it has a place in both. It would also be like taking away a responsibility, 'Well, stay calm, you don't have to continue publishing us [in the media], after all we have the books'. No. The book also has a much more elite reception. Journalism is a vocation of service, shall we say. I want to tell people a lot of stories not so that people say, 'wow how well this woman writes!', but to share that story, as good, cute, happy, sad, whatever it is. It is more possible to do that in a media outlet than in a book that only about 2,000 people are going buy, hopefully. [. . .]

What attracts you to documentary storytelling?

I don't know how to answer that. This is what I like to do. I don't know why I like this and I don't like writing poetry. I don't have the talent to write poetry.

But you would not practise everyday news writing either. . .

No. I think the papers should be better written, but let's say, to me there is something about the news, about the adrenaline rush for the news, which I find very attractive, but which I think is very beyond my means. I spend a lot of time observing, thinking, getting to know what I want to say, and I think I would be exercising violence against myself permanently if I got into such a thing [news writing]. Besides, I don't think I have the talent for news writing. There are people who do it wonderfully well; I don't like to be as outstanding. It takes a kind of practice, even a kind of permanent attitude of suspicion, I would tell you, that I do not have, it is not in my nature, and good news journalists do have it [. . .] the documentary format gives me freedom, within the enormous amount of limits that it imposes, I feel freedom within those limits: I have a clear border, I know where I can go, where I cannot, I know what I can do, what I cannot do [. . .]

* * *

Are there ethical limits on the investigations?

I believe that everyone, facing the loneliness of their research and their text, works as he works with the baggage of the rest of their lives. There are basic ethical rules, which you can imagine, what do I know? Not to betray an off-the-record account, there are also discussions about that. Obviously, you should not invent something that did not exist, not lying, at least not shamelessly; but well, what do I know? My rule, I would tell you, is to try to sit down and write only when I have something to say about the story and I feel that I have all the information [. . .] But the word 'ethics', I would not wish to use that card, not because I am planning to commit plagiarism in the future, but because it seems to me that it is vain, because one always at some point is wrong, screws up. You cannot ask a journalist what is not asked of another person with another foolproof trade. It seems to me that we all make mistakes, those mistakes can be awful in diverse degrees, sometimes you screw up even without realizing it. I know that I will never invent something, I know that I will always try to check the information. [. . .]

Do you follow any specific method for doing your investigations based on some journalism training, or any other method obtained in formal education?

No, I never took a journalism course, not a workshop or anything; everything I learned, I learned it in the newsrooms. But I have a method, like everyone else, which basically consists firstly in doing the whole stage of the investigation, the reportage; after that I do the transcripts of all the recordings myself – I transcribe everything, until the last word spoken – and, finally, I print all that, and, before I sit down and write, I read all that material, review the videos I have to review.
[. . .]

Is information a priority over style?

Yes, of course, it is journalism. You have to keep that in mind [. . .] When you write non-fiction, you never have to lose sight of what you are doing, which is transferring information, maybe in a very well-written form, but it is still information.

How much of your work is done because a job is commissioned and how much is about doing something that catches your eye or motivates you?

It depends. I would tell you that 70–75 per cent are my own proposals and the rest are commissions from editors, more or less. It depends on the times, sometimes it is more like 50–50.
[. . .]

How do you make the first approach to an informant?

Look, it is usually by a phone call. When I call on the phone, I introduce myself, I say who I am [...] And then, well, I propose a first encounter. Usually there is no problem with that, sometimes there are more complicated people [...] I am not offended at all that people want to meet me beforehand and have a coffee with me, after all we will live together for a while and not only that, but I will be repository of a story that for them is the story of their life. I don't think it is a bad thing that they want to know who I am. And those first encounters are not at all uncomfortable; in general, people relax. Of course, they are not interested in me at all, they don't care about me, luckily, and they talk more about other things. [...]

Do you consider that your personality has any influence on the conversations with your interviewees?

Mmm... I suppose so; you wear yourself all the time. I cannot be any different as I am as a person to the way I am as a journalist. I can probably recognize in myself a great listening ability, even before I was a journalist. I don't speak too much; well, now I speak because you are asking me and it would be horrible if I did not talk to you, but in intimate circumstances, with family or friends, I don't speak much. I am not a typical chatterbox; I am not telling my life to everybody. I mean, with my friends I have a nice relationship, but except under certain circumstances, I think they always talk more about themselves than I do about myself, and for some reason I think people feel they can trust me to tell me a story they would not tell anyone else. It seems to me that it has to do with a certain degree of discretion I have, but I think above it all that this is because of the ability I have since very young of not to judge.

Do you think that this way of being in a real dialogue with the informant differs from what you later represent in the texts, when you reproduce that conversation, and you include yourself?

I don't think so [...] Whenever I show up, it is for the question to reflect something of the interviewee, not of me, but I actually feel that if I don't put that question that doesn't happen [...] I don't believe in transforming the narrator when he appears into a more caustic, sarcastic or braver character than he was [...] Of course, at the time of editing there are questions that are made shorter, the dialogue is edited because, if not, it would be a court transcript.

What leads you to choose to transcribe a statement directly, to represent that dialogue with you in it or to simply present the interview as a source of information?

[. . .] I believe that when one perceives that there are things that have to have a stronger narrative tension, it is not a very good idea to give the voice to the protagonist of the matter, it depends. There are no rules with that. I evaluate that [. . .] how this story will be read better, how the weight of the information will be better perceived: whether the person tells it themselves, or if I tell it, or if we share the voice.

When you choose to reproduce a dialogue in your text, is it a dialogue that really happened that way?

Yes, of course [. . .] when these small dialogues appear, of course they happened in reality, and it seems to me that they can shed a little more light on the person whose life I am telling.

How would you define a successful or effective interview?

I think it is an interview in which one achieves connection with the interviewee, an interview that contains information, that has emotion [. . .] an interview that also generates in you as an interviewer the enthusiasm to keep asking, right? [. . .]

How do you decide who the character you want to talk about is? As in *Una historia sencilla* (A Simple Story), for example.

Well, *A Simple Story* was kind of unexpected, as you may have read in the book. I was going to tell the story of the Laborde Festival, and suddenly I met that man dancing on stage, and I think at that moment I was sure that the story needed to have him, in a rather kamikaze way let's say, because it meant following him for a year and a half without knowing what could happen [. . .] There is always something that moves my curiosity; there is always a dark spot or blind spot that, although one can read many news stories about those people, still generates curiosity, intrigue, and I cannot answer who that person is, what happened to that person. I think that is it: there is an unsatiated curiosity. I want to know, and journalism is like the best excuse to get you into places that for other people are prohibited.

Is this curiosity also generated because the interviewees are very different from you? How difficult is it to have a dialogue with a person so different from you?

Well... no, it is not hard for me. It seems to me that it is more difficult to talk about a person similar to me and then write about it because empathy is very strong [...] When people are really different and belong to a world that has nothing to do with my world, I have an attitude just as discreet, very humble, very cautious, I would tell you, because I do not want to be a demagogic person and chameleonize and become part of that person's world when I am not; and I also don't want to be offensive and contravene any of the little codes that are in people's lives and that one still fails to comprehend. [...]

How close is the relationship you establish with your informants?

During the stage when I am reporting, I am very close to people and then, well, it depends, I usually continue in a good relationship, but I think my work ends there, in the publication, and then there is common sense. There are people I have been very close to; for example, people from the Argentine forensic anthropology team, who are my friends, they come to have lunch at my home on weekends. [Guillermo] Kuitca is another person with whom I have stayed very close, not of friendship, I clarify, but he is a person for whom I have a lot of affection, I think it is a mutual affection, and every time I publish a book I go to his house and bring him a copy, he was here having dinner a few months ago too [...] they belong to worlds that I feel very close to mine, it was very difficult to write about these people precisely because of that. But in the case of Rodolfo, for example, the protagonist of *A Simple Story*, I have continued meeting him. I think he was one of the people I saw most assiduously after a text was published.

But you have not developed a friendship with him after that?

No, I could not say that we are friends [...] the truth is that in general terms, what I usually have with people after publishing a text is an affable relation of friendship, let's say. In fact, many times it happens that there are interviewees who have insisted on going for a coffee or so, and I am a little elusive in this, unless there is a certain reason, I do it very few times [...] When I see that there is someone who has some needs, I try to help if it is within my means, but I also take into account that this is not an exchange of favours; this is journalism: if you want to tell me your story, I will tell it, but do not wait in return for me to publish you a letter in the paper, or to help you solve your life or transform myself into your friend. For me, that distance is always very clear. If it happens, it happens, I don't object, but I know my role is another one. My role is to be there to tell a story.

[...]

Pierre Bourdieu said that an interview, so that it had less scope for error, had to be done between equals [. . .] I would like to know what you think about this and also to discuss a little about who the other is to you. . .

In principle I think it is a false assumption that there might be someone who is an equal. [. . .] people are super different. Even if one assumes that one has the same social, cultural, etcetera, extraction, the other is always an enigma [. . .] I think a journalist's job is to go against the commonplace and against the idea of comfort. Thinking that 'the other' has to be someone like me or someone very similar so I can understand him or for my interview to be true, well, it is out of my comprehension. I think I find it much more challenging when I get into realities that have nothing to do with my everyday reality than when I feel like I am with someone culturally closer.

In the case of Latin American writing, there are repeated topics, such as poverty, violence, prisons. Do you think that there are certain particularities of Latin American reality that attract journalists to write about these issues?

There are certain features in Latin American reality that are closely related to these issues, and that is why journalists try to make those stories visible. It seems to me that we exaggerate somewhat when we only tell those stories [. . .] it does seem to me that there is still an enormous inequality, that the situation in prisons is appalling, that the situation of women has been set aside, the situation of education is precarious, etcetera, so the reality of ours is very different from the reality of a continent like the European one; it is other than the Asian continent, distinct from American reality. It would be very rare for journalists not to want to relate to those realities because they are the things we have every day before our eyes [. . .] I think it is honourable [of journalists] to keep telling these stories, although I repeat it to you, it seems to me that they are not the only stories to tell.

But they are also stories that sell, if we consider the commercial part of the media. Thinking about the boom of stories about drug trafficking in Mexico, for example.

No, look, it would be very unfair to say that in the case of the stories of drug trafficking in Mexico, colleagues are doing them because they sell, because they are killing colleagues in Mexico. I think it is an atrocious reality. What happens in these stories is that there are no new points of view; that is, many of those stories don't contribute and end up like tolling the bell, which is like trivializing the subject: 'Well, they killed another one', and that is what doesn't have to happen. But well, within that kind of journalism there is well-done journalism and poorly done journalism. Good stories open their own way. At least in the kind of journalism that I do or try to do. I don't think you think in terms of how much you sell because the truth is that the magazines in which I publish do not sell 400,000 copies; they are small magazines, with financial problems. Books published within the genre are books of modest print runs; they do not sell anywhere near 8,000 copies, and 500 reprints are not made. I think the term 'sale' may be reflected in the news, but so is this idea that the news is the bad news; the good news doesn't matter much to anyone [. . .] Journalism is the best excuse to get anywhere, so journalists are usually curious, fearless people, etcetera, etcetera. Having the chance to get into the gang world in El Salvador with the perfect trade is also very attractive, isn't it?

Some Southern Cone academics, such as Beatriz Sarlo and Nelly Richard, have questioned the excess of testimony as a resource of plausibility [. . .] How do you believe in an interviewee's story?

[. . .] I think we all have a public story to tell about ourselves. In principle I depart from that assumption: the interviewee will tell me some things that his memory has also been avoiding. In some cases, he has done better or worse [than he remembers]; in some cases, it is not so true to what happened in his time, of course I am very interested in that version. Then I check out other material, when there are things written by journalists or biographers about that person and I am very good at choral testimonies: not only to have the testimony of the interviewee but also to have the testimony of his wife, his ex-wife, his enemy, his best friend, the boy with whom he went to school. All these testimonies somehow complete, contradict, and help give the reader nods about what is legend or confirmed truth within all that [. . .]

Would this be a difference between doing journalism and writing a testimonial novel?

I suppose the one who makes a novel can make the interviewee say whatever he wants in order to achieve plausibility. As a journalist one must also achieve plausibility, but on the basis of the facts that reality provides. I mean, you cannot create plausibility by saying 'here I could use a character, an old lady who says such a thing,' that cannot be done.

> In the end the journalist also struggles with language in that sense: he seeks to create plausibility even in telling a story that did happen; it is not enough that it is real.

No, it is not enough that it is real, it has to look real, and in that search for looking real – because reality can be implausible – you have to put into that text everything you have seen. You cannot invent anything to make it look real.

* * *

> Regarding *Los suicidas del fin del mundo* (The Suicidal Ones at the End of the World), I would like to know what motivated you to write the story and how you found out about it.

The book describes it very clearly: one day I got a press release from an NGO called Poder Ciudadano (Citizen Power), as it should have gone to the entire staff at *La Nación* newspaper. They said that they were going to implement a plan to train young negotiators, that it had been a human development plan created by Harvard University and that they were going to implement it in two or three sites in Argentina in order to provide people with tools to resolve conflicts without the need to reach hostility or violence. One of these places they were going to implement this programme was the city of Las Heras, which I had never heard of. [. . .] They mentioned a figure of twenty-two people who committed suicide. And I found it super interesting because, first of all, I am interested in the stories of the provinces; it seems to me that not everything has to happen in Buenos Aires; then because there were some issues that had to do with bigger things like the privatization of YPF, which I found attractive too and, well, finally [it involved] a social situation that seemed super precarious to me: the part of the employment, alcoholism, domestic violence, the suicidal ones. Then I went there and clearly the suicidal ones became the narrative thread to tell the story of this place so forgotten by God, I would tell you, so devoid of all kinds of citizens' rights.

> Was the story intended to be a book from the beginning?

No, not at all. I was going to make a piece for *Rolling Stone*. Then *Rolling Stone* finally ran out of budget, because it was the 2001 crisis here, so I went on my own, without knowing very well what I was going to do next with the information I gathered [. . .] I had a hard time finding a publishing house because publishers were not interested in a book about suicides, they thought it was going to be a very dark book that people would not be interested in [. . .] I found a place in a more unexpected publishing house because non-fiction was not a consolidated genre in Tusquets at the time, but it was my adored friend Sergio Olguín who suggested that I submitted the book and so I did.

Did you have an editor who worked closely with you during or after the writing process?

I really did not have one. Sergio Olguín looked at the text while I was writing it, because I had never written a book, I did not know how to write a book [. . .] I had taken a month and a half of vacation from the newspaper to write [. . .]

When you publish short stories or chronicles, do you usually work closely with an editor?

No, no, no, no, usually not. I usually submit the work and it gets published as it is, except for some minor doubts or some mistakes that there may be with dates.

When did you make the decision to use the first person in storytelling? It is something you don't do that much of in shorter pieces.

Yes, I never do, except in the opinion pieces because there I am interested in using a strong 'I' to take responsibility for what I am saying. I had the feeling that I had to write it in the first person and consulted it with Jordi Carrión, a very intelligent Spanish journalist, and he said, 'you have to write it in the first person, decidedly'. My decision to write it in the first person had to do with me needing that hostile landscape of life that for them was the most natural thing in the world [. . .] I needed to contrast all this with the gaze of someone for whom everything that seemed natural to them would be what it was: a monstrosity, let's say. The only one I had on hand was myself. So that is why I wrote it in the first person, to establish that contrast between the naturalized gaze of all those poor neighbours who were forgotten by the world, who had assumed that you just had to deal with it, and this big city-dweller character who acted as an axis [*she laughs*], who had internet in her house, who could move freely around the world and whose neighbours were not trying to kill themselves every three days. That contrast between someone for whom the brutal does not have to be part of everyday life and these people for whom the brutal was the only thing that was part of everyday life seemed super important to me for the book, so that the reader understood the degree of brutality, of the process of desensitization that these people were experiencing. That is why I wrote it in the first person. I also followed some of the advice of Homero Alcina Thevenet, who said that the only reason one had to use the first person was to talk about a non-transferrable experience, and I think this was a non-transferrable experience.

Did you somehow start building a character onto yourself? Who is that Leila Guerriero as narrator? How would you define the narrator?

Well, a little bit of what I told you before: I am not very different from what is in the texts. Uh... I think I am a tough chick, frugal with words, a discreet chick, a chick you are never going to see drunk, climbing onto a table dancing the chachacha, let's say. I don't think it is any different from what is in there. There are moments that are edited because no one is interested, what do I know? There are moments when I talk to my husband from Las Heras to Buenos Aires, what do people care about what I speak about or what I don't talk about? Also in *A Simple Story*, I think the essence of what I am is more or less reflected. There is always a narrator that is a bit of a construction, but it is an edited version of yourself rather. It is what the story needs, but it is not an invention.

[...]

How do you define the book [*Los suicidas*]?

Uh... now the word '*crónica*' is used a lot. We could say it is a *crónica*. I like 'a non-fiction book', I would say; a non-fiction report, if you like.

Well, the problem with *crónica* is that its definition includes everything...

Of course, isn't it? It is like a written documentary to me. For me there is no difference between making a documentary film and writing a text like these ones, that's it: it is a documentary, but in written form.

Did you get inspired by some other book for this story?

Look, I remember when I was writing it, I was reading something that has nothing to do with this so as not to contaminate me, which was a book by [John] Irving that I have read about 400,000 times, that is *The World According to Garp* [...] Jordi Carrión recommended that I read 'The Crime Part', of [Roberto] Bolaño's *2666*, and I looked at it superficially and I did not want to read it, because I felt like I was going to stay very attached to that [. . .] if I read more than that book I don't remember it, I worked many hours a day besides: from seven in the morning to twelve o'clock at night, unstoppably, because I had to take advantage of the time I had to write, so I did not have a lot of time left to read.

How much time did you have for writing the book?

I think a month and a week, a month and a half, a thing like that.

I find it very honest how you end up saying that you cannot give a single answer, an explanation for the suicide cases. I would like to know, then, what is the purpose of doing this kind of journalism for you? If the result can be so uncertain, what motivates you to conduct such an exhaustive investigation? And where can we find the truth of a story like this, if any?

It is just not about finding the truth, that is precisely the difference between this kind of journalism and investigative journalism. Investigative journalism investigates and tries to give an answer, tries to bring to light something that refuses to be brought to light and has to say, for example, 'the president so-and-so sold weapons to the country such-and-such in such a year and this is the evidence', there has to be a clear answer. In the kind of journalism I do, I find the answer less interesting the more reductionist it is. [. . .] Also, finally, I would like to mention that in every act of reading, in every act of writing, there is an aesthetic enjoyment that seems to me as though it is also part of an ethics. I think the aesthetic enjoyment when it comes to reading non-fiction is as important as when it comes to reading fiction. If they tell you a good story that is well told, you are not looking for an answer, you are enjoying it. Even if it is a terrible story.

Interview 6
Elena Poniatowska (Paris, France, 1932)

There were two interviews, on 3 September 2013 and 9 January 2015. Both were conducted in the author's house in the neighbourhood of Chimalistac, in Mexico City.

How did you begin your career as a journalist and literature writer?

Everything has been simultaneous. I started my journalistic career in 1953, but in 1954 I started publishing literature in the collection *Los presentes*, where Carlos Fuentes, José Emilio, Alvaro Mutis published.

Is the process different when you write journalism than when you write literature?

It is very difficult to say, because it certainly takes a long time to write literature. Not only do I write, but I rewrite, rework. I have full boxes filled with typed manuscripts of the same book, sometimes there are eight versions of the same book. Journalism is immediate: one makes an article that is published the next day or three days later; it does not work like fiction, it is totally different. [. . .]

What is your relationship with the interviewees like?

It is great, if it was not, I could not write books. It is a relationship of great affection, of camaraderie. Overall, the people I visit know I am doing a book.

How does contact with someone you have never met begin?

Just like you, who came through the door a minute ago. There are people who are nicer than others, or people with whom one feels an immediate sympathy and even complicity, but there are others with whom that does not happen. Anyway, I could never make a book about someone I did not love or admire.

What does a person have to have for you to be interested in them?

They have to be a warm-hearted person; of course, they have to be a loving person. They can also be very defensive, but deep down I know they are a loving person. For example, in Guillermo Haro's biography, I say that he was very defensive with me; he said that journalists were dropouts from all careers, that they were useless, that they knew nothing, but I took revenge on him by marrying him.

Do you think the relationship between the interviewee and the interviewer has to be loving?

It has to be because making a book in a condition other than love would be torture, punishment and I don't think that is the way it is.

Can't it be an objective relationship?

It can be too, but then the books made are drier. I don't think I make dry books, nor cold or distant ones.

How do you choose information? What happens when you have already gathered it?

I choose what motivates me, what excites me, that is the main guide. What tells me something I think will say something to the reader, but after all that there is a lot of work, a lot of research, lots of reading. As time goes on more and more, because when you are young you are more unconscious... [*her servant brings tea for us*] Thank you, Martincilla .. you think it is possible to do things with a certain naivety, spontaneity, that they will forgive you your faults, that it will be easy for them to forgive you, but when you are like me, eighty years old, you know they are going to get on you if you are wrong, if you give the wrong information, if you screw up, as you say vulgarly, that is why I do more and more research, I read more and more.

What have been the hardest interviews for you?

A lot of them have been difficult, because I started my career very young. I remember a Frenchman, Francois Mauriac. I remember he told me that if I had not read his books, that if I had not been prepared, he would have walked me to the door and told me to come back when I had read something. I wrote about what happened in that failed interview, as it happened. This was in France, I was twenty-one. I brought the text later to him and he really liked the interview, because it was the confession of my failure.

Is there a different kind of ethics in journalism than in literature?

In journalism you cannot invent, but in literature you can. [. . .]

Many of your interviewees are very different from you . . .

It has been very useful to me because I have entered totally unknown worlds. I was always interested in people who had nothing to do with me, like Jesusa Palancares, who had been in the [Mexican] Revolution and who is probably the person for whom I feel the greatest admiration, for how she led her life. Everything that she was provokes tenderness and sympathy in me [. . .]

Do you faithfully transcribe everything your interviewees tell you?

I have got the transcripts upstairs [*of her house*]. I have thousands of complete transcripts, but I use just what moves me, what I feel is going to be useful to write what I want to write.

Do you do this also in journalism or in a chronicle?

No, when it comes to journalism, my problem is that everything has to be as faithful to reality as possible. It happens also with the novel, but I put the feelings in the novel. [For example, when I describe] lovemaking: I don't know how Tina Modotti did it and I do depict her making love [in the novel]. [. . .] I have a good ear; I retain the way people speak, and that is how I write their speech in novels. I listen to a lot of popular speech because when I arrived from France, that was the language that hit me. I did not go to a school where people spoke Spanish, but French and English. I learned Spanish from the streets.

* * *

[...]

Is it difficult to interview marginalized people that have never been interviewed?

Sometimes marginalized people give great surprises and are much more coherent than a good posh girl who does not even know where the sun comes from [*long silence*] I was a good posh girl.
[...]

Did you leave aside much of your personal life for recording the lives of others?

In the end, your personal life is what you do in your home, and it is the loneliness of writing. You have to get used to being alone, to people rejecting you because you don't participate; they tell you, 'oh, how arrogant you are! What do you think of yourself? Things are not going to change because you are writing and writing, what does it matter what you are doing?' Besides, you have to think about it throughout your life. When you have children, you start blaming yourself and saying, 'I don't take enough care of my children, I am not with them all the time.' While your children are telling you something, you are distracted and thinking of something else.

* * *

To what extent is it enough to record reality?

What is important is to do what [Carlos] Monsiváis did. He made up conclusions, he analysed what he observed and he made eminently political and philosophical texts about what Mexico was like: from funky holes to the weight of religion. He fought hard for a secular state.

Would your fiction have been different if you had not done journalism?

Probably... [*she interrupts the conversation to get rid of her two cats, Monsi and Vais, as I told her I have zoophobia*]

How hard was it to be different from your interviewees?

Jesusa Palancares rejected me at first, but then she accepted me. It is difficult to go towards something that you do not know, that is not familiar, but I have all my life had a very large inclination towards things that are nothing like what I have lived [...] People tell me I should not say this, but at this point in my life I am so sorry I did not go to university. I feel like it would have helped me a lot. People tell me, 'your university was the street', but I feel like I have worked more than usual. The first year I did journalism, I did 365 interviews, one daily; I was, as they say, *picada*, obsessed.

Why didn't you go to college?

Because in my day in my family there was not so much that possibility. I studied at a nuns' convent in the United States, at The Sacred Heart. It would have been the equivalent to junior high school and high school; I did not revalidate it, I had to revalidate.[1] All I studied was typing at an academy in San Juan de Letrán [in Mexico City]; that is all I know how to do, what I studied. I think I'd have saved myself a lot of laps if I'd gone to college, I'd have acquired a methodology I don't have. My methodology is to work three times as hard as those who do know how to do things. Now the computer makes it much easier for you because you can change the position of paragraphs. The internet makes things much easier because you are looking for a character and all of a sudden he appears on the internet and that is it!

Do you use the internet for your work?

No, I use it a little, but I know I can turn to it. My informants are the voices in the street. [...]

* * *

---

[1] She is referring to the process for the recognition by Mexican institutions of a foreign certificate of education.

You were saying you have to prepare for your interviews...

Well, now, because when I was young, I went crazy without knowing anything about anything, but when you are young, I think people like you, even if you don't know anything and ask pure idiotic questions. You are liked because of your youth. Besides, at the time I did journalism, there were few journalists, so you would arrive, and people would accept you.

And what questions did you ask?

I asked Diego Rivera if his teeth were made out of milk because I had never seen a painting by him, I came from a nuns' convent. I said to myself, 'he is very tall, very big and his teeth [are] very small', and he said, 'yes, they are of milk and with these teeth I eat the nosy little Polish girls', and then I had an interview. And I got an audience that used to say, 'let's see what this silly girl is going to ask' [...]

Have you read works of the New Journalism when you wrote *Hasta no verte Jesús mío* (Here's to you, Jesusa)?

No, but the one who did have them was Monsiváis. He was younger than me, but he was a well-informed person, he had not been locked up in a nuns' convent praying. He would not suggest readings to me, but he would take care of me, he used to encourage me a lot. [...]

Was he your mentor?

Not at all. My mentor is the people on the street. [...]

What literary generation do you feel part of?

Well, [Enrique] Krauze and all of them always put us together: Monsi [Carlos Monsiváis], [José Emilio] Pacheco and I, but I am older than them. I don't know why they put us together, maybe because we care about social problems. [...]

Does a writer need to have a political commitment?

I feel that in Mexico it is very difficult not to have it. You really need to lock yourself in stone and mud, because reality enters your house and overwhelms you. I think that you can write about the states of your souls in New York or Paris, but in Mexico there is a reality that hits you every moment and in every corner.

What do you commit yourself to politically?

Since 2005 I have been politically linked with Andrés Manuel López Obrador. I do the tasks that he entrusts to me; usually it has to do with writing. I go to the rallies, the meetings that I have to go to and also other social causes: the causes of feminism, of women. I am a feminist, I am in favour of women doing better in this country. [. . .]

Which journalists do you admire?

I rather admire literary authors: Marguerite Yourcenar, Virginia Woolf. Journalists, too. I think there are great journalists in Mexico, but I would not know many journalists as I know writers, like Elvira Lindo, a very good Spanish author, or Rosa Montero.

Have you learned from some writers in particular?

I really like Katherine Mansfield, an Australian, an extraordinary storyteller who has never been overcome. The list of writers I admire is endless.

* * *

What does the interview mean to you?

I can only see it as a dialogue. There are thousands of interviews, you know better than I do: there is the interview to get a news story, which is to put the microphone in the interviewee's mouth, among many journalists, to get the interview; but I don't do those kinds of interviews. I do the kind of interview that Americans call *profile*, that is, to describe what the house is like, what the wife is like, what the cat is like, who comes in, who goes out, whether it is cold or hot. I describe the character in his environment or at least that is what I am trying to do.

You think that says more than a news piece?

I don't know, I can't judge. I know that writing is my craft [*she looks at my voice recorder*] It is already turned off, look! [*she looks again to the recorder*] Oh, no, it is not true! . .

. And I do it with the best will in the world, but I don't know what the outcome looks like for the readers. I guess if I have not been fired from the newspaper and if I have not been told to go to rest now, it is because I contribute somehow.

* * *

[...]

You and Monsiváis had a very particular perspective on Mexican reality. Do you notice differences between what you have done and what is now being done in narrative journalism in Mexico?

I think journalism has now been modernized a lot. I think Monsiváis at one point was the one who started doing a journalism of social justice, a journalism in which the truth was told, a very direct journalism and also very analytical of what was happening, what can be called 'investigative journalism'. He would ask what had happened; he would do things in the place of the events. I remember in 1985 we both stayed on the street. I stayed longer than him because he had other commitments, but I remember staying on the street for at least four months after the earthquake.

What was that reporting job like?

It was to do what you are doing: to ask questions, only in much more difficult circumstances, not sitting in an illuminated room, with flowers and books, waiting for tea, but on the street, standing, in circumstances of tragedy, because people were observing their own drama, their own tragedy.

Do you consider the 1985 Mexico City earthquake to be one of the main events that moved you at the time?

No, I consider everything I have seen to have moved me. There is the tale of the colony Rubén Jaramillo, near Atlixco, in Guerrero, because it was also something that shocked me. I was struck by the 1968 massacre. Several events: fires that broke out, the fireworks factory. In Mexico you get very used to little fireworks, the artificial lights. All those things were experienced at the very moment [they happened], of course they had a big impact on me.

I sense that your gaze in the chronicles of this period is a very surprised gaze at reality, as if you saw it for the first time, what were you experiencing?

I don't think I saw it as for the first time, but in order to write I had to give importance to what was happening.

Was there previous work on the investigation?

Yes, a lot. There were so many interviews. I have done a lot of research all my life. I talked to many people before I chose which character I was going to give more importance to than someone else.

What do you consider when you choose your informants?

It is just intuition or instinct, or interest in what is happening, or I look at the person there that is more alert or more affected by what is going on and more willing to talk. [...]

Bringing to mind your relationship with Jesusa Palancares, for example, do you maintain a relationship with the people you interview?

Of course, over the years, it goes on and on. For example, right now I have a very strong relationship with Evangelina Corona, who was the leader of the seamstresses in 1985. We visit each other, she comes here to have lunch, that kind of thing. [...]

There are authors who say that they never write anything that the interviewee has not said literally, because that would not be true.

Well, I use the tape recorder and transcribe. Obviously, if I use a tape recorder and transcribe, I am as loyal as possible to what the interviewee tells me.

About the controversy with *La noche de Tlatelolco*, regarding the testimonies. . .

No, that was a problem that arose after thirty years of the publication of *La noche de Tlatelolco*. Luis González de Alba waited thirty years to say that there was not a certain person on the third floor but on the fifth floor, that he had not said as such, or the word that was reproduced in the book. Rather than a problem for me, it is a problem for Luis González de Alba.

Yes, well, that is what I meant, there are authors who can go so far as to specify each piece of information, but perhaps the important thing is in the interpretation of the facts. . . Do you follow a methodology?

No, I don't follow methods, I do what I can, I don't have methods. [. . .]

* * *

[. . .]

I think there is a difference between your style and that of other authors who become one more character in their own chronicle. When I read your chronicles, it is very difficult to find the 'I'. I don't know if this is intentional. . .

Yes, it is intentional. The day I have time or want to write my biography I will use the 'I', but when I am doing a chronicle of something that happens outside of me, I don't see the need to insert myself, to talk about myself: whether my feet hurt or if I have been standing for twelve hours waiting, for example, in an earthquake or a tragedy, as in the many I have lived through.

Have you considered writing memoirs of what you have been through?

No, in what I write there is a lot of myself; in the interviews and chronicles there is a lot of my own life.

Do you consider the chronicle to be a particular way of representing reality today or is it a genre that has always existed as such?

I believe that in Mexico there have been exceptional chroniclers, such as Hermann Bellinghausen, Carlos Monsiváis, Héctor Aguilar Camín, Jaime Avilés. There are great chroniclers in Mexico, and they often make us think that no novelists are needed because Mexican reality far outweighs fiction. When one sees, for example, the murder in Tijuana of Luis Donaldo Colosio and then one sees how his wife, Diana Laura, died a month after, I believe that there is a Shakespearean tragedy, as in *Macbeth,* and that everything surpasses any novel that a writer would like to write. So there are many issues in Mexico; there is a very strong reality that deserves to be consigned [to record] and that many have decided to record and those have been the chroniclers whose names I have just mentioned.

Do you think the *crónica* is a better form to narrate reality?

No, I don't think anything. I think there are good chronicles and good novels, good stories and good poems. Not that one form is better than another. [...]

I would like to talk a little bit about *La herida de Paulina*. It took me a while to find it...

Yes, it is sold out.

Didn't you want a reprint?

Books don't depend on the author; they depend on whether the publisher wants to publish it or does not want to publish it. This is a book I constantly forget. It is a book I don't feel any love for.

Why did you write it?

Because Martha Lamas asked me to. Because it was a raped girl who had not been given access to abortion and they, the feminists, dealt a lot with the issue of abortion and, therefore, I did so out of friendship with Martha Lamas. But there are two books which I did a little bit to feel pious as they say. One is about Gaby Brimmer, who is a girl who has cerebral palsy, and I was asked to do it and I accepted, but I did not like doing it; and I liked doing Paulina's book even less. With Gaby Brimmer's book, well, it happened, but the other one for me was no joy, it was no pleasure to publish that book. Besides, I think they are two books that have nothing to do with literature. [...]

When you write chronicle, do you consider a different reader than for the novel?

No, I cannot think of the reader because I don't know who the reader is, right? When my mum was alive, I could think, 'my mother is going to read it', but since my mother died in 2001 I don't know who can be a reader anymore. One writes, but one cannot imagine one's audience. However, I do can imagine the audience of *La noche de Tlatelolco* because of the kids, because of the friendship of the young students that book brought me. [...]

Do you think a book changes its value when it is said to be based on real facts or that it is a true story?

I don't know, for me all the books are real. I don't understand why people have to say that all is fiction. I feel that everyone writes from their own self: when they are not describing their childhood, they are describing their adolescence or the present. [...]

Even in journalism, is the 'I' always present?

No, the 'I' is not present there, but there are many things. When you tell me that if I have not written my autobiography, I would say that in the books one writes, merely the fact of choosing certain events and leaving aside certain others is already a way of speaking of oneself. Anyway, you talk about yourself, even doing an article, don't you?

Where is your point of view?

I am inside, I cannot be outside; if I was outside, I could not write. I don't think anyone is objective, everyone writes departing from himself and from his circumstances.

Can you be a mere observer?

I never have been, but maybe someone will make it, I don't know.

* * *

Have you had any particular case of censorship before publishing your texts?

Well, when I started in journalism there were taboos: Our Lady of Guadalupe, the army, the president of the [Mexican] Republic and his family, the [Catholic] Church. There were issues you could not talk about in a negative way. [...]

In that case, could publishing books be an alternative to avoid censorship a little?

Yes, of course, *La noche de Tlatelolco* is a book made with censored articles only, it is a book not allowed by censorship. When it was published, it was also censored.

Would you have preferred to publish that story in newspapers?

No, I don't impose my preferences, as you say. Things happen, and if they don't happen, well, they don't. To me now my only serious problem that I have awareness of is that of old age, because at eighty-three I know that I do not have many years to do everything I have and want to do.

Do you still have topics you have not explored?

Yes, I have many topics that I want to do regarding my work, and I also want to protect my family somehow, to be aware of my family and my country [...]

Last year, when I came to visit you, we talked about how you started doing journalism. I am interested in analysing the journalist's conversation with the informants during fieldwork. I do think your style is very different to those journalists trying to impose a first-person narration [...] Do you deliberately try to keep a certain style or overall gaze in all your *crónicas* or each text is treated differently?

No, I think you work on your personal nature. The word 'deliberate' I don't think is part of my way of being, I just do a job which, since 1953, has been more or less the same. Of course, as a result of so many years, there is already a certain way of doing it; maybe there would be another that would be a hundred times better, but the path I found is the path on which I will always fall naturally because it is what I have practised all my life, whether that is good or bad. Sometimes one would want to reinvent oneself, or to be born or resurrect and be someone else, but God does not fulfil cravings nor straighten hunchbacks.

[...]

I think it is very difficult to balance the hard data or numbers with qualitative information that is left for the memory mostly, but many journalists prefer the figures...

Well, it depends, because they are also asked for figures in their papers, right? There is always a chief information officer, an editor-in-chief. Every newspaper has a way of being, some greatly reduce their information and some don't. Other newspapers can write 25,000 pages; it depends on the famous space: if there are no dead, there is more space; if there are no ads, there is more space. In a newspaper like *La Jornada*, which has very few advertisements, there is more space, but there are newspapers that what matters most to them is advertising, then the information is reduced to ten lines or twelve.

Interview 7

Santiago Roncagliolo (Lima, Perú, 1975)

The interview was conducted in three sessions on 7, 8 and 9 July 2014, in restaurants in El Borne neighbourhood, in Barcelona.

I would like to know how you started in literature and when did journalism come in, what came first?

It all started at the same time. I wanted to study journalism and my father told me, 'what are you going to study in journalism? Writing and spelling? Go and study another starving career and then you do journalism, that is what we all do', because he also did journalism, he was a columnist, even though he worked on other things. I studied literature, but I was always sure that what I liked was writing, not being academic or reflecting on texts but writing scripts, journalism, whatever.

And you expected to live on it?

Well, I never thought I was going to live on being a writer, this happened, but it was not planned. I always thought that what I could live on was writing, I am not very good at anything else either and I don't like anything else much either. So, while studying literature, I always dedicated myself to writing: I made television scripts, political speeches, all of it was writing work, and then I went forward and came to Spain with the idea of being a writer, but I came to write scripts [. . .] Then I started writing books and started living off them, but even now I like to keep writing journalism, columns and reportages because if I did not I would be a guy locked in my room all day with my ideas, self-absorbed. Journalism takes you out, puts you in touch with people, gives you stories, gives you a good life. My novels are also fed on what I do.

Do you think your fiction would have been different if you had not practised journalism?

Yes, of course, I cannot even think of how I could have written novels without being a journalist, because I usually do a lot of research, and, even if I don't necessarily investigate, there is a certain journalist's eye for looking at the details, to look at things and relate them, which is a trade that serves you a lot in being a writer. Being a foreigner is also good for that eh: I grew up in Mexico and then I had to go to Peru, which was my own country, and I had to learn again how to live in that country, what that society was like; and then I had to go to Madrid and redo everything; and then I came to Barcelona. Many times in my life I have been reformulating everything so that I can re-enter a society and that helps you a lot: knowing what can be done, what cannot be done.

Is the external gaze a given when you are a migrant?

Yes, and it is a gaze that is much present, I write a lot about places that are not Peru. Right now, I have been out of Peru for fifteen years. I have an outsider's gaze also about Peru. I am a foreigner everywhere, and that is good for writing.

What is journalism to you? How would you define it?

The art of telling real stories. For me the only difference between journalism and literature is that you make up some [stories] and investigate the others; there is no more difference.

And what happens when you investigate a story and then you write fiction with that information? Where is the limit?

If you put on a little fiction, it is already fiction, there is not much ambiguity for me. If your novel is full of real facts, but has dialogues, for example, that you have not recorded, that is fiction [...]

Do you have your own rules, your own ethics when reproducing information or reinterpreting it in your novels?

They are very basic rules, I have not invented anything: if it is true, it is true; and if it is not true, it is not true. It is not even a matter of ethics; it is my lawyer's advice.

Have you had any legal conflicts?

Thousands. With all my non-fiction books, legal and non-legal, and threats. In fact, right now I don't feel like making non-fiction books; there are a lot of problems with them, some very serious.

Would you rather point out, like [Elena] Poniatowska, 'this is a testimonial novel'?

I have said that sometimes, but when the material has been real, there have also been problems. The mafia people don't have a very sophisticated eye for fiction and non-fiction.

Why do you think people are so attracted to the fact that the work is based on real events?

'Based on real' facts already means that it is not real, it is based, it looks like a true story, but it is not real. Real is real. All my stories are based on real events, but the journalistic ones are real; that is the difference. When I write a novel, I usually do a lot of things that an investigative journalist does; what's more, my prose is very clear, essential, very journalistic, I don't do great formal deployments, I am not [Guillermo] Cabrera Infante or similar. And when I write a real story, I use many elements of the novel, such as dialogues, descriptions of place, storytelling, pivot points. It is the art of storytelling: some are real and others are not real, that is all. I have no ambiguity about it.
[. . .]

In the case of real stories, do you think there are particular topics that interest more or sell more in Latin America?

Well, everybody cares about the stories of their country; the rest of the world doesn't give a damn. [. . .]

Either way, I think your gaze is focused on Peru, towards understanding Peru. . .

I don't think so, because my previous novel happens in Miami, the last one in Tokyo, there isn't any Peruvian [in them]. *El amante uruguayo* does not have Peruvians either. In *Memorias de una dama*, the narrator is a Peruvian, but he never steps on Peruvian soil. *Pudor* (Modesty) happens in Peru but the film was made in Spain; the same story can occur in the middle class anywhere. Overall, I rather think I am an author, European publishers make me notice that I am an author who is not very close to the idea of the national intellectual, which is the image they have of a Latin American writer. I do not do that [. . .]

Do you feel part of a particular literary tradition?

Sure, but I feel part of a lot of them. Of the Peruvian one. I love the English and the Americans; I have a great sense of humour. Latin Americans are solemn, distant, pompous, but Americans have always gotten along very well with humour, they have always had a more popular literature, it is not elitist.

Do you think that humour is a more accessible way to approach literature?

Yes, especially because humour is a way of saying smart things about important issues. In my father's generation, there were two great ideologies: either you were on one side or the other, and those two great speeches organized the whole of reality, but that has become very misleading. [. . .] now the world has become harder to hold on to, and all these paradoxes are not understood from any ideological perspective, they don't have a place. So, humour is a way of highlighting these paradoxes without being a demagogue.

That humour that is nearer to irony is a feature of postmodern literature. Do you think you could be in this line of thought?

I have never been sure about what 'postmodern' means. It is a word that every time I hear it, it means something different, but yes, at least it is a post–Cold War thing.

Do you consider your generation to be the children of the Boom?

We are almost the grandchildren eh. [Mario] Vargas Llosa is forty years older than me. . .

Well, in the sense that you have been writing from another perspective on the same topics...

Well, a major change for me is the point of view. The novels of the Boom generation were obsessed with the dictator, the great historical process, the revolutionary, the leader, and I think in my generation we care more about 'small' people: the official who works in the basement archive of the courthouse, the middle-class family. [Alejandro] Zambra has a novel called *Formas de volver a casa* [Ways of going Home], which is simply about a Chilean middle-class family that did nothing, are neither heroes of the left nor right. The characters of Guadalupe Nettel are *clasemedieros* (middle-class people) of the DF, many like my parents, exiled from the dictatorships of the region. I think what has changed is that we care less about the big public figures and more about the common people.

Is it hard to face 'the fathers' speech', grandparents' speech or whatever you want to call it?

Well, I don't face it, I don't think anyone's up against it. Everyone does what they can and wants. When your parents are of the size of Vargas Llosa and García Márquez, you are going to have a hard time; they kill you. Three centuries from now people will continue to read them and probably they will not read you, but there is no need to do anything else either. Another thing that is changed is that I don't want to be a president, I don't want to go on a trip with Fidel Castro, I want to be a writer, I love being a writer. I go out, I write stories; sometimes I make them up, sometimes I investigate them. I don't know anyone in my generation who has claims to be a public figure, we don't want to be that important.

Does that offer your writing more freedom?

Without a doubt, and it is a better life too. It is a more normal life.

Do you think that the era of the writer as an intellectual figure, one who is close to power and who influences the fate of his country, is over?

I hope it is over, because what most people call 'political engagement' [...] is political lobbying: they have worked with a salary for powerful people who have told them what they had to say, and they have said everything [Joseph] Stalin or Margaret Thatcher or [Francisco] Franco wanted to say. There is always an old man who comes and tells me that he likes engaged writers, and I always think that they are the sellouts of writers. I am me. I also write about politics, it is not like I don't care about the subject, but I don't want to be associated with any ideology. [...]

What do you think is the difference between you and the writers of the 1970s who regarded testimony as an important tool in their texts, as a way of 'giving voice to the other' and had social commitment?

I like it.

Do you consider yourself part of that tradition?

I don't know. I consider myself a storyteller. I take it where it is good for me. In fact, in the case of journalism in particular, the tradition that I feel very close to is that of American journalism, of New Journalism. [Carlos] Monsiváis or even [Juan] Villoro, who are authors that I admire very much, are much more baroque than I am. I admire them because I read them, and of course their work is very good, but they have an interest in prose. Instead, Americans like Truman Capote, like Norman Mailer, use prose to try to hide prose; they try to make you forget what they are telling you. You have to do a very good job with prose to do that, but it is a very precise prose, very clear, with a great emphasis on the story over language and that seems very similar to what I do. In Peru, there was a very good chronicler, who I love, Guillermo Thorndike. I could also say that he is for me a reference, but within the known traditions in general I feel very close to the American one.

There is also [Martín] Caparrós and other FNPI professors who have been claiming the Latin American tradition of chronicle. Don't you feel a part of it?

Each thing influences me differently. I mean, I had read these New Journalists and I love them; they are great journalists. It is true that I have always liked Anglo-Saxon literature because I think it is much more direct, less elitist than Latino and Hispanic literature, which is more academic, more for a smaller group of people who read. But on the other hand, one of the reasons I have written books about real stories has been because I saw that Latin Americans were doing it; maybe I would not have thought of it if they had not been doing it. I am more or less close to the people of *Etiqueta Negra* (Black Label), to Dany Alarcón. I knew Caparrós more recently, but I also used to read him. I have read Monsiváis, Villoro and a lot more. I love women [chroniclers]: Leila Guerriero, Gaby

Wiener. At some point I was writing novels, but I saw that these people were doing this, and I said 'why don't I do it too, right? Can I do this?' I have always liked doing journalism, but I valued my journalistic books as novels are valued because Latin Americans were doing it. It would not have occurred to me if I had not seen people doing it around me.

What do you call what you do? Is it non-fiction?

Yes, non-fiction, journalism, reportage, *crónica* or novel.

Does it depend on your lawyer?

[*He laughs*] Yes, it depends on my lawyer. Just kidding, I am always very clear. They are different working methods: one involves going out searching and the other involves locking yourself in your room and inventing. I like the two things; they are just different. [...]

Could non-fiction books be an alternative to journalism that cannot be done in the daily press?

Well, I think the reportage is getting more and more place in the books and less in the newspapers, for reasons of space, money, editorial approach and risks. As the book is a more elitist medium, there is less anguish in a book editor than in a newspaper editor about what you are going to say and about what trouble you are going to get into. Normally a very good reportage needs space, many pages, a lot of development. Increasingly, the space for true reportage is books. The difference in calling a reportage 'literary' is whether you are going to read it because you need the information or if you are going to read it for the story. If you read it for the story itself, not for the information, you are already reading [literary] narrative.

How is it possible to maintain the balance between information and the story?

For me, when you read literature, you read it for pleasure, when you read journalism, you read it for other reasons in general. You read the paper because you want to know what new laws there are, what your government has decided, what your football team looks like, if there is a psychopath on the street who is killing in a particular way, if there is a natural catastrophe. This is information that helps you know what world you live in. Then you read novels that don't tell you anything directly from the world you live in, but make you think about the world you live in more indirectly [...]

One can also maintain an attitude of scepticism and question what is true...

But journalism tells you what things are true, there are ways to check what is true. There are things that are true and there are things that are not true. Academics love to say, 'the truth is relative', but if you get robbed at home and you go to the police station and the cop tells you, 'what is stealing? What is the truth?'; you get angry and shoot him twice [. . .] literary journalism is real, rigorously real and has to be documented, and, if not, it is illegal [. . .]

* * *

I would like you to tell me about your research process for a book about real facts.

There is nothing original about my method, it is pure journalistic curiosity: to go out, to investigate, to investigate, to investigate; to look for all the data, to talk to as many people as possible, to read all the books about the topic.

Do you always choose the topic?

Journalistic books have an important difference in comparison to fiction books: research costs; if there is no money, there is no research. [. . .]

Do you have any research models or books you like to follow?

No, because every story imposes different rules. In fact, what I like about journalistic stories is that they make me a different person in every book. I go and become a policeman in Peru for a while, a writer of the 1930s in Uruguay or a journalist in the Dominican Republic. I become a different person for each book, because I have to move in a different medium, gather information from different people and those people have to be shown that you understand their language, that you speak their language and that you are interested in what they are telling you. That is what I like the most. In fiction you live the life you want in a lonely and personal way, but in journalism you live another life; you go and you really become this person, you become the person who could have understood the protagonist, you look for his friends and enemies.
    [. . .]

What must a person have to interest you as an informational source and as a character?

You must be close to the person you are talking about. My non-fiction books are not about things or facts, but about people: the mafia's daughter, the loving poet of García Lorca, the terrorist leader. [...] I try to be deeply sympathetic. I try to make them feel confident, relaxed, that they feel that they can talk, that they don't have to convince me of anything, that they know that I am going to tell the story as they have told it to me, that I am not going to betray them.

Does that idea they get of you differ from what you later represent in the text?

I never know if it differs. Sometimes they have felt betrayed, that usually happens [...] You cannot use real characters like literary ones; they are real, flesh-and-blood people, and you are playing with their lives. I never deceive anyone, although it is subjective: it has happened to me that there are sources who feel deceived because their perspective on the subject was one and the perspective, they see on the book is another, but it is something that I cannot control. Besides, I cannot betray many of my sources because they can shoot me, it is better to respect them.
[...]

Have you had cases where you feel too different from the informant so that the dialogue doesn't flow?

It did not happen to me because by the time I meet the informant, he is no longer that different. I do not start with interviews, I usually look for all the written documentation, archived, on the internet. I try to meet the source when I am already very well-informed, otherwise you waste his time. [...]

How do you select and edit information for a book?

This is where I work just like with a novel: what I want is to build a good story. A good story has a good plot that keeps you reading. [...]

Do you usually record your interviews?

Yes, whenever I can. But in prisons, for example, they won't let you get in with voice recorders, or if I see that the person is going to get nervous I don't record it.

How faithful are you to your transcripts?

Well, faithful, that is not a matter of degree: you are faithful or you are not faithful. [...]

When do you decide to insert yourself through a dialogue in your texts? The 'I' can be a very loud voice when the other is the supposedly important character...

Of course, it depends on what is right for each case [...] On political issues, everything is usually so opinionated that if you don't want it to be a pamphlet or an ideological essay, you have to say, 'this is me, this is how I see things because this is my story'.

Could it be metajournalism?

No, just first-person journalism. [...]

Do you think first-person journalism can remain objective?

Yes, of course. Objectivity and subjectivity are not [the same as] using third and first person. On the contrary, especially in the case of *La cuarta espada*, using the first person was the only way to be objective, any other way would have been a way to disguise my subjectivity [...]

Do other people, such as editors, have influence in your editing process?

Not in interviews, not in the process, but there is an editor at the end. When you are lucky there is a *fact checker*, I prefer that there is one, but there is little tradition in Spanish of this [...]

* * *

I would like to talk about *Memorias de una dama*...

[*He stops my recorder, and we talk for a while off the record*]

Why did you write about Shining Path in *La cuarta espada* when you had already written about it in your novel *Abril rojo* (Red April)?

Well, one came from the other. When I released *Abril rojo* in Lima, it had a whole impact and an echo that I did not expect and that books normally did not have, and, well, I talked a lot about the subject, which for Peru was a national theme. Then a gentleman came to a book launch, and he said, 'I work in jails with the imprisoned terrorists.'

While writing *Abril rojo*, didn't you think of going to prisons?

I had gone before, because I worked in human rights in Peru for a while, so I had already been in prisons, I had already spoken to people, I was interested in the topic because of that. This man came to ask me if we could present *Abril rojo* in prisons. I had already tried before to do a reportage with the leaders of *Sendero*, and it was impossible, they did not speak, they were not allowed to talk, and even if they could let them speak, they would not speak. I said to this man, 'Can you take me to a prison and talk to such and such?', the leaders of *Sendero*, he said, 'that would be three prisons', and I said, 'let's go to all of them'.

But this was under the excuse that you were organizing a book launch...

Well, it was both, I presented my book, then we would talk and then we would have lunch, as would be normal anywhere, only in the meantime I was talking to all the leaders of *Sendero*, which was the version [of events] my book lacked. [...]

Did you want to write about it because you are Peruvian?

Yes, obviously I was interested in the subject personally; it was my subject, my story. I come from a generation that grew up within this context during childhood and that has only known the two radical versions, on one side or the other. All my books are a way of making sense of things that have happened in my life, they are a little therapeutic in that. [...]

How do you decide to insert yourself into that story?

Well, on the one hand, it is a very personal story. I grew up in a family that talked about revolution, and by the time we returned to Peru, a revolution had passed, and it was a horror, it was hell [. . .] Additionally, I thought, no one knows anything about Peru; this has been a silent war. There have been more dead than in Chile or Argentina, but no one knows, no one cares [. . .] it was a way to make the story more accessible to the reader.

Was it a stylistic resource?

If it were a stylistic resource, it would be justified too, but I think it has to do with personal things, with my process with the book, with trying to understand my own story within this book and at the same time with the need to make a book that was readable outside Peru, that could have translations, that could be published in several countries, that could serve to make understandable what had happened there, and that meant not assuming there was a Peruvian reader who already knows everything that has happened there. How do you tell things without them being boring? Well, by telling my own story, which is the story of someone who has grown up in that country, who has an emotional bond with that country and telling you that story allows you to understand what is going on there.

How do you differentiate between a text based on real facts and a real story?

Abril rojo is based on real facts, and this [*La cuarta espada*] is not, this is clearly real. Everything you find there has a source; you can verify that someone said that happened. And I was just another source, someone who grew up there and can tell you, not a New York correspondent.
[. . .]

* * *

Who is the 'other' for you?

Well, everyone is the other. The thing is that when you do the research, you have to take his side, even temporarily.
[. . .]

While meeting your sources, do you think you are different from the narrator who writes about them?

In fact, I think the narrator is the person I was at the time. Normally I am not that political, I usually try to be rather more frivolous than the man who writes that book, because I think your life is better that way, but when you do a journalistic investigation you become someone else, you have to become someone else.

Were you less authentic?

Yes, well, let's say, there are certain things about you that are enhanced in one case, and there are certain things about you that are enhanced in another, but we all have many facets.

I am talking about a 'narrator' because as a reader I don't know if you are him or not...

It is me! It is me! There is no ambiguity: that gentleman is me, everything he tells is true, everything he says is what happened to me.

Well, in a narrative he is a storyteller...

The narrative in a novel, but not in a newspaper book. The narrator is the author.

It can be a construction of yours...

All the data I tell has sources and they are real, also my personal history and opinions are based on that, besides I try to avoid stating my opinion a lot.

But does the person you were with your informants differ from your self-representation in the text?

Well, there was something that certain people may consider to be 'theatre', but I consider it to be legitimate and ethical. When I confronted the police I said, 'I am from the international press that wants to know about our glorious achievement against terrorism', and when I was with Shining Path, I said, 'the press wants to know the struggle of your comrades.' Now, let's see, it was pretty clear that I was a white, urban guy, who lived in Europe and was more or less a '*progre*'. I was not fooling anyone who was not very dumb, and not one of my sources was too dumb [to understand this], but I was trying to show them that I spoke their language and that I understood how they said things and that I was therefore able to reproduce their story as faithfully as possible. I think they knew; I don't think anyone thinks I am a Maoist Marxist just by

looking at me, come on, look at me! You won't get there and become someone else, but you do have to show your source that you understand their story and that you are interested in their story, that you are not going to judge him. If you go with your sources and tell them, 'you were miserable killers and you did everything wrong and I am going to ask you a few questions', well, they are not going to respond.
[. . .]

Do you make a difference when you write fiction in contrast with journalism?

They are always stories, some you make them up, some you investigate, but they are all stories. As a chronicler, I am a narrator and as a novelist too [. . .]

Interview 8

Juan Villoro (Ciudad de México, 1956)

The interview was conducted in Mexico City on 8 January 2015. It was held in a bookshop in Coyoacán, the author's neighbourhood.

How did you begin doing journalism and literature?

I have already told the story many times, and, at the risk of being repetitive, I started late, when I read *De perfil*, by José Agustín, a novel with which I fully identified because it was a kind of mirror: the protagonist was my age, he lived in the same city as me – in Mexico City – he was a middle-class boy, his parents were getting divorced – my parents had divorced – then this novel belatedly revealed to me that my life, to which I then gave no literary value, could be the subject of a story. It made me feel that the everyday environment, the environment I had, was literary.

What is journalism to you? How do you define the kind of journalism you do?

I was lucky enough to start reading newspapers when Julio Scherer García was running *Excélsior*, which was the best newspaper that ever existed in Mexico . . . by the way, Julio died yesterday. It was a newspaper that included many elements of the chronicle, it used caricature as one of its main resources [. . .] When I started reading newspapers, around fourteen years old, the *Excélsior* would be delivered to my house, and I was lucky enough to find a newspaper like that one. For example, on the front page it could have an interview with Julio Cortázar or Gabriel García Márquez. This kind of journalism was a great way of learning; in fact, many of those who still direct or work with media in Mexico learned there [at *Excélsior*]. So for me the idea of journalism was not restricted exclusively to pure and hard news reporting or to the management of information, it involved the chronicle, the profile, a series of very rich variants of news covering [. . .]

Do you consider yourself to be part of a specific generation of journalists?

Well, inevitably one corresponds per generation to a group of people who started publishing in the 1970s [...] in that time I met many journalists such as Jaime Avilés, René Delgado, well, many who have been in the journalistic career.

When we talk about chronicle in Latin America, we generally talk about two traditions or influences: the American New Journalism and the modernist chronicle, and if we go further back, the *Crónica de Indias*. Do you think that these influences have been part of your own tradition?

There are fashions to name what one does, and I believe that these labels, such as the 'chroniclers of the Indies', or the 'new chroniclers of the Indies' or the 'New Journalism', have to do with putting the emphasis on something that has always existed, which is narrative journalism. That is what Daniel Defoe writes in the seventeenth century; he was a journalist until he was sixty years old, and when he writes *A Journal of the Plague Year*, he was doing what is now called New Journalism, that is, journalism with narrative quality. And if we go further back, the Gospels are works of narrative journalism with a transcendent view of the world because they are covering the 'good news', and this news is the arrival of the son of God, especially the first three Gospels, except that of St John, are very narrative and deal with the same event from different points of view. So, I believe that in the narrative of real or purportedly real facts, the different chroniclers have always tried to incorporate a certain narrative quality, and this has happened since the beginning of the times. What happens now is that the value of narrative journalism has changed. For example, when I wrote my first *crónicas*, I did not know I was writing chronicles, because the word *crónica* was not fashionable, and I never thought a text like that could last, because journalism was ephemeral. [...]

What does *crónica* offer to an author who wants to talk about reality, that another genre cannot offer?

On the one hand, the chronicle represents, in a very straightforward way, what we can say about reality. I believe there is a greater appreciation for the testimonies of reality when the margins of freedom of speech increase and the environment in which we live is valued more [...] this also has to do with the fact that Latin American reality, being as varied, convulsive and surprising as it is, has given rise to many themes for the chronicle. [...]

Do you think that the space of the chronicle is moving from newspapers to books or the internet?

Yes, inevitably, because of the drift that journalism is having. As digital journalism predominates, the spaces of dissemination are being shortened, and this certainly harms investigative journalism, long-form journalism and, above all, it affects the length of texts. [...]

Beatriz Sarlo has reflected on the 'excess of testimony', about how testimony has suddenly been taken as the only criterion of plausibility to get to know the reality in our countries. What do you think of that? What value do you place on testimony within your texts?

Well, it depends on the cases and also depends on the quality of the testimony, because we move on to the area of the finest definitions. The chronicle is, as I said, a relationship between true facts and a significant narrative quality, then the chronicle aspires to be the enduring account of the real, and very significant examples of this would be *Operación Masacre* by Rodolfo Walsh, *Relato de un náufrago* by Gabriel García Márquez and *El águila y la serpiente* (The Eagle and the Snake) by Martín Luis Guzmán. Then there is the *testimonio*, which is, let's put it this way, a more documentary form to provide data from reality and it depends on the case. For example, the issue of the disappeared has been very much worked on in Argentina; the subject of the Spanish Civil War has been very much worked on in Spain; in Mexico, for a while the theme of 1968 was worked on quite a bit, although not so much work was done. Then, certainly, sometimes the overabundance of testimonies can lead to the lack of the most important thing, which is the interpretations of testimonies, because literature gives you not only facts about reality but the emotional meaning of reality [...]

Indeed, in fact there is a point of comparison between what you do and what Martín Caparrós does: between the essay and the chronicle...

Yes, well, there are different types of chroniclers and some are content to narrate the facts, right? That is a type of chronicler that can be related to the American school, one that has a close approach to events, which I think is certainly very valid, but there are other kinds of chroniclers who, along with the events, also need to narrate the opinions on the events, whether they are their own experiences or another's. In Mexico, we had a chronicler who was basically an editorialist of reality: Carlos Monsiváis. He created a type of chronicle in which the interpretation of reality was always more important than the storytelling. He is not a very anecdotal chronicler. I try to be much more anecdotal-based than him, but I write, as Julio Villanueva Chang once said, 'chronicles with opinions', annotated chronicles [. . .]

Could you somehow define a method you follow when you work on chronicles?

No! Every theme brings you different challenges. There are matters that are already very orderly in themselves: if you are going to cover, say, the final match of the football World Cup, well, that will last ninety minutes, plus the compensation time. You have to have a concrete outcome, a winner, the space where it happens is well defined, then you write a very narrow chronicle, in which of course many surprises can occur, but there the structure is given by the event itself. There are events that are totally unstructured, where what you have to look for is for a textual structure. A chronicle must seem like something concrete; it should not seem like a piece of interrupted life, but it must have a symbolic unity and it is often complex to find this symbolic unity. Then you have to look for a secondary character that appears at the beginning of the chronicle and contributes to the outcome. You have to look for some emotional gesture that gives you a sense of closure; it depends on that. Then there are things that are very close to you because you have experienced them a lot, right? I did an interview with Mick Jagger, and, well, I did not have to prepare but only to control my nerves and to have a certain emotional and psychological attitude to dialogue with him, but I did not have to study because I have lived listening to his music all my life, that is, it is already inside my veins, so it would have been false to study for that. [. . .] On the contrary, there are other types of characters that you have to study a lot in order to get to them [. . .] there the previous work is very important, it is like an actor who has to enter into character. The chronicler has to prepare, and often the preparation of the chronicler is much more interesting than his own characters; that is, in the famous meetings of journalists it is often more exciting to hear how someone prepared to do a chronicle and the difficulties it took than the result itself.

Well, in the case, for example, of your book about the earthquake in Chile, I sensed that there was an emphasis on your personal testimony. . .

Yes.

Obviously, you experienced it, you were there, but how do you decide how the 'I' comes in as the main character or when you prefer another protagonist?

Yes, it depends on the circumstances. For example, for the first and so far only time in my life I started writing the book of the earthquake in Chile as a kind of exorcism. I had been there and was obsessed with experience [. . .]I thought if I could not write about anything because I was just thinking about the earthquake, what I had left was to write about the earthquake. And there it had to be a very personal chronicle and written in a style and with an extension that no one would have published for me in a magazine; since it jumps from one subject to another, it becomes essayistic, then it enters as in the flow of consciousness of some characters, recovers *twitts*; in short, it uses many different resources and extends over eighty pages. I started writing without knowing that I was making a book, I just wanted to vent, so the result there was necessarily very personal. Of course, in other chronicles I have tried to put myself a little aside because I think it is very dangerous that the protagonist of the chronicle is the chronicler himself. There are chroniclers of high narcissism who consider themselves to be more important than the news, and sometimes these are people with such a colourful personality that you appreciate that they are in the foreground, but in general I distrust this procedure, and I think it is better for one to accompany the facts. Of course, I am very present, especially in metaphors, in comparisons, in quotations, that is, in the way things are told. I think I do have a very personal style, but not so much regarding interpretation, [it is not like] I do things, I open a door, I find a treasure.

The one who performs the action is the other. . .

The one who performs the action is the other one, isn't he? And I don't try to fully explain it either, I often ask questions and leave what might happen to chance. So, there is already an irony in most of my chronicles and that speaks of a personal temperament, but I would not want to be a character in the chronicle. Now, sometimes it is important what happens to you to get to the story and then it is a shame not to include it.

I am interested in this kind of dialogue between the chronicler and the informant, the other. How do you approach an informant or a person who is going to be perhaps the character of your chronicle?

I think you have to have absolute respect, and the first thing one should consider is that the person has no obligation to give you an interview. I think one of the great mistakes of journalists is that they consider everyone to have an obligation to speak, and they have a very invasive attitude. [. . .] I think another huge difficulty we have today is the recorder. I believe that the recorder greatly harms the testimony, precisely because of what Beatriz Sarlo said, because there is always a tension between literal truthfulness and interpretation. When you reproduce a dialogue, you are generally much more faithful to the spirit of that dialogue than when you transcribe it, because one speaks with flaws, with carelessness, with intonations that depend on body language, of the nuances of the voice, but all this is lost and literal interviews are usually the worst. So I think the ease of having the recorder has rather weakened the art of the interview.

Do you record your interviews?

No, I don't.

What is your technique?

I do record, but for legal reasons, because I think it is very important to have a backup because a lot of times you are getting troubled information [. . .] I find it very useful to reproduce the dialogue from my notes and then hear the interview to add some things that may have escaped and above all recover certain strategic words. Everyone uses some words that are their own, which give personality to that person.

Do you have any rules or certain code of ethics that you follow when reproducing what the other says?

Well, the main thing is that you cannot misrepresent anything you have been told in the same way that you cannot misrepresent the facts. [. . .]

There we could find a point of difference with the work of the fiction writer.

Of course, as a fiction writer you can do whatever you want! You can even be a lousy person and mistreat your characters. You don't respond to anyone but your imagination [. . .] I mean, you can be an unethical writer, but it is impossible to be an unethical journalist, in my view.

Is there an ethics over the aesthetic in this case?

Well, I think in journalism aesthetics is a form of ethics because you have to adjust to a truth in what you are narrating. [. . .]

Finally, why do you think the chronicle is booming in Latin America, academically at least?

It is a boom of perception, I think, because if you think of all the magazines that are here [*he points a finger at the shelves in the library*] I don't see many spaces especially novel or significant for the publication of chronicles. Specialized magazines have emerged, but they are heroic and often minority magazines, such as the famous *Etiqueta Negra*, in Peru, which is a legitimately cult magazine.

Yes, we say 'famous' because we know it [*Etiqueta Negra* magazine]...

Because we know it, because it has published some great things, hasn't it? Exactly. Then I go back to the same thing: the importance of the chronicle has to do with this. Now, for example, the world is organized around certain assessment criteria. Martín Caparrós's new book, *El hambre*, will be translated into many languages, but he told me that the first person interested in translating it was a great American publisher. So when you, in the world, have a very powerful American editor interested in a book of yours, there is already a snowball effect. These are the forms of access to culture and distribution of culture. It is not that the chronicle itself automatically enters [the international publishing market] [...] The importance of the chronicle is within the chronicle itself. How much is it valued today? It depends on academic, social, cultural misunderstandings, and compensation exercises. There are many newspapers that prefer to organize a chronicle seminar for their journalists provided that none of them later publish a chronicle. I myself have given these seminars and the editors claim, 'why are there no chronicles?' [...] Of course, journalists continue to write the same because they are encouraged to publish a chronicle.

References

'About Us', *International Association for Literary Journalism Studies*. Available online: http://ialjs.org/about-us/ (accessed 23 April 2017).
'La odisea del náufrago sobreviviente del "A.R.C. Caldas"' (1955), *El Espectador*, Second Section, Special Supplement, 28 April: 1.
'La verdad sobre mi aventura' (1955), *El Espectador*, Second Section, Special Supplement, 28 April.
'Natalia. Moldova, víctima del tráfico de personas' (2007), in L. Laski and S. Schellekens (eds), *Jóvenes en movimiento. Población mundial 2006 suplemento Jóvenes*, 25–9, New York: UNFPA.
'Polémica: Carlos Monsiváis-Octavio Paz' (2004), *Diccionario de literatura mexicana. Siglo XX*, ed. Armando Pereira, Mexico City: UNAM / Ediciones Coyoacán. Available online: http://elem.mx/estgrp/datos/268 (accessed 7 April 2017).
'The Nobel Prize in Literature 2015' (2014), Nobelprize.org. *Nobel Media*. Available online: http://www.nobelprize.org/nobel_prizes/literature/laureates/2015/ (accessed 23 April 2017).
Acosta Montoro, J. (1973), *Periodismo y literatura*, Madrid: Ediciones Guadarrama.
Aguilar, M. (2010), *Domadores de historias. Conversaciones con grandes cronistas de América Latina*, Santiago de Chile: Universidad Finis Terrae; RIL editores.
Aguilar, M., C. Darrigrandi, M. Méndez and A. Viu, eds (2014), *Escrituras a ras de suelo: crónica latinoamericana del siglo XX*, Providencia: Universidad Finis Terrae.
Alarcón, C. ([2003] 2008), *Cuando me muera quiero que me toquen cumbia. Vidas de pibes chorros*, Buenos Aires: Verticales de Bolsillo.
Alarcón, C. (2019), *Dance for me when I die*, trans. N. Caistor and M. López Levy, Durham: Duke University Press.
Alarcón, C., ed (2015), *Anfibia. Crónicas y ensayos/1*, Buenos Aires: UNSAM.
Alexander, R. J. (1952), *The Peron Era*, London: Victor Gollancz.
Alexander, R. J. (1979), *Juan Domingo Perón: A History*, Boulder: Westview Press.
Amar Sánchez, A. (1992), *El relato de los hechos. Rodolfo Walsh: testimonio y escritura*, Rosario: Beatriz Viterbo.
Angulo Egea, M., ed (2014), *Crónica y mirada. Aproximaciones al periodismo narrativo*, Madrid: Libros del K.O.
Angulo Egea, M. (2017), *Inmersiones. Crónica de viajes y periodismo encubierto*, Barcelona: Universitat de Barcelona Edicions.
Arfuch, L. ([2002] 2010), *El espacio biográfico. Dilemas de la subjetividad contemporánea*, Buenos Aires: Fondo de Cultura Económica.
Arfuch, L. (1995), *La entrevista, una invención dialógica*, Buenos Aires: Paidós.
Bak, J. (2011), 'Introduction', in J. Bak and B. Reynolds (eds), *Literary Journalism Across the Globe: Journalistic Traditions and Transnational Influences*, 1–20, Amherst: University of Massachusetts Press.

Bak, J. and B. Reynolds, eds (2011), *Literary Journalism Across the Globe: Journalistic Traditions and Transnational Influences*, Amherst: University of Massachusetts Press.

Bakhtin, M. (1987), 'The Problem of Speech Genres', in C. Emerson and M. Holquist (eds), *Speech Genres and Other Late Essays*, trans. Vern W. McGee, 60–102, Austin: University of Texas Press.

Bakhtin, M. ([1981] 2011), 'Discourse in the Novel', in M. Holquist (ed), *The Dialogic Imagination. Four Essays by M. M. Bakhtin*, trans. C. Emerson and M. Holquist, 259–422, Austin: University of Texas Press.

Barthes, R. ([1953] 1967), *Writing Degree Zero*, trans. A. Lavers, London: Cape.

Barthes, R. [1957] 2001), *Mythologies*, Paris: Éditions du Seuil.

Bartra, R. (1987), *La jaula de la melancolía*, Mexico City: Grijalbo.

Bastenier, M. A. (2009), *Cómo se escribe un periódico. El chip colonial y los diarios en América Latina*, Bogotá: Fondo de Cultura Económica / Fundación para un Nuevo Periodismo Iberoamericano.

Bencomo, A. (2002), *Voces y voceros de la megalópolis: la crónica periodístico-literaria en México*, Madrid; Frankfurt am Main: Iberoamericana–Vervuert.

Benjamin, W. ([1955] 1999), 'The Storyteller', in H. Arendt (ed), *Illuminations*, trans. H. Zorn, 83–107, London: Pimlico.

Benjamin, W. (1973), 'Some Motifs in Baudelaire', in *Charles Baudelaire: A Lyric Poet in the Era of High Capitalism*, trans. H. Zorn, 107–54, London: NLB.

Berger, P. and T. Luckmann (1967), *The Social Construction of Reality: A Treatise in the Sociology of Knowledge*, London: Penguin.

Beverley, J. (1996), 'The Real Thing', in G. Gugelberger (ed), *The Real Thing. Testimonial Discourse and Latin America*, Durham, NC; London: Duke University Press.

Beverley, J. (2004), *Testimonio. On the Politics of Truth*, Minneapolis: University of Minnesota Press.

Bielsa, E. (2006), *The Latin American Urban Crónica: Between Literature and Mass Culture*, Lanham: Lexington Books.

Blanco, J. (1982), *Crónica de la literatura reciente en México, 1950–1980*, Mexico City: INAH.

Bourdieu, P. (1993), *The Field of Cultural Production: Essays on Art and Literature*, Cambridge: Polity Press.

Bourdieu, P. (1998), *On Television and Journalism*, London: Pluto Press.

Bruner, J. (1990), *Acts of Meaning*, Cambridge, MA; London: Harvard University Press.

Burgos, E. and R. Menchú ([1983] 2005), *Me llamo Rigoberta Menchú y así me nació la conciencia*, Mexico City: Siglo XXI.

Butler, J. (1988), 'Performative Acts and Gender Constitution: An Essay in Phenomenology and Feminist Theory', *Theatre Journal*, 40 (4): 519–31.

Butler, J. (2005), *Giving an Account of Oneself*, New York: Fordham University Press.

Calvi, P. (2019), *Latin American Adventures in Literary Journalism*, Pittsburgh: University of Pittsburgh Press.

Caparrós, M. ([2006] 2014), *El interior*, Barcelona: Malpaso.

Caparrós, M. (2009), *Una luna. Diario de hiperviaje*, Barcelona: Anagrama.

Caparrós, M. (2010), *Contra el cambio. Un hiperviaje al apocalipsis climático*, Barcelona: Anagrama.

Caparrós, M. (2014), *El hambre*, Buenos Aires: Planeta.

Caparrós, M. (2017), *Hunger*, trans. K. Silver, London: Penguin Random House.

Carrión, J., ed (2012), *Mejor que ficción. Crónicas ejemplares*, Barcelona: Anagrama.

References

Cavarero, A. (2000), *Relating Narratives: Storytelling and Selfhood*. London: Routledge.
Chávez Díaz, L. (2017), 'Based on True Stories: Representing the Self and the Other in Latin American Documentary Narratives', PhD diss., Department of Spanish and Portuguese, University of Cambridge, Cambridge.
Chávez Díaz, L. (2018), 'Beyond Crónica: Journalism in Contemporary Latin American Documentary Narratives', *Textos Híbridos*, 6 (1): n.p. Available online: https://textoshibridos.uai.cl/index.php/textoshibridos/%20article/view/75 (accessed 28 February 2021).
Chávez Díaz, L. (2019), 'To Possess is to Belong: Carlos Monsiváis's Collection of Ephemera and Popular Culture in Mexico City', in R. Isking and B. Salsbury (eds), *Collecting Prints, Posters and Ephemera; Perspectives in a Global World*, 179–96, London: Bloomsbury Academic.
Chávez Díaz, L. (2020), 'Two True Stories of Survivors: Gabriel García Márquez and Rodolfo Walsh', in Y. Passos and M. Wiktoworska (eds), *Literary Journalism and Latin American Wars: Revolutions, Retributions, Resignations*, 71–94, Nancy: Éditions PUN – Université de Lorraine.
Chávez Díaz, L. (2021), *Viajar sola: Identidad y experiencia de viaje en autoras hispanoamericanas*, Barcelona: Universitat de Barcelona Edicions.
Chevigy, G. B. (1985), 'The Transformation of Privilege in the Work of Elena Poniatowska', *Latin American Literary Review*, 13 (24): 49–62.
Chillón, A. (1999), *Literatura y periodismo: una tradición de relaciones promiscuas*, Barcelona: Universitat Autònoma de Barcelona.
Chillón, A. (2014), *La palabra facticia. Literatura, periodismo y comunicación*, Barcelona: Universitat Autònoma de Barcelona.
Cleto, F. (1999), 'Introduction: Queering the Camp', in F. Cleto (ed), *Camp: Queer Aesthetics and the Performing Subject*: A Reader, 1–42, Edinburgh: Edinburgh University Press.
Corona, I. (2002), 'At the Intersection: Chronicle and Ethnography', in B. Jörgensen and I. Corona (eds), *The Contemporary Mexican Chronicle Theoretical Perspectives on the Liminal Genre*, 123–56, Albany: State University of New York Press.
Davies, L. H. (2007), *Projections of Peronism in Argentine Autobiography, Biography and Fiction*, Cardiff: University of Wales Press.
Davies, L. H. (2010), 'Tomás Eloy Martínez and the Literary Representation of Peronism: A Tale of Bifurcating Paths?' in V. Carpenter (ed), *(Re) Collecting the Past. History and Collective Memory in Latin American Narrative*, 113–43, Bern: Peter Lang.
Davis, L. (1983), *Factual Fictions: The Origins of the English Novel*, New York: Columbia University Press.
De Certeau, M. (1984), *The Practice of Everyday Life*, Berkeley: University of California Press.
Detwiler, L. and J. Breckenridge (2012), 'Introduction: Points of Departure', in L. Detwiler and J. Breckenridge (eds), *Pushing the Boundaries of Latin American Testimony: Metamorphoses and Migrations*, 1–6, New York: Palgrave Macmillan.
Dragas, A. (2014), *The Return of the Storyteller in Contemporary Fiction*, London: Bloomsbury.
Echeverría, B. (2017 [1998]), *La modernidad de lo barroco*, Mexico City: Ediciones Era.
Egan, L. (2001), *Carlos Monsiváis: Culture and Chronicle in Contemporary Mexico*, Tucson: University of Arizona Press.

Egan, L. (2011), 'Carlos Monsiváis, in Collective and Personal Memory', *Mexican Studies/Estudios mexicanos*, 27: 225–31.
Ferreira dos Santos, J., ed (2005), *As cem melhores crônicas brasileiras*, Rio de Janeiro: Objetiva.
Ferro, R. (1994), 'Operación Masacre: investigación y escritura', *Nuevo texto crítico*, 12/13: 139–66.
Ferro, R. (2009), 'Palabras liminares y criterios de edición', in Roberto Ferro (ed), *Operación Masacre. Seguido de la campaña periodística*, 9–13, Buenos Aires: Ediciones de la Flor.
Fickelscherer de Mattos, C. (2003), 'Tomás Eloy Martínez: una bibliografía', in *Espéculo. Revista de estudios literarios*, 23: n.p. Available online: http://www.ucm.es/info/especulo/numero23/bib_tem.html (accessed 28 February 2021).
Firpo, Norberto (N.d.), 'Tomás', Buenos Aires, Archivo TEM, SE-I-1.
Foley, B. (1986), *Telling the Truth: The Theory and Practice of Documentary Fiction*, Ithaca: Cornell University Press.
Fonseca, D. and A. El-Kadi, eds (2012), *Sam no es mi tío: veinticuatro crónicas migrantes y un sueño americano*, Buenos Aires: Alfaguara.
Fontaine, A. (2010), *La vida doble*, Barcelona: Tusquets.
Fontaine, A. (2014), *La Vida Doble: A Novel*, trans. M. McDowell, New Haven: Yale University Press.
Foster, D. W. (1984), 'Latin American Documentary Narrative', *PMLA*, 99: 41–55.
Foucault, M. (2012), *The Courage of the Truth: The Government of Self and Others II. Lectures at the College de France, 1983–1984*, Basingstoke: Palgrave Macmillan.
Franco, J. (2002), *The Decline and Fall of the Lettered City. Latin America in the Cold War*, Cambridge, MA; London: Harvard University Press.
Franco, J. (2013), *Cruel Modernity*, Durham: Duke University Press.
Frus, P. (1994), *The Politics and Poetics of Journalistic Narrative: The Timely and the Timeless*, Cambridge: Cambridge University Press.
Fuentes, C. (2007), 'Foreword. "La Poni"', in M. Schuessler (ed), *Elena Poniatowska: An Intimate Biography*, ix–x, Tucson: University of Arizona Press.
Fundación Gabriel García Márquez para el Nuevo Periodismo Iberoamericano. 'Nuevos Cronistas de Indias'. Available online: http://nuevoscronistasdeindias.fnpi.org (accessed 28 February 2021).
Gambini, H. (1999), *Historia del peronismo*, Buenos Aires: Planeta.
García Canclini, N. (1990), *Culturas híbridas. Estrategias para entrar y salir de la modernidad*, Mexico City: Conaculta / Grijalbo.
García Márquez, G. ([1970] 2013), *Relato de un náufrago que estuvo diez días a la deriva en una balsa sin comer ni beber, que fue proclamado héroe de la patria, besado por las reinas de belleza y hecho rico por la publicidad, y luego aborrecido por el gobierno y olvidado para siempre*, Barcelona: Tusquets.
García Márquez, G. (1981), 'Recuerdos de periodista', *El país*, section Opinión, 16 December. Available online: http://elpais.com/diario/1981/12/16/opinion/377305211_850215.html (accessed 23 April 2017).
García Márquez, G. (1986), *La aventura de Miguel Littín, clandestino en Chile: un reportaje*, Buenos Aires: Editorial Sudamericana.
García Márquez, G. (1989), *The Story of a Shipwrecked Sailor: Who Drifted on a Liferaft for Ten Days Without Food or Water, Was Proclaimed a National Hero, Kissed by Beauty*

Queens, Made Rich Through Publicity, and Then Spurned by the Government and Forgotten for All Time, trans. Randolph Hogan, New York: Vintage Books.

García Márquez, G. (1996), 'El mejor oficio del mundo: discurso de Gabriel García Márquez ante la SIP', *Fundación Gabo*, section Recursos, 7 October. Available online: https://fundaciongabo.org/es/recursos/discursos/el-mejor-oficio-del-mundo-discurso-de-gabriel-garcia-marquez-ante-la-sip (accessed 24 June 2021).

García Márquez, G. (1996), *Noticia de un secuestro*, Barcelona; Bogotá: Norma.

García Márquez, G. (1997), 'The Best Job in the World', *Index on Censorship*, 26 (3): 77–80. Available online: https://archivos.juridicas.unam.mx/www/bjv/libros/3/1132/2.pdf (accessed 28 February 2021).

García Márquez, G. (2002), *Vivir para contarla*, Barcelona: Mondadori.

García Márquez, G. (2004), *Living to Tell the Tale*, trans. Edith Grossman, New York, Vintage International.

Genette, G. (1997), *Palimpsests: Literature in the Second Degree*, Lincoln; London: University of Nebraska Press.

Gilard, J. (1987), 'Prólogo', in G. García Márquez (ed), *Textos costeños. Obra periodística I, 1948-1952*, Buenos Aires: Editorial Sudamericana.

Goffman, E. (1974), *Frame Analysis: An Essay on the Organization of Experience*, Cambridge, MA: Harvard University Press.

Goldman, F. ([2007] 2010), *The Art of Political Murder. Who Killed Bishop Gerardi?*, London: Atlantic Books.

González Echevarría, R. ([1990] 2006), *Myth and Archive. A Theory of Latin American Narrative*, New York: Cambridge University Press.

González, A. ([1993] 2006), *Journalism and the Development of Spanish American Narrative*, New York: Cambridge University Press.

González, A. (1983), *La crónica modernista hispanoamericana*, Madrid: Porrúa Turanzas.

Guerriero, L. (2006), *Los suicidas del fin del mundo. Crónica de un pueblo patagónico*, Barcelona: Tusquets.

Habermas, J. (1992), *The Structural Transformation of the Public Sphere: An Inquiry into a Category of Bourgeois Society*, Cambridge: Polity.

Halperín, J. ([1995] 2002), *La entrevista periodística. Intimidades de la conversación pública*, Buenos Aires: Paidós.

Hartsock, J. (2000), *A History of American Literary Journalism: The Emergence of a Modern Narrative Form*, Amherst: University of Massachusetts Press.

Hartsock, J. (2016), *Literary Journalism and the Aesthetics of Experience*, Amherst; Boston: University of Massachusetts Press.

Hellman, J. (1981), *Fables of Fact: The New Journalism as New Fiction*, Urbana; London: University of Illinois Press.

Herlinghaus, H. (2002), 'La imaginación melodramática. Rasgos intermediales y heterogéneos de una categoría precaria', in H. Herlinghaus (ed), *Narraciones anacrónicas de la modernidad. Melodrama e intermedialidad en América Latina*, 21–59, Santiago de Chile: Cuarto Propio.

Herrscher, R. (2012), *Periodismo narrativo. Cómo contar la realidad con las armas de la literatura*, Barcelona: Universitat de Barcelona.

Hersey, J. (1946), *Hiroshima*, Harmondsworth: Penguin.

Hutcheon, L. (1984), *Narcissistic Narrative. The Metafictional Paradox*, London: Methuen.

Hutcheon, L. (1988), *A Poetics of Postmodernism: History, Theory, Fiction*, New York: Routledge.

Hutcheon, L. (1989), *The Politics of Postmodernism*, London; New York: Routledge.
Informe Final (2003), Lima: Comisión de la verdad y reconciliación. Available online: http://cverdad.org.pe/ifinal/ (accessed 23 April 2017).
Jaramillo Agudelo, D. (2012), 'Collage sobre la crónica latinoamericana del siglo veintiuno', in D. Jaramillo Agudelo (ed), *Antología de crónica latinoamericana actual*, 11–4, Mexico City: Alfaguara.
Jaramillo Agudelo, D., ed (2012), *Antología de crónica latinoamericana*, Mexico City: Alfaguara.
Johnson, M. (1971), *The New Journalism; the Underground Press, the Artists of Nonfiction, and Changes in the Established Media*, Lawrence: University Press of Kansas.
Jörgensen, B. (1994), *The Writing of Elena Poniatowska: Engaging Dialogues*, Austin: University of Texas Press.
Jörgensen, B. (2011), *Documents in Crisis: Nonfiction Literatures in Twentieth-Century Mexico*, Albany: State University of New York Press.
Jörgensen, B. and I. Corona, eds (2002), *The Contemporary Mexican Chronicle: Theoretical Perspectives on the Liminal Genre*, Albany, NY: State University of New York Press.
Kapuściński, R. ([2000] 2005), *Los cínicos no sirven para este oficio. Sobre el buen periodismo*, Barcelona: Anagrama.
Kapuściński, R. (2007), *Encuentro con el Otro*, trans. A. Orzeszek, Barcelona: Anagrama.
Keeble, R. and J. Tulloch, eds (2012), *Global Literary Journalism: Exploring the Journalistic Imagination*, New York: Peter Lang.
Köhler, A., et al. (2010), *Slajel Kibeltik, tejiendo nuestras raíces*, Mexico City: Organización Sociedad Civil Las Abejas.
Kraniauskas, J. (1997), 'Introduction. Critical Closeness: The Chronicle–Essays of Carlos Monsiváis', in C. Monsiváis (ed), *Mexican Postcards*, trans. J. Kraniauskas, ix–xxii, London: Verso.
Krauze, E. (1985), *Caudillos culturales en la Revolución Mexicana*, Mexico City: SEP.
Lamas, M. (2010), 'Presentación. La puerta de la dignidad', in C. Monsiváis (ed), *Que se abra esa puerta. Crónicas sobre la diversidad sexual*, 11–15, Mexico City: Paidós.
Laski, L. and S. Schellekens, eds (2007), *Jóvenes en movimiento. Población mundial 2006 suplemento Jóvenes*, New York: UNFPA. Available online: http://www.unfpa.org/sites/default/files/pub-pdf/moving_young_spa.pdf (accessed 11 April 2017).
Lefebvre, H. (1991), *The Production of Space*, Oxford: Basil Blackwell.
Levinas, E. ([1972] 1996), 'Truth of Disclosure and Truth of Testimony', in A. T. Peperzak, S. Critchley, and R. Bernasconi (eds), *Basic Philosophical Writings*, 97–107, Bloomington, IN: Indiana University Press.
Levinas, E. (1984), 'Ethics and Infinity', *CrossCurrents*, 34-2: 191–203.
Lewis, O. (1964), *Pedro Martínez. A Mexican Peasant and His Family*, London: Secker & Warburg.
López Badano, C. (2010), *La novela histórica latinoamericana entre dos siglos. Un caso: Santa Evita, cadáver exquisito de paseo por el canon*, Madrid: Consejo Superior de Investigaciones Científicas.
Lozada, C. (2008), 'Love in the Time of Terror', *Foreign Policy*, 165: 86–8.
Lukács, G. ([1937] 1978), *The Historical Novel*, trans. H. and S. Mitchell, London: Penguin.
Mahieux, V. (2011), *Urban Chroniclers in Modern Latin America*, Austin: University of Texas Press.
Malcolm, J. ([1990] 2012), *The Journalist and the Assassin*, London: Granta.
Martin, G. (2008), *Gabriel García Márquez: A Life*, London: Bloomsbury.

Martínez-Richter, M. (1997), 'Tomás Eloy Martínez', in M. Martínez-Richter (ed), *La caja de la escritura. Diálogos con narradores y críticos argentinos*, 35–47, Madrid: Vervuert/Iberoamericana.

Martínez, E. (2014), Personal interview conducted by Liliana Chávez, Buenos Aires, 19 November.

Martínez, T. E. ([1973] 2007), *La pasión según Trelew*, Buenos Aires: Punto de Lectura.

Martínez, T. E. ([1985] 2004a), *La novela de Perón*, Buenos Aires: Alfaguara.

Martínez, T. E. ([1995] 2002), *Santa Evita*, Mexico City: Alfaguara.

Martínez, T. E. ([2004] 2009a), *Las vidas del general. Memorias del exilio y otros textos sobre Juan Domingo Perón*, Buenos Aires: Alfaguara.

Martínez, T. E. (1970b), 'Querido Norberto', Buenos Aires, Archivo TEM, SE–I–1.

Martínez, T. E. (1970c), 'Viaje a Bonn', Buenos Aires, Archivo TEM, SE–I–1.

Martínez, T. E. (1988), 'Ficción e historia en *La novela de Perón*', *Hispamérica*, 17 (49): 41–9.

Martínez, T. E. (1989a), 'Entrevista al Coronel Héctor Cabanillas', Buenos Aires, Archivo TEM, SE–I–E–1.

Martínez, T. E. (1989b), 'Entrevista del 10 de mayo de 1989, en el Café Tabac, Buenos Aires, con el Coronel Héctor Eduardo Cabanillas, el Brigadier Jorge Rojas Silveyra y el Suboficial Manuel Sorolla [Carlos Maggi]', Buenos Aires, Archivo TEM, SE–I–E–3.

Martínez, T. E. (1989c), 'La historia de Evita', Buenos Aires, Archivo TEM, SE–D–3.

Martínez, T. E. (1991), 'Entrevista al Suboficial Principal Sorolla (Carlo Maggi)', Buenos Aires, Archivo TEM, SE–I–E–4.

Martínez, T. E. (1991), 'Entrevista con la viuda de Moori Koenig', Buenos Aires, Archivo TEM, SE–I–E–5.

Martínez, T. E. (1994), 'Prólogo', in El credo de Carlos Fuentes (ed.), *Tres discursos para dos aldeas*, 7–19, Mexico City: Fondo de Cultura Económica.

Martínez, T. E. (1996), *Las memorias del General*, Buenos Aires: Planeta.

Martínez, T. E. (1997), *Santa Evita*, trans. H. Lane, London: Doubleday.

Martínez, T. E. (1998), *The Perón Novel*, trans. H. Lane, New York: Vintage Books.

Martínez, T. E. (2009b), 'Perón y sus novelas', in Tomas E. Martinez, (ed.), *Las vidas del general. Memorias del exilio y otros textos sobre Juan Domingo Perón*, 147–60, Buenos Aires: Alfaguara.

Martínez, T. E. (2009c), 'Las memorias de Puerta de Hierro', in Tomas E. Martinez, (ed.), *Las vidas del general. Memorias del exilio y otros textos sobre Juan Domingo Perón*, 13–146, Buenos Aires: Alfaguara.

Martínez, T. E. (2014), *Tomás Eloy Martínez: Juan Domingo Perón: Encuentro en Puerta de Hierro*, Buenos Aires: Fundación Tomás Eloy Martínez.

Martínez, T. E. (C. 1989), 'Evita Rest in Peace/Descanso eterno/Rest in Peace', Buenos Aires, Archivo TEM, TS SE–D–1.

Martínez, T. E. (N.d.), 'Cabanillas2', Buenos Aires, Archivo TEM, SE–I–E–2.

Martínez, T. E. (N.d.), 'Curriculum Vitae', San Miguel de Tucumán, Private archive of *La Gaceta*, 13742.

Martínez, T. E. (1970a), 'Las memorias de Juan Perón (1895–1945)', *Panorama*, 14 April: 20–25.

Martínez, T. E., ed. (2006), *Lo mejor del periodismo de América Latina*, Mexico City: Fondo de Cultura Económica; Fundación para un Nuevo Periodismo Iberoamericano.

Mayer, M., ed (1994), *El peronismo: historias de una pasión argentina*, Buenos Aires: Ediciones Instituto Movilizador de Fondos Cooperativos.

McHale, B. (1987), *Postmodernist Fiction*, New York: Methuen.

Méndez, J. (1992), *Cómo leer a García Márquez: una interpretación sociológica*, Río Piedras: Editorial de la Universidad de Puerto Rico.
Menton, S. (1993), *Latin America's New Historical Novel*, Austin: University of Texas Press.
Molloy, S. (1991), *At Face Value: Autobiographical Writing in Spanish America*, Cambridge: Cambridge University Press.
Monsiváis, C. ([1970] 2010b), *Días de guardar*, Mexico City: Era.
Monsiváis, C. ([1987] 1994), *Entrada libre: Crónicas de la sociedad que se organiza*, Mexico City: Era.
Monsiváis, C. ([1995] 1998), *Los rituales del caos*, Mexico City: Era.
Monsiváis, C. ([1995] 2000a), *Los rituales del caos*, Mexico City: Era.
Monsiváis, C. ([2005] 2006), *"No sin nosotros". Los días del terremoto 1985-2005*, Mexico City: Era/Editores Independientes.
Monsiváis, C. ([2006] 2010a), 'Prólogo', in C. Monsiváis (ed), *A ustedes les consta. Antología de la crónica en México*, 15–12, Mexico City: Era.
Monsiváis, C. (1966), *Autobiografía*, Mexico City: Empresas Editoriales, Scribd.
Monsiváis, C. (1977), 'Isela Vega. ¡Viva México hijos de la decencia! Del nuevo status de las 'malas palabras', in *Amor perdido*, 319–46, Mexico City: Era.
Monsiváis, C. (1978), 'Notas sobre cultura popular en México', *Latin American Perspectives*, 5 (1): 98–118.
Monsiváis, C. (1988), *Escenas de pudor y liviandad*, Mexico City: Era.
Monsiváis, C. (1997), *Mexican Postcards*, trans. J. Kraniauskas, London: Verso.
Monsiváis, C. (2000b), *Salvador Novo: lo marginal en el centro*, Mexico City: Era.
Monsiváis, C. (2007), *A New Catechism for Recalcitrant Indians*, trans. J. Browitt and N. Castrillón, Mexico City: Fondo de Cultura Económica / Fundación para las Letras Mexicanas.
Monsiváis, C. (2010c), *Que se abra esa puerta. Crónicas sobre la diversidad sexual*, Mexico City: Paidós.
Monsiváis, C., ed ([1980] 2010), *A ustedes les consta. Antología de la crónica en México*, Mexico City: Era.
Moraña, M. and I. Sánchez, eds. (2007), *El arte de la ironía: Carlos Monsiváis ante la crítica*, Mexico City: Ediciones Era.
Mudrovcic, M. (1999), 'El arma periodística y una literatura "necesaria". El caso de Primera Plana', in N. Jitrik and S. Cella (eds), *Historia crítica de la literatura argentina*, vol. 10, 295–311, Buenos Aires: Emecé.
Mudrovcic, M. (2005), 'Nombres en litigio: Velasco vs. García Márquez', *Arizona Journal of Hispanic Cultural Studies*, 9: 161–70.
Nance, K. (2006), *Can Literature Promote Social Justice? Trauma Narrative and Social Action in Latin American Testimonio*, Nashville: Vanderbilt University Press.
Ortiz, F. ([1963] 1987), *Contrapunteo cubano del tabaco y el azúcar*, Caracas: Fundación Biblioteca Ayacucho.
Osorno, G. (2014), *Tengo que morir todas las noches. Una crónica de los ochenta, el underground y la cultura gay*, Mexico City: Penguin Random House.
Páez de la Torre, C. (2002), 'El periodismo', in Daniel James (ed.), *Nueva historia de la nación argentina*, vol. IX, 333–61, Buenos Aires: Academia Nacional de la Historia / Planeta.
Page, J. (1983), *Perón, a Biography*, New York: Random House.
Paz, O. (1974), *Los hijos del limo*, Barcelona: Seix Barral.

Paz, O. (1977), 'Aclaraciones y reiteraciones', *Proceso*, 51. Available online: http://hemeroteca.proceso.com.mx/?page_id=278958&a51dc26366d99bb5fa29cea4747565fec=122086 (accessed 7 April 2017).
Perilli, C. (2010), 'Ciudades blancas. Crónicas rojas: las historias de Cristian Alarcón', *INTI, Revista de literatura hispánica*, 71/72: 335–44.
Perón, E. (1951), *La razón de mi vida*, Buenos Aires: Ediciones Peuser.
Pitman, T. (2008), *Mexican Travel Writing*, Oxford; New York: Peter Lang.
Polit, G. (2013), *Narrating Narcos: Culiacán and Medellín*, Pittsburgh: University of Pittsburgh Press.
Polit, G. (2019), *Unwanted Witnesses. Journalist and Conflict in Contemporary Latin America*, Pittsburgh: University of Pittsburgh Press.
Poniatowska, E. ([1954] 1987), *Lilus Kikus*, Mexico City: Era.
Poniatowska, E. ([2013] 2014), *El universo o nada: biografía del estrellero Guillermo Haro*, Barcelona: Seix Barral.
Poniatowska, E. (1969), *Hasta no verte Jesús mío*, Mexico City: Era.
Poniatowska, E. (1971), *La noche de Tlatelolco. Testimonios de vida oral*, Mexico City: Era.
Poniatowska, E. (1979), *Gaby Brimmer*, Mexico City: Grijalbo.
Poniatowska, E. (1980), *Fuerte es el silencio*, Mexico City: Era.
Poniatowska, E. (1988a), *La "Flor de Lis"*, Mexico City: Era.
Poniatowska, E. (1988b), *Nada, nadie. Las voces del temblor*, Mexico City: Era.
Poniatowska, E. (1991), 'Jorge Luis Borges', *Todo México*, 1, 3rd reprint, 115–54, Mexico City: Diana.
Poniatowska, E. (1992), *Tinísima*, Mexico City: Era.
Poniatowska, E. (1994), *Luz y luna, las lunitas*, Mexico City: Era.
Poniatowska, E. (1997), '¿De qué quiere su domingo?' in Elena Poniatowska (ed.), *Todo empezó el domingo*, 13–16, Mexico City: Océano.
Poniatowska, E. (2000a), *Las mil y una… la herida de Paulina*, Barcelona: Plaza y Janés.
Poniatowska, E. (2000b), *Las siete cabritas*, Mexico City: Era.
Poniatowska, E. (2007), *Amanecer en el Zócalo: los 50 días que confrontaron a México*, Mexico City: Planeta.
Poniatowska, E. (2019), *El amante polaco. Libro 1*, Mexico City: Seix Barral.
Pratt, M. L. (1992), *Imperial Eyes: Travel Writing and Transculturation*, London: Routledge.
Quattrocchi-Woisson, D. (2003), 'Las revistas en la vida intelectual y política', in Miguel Ángel de Marco (ed.), *Nueva historia de la nación argentina*, vol. X, 13–16, Buenos Aires: Academia Nacional de la Historia / Planeta.
Rama, A. ([1982] 2004), *Transculturación narrativa en América Latina*, Mexico City: Siglo XXI.
Randall, M. (1992), '¿Que es, y como se hace un testimonio? *Revista de Crítica Literaria Latinoamericana*, 18 (36): 23–47.
Reynolds, A. (2012), *The Spanish American Crónica Modernista, Temporality, and Material culture: Modernismo's Unstoppable Presses*, Lewisburg: Bucknell University Press.
Riffaterre, M. (1990), *Fictional Truth*, Baltimore: Johns Hopkins University Press.
Rivas Hernández, A. (2011), '¿Ficción o realidad? El valor sociológico de *Relato de un náufrago* de Gabriel García Márquez', *Acta Literaria*, 42: 45–59. Available online: https://scielo.conicyt.cl/scielo.php?script=sci_arttext&pid=S0717-68482011000100004 (accessed 28 February 2021).
Rivera Garza, C. (2013), *Los muertos indóciles*, Mexico City: Tusquets.

Rodríguez-Luis, J. (1997), *El enfoque documental en la narrativa hispanoamericana: estudio taxonómico*, Mexico City: Fondo de Cultura Económica.

Roffé, R. (2003), 'Entrevista con Tomás Eloy Martínez', *Cuadernos hispanoamericanos*, 633: 101–06.

Romero de Terreros, M. (1926), *Bibliografía de cronistas de la Ciudad de México*, Mexico City: Imprenta de la Secretaría de Relaciones Exteriores.

Roncagliolo, S. (2005), 'La cuarta espada del comunismo', *El país*, 11 October. Available online: http://elpais.com/diario/2005/10/11/espana/1128981601_850215.html (accessed 3 May 2021).

Roncagliolo, S. (2007), *La cuarta espada. La historia de Abimael Guzmán y Sendero luminoso*, Barcelona: Debate.

Roncagliolo, S. (2009), *El amante uruguayo. Una historia real*, Alcalá la Real: Alcalá Grupo Editorial.

Roncagliolo, S. (2009), *Memorias de una dama*, Madrid: Alfaguara.

Rotker, S. ([1992] 2005), *La invención de la crónica*, Mexico City: Fondo de Cultura Económica / Fundación para un Nuevo Periodismo Iberoamericano.

Rotker, Susana, ed (2002), *Citizens of Fear: Urban Violence in Latin America*, New Brunswick: Rutgers University Press.

Said, E. ([1978] 2003), *Orientalism*, London: Penguin.

Said, E. (1984), 'Introduction: Secular Criticism', in Edward Said (ed.), *The World, the Text, and the Critic*, 1–30, London: Faber and Faber.

Sáizar, C. (2016), Personal interview conducted by Liliana Chávez, Cambridge, UK, 19 January.

Salinas Plaza, D. (2010), 'La preocupación de los marinos chilenos que viajan en el Esmeralda', *La nación*, 6 March, section Exterior: 4. Available online: http://servicios.lanacion.com.ar/archivo/2010/03/06/004/DT (accessed 11 April 2017).

Samper Ospina, D., ed (2008), *Soho. Crónicas*, Bogotá: Aguilar.

Sarduy, S. (1974), *Barroco*, Buenos Aires: Sudamericana.

Sarduy, S. (2013 [1988]), 'El barroco y el neobarroco', in Severo Sarduy (ed.), *Obras III. Ensayos*, 399–439, Mexico City: Fondo de Cultura Económica.

Sarlo, B. ([2005] 2006), *Tiempo pasado. Cultura de la memoria y giro subjectivo. Una discusión*, Mexico City: Siglo XXI.

Sarlo, B. (1995), 'Presentación', in L. Arfuch (ed), *La entrevista, una invención dialógica*, 11–15, Buenos Aires: Paidós.

Sarlo, B. (2003), *La pasión y la excepción*, Buenos Aires: Siglo XXI.

Sarmiento, D. F. ([1845] 1990), *Facundo: civilización y barbarie*, ed. Roberto Yahni, Madrid: Cátedra.

Schabert, I. (1990), *In Quest of the Other Person: Fiction as Biography*, Tübingen: Francke.

Schuessler, M. (2007), *Elena Poniatowska: An Intimate Biography*, Tucson: University of Arizona Press.

Shugart, H. and C. Waggoner (2008), *Making Camp: Rhetorics of Transgression in U.S. Popular Culture*, Tuscaloosa: The University of Alabama Press.

Silva, M. and R. Molano, eds (2006), *Las mejores crónicas de Gatopardo*, Bogotá: Debate.

Sims, N. (1990), *Literary Journalism in the Twentieth Century*, New York; Oxford: Oxford University Press.

Sims, N. (2007), *True Stories: A Century of Literary Journalism*, Evanston: Northwestern University Press.

Siskind, M. (2014), *Cosmopolitan Desires: Global Modernity and World Literature in Latin America*, Evanston: Northwestern University Press.

Siskind, M. (2019), 'Towards a Cosmopolitanism of Loss: An Essay About the End of the World', in G. Müller and M. Siskind (eds), *World Literature, Cosmopolitanism, Globality. Beyond, Against, Post, Otherwise*, 205–35, Berlin: De Gruyter. Available online: https://iberian-connections.yale.edu/wp-content/uploads/2020/03/Mariano_Siskind_Towards_a_cosmopolitanis.pdf (accessed 28 February 2021).

Sklodowska, E. (1993), 'Testimonio mediatizado: ¿ventriloquia o heteroglosia? (Barnet/Montejo; Burgos/Menchu)', *Revista de crítica literaria latinoamericana*, 38: 81–90.

Sommer, D. (1990), 'Irresistible Romance: The Foundational Fictions of Latin America', in H. K. Bhabha (ed), *Nation and Narration*, 71–98, New York: Routledge.

Sontag, S. ([1964] 2009), 'Notes on "Camp"', in Susan Sontag (ed.), *Against Interpretation*, 275–92, London: Penguin.

Steele, C. (1989), 'Entrevista. Elena Poniatowska', *Hispamérica*, 53/54: 89–105.

Stoll, D. (1999), *Rigoberta Menchú and the Story of All Poor Guatemalans*, Boulder; Oxford: Westview.

Todorov, T. ([1984] 1992), *The Conquest of America. The Question of the Other*, trans. R. Howard, New York: Harper Perennial.

Tomas, M., ed (2007), *La Argentina crónica, historias reales de un país al límite*, Buenos Aires: Planeta.

van Dijk, T. A. (1988), *News as Discourse*, Hillsdale, NJ: Erlbaum Associates.

Vargas Llosa, M. (1971), *García Márquez: historia de un deicidio*, Barcelona: Seix Barral.

Vargas Llosa, M. (1990), 'La verdad de las mentiras', in Mario Vargas Llosa (ed.), *La verdad de las mentiras. Ensayos sobre literatura*, 5–20, Barcelona: Seix Barral.

Vega, P., ed (2008), 'La autobiografía que Monsiváis quisiera sepultar', *Emeequis*, 5 May: 40–52. Available online: http://www.m-x.com.mx/2008-05-04/la-autobiografia-que-monsivais-quisiera-sepultar/ (accessed 7 April 2017).

Vera León, Antonio (1992), 'Hacer hablar: La transcripción testimonial', *Revista de crítica literaria latinoamericana*, 36, La voz del Otro: testimonio, subalternidad y verdad Narrativa: 185–203. Available online: http://jstor.org/stable/4530629 (accessed 23 April 2017).

Villalobos, J. (2009), *Con la sangre despierta. El primer arribo a esa ciudad narrado por once escritores latinoamericanos*, Mexico City: Sexto Piso.

Villanueva Chang, J. (2011), 'El que enciende la luz', in D. Jaramillo Agudelo (ed), *Antología de crónica latinoamericana actual*, 583–606, Mexico City: Alfaguara.

Villoro, J. (1989), *Palmeras de la brisa rápida. Un viaje a Yucatán*, Mexico City: Alianza.

Villoro, J. (2007), 'La cultura de masas imita a su profeta', in M. Moraña and I. Sánchez (eds), *El arte de la ironía: Carlos Monsiváis ante la crítica*, 375–81, Mexico City.

Villoro, J. (2010a), *8.8: El miedo en el espejo. Una crónica del terremoto en Chile*, Oaxaca de Juárez: Almadía.

Villoro, J. (2010b), 'El sabor de la muerte', *La nación*, section Exterior, 6 March: 4. Available online: http://servicios.lanacion.com.ar/archivo/2010/03/06/004/DT (accessed 11 April 2017).

Villoro, J. (2011), 'La crónica, ornitorrinco de la prosa', in D. Jaramillo Agudelo (ed), *Antología de crónica latinoamericana actual*, 577–82, Mexico City: Alfaguara.

Walsh, R. ([1969] 2009a), 'Prólogo de la tercera edición', in R. Ferro (ed), *Operación Masacre. Seguido de la campaña periodística*, 19–25, Buenos Aires: Ediciones de la Flor.

Walsh, R. ([1972] 2009b), 'Epílogo de la 2a edición de 1964', in R. Ferro (ed), *Operación Masacre. Seguido de la campaña periodística*, 312–14, Buenos Aires: Ediciones de la Flor.

Walsh, R. ([1972] 2009c), *Operación Masacre. Seguido de la campaña periodística*, ed. Roberto Ferro, Buenos Aires: Ediciones de la Flor.

Walsh, R. (1957), 'La Operación Masacre (1ª nota)', *Mayoría*, 27 May: 8–11.

Walsh, R. (1969), *Operación Masacre*, Buenos Aires: Editorial Jorge Álvarez.

Walsh, R. (1977), *Open Letter from a Writer to the Military Junta. Bilingual Edition English/Spanish*, Buenos Aires: Archivo Nacional de la Memoria / Secretaría de Derechos Humanos. Available online: http://www.jus.gob.ar/media/2940455/carta_rw:ingles-espa_ol_web.pdf (accessed 28 February 2021).

Walsh, R. (1981), 'Esa Mujer', in Rodolfo Walsh (ed.), *Obra literaria completa*, 163–71, Mexico City: Siglo XXI.

Walsh, R. (2013), *Operation Massacre*, trans. Daniella Gitlin, foreword Michael Greenberg, afterword Ricardo Piglia, New York: Seven Stories; Apple Books digital version.

White, H. (1978), *Tropics of Discourse. Essays in Cultural Criticism*, Baltimore: The John Hopkins University Press.

Wiktorowska, A. (2020), 'Introduction', in Y. Passos and M. Wiktoworska (eds), *Literary Journalism and Latin American Wars: Revolutions, Retributions, Resignations*, 1–10, Nancy: Éditions PUN – Université de Lorraine.

Roberts, W. and F. Giles (2014), 'Mapping Nonfiction Narrative: A New Theoretical Approach to Analysing Literary Journalism', *Literary Journalism Studies*, 6: 101–17. Available online: http://ialjs.org/wp-content/uploads/2014/12/101-118-LJS_v6n2.pdf (accessed 23 April 2017).

Williams, R. (1997), *The Postmodern Novel in Latin America: Politics, Culture, and the Crisis of Truth*, Basingstoke: Macmillan.

Wittgenstein, L. (2002 [1921]), *Tractatus Logico-Philosophicus*, trans. D. F. Pears and B. F. McGuiness, London: Routledge Classics.

Wolfe, T. (1973), 'The New Journalism', in T. Wolfe and E. W. Johnson (eds), *The New Journalism*, 3–52, New York: Harper and Row.

Woolf, V. (1929), *The Common Reader*, London: Hogarth Press.

Woolf, V. (1967), 'The New Biography', in Virginia Woold (ed.), *Collected Essays*, vol. 4, 229–35, London: The Hogarth Press.

Young, D. and W. Young (1983), 'The New Journalism in Mexico: Two Women Writers', *Chasqui*, 12 (2/3): 72–80.

Yudice, G. (1991), 'Testimonio and Postmodernism', *Latin American Perspectives*, 18: 15–31.

Zapaterra, Y. (2007), *Art Direction and Editorial Design*, New York: Abrams.

Zavarzadeh, M. (1976), *The Mythopoetic Reality: The Postwar American Nonfiction Novel*, Urbana: University of Illinois Press.

Index

8.8 El miedo en el espejo   135–7, 140, 145–8, 151–2

Alarcón, C.   7, 9–10, 18, 22, 37, 41–2, 101, 159–60, 166, 172–6, 180, 182–3
Anfibia   22 n.12, 192
autobiography
   and *crónica*   83
   genre   5, 27
   Martínez   112
   Monsiváis   91, 97, 101
   Poniatowska   85, 249

Bakhtin, M. M.
   carnival   95, 98, 105
   heteroglossia   40 n.42, 98
   speech genres theory   39–40, 43–4, 99
Barnet, M.   28, 50
baroque, *see also barroco*
   aesthetics   99, 101
   culture   95
   definition   2, 184
   in documentary narratives   2, 9, 105, 157, 184, 195, 226, 257
   in literature   96–8
   rhetoric   78
barroco
   ethos   95
   neo-   2 n.1, 35, 98–9, 184
Barthes, R.   36, 93
Bartra, R.   77, 93 n.39, 95
Benjamin, W.   3–4, 20, 39, 104, 119, 168–9, *see also* storyteller
Bourdieu, P.   36–7, 232
Butler, J.
   account of the self   5, 158, 162, 164, 181
   confession   5, 34, 161–2
   gender   101, 176
   truth-telling   156–7, 161
   vulnerability   5, 164, 172

Calvi, P.   6, 16–17, 23, 26–8
camp
   characteristics   96
   in Latin American literature   2 n.1
   Mexican   105
   in Monsiváis   98–101
   self-fashioning   96
Caparrós, M.   7, 9–10, 19, 22, 37, 57, 135–45, 152–7, 167, 170, 190, 218, 225–6, 257, 268, 272
Cavarero, A.
   desire   179–81
   narratable self   42–3, 162–3
   vulnerability   5, 164
censorship
   in Argentina   106, 111, 114
   in Latin America   9, 17
   of the press   33–4, 50, 60, 131, 184, 223, 250
   self-   37, 54, 77, 104, 209
chronicle, *see crónica*
chronicler   4, 7, 18, 24, 35, 37, 75, 77–80, 96
confession
   and autobiography   91
   cultural act   5, 33–4, 44, 161–2
   in documentary narratives   177–8
   genre   27
   legal practice   156
   of the other   129
   and *testimonio*   164
Corona, I.   21, 39
crónica
   Alarcón   188, 191–3
   Caparrós   198–202, 208–9, 220, 223, 225
   contemporary   16–18, 23, 36–8, 157–8, 178
   de Conquista or *de Indias*   95, 136, 157, 225, 267
   definition   6–8, 10, 23–4, 26–7, 79, 83, 152–6, 176

Fontaine 213
football 135
Goldman 223
Guerriero 225–7, 236
Martínez 128
modernista 21–2, 63 n.36, 76
Monsiváis 91–3, 97–105
origins 20–2, 26
Poniatowska 73, 83–4, 88, 90, 248–50, 258
and public space 104–5
urban 77, 101, 104, 105
Villoro 145–6, 267–72
Cuando me muera quiero que me toquen cumbia 159–60, 193, 195
cultural field
authorial role in 11, 16, 34, 37, 38, 78, 170
intersections of 2, 11, 87, 169
in Latin America 24, 37, 39, 79, 156
in Mexico 93

dialogue
definition 5, 39–40, 161, 193, 204, 216, 244
ethics of 162–76, 179–84, 192, 233, 238–44, 246, 253–4, 261, 271
face-to-face 3, 10, 179–80, 216, 229, 231
as intertextuality 136, 149
as interview 5 n.4, 39, 41–3, 48, 53–9, 81–4, 139–44
in journalism 6, 11, 39, 46, 88–90, 106–30, 155, 203, 244, 260
as literary device 25, 34, 36, 38, 42, 91, 125, 142–4, 154–8, 163–4, 170–2, 176, 183–5, 210, 215, 230, 261, 269
methodological strategies 193–5, 204, 214, 218, 229–32, 260–1, 269–71
with reader 103
theory 1, 43–4
Días de guardar 79, 92, 93, 100
dictatorship
Aramburu 56
Argentina 31, 60–1
Batista 15

novels 109
Pinilla 48
Pinochet 51, 163, 165, 220
Southern Cone 9, 27, 256
Videla 7, 60

El Espectador 46–8, 64
El País 36, 109
empathy 10, 38, 129, 154, 166, 179, 185, 231
erotics 178–9, 182
ethnography 6, 24, 36, 39, 41 n.44, 66, 92, 101, 152
Excélsior 81, 92, 266

fact-checking 19 n.5, 42
flâneur 4, 96
FNPI, *see* Fundación para un Nuevo Periodismo Iberoamericano
Fontaine, A. 7, 10, 42, 161–5, 180–2
Foucault, M.
author-function 156, 177
parrhesia 33–4
truth-telling 33, 156, 161–2, 181
Fundación Gabo, *see* Fundación para un Nuevo Periodismo Iberoamericano
Fundación para un Nuevo Periodismo Iberoamericano 10, 22, 37, 135, 257

García Márquez, G., *see also Relato de un náufrago*
FNPI 10, 22, 192
journalism 79, 190, 199, 219, 221–2, 266
public figure 256
and Walsh 15–16, 45–6, 57, 64
Gatopardo 22 n.12, 202
Genette, G. 107, 108, 112, 119
Goldman, F. 7, 10, 22, 32–3
González, A. 1, 39, 55, 63 n.36
González Echevarría, R. 3–4, 29
Guerriero, L. 7, 9–10, 16, 18, 22, 37, 41–2, 160, 165–75, 180–2, 257

Herrscher, R. 26
Hutcheon, L. 5, 112, 114, 151, 179
hybrid, *see* hybridity

hybridity
  in *crónica* 22, 24, 104–5
  in genres 30, 41, 131, 135, 152, 163, 178
  methodology 8–11, 24
  in style 7, 93
  in texts 2, 16, 25, 35, 147, 151, 169, 185

intellectual
  accessible 16, 105
  anti- 21
  Argentinian 106
  chronicler 20, 36, 148
  elite 9, 77, 177
  journalist 38
  Mexican 76–7, 81, 82, 85, 90, 93, 95–6
  national 255
  pole 37
  public 6, 9, 11, 19, 80, 84, 87, 92–4, 96, 104
  socially committed 28, 256
  women 85–6
interview, *see* dialogue
investigative journalism 10, 16, 63, 68, 105, 117, 120, 123, 131, 154, 161, 180, 237, 245, 254, 268

Jörgensen, B. 2, 21, 24, 81
journalistic field 2, 35, 37–8, 122, 184
justice
  in documentary narratives 6
  moral value 63, 68–9, 100
  social 16, 30, 80, 174, 202, 245
  system 32, 57

kitsch 91, 101

La Flor de Lis 73, 86, 90
La Nación 108–9, 136, 145–8, 234
La noche de Tlatelolco 80, 84, 247, 249, 250
La vida doble 161–4, 180, 213
Lemebel, P. 101, 190, 218
Levinas, E. 6, 162
Lilus Kikus 81, 86
listening

  act of 3, 55, 69, 84, 155, 177
  research technique 33, 153–4, 165, 168, 204, 211, 229
  in storytelling 39, 118, 157, 169, 178, 182
literary journalism
  and *crónica* 26, 105, 157, 223–4
  definitions 24–7, 259
  as documentary narratives 184
  in Latin America 5–7, 16–17, 23, 26–7, 160
  as literature 40 n.42, 55–6
  as non-fiction 20, 23, 25, 27
  and testimonio 28, 30
long-form journalism 16, 25, 198, 268
Los rituales del caos 75–6, 92, 101–2
Los suicidas del fin del mundo 160, 169, 171–3, 175, 181, 234–6
Luz y luna, las lunitas 73, 88, 103

Mahieux, V. 16, 20
Mayoría 59–64, 68
memoir
  Caparrós 141, 208
  García Márquez 51, 53
  genre 5, 27, 218
  Perón 110–16
  Poniatowska 83, 247
memory, *see also* memoir
  ability 49, 54, 66, 116–17, 137, 140, 203, 233, 251
  collective 57, 104, 184
  cultural 29, 103–4
  post- 31
  as remembrance 150, 155
Menchú, R. 29, 50
metadocumentary narratives
  characteristics 161–2, 176, 179
  definition 11
  and storytelling 157
  themes 141, 156
metafiction
  devices 161, 174, 178
  in documentary narratives 33, 38, 160, 182
  narrator 5, 20, 36, 117, 136, 153
  in nonfiction 7
  postmodern 25, 112

metajournalism   114, 140, 261
Monsiváis, C., *see also* autobiography; camp; *Días de guardar*; *Los rituales del caos*
　career   91–4
　as chronicler   156
　chronicle theorization   21, 79, 91, 94–6
　influence in other authors   241, 243, 245, 248, 257
　national culture   77–8, 95
　style   93, 97–8, 105

narrative journalism
　Caparrós   198–9, 202
　and *crónica*   23
　definitions   23, 25–6
　Goldman   223
　in Latin America   27
　Poniatowska   245
　Villoro   267
New Journalism   7, 16, 18, 25–6, 28, 33, 92, 140, 160, 190, 199, 220, 223, 225, 243, 257, 267
non-fiction
　American   26, 223
　based on journalistic investigation   177
　biography   120
　and *crónica*   23–4, 188, 191, 202, 225
　ethics   53, 193, 254
　exemplary works   51, 58, 109, 128, 152, 189, 198, 235–6, 260
　and fiction   3, 32, 131, 191–2, 200, 222, 237
　history   17–18
　literary devices   185, 228
　and literary journalism   25–6
　narratives   38
　postmodern   5
　story   11, 119
　subgenres   6, 19–20, 258
　and *testimonio*   27

Operación Masacre   28, 45–6, 54–69, 189, 198, 268

orality
　culture   185
　in oral history   225
　sources   11, 63, 66, 219
　speech   9, 40 n.42 n.43, 41, 43
　transcripts   27
otherness
　definition   6
　desire for   174–5
　encounters with   139, 155, 185, 210
　as foreign   135, 154, 157
　representation   42, 44, 83, 86, 90, 93, 98, 152, 156, 184
　theory   28, 99

Panorama   57, 109–11, 116, 121
performative
　ability   115
　act   40, 101, 154, 162, 176
　philosophy   162–3
　rhetoric strategy   99, 105, 183
Peronism
　Evita (*see* Perón, E.; *Santa Evita*)
　history   56
　in journalism   121–2
　in literature   106, 113
　Perón, E.   9, 108, 115–27
　Perón, J. D.   56, 106–10, 115–16, 121–2, 131
　Santa Evita   107–9, 116–30, 190
　and Walsh   59
Polit, G.   16–17, 24, 38, 68, 69, 169
Poniatowska, E., *see also* autobiography; *Luz y luna, las lunitas*; *La Flor de Lis*
　and Borges, J. L.   82–3
　career   80–1
　as chronicler   23, 74–7
　and popular culture   77–8
　and Rivera, D.   81–2
　style   84
　work methods   41, 81–2, 84
popular culture
　American   104–5, 150, 185
　and journalism   43, 185
　melodrama   35–6
　Mexican   91, 93–6, 99–100

and *modernismo* 9
and nationalism 77–80
postmodern
   journalism 12, 19, 25
   literature 5, 28, 113, 119, 255
   narrative strategies 20, 36, 99
   setting 17–20, 96, 120, 184
   trends 4, 7, 157
   turn 10
   worldview 94–5, 113, 136
postmodernism 28 n.25, 113, 184,
   see also postmodern

Rama, A. 24
realism 24, 26, 29, 128, 160 n.4, 219
Relato de un náufrago 8, 28, 45–7, 268
reportage
   and *crónica* 36, 79, 258
   definition 9 n.7, 59 n.28
   Latin American tradition of 9–10
   literary 18–19, 25–7, 258
   as long-form journalism 25
   in Martínez 128
   in Roncagliolo 35, 262
   in Walsh 59, 63–8, 125
reporter
   as chronicler 22–3, 157
   definition 9 n.7
   investigative 16, 32, 206
   news 37, 197
   representation of 39, 75, 79, 82–3, 91, 104, 112–14, 121, 147, 166, 171, 221
   undercover 15
Roncagliolo, S. 7, 10, 18, 35–7, 160, 165–70, 173–4, 180

Sarduy, S. 35, 99, 184
Sarlo, B. 4–5, 27, 31, 115–16, 233, 268, 271
self-representation
   Alarcón 159
   Caparrós 154
   and documentary narratives 9, 40
   of elites 11, 37
   genres 5
   Guerriero 166, 173
   Martínez 117

Poniatowska 85
Roncagliolo 173, 264
and storytelling 162
Villoro 158
Walsh 58
Siskind, M. 1, 24, 35, 174
Sontag, S. 92, 96, 99–101, 105
storyteller
   Benjamin, W. 4, 39, 119, 169
   contemporary 5, 10, 17
   in documentary narratives 33, 161, 169, 184, 264
   as informant 49, 55–6
   as journalist 3–5, 18, 39, 56, 104, 126, 171, 173, 183, 190–1, 257
storytelling, *see also* Benjamin, W.
   act of 157, 162, 169
   definition 119, 168
   in documentary narratives 169, 174, 177, 227, 254, 269
   as personal account 11, 38, 42, 162, 179, 219, 235
   return to 2–3, 45 n.1
   techniques 34, 36, 57, 63
   uses of 10, 16, 30, 131, 152, 155

testimonial narratives 4–7, 12, 23, 27–31, 68, 136, 157, 160, 164, 173, 178–9, *see also testimonio* genre
testimonio genre 5, 8, 16, 27–32, 34, 45, 50, 73, 88, 92, 153, 156, 164, 213, 218, 225, 233, 254, 268
testimony, *see also testimonio* genre
   in documentary narratives 39, 43, 84, 144, 149, 152, 165, 170, 173, 184, 218, 233, 257, 271
   erotics of 178–82
   as evidence 27, 31, 66, 68, 128, 268
   as personal account 4–5, 29, 51, 53, 104, 107, 127, 137, 148, 164, 183, 269
   uses of 6, 48, 142, 156, 208, 218–19
travel writing 23, 135–6
truthfulness
   claim of 8
   in journalism 17, 29, 124, 147, 271
   notion of 10
   pact of 56, 167

in philosophy   34
textual marks of   56, 110, 148
truth-telling, *see also* Foucault, M.
   act of   8, 156, 185
   ethics   19, 162, 178
   intentions for   158
   in journalism   46
   modes   34, 44, 177
   procedures   178
   rhetoric   1

Una luna   135–7, 140–4, 152, 206–8

verisimilitude   38, 41, 84, 93, 147, 155, 170, 176, 191, 205
Villoro, J.   7, 9–10, 21–2, 37, 97, 135–41, 145–58, 167, 257
vulnerability   5, 34, 164, 172

Walsh, R., *see also* García Márquez; *Operación Masacre*

'Esa mujer'   123–5
   influence in journalism   189, 198–9, 225–6, 268
   and Martínez, T. E.   125–7
and parrhesia   34
Wiener, G.   101, 190, 258
witness
   eye-   30, 39
   as informants' testimonies   29, 66, 109, 117, 147
   integral   139
   in journalism   16, 54, 68–9, 94, 110, 148, 152, 166
   in judicial process   27, 63, 174
   as literary character   20, 116, 176
   as narrator   4, 20, 24, 33, 38, 65, 84, 95–7, 141, 153–5, 170, 172, 177, 184
women
   chroniclers   23, 257
   representation   73, 85–6, 115, 142, 174, 182
   situation   232, 244

www.ingramcontent.com/pod-product-compliance
Lightning Source LLC
Chambersburg PA
CBHW052152300426
44115CB00011B/1629